FEAR *and* LEARNING

FEAR *and* LEARNING

FROM BASIC PROCESSES TO CLINICAL IMPLICATIONS

EDITED BY

Michelle G. Craske, Dirk Hermans,
and Debora Vansteenwegen

AMERICAN PSYCHOLOGICAL ASSOCIATION
WASHINGTON, DC

Published by
American Psychological Association
750 First Street, NE
Washington, DC 20002
www.apa.org

To order
APA Order Department
P.O. Box 92984
Washington, DC 20090-2984
Tel: (800) 374-2721; Direct: (202) 336-5510
Fax: (202) 336-5502; TDD/TTY: (202) 336-6123
Online: www.apa.org/books/
E-mail: order@apa.org

In the U.K., Europe, Africa, and the Middle East, copies may be ordered from
American Psychological Association
3 Henrietta Street
Covent Garden, London
WC2E 8LU England

Typeset in Goudy by Stephen McDougal, Mechanicsville, MD

Printer: Port City Press, Baltimore, MD
Cover Designer: Berg Design, Albany, NY
Technical/Production Editor: Tiffany L. Klaff

The opinions and statements published are the responsibility of the authors, and such opinions and statements do not necessarily represent the policies of the American Psychological Association.

Library of Congress Cataloging-in-Publication Data

Craske, Michelle Genevieve, 1959–
   Fear and learning: from basic processes to clinical implications / Michelle G. Craske, Dirk Hermans, and Debora Vansteenwegen.—1st ed.
     p. cm.
   ISBN 1-59147-414-0
   1. Fear. 2. Phobias. I. Hermans, Dirk. II. Vansteenwegen, Debora. III. Title.

   RC535.C732 2006
   616.85'225—dc22
                                           2005036271

British Library Cataloguing-in-Publication Data
A CIP record is available from the British Library.

Printed in the United States of America
First Edition

CONTENTS

CONTRIBUTORS

Mark Barad, MD, PhD, Department of Psychiatry and Biobehavioral Sciences, University of California, Los Angeles

Velma Barrios, BA, Department of Psychology, University at Albany, State University of New York, Albany

Mark E. Bouton, PhD, Department of Psychology, University of Vermont, Burlington

Michelle G. Craske, PhD, Department of Clinical Psychology, University of California, Los Angeles

Graham C. L. Davey, PhD, Department of Psychology, University of Sussex, Brighton, England

Trinette Dirikx, PhD, Department of Psychology, University of Leuven, Leuven, Belgium

Paul Eelen, PhD, Department of Psychology, University of Leuven, Leuven, Belgium

Georg H. Eifert, PhD, Department of Psychology, Chapman University, Orange, CA

Michael S. Fanselow, PhD, Department of Psychology, University of California, Los Angeles

John P. Forsyth, PhD, Department of Psychology, University at Albany, State University of New York, Albany

Ana García-Gutiérrez, PhD, Department of Psychology, University of Vermont, Burlington

Dirk Hermans, PhD, Department of Psychology, University of Leuven, Leuven, Belgium

Ottmar V. Lipp, PhD, School of Psychology, University of Queensland, St. Lucia, Australia

Peter Lovibond, PhD, School of Psychology, University of New South Wales, Australia

Susan Mineka, PhD, Department of Psychology, Northwestern University, Evanston, IL

Erik W. Moody, PhD, School of Social and Behavioral Sciences, Marist College, Poughkeepsie, NY

Jayson L. Mystkowski, PhD, Department of Psychology, University of California, Los Angeles

Jennifer J. Quinn, PhD, Department of Psychiatry, Yale University, New Haven, CT

Ceyhun Sunsay, PhD, Department of Psychology, Indiana University, Bloomington

Jon Sutton, PhD, Department of Psychology, Northwestern University, Evanston, IL

Debora Vansteenwegen, PhD, Department of Psychology, University of Leuven, Leuven, Belgium

Bram Vervliet, PhD, Department of Psychology, University of Leuven, Leuven, Belgium

Amanda M. Woods, BA, Department of Psychology, University of Vermont, Burlington

PREFACE

The goal of this volume is to bring together the most recent empirical and theoretical developments in the basic science of fear learning and to translate these developments to the clinical understanding and treatment of fears and phobias. A major impetus for the volume was the recognition that basic science in fear learning is advancing far more rapidly than the clinical application of this knowledge. This is especially true in the case of biobehavioral mechanisms of fear learning. Consequently, applications of fear learning to the understanding and treatment of fears and phobias are often based on outdated and oversimplified models. We believed there was a need to update the clinical field and that presentation of the most recent advances and debates in basic science would highlight directions for clinical application in terms of both research and practice. By the same token, presentation of the latest developments in clinical applications is expected to stimulate pursuit of new directions in basic science. Therefore, this volume is intended for both basic scientists and clinical scientists at undergraduate, graduate, and more advanced levels, as well as practicing clinicians who are interested in gaining an in-depth understanding of learning theory as it applies to fear and anxiety.

The book is structured to cover three main areas. The first presents the history of fear learning theory and fear measurement. The second area examines the acquisition and maintenance of fear, including neural circuitry, associative pathways, and cognitive mechanisms; the role of avoidance; and individual differences in fear learning. The third area covers the extinction, renewal, and reinstatement of fear, including neural circuitry and context dependency. The volume developed out of the Special Interest Meeting on Fear and Learning in Lignely, Belgium (May 2003), sponsored by the Fund for Scientific Research in Flanders, Belgium, and inspired by Paul Eelen.

ACKNOWLEDGMENTS

We would like to thank Florence Crestani for reviewing this book and Najwa Chowdhury for her assistance in administrative matters. Preparation of this book was supported by National Institute of Mental Healh Grant 1 R21 MH072259-1 (Co-PI Michelle G. Craske) "Translating Extinction of Fear to Anxiety Disorder Treatment," K. U. Leuven Grant GOA/2001/01 "Extinction and the Return of Conditioned Responses," and by the "Scientific Research Network on the Acquisition, Representation, and Activation of Evaluative Judgments and Emotion" of the Research Foundation—Flanders (Fonds voor Wetenschappelijk Onderzoek—Vlaanderen).

FEAR *and* LEARNING

INTRODUCTION: ETIOLOGICAL FACTORS OF FEARS AND PHOBIAS

MICHELLE G. CRASKE, DEBORA VANSTEENWEGEN,
AND DIRK HERMANS

The understanding of fears and phobias and their treatment has always been closely tied to basic science in learning and emotion, perhaps more so than any other emotional disorder. Nonetheless, clinical application of the significant advances that have been made over the last few years in the biobehavioral mechanisms of fear learning has been lagging. The goal of this volume is therefore to provide comprehensive coverage of the most recent advances in the basic science of fear learning, to offer directions for future research that are of most relevance to the basic scientist, and to outline the clinical implications of these advances that are of most relevance to the clinician. The book is divided into three sections. The first covers the history of fear learning and the methods for investigating this topic in humans. The second section covers the neurobiological and behavioral advances in the acquisition and maintenance of animal and human fears. The third section covers corresponding advances in the extinction of animal and human fears.

FEARS, PHOBIAS, AND ANXIETY DISORDERS

During childhood, fears of circumscribed objects or situations are common and are considered developmentally appropriate and even adaptive because they constitute protective responses to stimuli that are neither comprehensible nor controllable (Ollendick, Yule, & Ollier, 1991). That is, fears are purported to develop as children increasingly perceive potential dangers but are not yet sufficiently advanced to be able to understand or exercise control over the situation. Once those developmental transitions have been achieved, fears naturally subside for most, but some youths develop long-lasting phobias (e.g., McGee et al., 1990). Fears are also common in adults, with anywhere from 25% to 85% of the adult population experiencing occasional panic attacks (e.g., Norton, Cox, & Malan, 1992), public-speaking anxiety, and other social fears (e.g., Stein, Walker, & Forde, 1996), as well as specific fears of circumscribed objects (Agras & Jacob, 1981). Fears transform into phobias when they become persistent over time and are associated with avoidance behavior that places limits on functioning.

Most of the anxiety disorders are characterized by phobic fear, anxiety, and avoidance. Although the terms *fear* and *anxiety* have been suggested to denote responses that differ in relation to the imminence of threatening stimuli, with anxiety responding characteristic of more distal stimuli and fear responding more characteristic of proximal stimuli (e.g., Bouton, Mineka, & Barlow, 2001), they are used interchangeably in the chapters that follow. As categorized by the diagnostic nosology of *Diagnostic and Statistical Manual of Mental Disorders*, (4th ed.; American Psychiatric Association, 1994), the anxiety disorders include the following: panic disorder with or without agoraphobia, in which the phobic stimuli are physical sensations and the situations associated with such sensations; social phobia, involving fears of social evaluation and situations associated with such evaluation; specific phobias, in which the phobic stimuli are circumscribed situations (e.g., driving), animals, environments (e.g., storms), and blood, injury, or injections; obsessive–compulsive disorder, involving fears of unwanted intrusive images or thoughts and situations associated with such intrusions; and posttraumatic stress disorder, in which the phobic stimuli are the memory of the trauma and situations associated with the trauma. Only generalized anxiety disorder is not clearly characterized by well-circumscribed fear stimuli.

Anxiety disorders are one of the most commonly occurring forms of psychological disturbance. In the National Comorbidity Survey replication (Kessler et al., 1994), approximately 29% of respondents reportedly met criteria for a lifetime history of at least one anxiety disorder. Also, when left untreated, anxiety disorders and especially phobic avoidance (Tyrer, Alexander, Remington, & Riley, 1987) tend to be chronic and self-perpetuating (e.g., Keller et al., 1994). In addition, anxiety disorders have disabling effects (e.g., Olfson et al., 1997) and increase the likelihood of other forms of emotional distress, especially depression (e.g., Hayward, Killen, Kraemer, & Taylor, 2000). Anxiety may also contribute to substance-use-related disorders (Swendsen et al., 1998). In summary, phobic disorders are common, chronic if untreated, and contribute to the development of other mental disorders. Therefore, it is essential that we remain abreast of the advances made in basic science that inform not only the theory and constructs of fear learning but also the etiology and treatment of human fears and phobias.

THREE FEAR RESPONSE SYSTEMS

Some time ago, a gradual accumulation of empirical evidence contradicting features of Mowrer's (1960) two-factor theory (which implied that autonomic responses regulate avoidance behavior and must be reduced to eliminate avoidance; see chap. 1, this volume) led P. J. Lang (1971) to suggest that fear reactions comprise three loosely coupled response systems: self-report (or verbal), behavioral, and physiological. The verbal system of fear refers to self-reports of fear or panic and self-statements of danger and threat, including erroneous interpretations, irrational beliefs, self-preoccupation, report of internal physiological cues, and catastrophizing statements. The behavioral system includes passive avoidance on anticipated confrontation with feared stimuli, escape and active avoidance from feared stimuli, and learning and performance deficits (most relevant to social and performance phobias). Recognition has been given more recently to the role of safety signals (i.e., objects that diminish fear responding in the presence of the phobic stimulus) and behaviors oriented toward safety seeking in maintaining phobic responding.

Response in the physiological system refers to sympathetic and parasympathetic innervation of the autonomic system (as an index or arousal and behavioral activation), fear-potentiated blink startle (as an index of emotional valence), and increased blood flow in those areas of the brain that mediate the fear response (e.g., amygdala).

The response systems are interactive, and because of their influence on each other, they can be viewed as stimuli as well as responses. That is, Lang (1971) described a mutually augmenting feedback loop among the response systems. For example, anxious thinking might enhance awareness of autonomic feedback that in turn generates more danger-laden thinking. Autonomic activity may then feedback to influence striated muscle reflexes and cortical activity, which in turn disrupts the behavioral response system by producing unskillful performance or by blocking motor activity; such behavioral impairments may be perceived and contribute to an ascending spiral of verbal, behavioral, and autonomic activation.

Lang (1971) also viewed the response systems as partially independent, and hence it is not uncommon for individuals to report fear in the absence of physiological changes or to exhibit physiological changes in the absence of reported fear or behavioral changes. The independence of response systems was originally attributed to different levels of central nervous system (CNS) modulation and then to contextual and environmental influences, such as the opportunity to escape (P. J. Lang, Bradley, & Cuthbert, 1990). Subsequently, Fanselow (1994) concluded that prior research had confounded variations in environmental context with fear intensity and that situational parameters (i.e., opportunity to escape) are less important in determining behavioral and physiological responses (at least in nonprimates) than is the extent to which the situation is perceived to be dangerous, termed *imminence of threat*.

ETIOLOGY OF HUMAN PHOBIAS

Etiological factors of human fear and phobias include constitution—that is, temperament and genetics that influence the proneness to developing phobias—as well as learning experiences that define if (and which) specific stimuli become fearful.

The temperament most associated with anxiety disorders is neuroticism and emotional stability (Eysenck, 1967). Gray (1987) attributed proneness to anxiety to a lowered threshold for behavioral inhibition system activation (a defensive motivational state to which neuroticism, and to a lesser degree extraversion, contribute) in response to signals of punishment, frustrative nonreward (i.e., expected positive reinforcement is not received), extreme novelty, and intense and innate fear stimuli. Neuroticism is believed to contribute to both anxiety and depression.

The *contributory* role of neuroticism is demonstrated by positive relationships between measures of neuroticism and subsequent symptoms of anxiety and depression across all ages (e.g., Hayward et al., 2000), and several prospective studies indicate that behaviorally inhibited youth (behavioral inhibition is closely tied to the construct of neuroticism) develop multiple phobias and anxiety disorders more often than uninhibited peers (e.g., Schwartz, Snidman, & Kagan, 1999). The general factor of neuroticism is most closely connected with generalized anxiety disorder loading more heavily, with moderate connections with panic disorder–agoraphobia and lesser connections with social phobia (T. A. Brown, Chorpita, & Barlow, 1998). In the absence of data, specific phobias are hypothesized to be least connected to neuroticism. That is, the development of specific phobias may be less dependent on general neurotic vulnerabilities and more dependent on specific learning experiences than is the case for more pervasive anxiety disorders.

Numerous multivariate genetic analyses of human twin samples consistently attribute approximately 50% of variance in neuroticism to additive genetic factors (e.g., Lake, Eaves, Maes, Heath, & Martin, 2000). The observed phenotypic covariation among anxious symptoms, depression symptoms, and neuroticism is due largely to a single common genetic factor (Kendler, Heath, Martin, & Eaves, 1987). That is, anxiety and depression appear to be variable expressions of the heritable tendency toward neuroticism, although symptoms of fear (i.e., breathlessness, heart pounding) may be additionally explained by a unique source of genetic variance (e.g., Kendler et al., 1987). One of the most important conclusions from the body of genetic research to date is that genetic contributions to the etiology of anxiety are general and are not disorder-specific. As such, there is much room for individual learning experiences in the generation of specific types of anxiety disorders.

SPECIFIC RISK FACTORS: ASSOCIATIVE LEARNING

Pairing an initially neutral stimulus, such as a noise (conditional stimulus [CS]), with an intrinsically aversive stimulus, such as a mild footshock (unconditional stimulus [US]), generates robust conditional fear in rodents. Such Pavlovian fear conditioning has served as an important model for the study of molecular mechanisms underlying learning and memory for many decades (McGaugh, 2000). In addition, fear conditioning has long been an important experimental model for the pathogenesis of human anxiety disorders (Eysenck, 1968). Associative models attribute fears and phobias to aversive events, direct or vicarious (i.e., observing a model respond fearfully or be traumatized), including fear itself, that lead to conditioned anxiety over associated stimuli. Experimental evidence for conditioning models derives from laboratory studies with humans and rhesus monkeys, including the many examples of direct aversive conditioning of electrodermal and blink-startle reflex in humans (e.g., Grillon & Morgan, 1999; Öhman & Soares, 1998), and vicarious fear acquisition in laboratory-reared rhesus monkeys (Mineka, Davidson, Cook, & Keir, 1984).

Evidence to support the role of conditioning in the onset of chronic phobias derives from self-report and clinical observation, because, naturally, it is unethical to conduct the type of human experimental research necessary to demonstrate the causal role of associative learning in the development of excessive and chronic phobias. Prospective longitudinal research is rare and beset with its own sources of error in the absence of verification of surrounding contexts and the precise conditions of the aversive experiences. Some of the most compelling evidence in support of a conditioning model for chronic phobia acquisition is the development of fears and phobias following a trauma that were not present before the trauma, as is captured by the diagnosis of posttraumatic stress disorder.

As noted, fear can serve as an aversive stimulus, and this is particularly applicable to the conditioning model of panic disorder. Panic attacks (i.e., abrupt episodes of intense fear, often unexpected) are presumed to lead to acquisition of a learned fear of signals of panic, at least in vulnerable individuals, through a process of interoceptive conditioning, whereby low-level somatic sensations of arousal or anxiety become conditional stimuli (Razran,

1961) so that early somatic components of the anxiety response come to elicit anxiety or panic (Bouton et al., 2001). An extensive body of experimental literature attests to the robustness of interoceptive conditioning (e.g., Sokolowska, Siegel, & Kim, 2002). In addition, interoceptive conditional responses are not dependent on conscious awareness of triggering cues (Razran, 1961), and once acquired, these responses can be elicited under anesthesia, even in humans (e.g., Block, Ghoneim, Fowles, Kumar, & Pathak, 1987). Consequently, changes in relevant bodily functions that are not consciously recognized may elicit conditional fear because of previous pairings with panic, thereby accounting for the apparent spontaneity of panic attacks.

FEAR LEARNING: BASIC ISSUES (PART I) AND ACQUISITION AND MAINTENANCE OF FEAR (PART II)

Part I of this volume covers the history and measurement of conditioned fear. Chapter 1 by Paul Eelen and Bram Vervliet covers the philosophical (Locke and the traditions of empiricism and associationism), physiological (Sechenov, Bechterev, & Pavlov), and behavioral (Watson & Rayner; Mary Cover Jones; Dollard & Miller; Wolpe & Eysenck) backgrounds of classical conditioning as a paradigm, and the origins of behavioral therapy. This chapter is essential for those who wish to acquire a complete understanding of the evolution of learning theory and behavioral therapy. It not only is a historical resource but also enables a fuller appreciation of the constructs and procedures described in the subsequent chapters. Chapter 2 by Ottmar V. Lipp provides a gold standard for the measurement of experimentally induced fear. The author provides detailed descriptions of the CS and US conditioning procedures (i.e., differential delay and single cue or trace conditioning) and measures of verbal (including the importance of online measurement of expectancies and valence), behavioral (including approach tests and reaction time measures of attentional bias and affective priming), and physiological (blink-startle and autonomic indices) responding. This methodological overview is equally suited to the basic scientist studying nonphobic subjects and to the clinical scientist studying phobic subjects. As with chapter 1, Lipp's chapter enhances appreciation of those to follow by operationalizing the various constructs that are subsequently described.

Part II covers issues pertaining to the acquisition and maintenance of fear. Chapter 3 by Jennifer J. Quinn and Michael S. Fanselow presents knowledge gained from years of researching the functionality and neurobiology of fear in rodents, a valuable topic because the fear system is conserved across species and thereby of relevance to human fears and phobias. The role of the amygdala, and in particular, the frontotemporal amygdala, in fear conditioning and the role of the hippocampus in representation of contexts associated with conditioning, as well as the various afferent (input to CNS) and efferent (output from CNS) pathways are described in a way that provides a comprehensive overview of the entire neuroanatomical process; from sensory perception of CS and US, to association of CS (and associated contexts) with US, to fear response output. Also described are the molecular mechanisms of synaptic plasticity that underlie changes as a result of associative learning. Quinn and Fanselow suggest pathways through which the neurobiology of the fear system may be dysregulated and contribute to the development of phobias and anxiety disorders; these are immediately testable hypotheses for the basic and clinical scientist.

Chapter 4 by Susan Mineka and Jon Sutton moves the discussion from rodents to primates and considers the additional layers of complexity that are involved in human fear responding. After reviewing the evidence for direct, vicarious, and informational pathways to fear conditioning acquisition, reasons individuals respond differently to a given traumatic event are presented. These include temperament, prior exposure to a CS (latent inhibition and immunization), history of control and experience of control in relation to the trauma, and aversive events subsequent to the target trauma. In addition, Mineka and Sutton address the issue of preparedness as a model for the nonrandomness of phobias and cover the most recent developments in the experimental investigation of conditioning to fear-relevant stimuli and demonstrations of the nonconscious activation of such fear responding. Also, they provide an update of the debate regarding associative versus nonassociative means of human fear acquisition and speak to the various biases that intrude on retrospective recall of events, which, along with the notion of nonconscious fear activation, is directly relevant to the practicing clinician.

Chapter 5 by Graham C. L. Davey focuses on cognitive mechanisms involved in the acquisition and maintenance of human fears and phobias. An update is given of the experimental developments in information-processing biases that pertain to phobic and anxious responding; these include attentional biases, judgment biases, interpretation biases, and memory biases—or lack thereof. In addition, Davey describes the role of beliefs and expectations about fear-relevant stimuli as a factor that may contribute to the acquisition of long-lasting phobias. This chapter thus provides an alternative approach to the model of preparedness presented in chapter 4.

In chapter 6, Peter Lovibond pays special attention to the avoidance component of fear responding (in animal and human studies). He first presents historical views of avoidance learning, or the two-factor theory in which avoidance is understood as motivated by fear and reinforced by fear reduction. Although central to the development of behavioral therapies, Lovibond outlines the difficulties with the two-factor theory and reasons for its replacement by a conditioned inhibition model of avoidance learning, or a safety signal model, in line with recognition of the signal value of stimuli in relation to events (i.e., the Rescorla–Wagner model). The author also presents variants of this model. Extending further into the realm of informational models of conditioning, this chapter explores the possibility of all human fear learning (and avoidance learning) being propositional in nature rather than involving automatic or mechanistic conditioning and presents an expectancy-based model of human avoidance learning and the supporting experimental data. The chapter gives explicit clinical implications from an expectancy-based model for the treatment of human phobias.

In chapter 7, John P. Forsyth, Georg H. Eifert, and Velma Barrios offer a different point of view on avoidance learning by presenting a model of human phobias that de-emphasizes the conditioning experience relative to individual differences in willingness to tolerate the discomfort associated with aversive conditioning. The basic premise is that fear learning develops into a phobia when individuals attempt to down-regulate, escape, or avoid the effects of fear learning and thereby display poor emotion regulation and experiential avoidance, and when the attempts to down-regulate interfere with other ongoing activities. Thus, a trait of experiential avoidance is viewed as equally if not more important than the trait of neuroticism in generating a proneness to the development of phobic disorders. This chapter has direct relevance to understanding the etiology of phobias and raises the possibility of treating phobias by relinquishing attempts to control emotions.

TREATMENT FOR FEARS, PHOBIAS, AND ANXIETY DISORDERS

Extinction is the gradual reduction in conditional fear generated by the repeated presentation of the CS without any paired US. This process has enormous clinical importance because it has long served as the explicit model of behavior therapy. Extinction-like exposure continues to form the core of modern behavior and cognitive–behavioral therapies, which have demonstrated efficacy in the treatment of a variety of human anxiety disorders, including not only specific phobias but also panic disorder with agoraphobia, social phobia, posttraumatic stress disorder, and obsessive–compulsive disorder (see Craske, 1999).

The method of exposure therapy has undergone several revisions. Originally, Wolpe (1958) attributed extinction to counterconditioning or reciprocal inhibition. Thus, he developed his method of systematic desensitization from the premise that when a response antagonistic to anxiety is made to occur in the presence of anxiety-provoking stimuli and results in a complete or partial suppression of the anxiety response, then the bond between the stimulus and the anxiety response is weakened. Hence, in systematic desensitization, individuals progress through increasingly more anxiety-provoking, imagined encounters with phobic stimuli while using relaxation as a reciprocal inhibitor of rising anxiety. A body of research subsequently showed, however, that exposure therapy proceeded as well whether or not it was combined with relaxation or other cognitive coping tools designed to compete with anxiety (e.g., Foa, 1997; Marks, Lovell, Noshirvani, Livanou, & Thrasher, 1998).

Exposure therapies have since taken various forms, including controlled escape exposure involving encouraged escape from phobic situations when anxiety reaches high levels, followed by a return to the situation (e.g., Rachman, Craske, Tallman, & Solyom, 1986) and, conversely, graduated or intense (flooding) exposure therapy involving instructions to remain in the phobic situation until fear peaks and then subsides, as would be consistent with an emotional processing theory of exposure therapy (Foa & Kozak, 1986; Foa & McNally, 1996). In the latter theory, exposure to fear-provoking stimuli is purported to lead to short-term physiological habituation that dissociates the stimulus from the fear response, and in turn dismantles the original set of fearful associations among stimuli, responses, and meanings. More recent psychological models suggest that rather than "changing" the fear structure, a new competing structure is formed during exposure and extinction.

Exposure therapy is also a central element to cognitive therapy, which assumes that emotions are based on cognitive processes that can be corrected or manipulated through conscious reasoning; "one of the most effective ways of deactivating the primal threat mode is to counter it with more elaborative, strategic processing of information resulting from the activation of the constructive, reflective modes of thinking" (Beck & Clark, 1997, p. 55). Cognitive therapy represents elaborative, strategic processing. Behavioral experimentation provides the means for collecting information or data that serve to disconfirm conscious misappraisals of the dangers in any given experience or situation. Behavioral experimentation is akin to exposure therapy. Hence, the natural debate that arises is the degree to which the effects of cognitive therapy can be directly attributed to shifts in conscious appraisals as opposed to associative learning that may effect change, at least partially, through less elaborative, strategic processes as a result of the behavioral exposure.

Of late, the understanding and implementation of exposure therapy has lagged behind the advances being made in the basic science of extinction learning, and research questions have become more directed at outcomes at the cost of ongoing research into the mechanisms of exposure-based fear reduction. There is a need for more experimental investigation, guided by theoretical principles regarding the duration of exposure trials, intervals between exposure trials, level of fear or excitation during exposure, variation in the CS during exposure, safety signals during exposure, and ways of structuring exposure to minimize return of fear. The purpose of the third part of this volume is to outline the most recent developments in basic and clinical science regarding extinction and its application to exposure therapy for phobias.

EXTINCTION, RENEWAL, AND
REINSTATEMENT OF FEAR (PART III)

This part begins with chapter 8 by Mark Barad, who describes the neurobiology of fear extinction. In line with the behavioral evidence that extinction does not represent unlearning, Barad presents neurobiological evidence that extinction involves new learning given that similar anatomical structures and synaptic processes are involved in acquisition and extinction. As a counterpart to chapter 3 of this volume, which describes the neuroanatomical basis of fear acquisition, Barad describes cellular mechanisms of extinction and the role of the amygdala, infralimbic prefrontal cortex, and hippocampus in fear extinction and renewal of fear. This chapter not only presents the latest advances in the neurobiology of extinction that is of direct theoretical and empirical relevance to basic science but also has direct implications for clinical practice. The more clearly the cell biological processes involved in extinction are understood, the more likely it is that specific drugs can be designed to facilitate the extinction process; this type of pharmacological facilitation is already progressing in the form of d-cycloserine.

In chapter 9, Mark E. Bouton, Amanda M. Woods, Erik W. Moody, Ceyhun Sunsay, and Ana García-Gutiérrez review their extensive body of nonprimate behavioral evidence showing that extinction is not unlearning. Extinction is conceptualized as the development of a second context-specific inhibitory association that, in contrast to fear acquisition, does not easily generalize to new contexts. This extinction model has profound implications for clinical practice because it suggests that exposure effects will not readily generalize beyond the treatment context. Another consequence of this model is that factors enhancing extinction during a session (e.g., trial spacing, multiple contexts, and chemical adjuncts) are not necessarily the same as factors that enhance generalization of extinction in the long term because short-term and long-term effects are driven by partially different mechanisms. This, too, has direct clinical implications because it raises the possibility that attempts to facilitate fear reduction during exposure therapy, for example, may have little relevance for the return of fear at a later point in time. Bouton et al. advocate methods that would bridge the gap between new contexts and the exposure context, such as retrieval cues and conduct of extinction in the context most likely to be associated with return of fear. This chapter addresses fundamental issues about extinction that will be of interest to basic scientists and also serves as a guideline for exposure for the clinical scientist and practitioner.

In chapter 10 by Debora Vansteenwegen, Trinette Dirikx, Dirk Hermans, Bram Vervliet, and Paul Eelen, the methodology and principles developed by Bouton and colleagues in chapter 9 using nonprimates is extended to human samples. Vansteenwegen et al. provide an overview of the evidence for return of fear after extinction in human fear-conditioning studies. Then, following the paradigms established by Bouton and colleagues in laboratory-based conditioned fear, Vansteenwegen et al. present evidence for a context change after extinction (renewal) and unpredicted USs after extinction (reinstatement) to evoke a return of fear in humans. Investigation of the underlying mechanisms that might explain these effects is just beginning. Consistent with the suggestions of Bouton et al., Vansteenwegen et al. present preliminary evidence for the value of retrieval cues in helping to offset the context-specificity effect of extinction in human fear conditioning. In contrast to Bouton et al., they also report that the context-specificity effect is offset by inclusion of multiple contexts throughout extinction training.

Chapter 11 by Michelle G. Craske and Jayson L. Mystkowski moves even further into the clinical realm by presenting an overview of the latest experimental findings regarding extinction as a mechanism of exposure therapy in human phobic samples. Similar to the findings presented by Vansteenwgen et al. in chapter 10, Craske and Mystkowski describe a series of studies demonstrating context specificity of exposure effects when spider-phobic individuals are treated in one context and retested at a later point in time in another context, whether the context is an external location or an internal state. Also, Craske and Mystkowski pose the issue that extinction through exposure therapy may be facilitated by procedures designed to violate expectancies for aversive outcomes, as might be operationalized through the duration of a given exposure trial and by procedures designed to sustain levels of excitation throughout exposure, both of which suggest directions for future research and new ways to implement exposure therapy. Finally, consistent with the suggestions of Bouton and colleagues (chap. 9) and the findings described by Vansteenwegen et al. with laboratory conditioned fear, Craske and Mystkowski present evidence for the value of retrieval cues for offsetting return of fear.

The final chapter is a summary of the issues presented throughout, areas of debate, directions for future research, and clinical implications.

I

FEAR AND LEARNING: BASIC ISSUES

1

FEAR CONDITIONING AND CLINICAL IMPLICATIONS: WHAT CAN WE LEARN FROM THE PAST?

PAUL EELEN AND BRAM VERVLIET

One of the intriguing themes within philosophy, biology, and psychology has always been the "nature versus nurture" debate. This debate has had an impact not only on psychology in general but also on conceptualizations and theories about the origin of so-called abnormal behavior, or psychopathology. The different standpoints within this discussion are well known, although seldom clearly articulated. The extreme nature position defends a sort of biogenetically prepared hardwiring of behavioral output. Favorite research themes within this tradition are topics such as typology (as old as Greek philosophical ideas), personality traits, and, more recently, the genetic basis of behavior. The extreme nurture position assumes a *tabula rasa*: Nothing is programmed, and behavior of the individual is shaped as a result of experiences. Although virtually nobody today adheres to either extreme, most current behavioral research is a mixture of the two positions.

This chapter is written mainly from a nurture position, in which the psychology of learning has its roots. Indeed, learning is generally defined as a relatively permanent change in behavior as the result of experiences, either successful or unsuccessful. This point of view started within empiristic philosophy tradition and was a general theme within behaviorism and neobehaviorism.

We do not intend to summarize the complete history of behavior and cognitive–behavioral therapies or behavior modification and their impact on the treatment of anxiety disorders. Such a goal would be too broad for a single chapter, and there are other excellent sources available on the topic (e.g., Barlow, 2002).

The first section of this chapter focuses on the philosophical, physiological, and behavioral backgrounds of the classical conditioning paradigm, which has always been central to an understanding of the etiology and the eventual treatment of anxiety disorders. We do not underestimate the impact of the operant tradition in the psychology of learning, but in this chapter, it is treated only as part of the two-factor theory of avoidance learning, most clearly formulated by Mowrer (1947). This theory, discussed in more detail subsequently, affirms that a conditioning stimulus evokes a conditioned emotional reaction of fear, which leads to escape and eventually to avoidance of the stimulus—a conditioned avoidance response. Anxiety disorders are based not only on classical emotional conditioning but also on the way in which emotionally conditioned stimuli are managed.

The second section of the chapter considers the origins of behavior therapy and cognitive–behavioral therapy, especially theories (and related problems) on the etiology and treatment of anxiety disorders. More recent developments of theories and research are not addressed here because they are well documented elsewhere in this volume.

PHILOSOPHICAL TRADITIONS

Although there was a large tradition before him, John Locke (1632–1704) can be considered the father of empiricism, a tradition that would become extremely influential in the development of psychological science and especially the psychology of learning. In his major philosophical work, *An Essay Concerning Human Understanding* (1894/1690), he defended the position that human understanding and knowledge of things, the world, and the self derives only from sensory experience. The senses build knowledge of the outside world. Locke did not deny that the human mind has some innate capacities—for example, the ability to learn a language—but he strongly rejected the idea that some contents of the mind, such as the idea of God or of moral principles, were inborn. For Locke, sensory input from physical objects in the environment consists originally of simple sense impressions. These impressions are transmitted in the mind to form simple ideas. Through experience, these become organized into more complex ideas, leading to the perception of objects. Up to this point, Locke described the role of the mind as a passive registration of the outside world attained through the senses. In the fourth edition of the *Essay*, however, he was obliged to introduce the notion of *association* to explain the existence of fantasies (which have no replica in the outside world) and also to understand what he called "the wrong connexion of ideas." In this context, he gave several examples of how irrational anxiety can originate through association.

> An instance: The ideas of goblins and spirits have really no more to do with darkness than light: yet let but a foolish maid inculcate these often on the mind of a child, and raise them together, possibly he shall never be able to separate them again so long as he lives, but darkness shall ever afterwards bring with it those frightful ideas, and they shall be joined, that he can no more bear the one than the other. (Watson, 1979, p. 40)

Apart from its old-fashioned language, this citation could have been written by a contemporary cognitive–behavioral therapist as a case illustration of the etiology of phobic anxiety related to darkness.

Locke's basic philosophical position was further elaborated, in an even more extreme form, by George Berkeley and David Hume, and the importance of association became fully articulated by the next generation of the philosophers of associationism: David Hartley, James Mill, his son John Stuart Mill, and Thomas Brown. These philosophers formulated the basic laws of association, including contiguity, resemblance, frequency, and vividness— laws that formed the basic dimensions and discussions in the later psychology of learning. A common theme for these thinkers was the central role of experience and education in building knowledge and personality. In the central and practically unlimited role of learning in the development of normal and abnormal behavior, some writings from these authors are as extreme as the subsequent tradition of early behaviorism: The kind of person one becomes is almost wholly based on the experiences to which he or she is exposed and how the links between these experiences are created according to the basic laws of association.

The philosophical traditions of empiricism and associationism provided the impetus to better understand the mechanisms behind people's sensory experiences and the influence of external stimuli in building the "mind." It is not by accident that in the 18th and 19th centuries, the first discoveries were made about the working of the senses and the nervous system. In retrospect, some of these findings and theories are still valid, such as the basic distinction between the afferent and efferent systems in the Bell–Magendie law, which can be considered the foundation of a stimulus–response vocabulary (in more modern terms, the organism as an input–output system). Other theories are outdated but were nevertheless influential in creating a new way of thinking about behavior and the mind. Among others is the highly speculative phrenology of Franz Gall, which formed the basis of localizing the mind in material structures of the brain. This neurophysiological interest is another important root of later associative explanations of normal and abnormal behavior.

NEUROPHYSIOLOGICAL TRADITIONS

Hartley (1705–1757), a physician, was perhaps the first to attempt to draw a parallel between the associationistic philosophical doctrine and brain mechanisms: Sensory sensations lead in parallel to what he called "miniature vibrations" in the brain, which become, over time, connected to each other. In his day, however, the working of the brain was poorly understood, and there was no methodology available to test his speculations.

The true revolution in the neurophysiological tradition came from Russia with three important contributors: Ivan Sechenov (1829–1905), his student Vladimir Mikhaïlovitch Bechterev (1857–1927), and finally Ivan Pavlov (1849–1936), the most well known from this Russian school.

Sechenov, the founder of modern Russian physiology, published *Reflexes of the Brain* (1965/1863). It includes his hypothesis (mostly undocumented by empirical evidence) that all activities, including the complex processes of thinking and language, can be reduced to reflexes: The excitatory and inhibitory mediational role of the cerebral cortex is the central locus of reflexive actions. He believed that the cause of all intellectual and motor activity involved external stimulation. Thus, the entire repertoire of behavior is the result of responses to environmental stimuli, mediated at the cortical level. At the same time, he believed that the constructs of psychology (at that time mostly based on introspective reports) would gradually disappear because they were unnecessary to explain behavior. Over time, these constructs would be replaced by neurophysiological explanations, a point of view that, given the actual development of neuroscience, does not seem unfounded. Sechenov was hindered in developing experimental validation of his hypothesis, however, because the imperial government of the day considered it purely materialistic, and thus his work was heavily censored. He did not survive the revolution from which Pavlov would emerge, offering basically the same ideas as Sechenov before him.

Bechterev introduced the term *reflexology* and was influential in the later development of behaviorism, partly because of his book on *objective psychology*, published serially from 1907 to 1912 (and immediately translated into French; Bechterev, 1913). He influenced Watson in writing his behavioristic manifest (Watson, 1913). Bechterev concentrated on the role of what he called associative reflexes in motor responses: the striated muscles, rather than the glands or smooth muscles of the digestive system on which Pavlov focused. Bechterev began studying these associative reflexes in dogs but eventually used human subjects. His favorite experimental paradigm to study associative reflexes in human subjects consisted of applying shock to the palm of the hand, fingertips, or foot, preceded by various visual, auditory, or tactile neutral stimuli. Over numerous applications, the reflexive withdrawal reflex related to the shock was transferred to the neutral stimuli.

Today we no longer call this a pure procedure of classical or Pavlovian conditioning because the withdrawal response to the neutral stimuli might also be seen as a voluntary avoidance reaction, but in Bechterev's view, these voluntary reactions had the same status as reflexes. It inspired the experimental designs and apparatuses used by Watson and Lashley at Johns Hopkins University to study reflexes. It was less cumbersome than Pavlov's paradigm, and by using aversive stimuli, it avoided the problem of deprivation and satiation being a possible influences on salivary conditioning.

Although the work of Sechenov and Bechterev was influential, it is Pavlov whose name virtually became a synonym for conditioning and associative learning. It is remarkable that Pavlov started conditioning research at age 55 after having received the Nobel Prize in 1904 for his work on the digestive system, which concentrated mostly on the role of gastric secretions in the stomach. Thanks to some observations of his students, he undertook the study of the role of salivation within the digestive process, and in this study he discovered what he called the *psychic reflex*. In this context, the original observations of the psychic reflex came from dogs salivating when they saw or smelled food, or even when they heard the footsteps of the person who fed them. Pavlov decided to replace these "natural" conditioned stimuli linked to food with arbitrary stimuli; the result was that the situations required to obtain a conditioning effect became more stringent (e.g., strict temporal contiguity) and the phenomenon lost some of its ecological validity (Domjan, 2005).

Pavlov considered the salivary reflex an ideal objective measure, although it required surgery on the salivary glands so that the saliva drops could be quantified. He and his students used two types of unconditioned stimuli: either food or acid in the mouth. In both instances, an immediate reflexive salivary response occurred. On this basis, they went on to discover and describe the fundamental laws of what is now called classical conditioning: extinction, generalization, differentiation, and higher order conditioning, as well as conditioned inhibition, which was, according to Pavlov, as important as excitatory conditioning. Whereas in excitatory conditioning, the conditioned stimulus (CS) evokes a preparatory or even a similar reaction to the unconditioned stimulus (US), in inhibitory conditioning, the CS actively suppresses these reactions. Therefore, conditioned inhibition was neglected in the later conditioning literature: It is not easy to observe the difference between no response because of no learning occurred and active suppression of response. It is only in recent decades that the study of inhibition has been revived, especially with the renewed interest in the process of extinction and the role of context (see, e.g., chap. 9, this volume).

Pavlov's (1927) lectures reported in *Conditioned Reflexes* remain fresh. One can understand why he was, at a scientific level, on close terms with Bechterev: He found Bechterev's motoric studies too complex as an experimental paradigm. Although Pavlov, like Sechenov, was convinced that all behavior was reducible to a chain of reflexes, evoked by external or internal stimuli, he wanted to stay within an experimental paradigm that would provide more direct insight into the brain's functioning. Hence, the subtitle of his book was *The Physiological Activity of the Cerebral Cortex*.

For the context of this volume, it is important to note that Pavlov and his students gave first impetus to the study of what they called "experimental neuroses" and the linkage of conditioning studies to psychopathology. The circle–ellipse experiment of one of his students, Shenger-Krestovnikova, remains prototypical. A luminous circle (CS+; an excitatory CS) was projected on a screen in front of a dog, with food following the projection each time. When the conditioned reaction was well established, the projection of the circle was intermixed with the projection of an ellipse (CS–; an inhibitory CS), which was never followed by food. The ratio of the semiaxes of both figures was originally 2:1. A clear differentiation between the CS+ and the CS– was the expected result. Gradually, the experimenter changed the ratio between the two figures until a ratio of 9:8 was reached. Differentiation thus became more difficult, even with prolonged training. When the dog could no longer differentiate between the projections, its behavior underwent an abrupt change: It barked violently and became restless and aggressive. In short, it presented all the symptoms of a condition of acute neurosis (Pavlov, 1927, p. 291). For Pavlov, these neurotic symptoms were caused by a clash between excitatory and inhibitory processes. Formulated from another conceptual framework, Mineka later mentioned this experiment as an illustration of the role of unpredictability, or at least the loss of predictability, as a common characteristic in several studies of experimental neurosis (Mineka & Kihlstrom, 1978), which is congruent with other demonstrations in Pavlov's group of experimental neurosis. It is interesting to note that in this circle–ellipse experiment, no aversive stimuli (shock or strong noises) were applied, in contrast to several later experimental designs for modeling anxiety disorders.

One final finding of Pavlov's rich work should be mentioned: the first description of an exposure therapy based on the principle of a fear extinction learning in traumatized dogs. In 1924, a great flood occurred in Petrograd (Leningrad or St. Petersburg), and the kennels of the dogs that were located on the ground floor were flooded. The dogs were liberated from their kennels and swam in small groups in the midst of the heavy storm to the main building where the laboratories were located on the first floor. Over the next few days, the behavior of the dogs was completely disturbed, and it was practically impossible to retrain the conditioned reactions, learned before the flooding. The recovery came gradually, but only when the usual experimenter was physically present in the lab. As soon as the experimenter left, the learning was again disrupted. Two months later, everything seemed to have returned to normal. Water was then spilled beneath the door of the laboratory until the floor was covered with water (literally a "flooding procedure"). The experimental dogs became agitated and restless, and once again it was only the presence of the usual experimenter that restored the learned reflexes. Gradually, the presence of the experimenter was faded out by leaving only his clothes in the room, out of the dogs' sight but serving as olfactory stimuli. One can hardly imagine a nicer metaphor for the role of a therapist in later applications of flooding and exposure in behavior therapy.

EARLY BEHAVIORAL APPROACHES

Given the conceptual and empirical richness of the conditioning research by Pavlov (albeit mostly limited to salivary reflexes), it is sometimes frustrating to realize that a behavioral approach to the origin of fears, phobias, and anxiety states is often exclusively identified with John Watson and Rosalie Rayner's (1920) famous case study. They coined the term *conditioned emotional reaction*, a concept that became central in the later two-factor theory. Watson had already tested in babies what sort of stimuli evoked spontaneously (unconditional) emotional reactions. They were reduced to three: fear, rage, and love. The range of stimuli evoking these emotional reactions was small in comparison to the large range of emotionally evocative stimuli in later life. Watson and Rayner believed that conditioning could be one of the mechanisms that expanded this range of emotional stimuli.[1]

Watson and Rayner induced a phobic reaction in an 11-month-old baby, Albert B., by pairing a neutral stimulus (a white rat) with a strong aversive reinforcer (an intensive noise).[2] After a few pairings, it became clear that Albert became afraid when the rat was introduced, and this fear generalized to other similar stimuli, including a rabbit, dog, fur coat, and a Santa Claus mask. The child, who was an inpatient in the hospital, was observed until he was 1 year and 21 days old, and the fear reactions toward these stimuli did not disappear. Unfortunately, Albert was dismissed from the hospital, so Watson and Rayner did not have an opportunity to treat that fear. At the end of their case study, they mentioned some possible treatments that could

---

[1]Watson shared the belief of the philosophers of associationism on the unlimited role of learning processes in shaping personality. Of course, for Watson it was not a question of association between mental "ideas" but between stimuli and responses, the formation of habits. The most cited quotation in this context is from Watson (1924, p. 104): "Give me a dozen healthy infants, and my own specialized world to bring them up in and I'll guarantee to take any one at random and train him to become any type of specialist I might select—doctor, lawyer, artist, merchant-chief and, yes, even beggar-man and thief, regardless of his talents, . . . vocations, and race of his ancestors." In most citations of this fragment, however, they forget to quote the following sentence: "I am going beyond my facts and I admit it, but so have the advocates of the contrary and they have been doing it for many thousands of years."

[2]In fact, it was not a pure classical conditioning procedure but today would be described as an operant procedure of punishment because the aversive noise was given when Albert was touching the rat, which he did before without hesitation.

have been tried, among them pure exposure or extinction, reconditioning, and observational learning (i.e., watching another person handling the object of fear). They made a concluding, ironic comment regarding Freud and the psychoanalysts:

> The Freudians twenty years from now, unless their hypotheses change, when they come to analyze Albert's fear of a seal skin coat—assuming that he comes to analysis at that age—will probably tease from him the recital of a dream which upon their analysis will show that Albert at three years of age attempted to play with the pubic hair of the mother and was scolded violently for it. (We are by no means denying that this might in some other case condition it). . . .Albert may be fully convinced that the dream was a true revealer of the factors which brought about the fear. (Watson & Rayner, 1920, p. 14)

Watson and Rayner knew that psychiatrists practicing the dominant psychoanalytic treatment at that time would not accept their conditioning interpretation of acquired fear.

The same was true for the work of Mary Cover Jones who graduated after her studies at Vassar College at Columbia University under the indirect supervision of Watson. He had been forced to leave Johns Hopkins after his divorce, which was at that time a public scandal in Baltimore. He got a job at the J. Walter Thompson Advertising Company in New York City and was appointed to a consulting position at Teacher's College of Columbia University. Mary Cover Jones was a good friend of Rayner, the new wife of Watson. She attended a lecture of Watson and was impressed by the story of the Albert case and the general idea of the role of conditioning in the development of fear reactions. She decided to focus her studies on the topic of how to eliminate fears in children, a problem that had remained unfinished in Watson's work. She set up a genetic study of emotions, covering 70 children ranging from 3 months of age to 7 years of age. Careful observations of each child were made to discover what sort of stimuli evoked fear reactions and to determine the most effective methods of removing fear responses. The published report of this study is vague (M. C. Jones, 1924a), but remarkably, she did describe most of the later treatment methods in behavior therapy: verbal appeal (cognitive therapy), negative adaptation (now called exposure to the feared object), distraction, counterconditioning, and observational learning or "social imitation." According to Jones, the last two methods were the most efficient.

A more detailed description of both methods is reported in the case study of little Peter (M. C. Jones, 1924b). Peter was 2 years and 10 months old at the beginning of treatment. For Jones, Peter was the little Albert of Watson's study, grown a bit older. Like Albert, Peter was afraid of rats, fur coats, wool, and similar items, but he particularly feared rabbits. The difference from Albert's case, however, was that the origin of Peter's fear reactions was unknown. Jones decided to try out the principles that Watson had suggested for eliminating fear. In the first phase of treatment, Peter watched three other children playing with a rabbit; his fear diminished when he was tested alone, but it did not disappear completely. In a second phase, the method of "direct conditioning" (counterconditioning) was used. Peter was given some preferred food and while he was eating, the rabbit was brought into the room in a wire cage as close as possible to Peter without arousing a response that would interfere with the eating. "Through the presence of the pleasant stimulus (food) whenever the rabbit was shown, the fear was eliminated gradually in favor of a positive response" (M. C. Jones, 1924b, p. 313).

At about the same time, Guthrie (1935) noticed the general therapeutic applicability of the counterconditioning method. His theory on the process of learning is simple: Learning depends on the contiguity between a stimulus and a response. This theory formed the basis of later stochastic models of learning developed by Estes (1959). From his theory, Guthrie deduced several practical applications for breaking unadaptive habits. The general rule is "to find the cues that initiate the action and to practice another response to these cues" (Guthrie, 1935, p. 138).

The time was not ripe for new developments in clinical treatment, however. Examples of this is the relatively minor impact of Salter's (1949) work[3] and the general hesitation to apply the treatment method for enuresis developed by Mowrer and his wife (Mowrer & Mowrer, 1938), which was based on Mowrer's two-factor theory of learning but was considered a purely symptomatic treatment at that time.

In retrospect, it is amazing that the work of Pavlov, Watson, or Jones and so many other psychologists with similar ideas had so little impact on clinical practice during their own time, despite this being the golden period of the behavioral approach and of major learning theories. Nonetheless, there remained in this period a strong interest in translating the psychology of learning to the clinical field, in terms of creating new experimental paradigms for modeling neurotic behavior in animals (e.g., Dollard & Miller, 1950; Gantt, 1944; Liddell, 1949; Masserman, 1943), even though they rarely led to new clinical interventions and treatment methods.[4] One of the reasons might be that therapy was almost exclusively the domain of psychiatry. In their study curriculum, psychiatrists were influenced almost exclusively by Freudian psychoanalysis and related methods. Therefore, these experi-

---

[3]Salter was a psychologist who started his private practice by applying hypnosis, based on Hull's behavioristic interpretation of hypnosis. Salter extended these principles to autohypnosis, referring to the work of Pavlov and Bechterev. He went beyond hypnosis and believed that abnormal behavior, including anxiety, could be understood and treated by applying learning principles. Salter coined the term *conditioned reflex therapy* and published a book on the various applications of this approach (Salter, 1949).

[4]One important exception is the method of treating enuresis developed by the Mowrers, which is still considered the treatment of choice for most children with enuresis and later served as a behavior therapy success story.

mental models of neurosis were intended to offer a more experimental basis for the conceptual framework of psychoanalysis. This is the case for the work of Masserman (1943) and especially for the book by Dollard and Miller (1950), *Personality and Psychotherapy*. Dollard was a sociologist and Miller an experimental learning psychologist. Both were affiliated with the Institute of Human Relations at Yale University directed by Clark Hull, the most influential learning psychologist at that time. Hull even had advised Neal Miller to spend a year in Vienna to learn more about Freudian theory. In fact, Hullian learning theory is highly influenced by both Pavlovian and Freudian concepts, and Hull wanted to reconcile these seemingly different orientations (and many others) into a single, global scientific behavior theory (Hull, 1935). It resulted finally in his hypothetico-deductive system (Hull, 1952), a theoretical framework that the next generation of psychologists struggled to understand but that is still the prototypical example of what is now called neobehaviorism.

There were, however, several reasons to create new interventions. First, a growing number of clinical psychologists wanted to play an active role in therapeutic interventions, instead of being involved only in the diagnostic process. Psychologists brought a scientifically based knowledge in the various domains of psychology and empirical research, which was mostly superior to the psychological training of psychiatrists. Also, after World War II, there was an increased demand for therapeutic interventions for disorders that were too numerous to be treated by classical Freudian therapy and psychiatrists. The time was ripe for the growing number of clinical psychologists to receive psychotherapeutic training and for the construction of new methods of interventions. The end result was behavior therapy.

THE GROWTH OF BEHAVIOR THERAPY

The origins of behavior therapy cannot be attributed to one "father," as can some other orientations of psychotherapy (e.g., Freud, Rogers).[5] Rather, it is linked to a parallel development in three geographic centers: South Africa with Joseph Wolpe (and others), the United Kingdom with Hans Eysenck at Maudsley, and finally the United States with figures such as Mowrer and Skinner. These centers and figures all strongly influenced, with different emphases, the development of behavior therapy. They had a common intention: the application of learning principles and theories to gain a better understanding of the etiology and the treatment of maladaptive behavior.

In South Africa, Wolpe was as a psychiatrist trained in psychoanalytical treatment but was deeply dissatisfied with its therapeutic efficacy. He came into contact with two learning psychologists. First was James G. Tay-

---

[5]There is even discussion about who first used the term *behavior therapy*.

lor, a South African experimental psychologist and an avid follower of Hull, who introduced Wolpe to the Hullian analysis of perception. Even more important was Wolpe's contact with Leo Reyna, a graduate student of Kenneth Spence. Apart from Hull, Spence was the second most important figure in the neobehavioristic tradition. Reyna gave regular seminars in Johannesburg on the Hull–Spence learning theory and figured as a reader for Wolpe's MD dissertation (Wolpe, 1948). They remained close friends for the rest of their lives and were long-time editors of the influential *Journal of Behavior Therapy and Experimental Psychiatry*.

Through his contacts with Taylor and Reyna, Wolpe grew interested in the experimental foundations of learning principles and their applicability toward explaining pathological behavior. Wolpe decided to replicate some of the paradigms that had been used to create experimental neuroses but with the specific intention of finding methods to overcome and to treat these symptoms. His starting point was the paradigm of Masserman (1943) who had created experimental neurosis in cats by inducing an approach–avoidance conflict. Cats were trained to approach a food tray, but the same behavior led sometimes to the application of a punishing stimulus (a strong air puff in the cats' eyes), with the result that after a while the cats displayed "neurotic behavior" (agitation without an apparent cause, refusal to eat, etc.). Wolpe did not concur with Masserman's interpretation of these findings, however, which centered on the psychodynamic notion of the role of conflict. Wolpe wanted to demonstrate that conflict is not necessary to produce similar neurotic symptoms.

As a hospital psychiatrist, it was difficult for Wolpe to create an environment for experimentation on cats. He built an experimental cage in his office to deliver intense shocks, and the cats' home cage was constructed on the roof of the hospital. In this primitive setting, Wolpe made an observation that became important in his reciprocal inhibition principle. Each time he or his assistant carried a cat from the home cage to his office for an experimental trial, they noticed increasing nervousness and anxiety symptoms the closer they came to the office, where the cats had previously experienced the aversive trials. Once in the experimental cage, the cats showed signs of neurotic behavior. Even when the cats were extremely hungry, they hardly touched the food while in the experimental cage. There were no signs of extinction when the aversive shock was discontinued. Wolpe attributed these patterns of behavior to the Hullian principle of extinction. According to Hull, extinction is caused by reactive inhibition: The performance of any response is accompanied by an inhibitory tendency, and this inhibition leads to extinction (which was similar to Pavlov's theorizing about extinction, but with different explanations).

Wolpe thought that in the case of his cats, Hull's principle could not hold true because of the negligible reactive inhibition the autonomic responses evoked (compared with more molar motoric responses). To overcome this difficulty, Wolpe used another Hullian learning principle, the gradient of generalization: Fear reactions were clearly present in the original conditioning situation but were less pronounced in places or situations that were less similar to the original context. The purpose was now to overcome the first signs of fear by allowing the cats to perform a response, antagonistic to fear: eating. When the anxiety was no longer evident, the cats were moved to a situation that was more similar and closer to the original context. The rest of the story is well known: Wolpe and his team succeeded in feeding the cat in the original traumatic situation. These experiments formed the basis of Wolpe's reciprocal inhibition principle and the technique of systematic desensitization (Wolpe, 1958). In itself, the technique was not new, and Wolpe recognized his debt to the ideas of Pavlov, Watson, and Rayner, and Mary Cover-Jones's treatment of Peter (Wolpe, 1973).

Times had changed: Psychoanalysts were no longer dominating psychotherapy, and a large number of clinical psychologists were eager to discover new methods of intervention. The only difficulty for applying the principles of systematic desensitization to human fear was finding an appropriate antagonistic response to fear. Wolpe suggested several methods—assertive responses, sex, eating. The most successful and applicable method, however, was relaxation, in particular, a relaxation method developed by Jacobson (1938). Now all the ingredients were in place to develop an intervention for anxiety disorders. First, the therapist would help the client construct a hierarchy of anxiety-provoking stimuli and situations (i.e., a fear thermometer). Next, the therapist would provide explicit training in relaxation. Finally, the client would use the relaxation techniques to take successive steps in overcoming fears within the hierarchy. In most cases, the relaxation and steps were combined "in vitro" (i.e., by imagination).[6]

The method lent itself to a manualized presentation that could easily be applied. There were even instructions for the duration of evoking an anxiety-provoking situation, followed by instructions to relax (the therapist had a chronometer in his or her hand!). It was perhaps the first time in the history of psychotherapy that an intervention was described in operational terms, which still remains the great merit of Wolpe's ideas. It is thus not surprising that his intervention was the source of many empirical investigations. An extensive review by Kazdin and Wilcoxon (1976) made it clear that many of the steps in the procedure were not as necessary. Gradually the practice of systematic desensitization disappeared and was replaced by the concept of exposure, a purely descriptive concept.

---

[6]Wolpe warned about a superficial analysis of the relevant dimension for a stimulus analysis in setting up a hierarchy. He called it the "Achilles' heel" of behavior therapy. In applying his favorite technique, Wolpe devoted much time to finding the right dimension of a client's anxiety to construct an appropriate hierarchy. Of course, his reported successes (Wolpe, 1973) might have been in part caused by nonspecific factors (i.e., he was an excellent therapist).

Wolpe developed his technique in collaboration with others who later became the forerunners of behavior therapy, such as Arnold Lazarus as a postgraduate and Stanley Rachman and Terence Wilson as undergraduates. In 1956, Wolpe accepted a fellowship at the Center for Advanced Studies of Behavioral Sciences at Stanford University. During this sabbatical, he wrote *Psychotherapy by Reciprocal Inhibition* (Wolpe, 1958) and gave lectures at various universities at which his psychoanalytical colleagues constantly challenged him. As a result, Wolpe retained his defensive attitude toward psychoanalysis, even after the clinical community had widely accepted behavior therapy.

In 1962, he left South Africa permanently to join the faculty of the University of Virginia School of Medicine. In 1965 he became professor of psychiatry at Temple University and spent the most active period of his life at the Eastern Pennsylvania Psychiatric Institute. Under his directorship, the institute became a leading center for training in behavior therapy, and Wolpe worked with a number of excellent collaborators including Edna Foa, Alan Goldstein, Diane Chambless, Gail Steketee, and many others. Throughout his career, Wolpe remained confident in the validity of the Hullian and Pavlovian learning principles, even as behaviorism and neo-behaviorism lost their following. He was skeptical about the evolution toward cognitive therapy.

The other center of the beginning of behavior therapy and treatment based on learning principles was the Maudsley Hospital in London, under the directorship of Hans Eysenck. Eysenck had attained renown in the field of personality studies (an interest he maintained throughout his life). He was asked to construct a training program for clinical psychologists, which at that time scarcely existed outside of psychiatric programs. In his autobiography, he confessed, "I knew nothing of psychiatry or clinical and abnormal psychology . . . a field of study that I . . . did not particularly like" (Eysenck, 1980, p. 160). As an empirically oriented psychologist, he made a survey of the efficacy of existing psychotherapy methods according to available data. It resulted in an article, "The effects of psychotherapy: An evaluation" (Eysenck, 1952). Although the article is only five pages long and not at all polemical, it inspired, according to Bergin (1971), "two decades of vitriol." In fact, one might say it inspired several decades more!

On the basis of empirical evidence, Eysenck claimed that the traditional psychotherapies for mental disorders were no better than what could be expected from "spontaneous remission," a message that the clinical community certainly could not accept. Eysenck did not change his view in his follow-up studies on the effects of psychotherapy, however, and in fact added more controversy to the debate when he came to the conclusion that the only effective therapy was one "based upon modern learning theory" (i.e., behavior therapy; Eysenck, 1960).

The trend was set for the clinical program at Maudsley: It must provide training in methods derived from scientific psychology, and the Maudsley-trained clinical psychologist must do therapeutic work independent of a psychiatrist. One of the instigators for Eysenck in defining methods for treatment was, ironically enough, a refugee German psychoanalyst, Alexander Herzberg, who promoted, especially for anxiety problems, an "active psychotherapy," in which he incorporated tasks of graduated confrontation with the fearful situations—a therapy that was in sharp contrast to traditional psychoanalysis. Its emphasis on "exposure" (based on the learning principle of extinction) remained a hallmark of the early treatment methods of the Maudsley group and was reinforced with the arrival of Stanley Rachman, who became responsible for the clinical section, and Isaac Marks, head of the psychiatry department. In 1963, Eysenck edited the first volume of *Behaviour Research and Therapy*, which remains one of the most influential journals in the field. In his first editorial, Eysenck formulated the general philosophy of the new journal:

> The application of learning theory and the experimental method to clinical psychology also promises to carry this discipline beyond mere psychometry and close the gap between the laboratory and the clinic. . . . Contributions will stress equally the application of existing knowledge to psychiatric and social problems, experimental research into fundamental questions arising from these attempts to relate learning theory and maladaptive behaviour, and high level theoretical attempts to lay more secure foundations for experimental and observational studies along these lines. (Eysenck, 1963, p. 1)

This general philosophy has remained characteristic of the journal since its inception—more than 40 years ago as of this writing.

Finally, we consider developments in the United States, which may be considered the birthplace of learning theories and the home of the early applications we have already described. Apart from all insights into the use of classical conditioning, a major contribution came from the Skinnerian tradition in applying operant principles for populations that existing therapies generally failed to help (e.g., the first use of token economies with chronic psychiatric patients). We do not elaborate on these developments here, but the topic is considered in the discussion of avoidance behavior, a central topic in behavioral treatments based mainly on Mowrer's two-factor theory. Mowrer did not consider the application of learning theory to behavior therapy as being significantly different from psychoanalysis, however.[7]

CRITICISMS OF THE CONDITIONING APPROACH

Although the early behavioral therapists claimed to have developed superior methods with those of clinicians in other domains of psychopathol-

---

[7]He ultimately arrived at a semireligious belief system that stressed the role of confrontation offering relief from the guilt of ones "sins" (Mowrer, 1960, 1963).

ogy (phobias, obsessive–compulsive disorders, depression), the application of learning principles to clinical phenomena posed certain problems. In particular, the classical conditioning model of anxiety disorders evoked various criticisms, and these shaped the development not only of theories of anxiety disorders but also of more appropriate interventions. This continuous interaction between clinical findings and the more theoretical developments within the psychology of learning is one of the attractive hallmarks of behavior and cognitive–behavioral therapies. We briefly address the main critiques of the classical conditioning model of anxiety, which are discussed in more detail in later chapters of this volume (see chaps. 4, 5, 6, and 9, this volume).

The Problem of Extinction

The first critique concerns the relative resistance of clinical anxiety to extinction. The Albert and Peter cases (as reported by Watson and Rayner and by Jones, respectively) and Wolpe's cats were seemingly insensitive to extinction and required counterconditioning. In contrast, a rapid extinction of fear reactions would be predicted by the conditioning model when the aversive stimulus is no longer applied. Various ways to incorporate this resistance-to-extinction effect in the conditioning model have been developed in the literature. One solution came from the studies on avoidance learning by Miller and Mowrer, who were both associated with Hull's Institute of Human Relations at Yale University. The experimental paradigm is well known: An animal subject is placed in a shuttle box (of which there are many variants), and in one compartment a neutral stimulus (tone or light) is followed by an aversive stimulus (shock). As soon as the shock is applied, the animal tries to escape it and eventually jumps to the other compartment. After a few similar trials, the animal will no longer wait for the shock but will jump to the "safe side" as soon as the light or the tone is delivered. From then on, the animal displays avoidance behavior. The problem with explaining avoidance behavior from a Hullian perspective is well formulated by Mowrer: "How can a shock which is not experienced, i.e. which is avoided, be said to provide a source of motivation or of satisfaction?" (Mowrer, 1947, p. 108). It is easy to understand how the termination of shock reinforces the *escape* behavior earlier in the experiment; the surprising feature of *avoidance* behavior is that the omission of this reinforcer (as the shock and its termination are no longer experienced) does not extinguish that behavior. As noted in brief earlier, the two-factor theory states that the CS (signaling stimulus) evokes a CER (a conditioned emotional reaction of fear), which leads (by drive reduction) to escape and eventually to avoidance: the CAR (the conditioned avoidance response). This schema, CS–CER–CAR, has played an important role in the etiology and treatment of anxiety disorders (e.g., the technique of implosive therapy; Levis, 1985). It stimulated much research, and it extended learned fear beyond the unitary model of Pavlovian conditioning by stressing the importance of coping behaviors (or lack thereof). Nevertheless, the two-factor theory faces a number of problems (e.g., it fails to explain why the CER should not extinguish in avoidance learning). The chapter by Peter Lovibond later in this volume focuses on the developments in this field.

Apart from the studies on avoidance behavior, there have been other approaches to the difficult extinction of fear. The most controversial solution came from Eysenck (1979) with the concept of *incubation of fear*, on the basis of a rather obscure experiment by A. V. Napalkov in which a CR became more intense in response to a *nonreinforced* CS, which contradicts the usual extinction effect. Eysenck (1979) argued that there is much more empirical evidence for the incubation effect, especially with short CS durations and an intense original US. Although several critical commentators did not completely accept this concept, incubation effects found plausibility within a totally different domain of social psychology. Tesser (1978) demonstrated that repeatedly thinking or imagining positive or negative evaluated stimuli can have an incubation effect if there is no direct, actual confrontation with the stimulus. If a CS evokes a representation of the US, as is commonly accepted in most contemporary conditioning theories, the incubation effect is a plausible contributor to the resistance-to-extinction of pathological fear.

Another explanation for the resistance to extinction is linked to the notion of preparedness, introduced in the fear literature by Seligman (e.g., Seligman, 1971). The general idea is that there are some stimuli in our environment that are evolutionarily prone to becoming objects of conditioned fear (e.g., spiders, snakes, etc.) and are resistant to extinction. The notion inspired Öhman to set up an impressive research program (a recent overview is reported in Öhman & Mineka, 2001). One of the cardinal features of preparedness is the slow extinction rate of conditioned fear reactions to prepared stimuli. Preparedness theory has not been without criticism (see, e.g., McNally, 1987), in part because of Seligman's speculative definition of what can be considered as a criterion for "prepared stimuli": evolutionary significance of a specific species. Almost exclusively inspired by the original experiments of Öhman, pictures of spiders and snakes became prototypes of prepared stimuli, whereas pictures of flowers and mushrooms were typical unprepared stimuli.

One of the merits of preparedness theory is that it redirected attention to the ecological or functional role of Pavlovian conditioning in general (Domjan, 2005) and specifically in the domain of fear (Öhman & Mineka, 2001, see chap. 4, this volume). After all, Pavlov's work did not start with an arranged, contiguous relation between an arbitrary stimulus and food, but with the observation that the dogs were salivating in response to the sight or the smell of food.

Perhaps the most promising evolution in understanding resistance to extinction is the innovative research by Bouton (2002) and Rescorla (2001), who demonstrated that an extinction procedure renders the learned CS–US association behaviorally silent without erasing it. Under the right conditions, this association can again control the behavior. The consequence of this evolution for the extinction and return of fear are well documented in this volume (see chaps. 9, 10, 11, this volume).

The Problem of the Unconditioned Stimulus and Conditioned Stimulus

A classical conditioning approach is based on a model in which an original neutral stimulus (conditional stimulus; CS) is followed by a stimulus that evokes a strong, mostly emotional reaction (US–UR [unconditioned response]). A number of problems are encountered when fitting anxiety disorders into this model, however. These problems are related to the following questions: (a) What are the limits for defining an event as a US–UR, or as a CS–CR (conditioned response)? (b) Why is it not always clear to the patient whether a US–UR event occurred? (c) Why do victims of traumatic experiences often not develop anxiety symptoms? (d) Are there more pathways to the conditioning of fear?

It is beyond the scope of this chapter to elaborate on these issues, but the interested reader is referred to chapters 4 and 5 of this volume.

In relation to the formulated critiques, the conditioning model of anxiety disorders may not be falsifiable. But must it to be proved false? A model is not a theory, and there are many theories about conditioning that have been proved false in the past. We regard conditioning more as a basic assumption with regard to anxiety problems (Eelen, Hermans, & Baeyens, 2001).

THE GROWTH OF COGNITIVE–BEHAVIORAL THERAPY

It is ironic that behavior therapy (heavily inspired by neobehaviorism) came to its apex at the moment when behaviorism was no longer the leading theoretical model within psychology and had been replaced by what some have called "a cognitive revolution." It was as if the psychological community suddenly discovered that studying the behavior of rats and pigeons could not be directly applied to human functioning. Conditioning and learning in general were no longer central topics of interest and were replaced by processes of attention, memory, representation, and attribution. At the beginning of this (r)evolution, it looked as though we were back to psychology being an introspective enterprise. This was due in part to the way *cognition* was defined primarily as being the content of our conscious thoughts. The impact of this evolution became apparent in different fields of psychology and, of course, also within behavior therapy. Promoters were Beck (1972) and the less popular Ellis (1962) with his rational emotive therapy. Both had analytical backgrounds and felt that the impact of conscious thoughts within psychoanalysis was being underestimated as a by-product of unconscious processes. They emphasized the irrationality of certain thoughts and that the primary intervention within psychotherapy could be regarded as convincing (through Socratic dialogue but also through behavioral exercises) the patient that his or her thoughts in certain anxiety-inducing situations were indeed irrational. For some psychologists, this philosophy, which seemed to imply that therapy was simply an exercise in logical thinking that should change emotional responses, was unacceptable.

The real contributions of the cognitive evolution came from the more theoretical models developed within cognitive psychology, which encompass a larger field than simply the study and description of conscious thoughts. New methods were used to detect the mostly unconscious cognitive processes, but behavioral and empirical indices were used to describe them. The classical Stroop test (1935) became a central research method for studying anxiety disorders. Other indirect measures for studying cognitive processes such as priming, subliminal perception, and attentional biases also developed. This movement within cognitive therapy upholds the original philosophy of behavior therapy by linking clinical phenomena with the knowledge acquired in general theoretical and experimental psychology.

One could argue that the term *cognitive–behavioral therapy* is a misnomer, or at least a tautology. It is difficult to imagine a behavior that is not influenced by cognitive processes (even in Pavlov's dogs) or to detect the role of cognitive processes without looking for a behavioral expression. At least the addition of the term *cognitive* to behavior therapy has resulted in more general acceptance but at the expense of losing contact with the original basis and interest in conditioning studies.

CONCLUSION

In this chapter, we have focused on the evolution of understanding anxiety problems within the development of conditioning models. Readers will note that other emphases and approaches in the rich 100-year history of behaviorism exist but could not be covered in a single chapter. What we have hoped to do is to highlight what we consider the major developments for researchers and clinicians interested in behavior therapy for anxiety disorders.

The danger exists that we lose track of the rich empirical research inspired by an associative account of anxiety disorders. It would be unwise to abandon this learning approach by assuming it is outdated. It still offers the clinical psychologist a strong heuristic framework for conceptualizing therapeutic endeavors and remains an ideal meeting ground for theory and practice (Eelen et al., 2001).

We end this chapter with a few words from Wolpe:

"conditioning" equals "learning.". . . If conditioning is the basis of thera-peutic change, it is likely that all therapists would have better control of change within their own frameworks, if, like the behavior therapists, they made use of available knowledge of the learning process and the factors that influence it. *To those who deny that learning is the mechanism on which therapeutic change depends, the question must be put: If it is not learning, what is it?* (Wolpe, 1976, p. 67, italics added)

It is hoped that learning theories and experimental psychology will re-main an inspiring foundation for behavior and cognitive–behavioral thera-pies.

2

HUMAN FEAR LEARNING: CONTEMPORARY PROCEDURES AND MEASUREMENT

OTTMAR V. LIPP

Has there ever been a better time to be a researcher interested in the acquisition and maintenance of human fear? Given recent developments in fear research on the molecular, neural, and behavioral levels, it seems difficult to answer this question in the negative. On the molecular and neural levels, basic neuroscience research has not only documented the neural circuits involved in unconditioned fear and fear learning (for review, see P. J. Lang, Davis, & Öhman, 2000; chap. 3, this volume) but has also begun to illuminate the biochemical processes that mediate learning at the neural level (chap. 8, this volume). This research has already resulted in the development of interventions that seem to enhance the effectiveness of traditional exposure therapies (Ressler et al., 2004). On the behavioral level, our understanding of the conditions that generate and maintain fear learning has seen a major revision. Due largely to the seminal work of Robert Rescorla (2001) and Mark Bouton (1993, chap. 9, this volume) and their colleagues, a shift has occurred in the manner in which extinction, the process thought to underlie many behaviorally based interventions, is conceptualized. Rather than viewing extinction as the unlearning of previously established associations, we now regard extinction as the acquisition of new learning that masks the original association without eliminating it; a view that has considerable implications for the design of effective behavioral interventions (for a different view on the nature of extinction suggesting, on the basis of molecular data, that extinction comprises erasure of learning at some sites and maintenance at others, see chap. 8, this volume). These developments are currently based almost exclusively on research with nonhuman animal participants, however. Given that the extent to which we can generalize across species is limited not only by gross anatomical differences but also by the fact that humans can acquire knowledge in a number of ways that are not open to rodents (e.g., verbal instruction), it is imperative that we investigate the extent to which findings from nonhuman animal research are of relevance to human fear learning.

It is fortuitous that the increased need for research on human fear learning has coincided with the development of a number of procedures and techniques that render such experimentation more reliable. It is the purpose of this chapter to review the procedures that are currently used to investigate fear learning in humans as well as the basic methodologies used for the measurement of experimentally induced fear. The latter have been designed to tap the three levels of fear reactions, verbal (cognition and affect), behavioral, and physiological (P. J. Lang, 1985). In particular, the use of physiological measures, such as changes in autonomic nervous system activity or reflex parameters, offers the opportunity to conduct research that closely parallels the paradigms used in animal experimentation.

STIMULI AND PROCEDURES IN HUMAN FEAR LEARNING

In the prototypical nonhuman animal fear-learning study, a neutral conditioned stimulus (CS) is paired repeatedly with an aversive electric shock unconditioned stimulus (US) until fear reactions can be observed to the originally neutral stimulus alone. The CS can be a discrete event such as a brief presentation of a tone or light or the context in which the experiment is conducted. Human studies on fear learning have frequently copied these stimulus conditions, pairing neutral CSs with aversive stimuli such as loud noises, electric shock, or aversive visual stimuli (pictures, words) and can thus be regarded as analogues.

Conditioned Stimuli

Conditioned stimuli are those that elicit a conditioned response only after repeated pairing with the US. Thus, within the context of fear learning, a CS is affectively neutral prior to acquisition training. CSs have been drawn from a variety of sources, although the majority of studies seem to rely on visual

CSs, most likely because of the ease with which many distinct stimuli can be created and presented. Stimuli include lights of different color (e.g., Grillon & Ameli, 1998), simple geometric shapes (e.g., Lipp, Siddle, & Dall, 2003) and pictures of human faces that have been rated as neutral prior to the experiment (e.g., Hermans, Crombez, Vansteenwegen, Baeyens, & Eelen, 2002). In addition, tones of different pitch and simple tactile stimuli have been used (e.g., Lipp, Siddle, & Dall, 1998). Fewer studies have investigated the effects of context on conditioned responding, although contextual stimuli can be implemented in a similar fashion (Lachnit, 1986; see Baas, Nugent, Lissek, Pine, & Grillon, 2004, for use of virtual reality to create experimental contexts).

A special case is constituted by the use of fear-relevant CSs, for example, pictures of snakes, spiders, or angry facial expressions (for a review, see Öhman & Mineka, 2001). Pairing of these CSs with aversive USs has been shown to promote conditioning that differs from conditioning with neutral CSs in that it is resistant to extinction, seen after a single trial, and less affected by verbal instructions. Moreover, recent studies have shown that electrodermal conditioning can be observed even if these CSs are presented outside conscious perception (e.g., Öhman & Soares, 1998). Most of the studies that investigated fear learning with fear-relevant stimuli used electrodermal responses, a dependent measure that is not selectively sensitive to emotional learning (P. J. Lang, Greenwald, Bradley, & Hamm, 1993; Lipp & Vaitl, 1990). Hence it is difficult to interpret the results as unambiguously reflecting the acquisition of fear rather than the cognitive processes involved in associative learning.

Unconditioned Stimuli

The most frequently used procedure in human fear learning involves, as in animal conditioning, the application of electrotactile stimuli as the USs. These stimuli can be generated with either commercially available or custom-built equipment (e.g., Kimmel, King, Huddy, & Gardner, 1980) and are best presented through concentric electrodes that limit the current flow to a small area of skin (Tursky, Watson, & O'Connell, 1965). The application of these stimuli is unproblematic and acceptable to ethics review boards if a number of basic directions are followed. The maximal current output of the devise has to be limited, the intensity of the stimulus is to be determined individually by the participant, and the chosen intensity is to remain constant. Individual determination of the US intensity involves the presentation of stimuli of increasing intensity starting at zero and terminating at an intensity that is perceived as "unpleasant, but not painful." This procedure leaves the participant in control and avoids presentation of stimuli that are too strong. Moreover, the matching to an individual intensity level permits the control of subjective US salience, which is not possible if a physically defined intensity is used for all participants. The perceived intensity will vary with factors other than physical intensity, such as quality of contact with skin, location of electrodes, and skin anatomy. The duration of the electric stimuli varies across studies, ranging from a few milliseconds to 500 milliseconds. A potential shortcoming of the workup procedure is that preexposure of the US may limit its effectiveness because of habituation and can retard subsequent learning because of the US preexposure effect (A. G. Baker, Mercier, Gabel, & Baker, 1981). These limitations are outweighed, however, by greater participant acceptance and the opportunity to match the subjective intensity across participants.

Alternatively, researchers have used auditory stimuli such as loud noise, pure tones, or more complex events such as human screams (Hamm, Vaitl, & Lang, 1989) as USs. Calibration of the stimulus presentation system is essential when using acoustic stimuli to confirm the actual sound pressure levels (SPLs). The U.S. Occupational Safety and Health Act standards (occupational noise exposure, 1910.95) state that hearing protection is not required if, at a stimulus intensity of 115 dB(A) SPL, the sound is presented for less than 15 min per day. This standard refers to continuous noise, not to the impulse stimuli of a few seconds that are used as USs. Thus, care is required when selecting a stimulus intensity, and lower intensities of 100 to 105 dB(A) SPL are preferable. It should also be noted that the salience of acoustic USs varies with participants' hearing, which may vary considerably given the extent of noise pollution or differences in participant age. As an alternative to shocks and loud noises, Grillon and Ameli (1998) suggested the use of air blasts directed at the participants' larynx, in particular, for research with younger participants.

Studies that aim to avoid the use of intense physical stimuli have used visual stimuli such as pictures selected from the International Affective Picture System (Center for the Study of Emotion and Attention, 1999), a set of color photographs that were rated for valence and arousal. Unfortunately, the results from these studies are inconsistent. Whereas verbal ratings of CS valence and behavioral measures seem to indicate the effectiveness of the picture USs, physiological measures, in particular, blink startle modulation, have yielded mixed results, with some indicating the presence of fear learning (Allen, Wong, Kim, & Trinder, 1996) whereas others do not (Lipp, Cox, & Siddle, 2001). More work is required to confirm the utility of picture USs in the context of fear conditioning.

An interesting alternative is the use of CO_2-enriched air as a US (e.g., Forsyth & Eifert, 1998). The CO_2-enriched air is presented through a breathing mask at concentrations between 7.5% and 20%. Pairing either olfactory or visual CSs with this US has yielded reliable differential conditioning of autonomic and skeletomuscular parameters and of verbal reports of discomfort. The CO_2 procedure has the advantage of mimicking restricted breathing, a stimulus condition that is associated with experiences of anxiety.

In summary, a number of US procedures are available for the establishment of fear analogs in human experimentation. Procedures that involve intense physical stimuli such as shock, loud noise, or air blasts have yielded reliable conditioning effects across verbal, behavioral, and physiological indices. Moreover, the physiological changes seen during aversive conditioning mirror those established during fear conditioning in rodents: sympathetic activation (Öhman, Hamm, & Hugdahl, 2000), fear-potentiated startle (Hamm & Vaitl, 1996), and increased blood flow in brain areas involved in the mediation of fear reactions (Büchel & Dolan, 2000).

Conditioning Procedures

The majority of human fear-learning studies uses a simple differential delay conditioning procedure in which the offset of one CS (CS+) coincides with or is preceded by the onset of the US, whereas a second CS is presented alone (CS–). Conditioning is evident in differential responding to the two CSs and can usually be found within as few as four trials. This paradigm differs from the single-cue conditioning designs preferred in animal work. In a single-cue design, animals are presented with only one CS paired with the US. Conditioning is assessed in comparison to a control group that is trained with a random sequence of CSs and USs or with an explicitly unpaired stimulus sequence (e.g., Lipp, Sheridan, & Siddle, 1994). The latter can result in inhibitory conditioning, which may confound the interpretation of results (Rescorla, 1967). The preference for the differential conditioning procedure in human research reflects on its enhanced power, within- versus between-subject comparisons, and economy because it requires fewer participants. Moreover, it permits control for orienting and other responses mediated by nonassociative processes, which is important if autonomic nervous system responses, such as electrodermal or cardiac responses, serve as dependent variables (Prokasy, 1977).

Decisions about specific parameters such as CS duration, interstimulus interval (ISI), intertrial interval (ITI), or number of trials are driven largely by pragmatic considerations and reflect a compromise between the desire to obtain reliable conditioning and the interests of the participants because the experiment should not consume more of the participants' time than necessary. Studies that measure autonomic responses (electrodermal, cardiac, etc.) require CSs of typically 6 to 8 seconds and an ITI (CS onset to CS onset) of more than 20 seconds to avoid response interference. Studies that involve verbal measures only can be performed with CSs lasting 1 or 2 seconds and ITIs of 4 to 5 seconds, just longer than the ISI. The basic paradigm can be modified by the addition of contextual stimuli (e.g., Lachnit, 1986) or occasion setters (e.g., Hardwick & Lipp, 2000) to create more complex procedures. In Lachnit's (1986) context-conditioning procedure, room illumination signaled whether a tone CS was followed by the US. Illuminations lasted for several minutes and were alternated in a pseudorandom sequence. Conditioned responses to the CS differed between contexts; moreover, the context stimuli elicited differential responses. Hardwick and Lipp (2000) used a sequential feature positive (A → B-US/B) or negative paradigm (B-US/A → B) in which the presence of a feature stimulus A disambiguated the relationship between a subsequently presented target stimulus B and the US. Here, startle potentiation during the target was restricted to trials in which the feature had indicated the occurrence of the US. It should be noted that some conditioning phenomena, in particular, those reflecting stimulus competition (blocking, inhibitory conditioning), may be difficult to observe in humans (but see Neumann, Lipp, & Siddle, 1997). This may reflect differences in the manner in which multicomponent stimuli are processed (D. A. Williams, Sagness, & McPhee, 1994).

Although its power is one of the major advantages of the differential conditioning procedure, this can become a disadvantage if one is interested in subtle differences in the speed of learning because differential learning may be acquired too quickly. Under these circumstances, it is advisable to use a less powerful procedure such as single-cue conditioning (Lipp et al., 1994) or use a trace instead of a delay conditioning procedure. In trace conditioning, the onset of the US is separated from CS offset by a brief time interval, the trace interval. Alternatively, USs may be presented after only a portion of CS+ presentations reducing the contingency between CS+ and US. Finally, differences in conditioning may be assessed during extinction rather than acquisition if acquisition progresses too rapidly (Öhman, 1986).

An interesting variant of the basic conditioning procedure is the threat of shock paradigm (Grillon, Ameli, Woods, Merikangas, & Davis, 1991) in which the US is said to occur after one CS but does not eventuate, or eventuates less than participants expected. The conditioned responses in this procedure resemble those in simple Pavlovian conditioning and may even be superior in size because the US is not subject to habituation. Grillon (2002) describes a modification of the *threat of shock* paradigm with three experimental conditions: a safe conditioning in which no aversive stimuli are presented, a predictable condition in which the aversive event may occur after the CS, and an unpredictable condition in which the aversive event may occur at any time. The unpredictable condition is said to support contextual conditioning and to permit the assessment of anxiety in addition to that of fear of a discrete stimulus as seen in the predictable condition.

THE MEASUREMENT OF EXPERIMENTALLY INDUCED FEAR

Following P. J. Lang's (1985) bioinformational model, human fear is expressed on three levels: verbal, behavioral, and physiological. Verbal measures include subjective ratings of CS valence or fear of the CS as well as reports of US expectation or contingency knowledge. On the behavioral level, response time (RT)-based measures can reflect changes in CS valence (e.g., Fazio & Olson, 2003) and cognitive resource allocation during conditioning (secondary probe RT; Dawson, Schell, Beers, & Kelly, 1982). Physiological measures reflecting activity of the autonomic or skeletal nervous system have a long tradition in studies of human fear learning (M. M. Bradley, 2000; Öhman et al., 2000). One of the main advantages of physiological measures is the comparison with studies involving nonhuman animal participants. Contrary to earlier studies of human fear learning, which often used only single dependent measures, contemporary research attempts to assess fear on all three response levels. This change is driven by the desire to provide a more complete picture of the learning process in question as well as the realization that single measures have specific limitations that can be overcome in a process of converging operations.

Verbal Measures

Given the limitations imposed by common sense and experimental ethics on the extent of fear conditioned in a laboratory analogue, it is unlikely that one will observe fear responses resembling those seen in clinical practice (but see Campbell, Sanderson, & Laverty, 1964; Watson & Rayner, 1920). Thus, verbal reports are more likely to indicate the acquisition of unpleasantness rather than of fear of the CS. Verbal assessments of CS valence or fear are easily obtained using paper and pencil or computer-based rating scales (e.g., Hermans et al., 2002). Usually, participants are asked to indicate their evaluation of the CSs used during training, and of control stimuli not presented during training to control for mere exposure effects (Zajonc, 2001). These assessments are collected on visual analog or Likert scales before and after acquisition and then after extinction. The verbal measures are sensitive to changes in CS valence, negative or positive.

Verbal measures can also be used to assess the extent to which participants have learned and can verbalize the CS–US relationship. Dawson and Reardon (1973) compared recognition and recall questionnaires used to assess CS–US contingency awareness in postexperimental test sessions. Recall measures comprised questions such as "Were you ever able to tell when the US occurred?" whereas recognition measures comprised multiple choice items such as "The US followed the (a) picture of a square, (b) picture of a circle, (c) no picture in particular, (d) I could not tell." Recognition measures had the highest hit rate and the lowest percentage of false alarms, which, together with their ease of application, render them superior. Dawson and Reardon (1973) also concluded, however, that postexperimental measures of contingency awareness are not optimal and that contingency awareness is best assessed during conditioning training. Inability to report the contingency in a postexperimental questionnaire may reflect on a genuine failure to learn the CS–US relationship. However, it may be that simple forgetting, effects of extinction training, or characteristics of the posttraining test procedure itself interfered with contingency knowledge between acquisition training and testing (for more detail see Shanks & St. John, 1994).

An alternative to pre- and postexperimental questionnaires is the collection of verbal reports during acquisition or extinction. Several devices, such as dial and pointer setups or choice-button boxes have been used to collect participants' moment-by-moment knowledge of the experimental contingencies (e.g., Purkis & Lipp, 2001) or evaluation of the CSs (Lipp, Oughton, & LeLievre, 2003). Although permitting a fine-grained analysis of the acquisition of US expectancy or conditioned fear, these measures have the disadvantage of focusing participants' attention on the dependent measure and thus facilitating the learning process. This potential interference can be compensated for by embedding the Pavlovian conditioning contingency in a masking task (e.g., Purkis & Lipp, 2001).

The problems associated with postexperimental testing sessions were illustrated by Lipp and colleagues (2003), who found differential valence ratings for CS+ and CS– in the postextinction test although they had been absent toward the end of extinction training. Previous findings of differential evaluations of CS+ and CS– in postextinction tests have been taken to indicate that acquired valence does not extinguish. The failure to find differential evaluations during extinction training is inconsistent with such an interpretation. The differences between measures taken during extinction and in postextinction tests may reflect different evaluation strategies used at different times of the experiment. Collins and Shanks (2002) have shown that participants integrated causal judgments across the entire experiment when asked only after the experiment, whereas they provided judgments of the momentary predictive value of a cue if asked at different stages of training. However, these results may reflect renewal of fear learning caused by context change (Bouton, 1994), that is, a genuine reappearance of conditioned fear that was reduced or lost during extinction training. A distinction between the two accounts is currently not possible, mainly because research on renewal in human fear learning (see chap. 10, this volume) and the role of evaluation strategies has begun only recently. However, the mechanisms that affect fear reports in postextinction tests are of interest in applied settings as follow-up measurements after therapy are an example of postexperimental rating sessions.

A second major disadvantage of verbal measures, whether collected during or after conditioning, is their susceptibility to demand characteristics. Most standard conditioning procedures are transparent, using only a small number of CSs and USs. Thus, participants may have little difficulty determining the purpose of the experiment and may feel compelled to respond in a manner that does or does not support the experimenter. Thus, reliance on verbal measures alone can render the interpretation of results difficult.

Behavioral Measures

The behavioral measure of choice for the assessment of fear—for instance, in the study of the effectiveness of therapeutic interventions—is the approach test (e.g., Craske, DeCola, Sachs, & Pontillo, 2003). Participants are asked to approach the feared stimulus, and distance is taken as an index of fear. Similar procedures have been used in laboratory-based studies of human fear learning, albeit infrequently (e.g., Foa, McNally, Steketee, & McCarthy, 1991; Malloy & Levis, 1988). Recent developments of implicit measures for the assessment of attitudes (Fazio & Olson, 2003) and of attentional biases in anxiety (E. Fox, 2004) have provided a number of RT-based measures that are promising as behavioral indices of fear learning. The affective priming paradigm (Fazio & Olson, 2003) assesses the extent to which a valence match between a prime and target stimulus facilitates classification of the target as positive or negative or target naming (Spruyt, Hermans, De Houwer, & Eelen, 2004). In the classification, variant primes are presented briefly followed by the target (for more detail, see Klauer & Musch, 2003). Target classification is faster with fewer errors if the valence of prime and target match (i.e., positive prime–positive target) than when they are mismatched (e.g., positive prime–negative target). Hermans et al. (2002; Hermans, Baeyens, & Eelen, 2003) used an affective priming task after conditioning training and confirmed that affective priming can track the acquisition of CS valence.

Studies of attentional bias in anxiety have shown that anxious participants allocate attention preferentially to threatening stimuli relative to nonthreatening stimuli (Mogg & Bradley, 1999). This preferential processing has been assessed in a number of procedures. MacLeod, Mathews, and Tata (1986) presented anxious participants with two words at different locations on a computer screen, which were followed by the presentation of a probe stimulus, a dot, which replaced one of the word stimuli. Participants were faster to locate the dot if it was presented after a threatening word than after a nonthreatening word. Similar results have been obtained in studies using pictorial stimuli, for example, threatening and nonthreatening faces (Mogg & Bradley, 1999). Purkis (2004) used the dot probe task to index conditioned fear and found evidence for attentional biases toward animal picture CSs, birds and horses, and neutral geometric shape CSs after pairing with an aversive US.

In addition to the dot probe task, Purkis (2004) used a visual search task that has been used to assess the preferential processing of fear-relevant stimuli such as pictures of snakes or spiders (Öhman, Flykt, & Esteves, 2001). Participants are presented with, for instance, a matrix of nine pictures and asked to decide whether all pictures come from one category (e.g., all snakes) or whether there is a deviant among them (e.g., a snake among flowers). Öhman and colleagues (2001) found that fear-relevant deviants are found faster among non-fear-relevant backgrounds than vice versa; participants find a spider faster among mushrooms than a mushroom among spiders. Purkis (2004) replicated this finding using neutral geometric shape CSs. Participants found the CS+ faster among CS– backgrounds than vice versa.

Fox and colleagues (for a review, see E. Fox, 2004) used an exogenous cuing task to assess whether threat stimuli preferentially capture or hold attention in anxiety. In this task, a single cue is presented on either side of the screen while participants are instructed to focus on its center. Presentation of the cue is followed by the presentation of a target either in the cued location (valid trials) or in the uncued location (invalid trials). On valid trials, there was no difference between threat and nonthreat cues, angry versus neutral faces. On invalid trials, however, performance was slower after a threatening cue. This finding suggests that the threatening stimuli hold attention for longer than do nonthreatening stimuli. Koster, Crombez, Van Damme, Verschuere, and de Houwer (2004) adapted the exogenous cuing paradigm to assess whether CSs will preferentially attract or hold attention. Colored rectangles, pink or green, served as CSs in a differential conditioning procedure with a loud-noise US. Koster et al. (2004) found evidence for faster target detection after the CS+ on valid trials and for slower target detection after CS+ on invalid trials. Thus, contrary to the results with a prior threatening stimulus, CS+ seemed not only to hold attention longer but also to capture attention preferentially.

In summary, the RT-based measures of stimulus valence, affective priming, dot probe, visual search, or exogenous cuing offer an alternative for the assessment of conditioned fear that is less subject to demand characteristics than are verbal measures. However, these measures are not without problems. Affective priming, dot probe, and visual search require testing in a postexperimental test session, which may be subject to interference because of renewal by context change, spontaneous recovery, or lack of generalization across different modes of stimulus presentation. Koster et al. (2004) avoided this problem by embedding the conditioning procedure in the exogenous cuing task. This, however, raises the possibility of interference between tasks. A second disadvantage of RT-based procedures is the need to aggregate RTs across trials to obtain stable indices. This prevents the analysis of changes within, for instance, acquisition or extinction sessions. This disadvantage can be alleviated by scheduling the tasks at different times during the experiment, for example, complete affective priming tasks before and after acquisition and after extinction to track changes in conditioned fear while maintaining the continuity of the experiment to avoid renewal. It is currently unknown whether the sensitivity of the tasks will be stable across repeated presentations, however.

RT-based measures have also been used to map the cognitive processes that occur during conditioning itself. M. E. Dawson et al. (1982) used a secondary task RT technique to assess the extent to which attentional resources are allocated to the processing of CSs during fear learning. In this technique, an increase in the cognitive resources taken up by the primary task, conditioning, is indicated by the deterioration of the performance on the secondary task, slower RTs. Dawson et al. (1982) presented probe stimuli in a differential conditioning procedure and found slower probe RTs during CS+ than during CS–, indicating larger resource allocation during CS+. Dirikx, Hermans, Vansteenwegen, Baeyens, and Eelen (2004) used the secondary task technique in an experiment on reinstatement of fear conditioning in humans. Slower probe RTs during CS+ than during CS– were observed during acquisition but not during extinction. The presentation of two USs alone after extinction reinstated the differential RT slowing, whereas no such effect was seen in a control group. It is interesting that the extent of reinstatement of differential RT slowing was related to the evaluations of the CSs at the end of extinction. The larger the difference in evaluations of CS+ and CS–, the larger was the reinstatement of differential RT slowing. This interesting finding hints at a relation between emotional and cognitive indices of fear learning and requires further investigation.

Physiological Measures

Physiological measures—in particular, measurements of autonomic nervous system activity—have long been central to research in human fear learning. This reflects on their sensitivity to associative learning as well as on the fact that autonomic nervous system responses are prominent in fear symptomatology. Their usefulness is limited, however, by the fact that autonomic responses are not selectively sensitive to fear, a shortcoming that led to the inclusion of other physiological measures associated with the fear response, such as blink-startle modulation or changes in cerebral blood flow. The chief advantage of physiological measures is that they can be recorded at the same time that learning occurs. Moreover, some physiological measures are outside conscious control and thus less vulnerable to demand characteristics. Blink startle, for instance, is a brain-stem reflex mediated by two to three synapses, which cannot be consciously influenced. Responses mediated by the autonomic nervous system, however, are readily affected by voluntary or involuntary maneuvers such as movements or changes in breathing patterns. The chief disadvantages of physiological measures are cost (in terms of equipment and time required to collect and score) and demand on the participant (for issues relating to safety, see Putnam, Johnson, & Roth, 1992). Moreover, their recording may interfere with the acquisition or extinction of fear because of reactivity to the measurement devices or the requirement to present intense probe stimuli. Blink-startle measurement, for instance, requires the placement of two electrodes under the participant's eye, a procedure that can be perceived as irritating, and requires the presentation of reflex-eliciting stimuli, usually brief loud noises. Nevertheless, physiological measures have the potential to provide unique information that otherwise might not be accessible.

Autonomic Measures

The most frequently used measure in the study of human fear learning is electrodermal activity (for details, see M. E. Dawson, Schell, & Filion, 2000; Fowles et al., 1981). Electrodermal activity is measured easily and is highly sensitive to psychological processes such as orienting to signals and anticipation of salient events that are central to learning in general and fear learning in particular (Öhman et al., 2000). In conditioning paradigms that use ISIs of 6 to 8 seconds, three discrete electrodermal responses can be distinguished, the first reflecting orienting to CS onset, the second reflecting anticipation of the US, and the third reflecting the unconditioned response to the US during acquisition and the omission of the US during extinction (Prokasy & Kumpfer, 1973). Of the two anticipatory response components, the first is usually larger than the second and, because it is highly sensitive to conditioning manipulations, it is frequently the only one reported. There are, however, instances when effects of the experimental manipulations emerged only in the second component, most likely because the first component also reflects nonassociative processes such as orienting (Prokasy, 1977).

The main disadvantage of electrodermal activity is that it is not selectively sensitive to fear learning. A CS paired with an aversive US (e.g., electrotactile stimulus) will elicit the same patterns of electrodermal responding as a CS paired with a nonaversive US (e.g., the "go" signal of an RT task; Lipp & Vaitl, 1990). Moreover, aversive and appetitive stimuli will elicit electrodermal responses of similar size if they are equated for arousal (M. M. Bradley, 2000).

The cardiovascular system provides a number of indices that have been used in human fear conditioning (see Brownley, Hurwitz, & Schneiderman, 2000). Heart rate, derived from the interbeat interval measured as the time between successive R-waves in the electrocardiogram, is the most frequently used cardiovascular index in conditioning. Heart rate responses to CSs in anticipation of a US display a characteristic three-phasic response pattern of initial deceleration, followed by a transient acceleration and subsequent deceleration (Bohlin & Kjellberg, 1979; for details, see Jennings et al., 1981). Similar to electrodermal responses, the first component of the heart rate response is thought to reflect orienting to the CS, whereas the acceleration and second deceleration are thought to reflect anticipation of the US. In contrast to electrodermal responses, conditioned and unconditioned heart rate responses seem to be sensitive to the affective valence of the eliciting stimuli. The unconditioned response to an aversive electrotactile stimulus is a brief acceleration of heart rate (Lipp & Vaitl, 1990). E. W. Cook, Hodes, and Lang (1986) found an enhancement of the accelerative response component during fear-relevant CSs (pictures of snakes and spiders) paired with an aversive US but not for non-fear-relevant CSs (pictures of flowers and mushrooms). This dissociation in conditioned response topography was not replicated in a study that used neutral CSs but varied the aversiveness of the US and observed conditioned decelerations with both US types (Lipp & Vaitl, 1990). Thus, it seems likely that the enhanced acceleration is restricted to studies that use intense USs or fear-relevant CSs. Aversive pictorial stimuli elicit a larger second deceleration than do pleasant stimuli (M. M. Bradley, 2000); however, increases in heart rate have been observed in phobic participants when confronted with their feared stimuli (Globisch, Hamm, Esteves, & Öhman, 1999). This difference seems to reflect the larger threat value of the phobic stimuli, which seems to trigger a defense reflex in contrast to less intense unpleasant pictures.

The increased availability of brain imaging techniques, in particular, functional magnetic resonance imaging, to psychological research has prompted the assessment of cerebral blood flow during fear conditioning in humans (Büchel & Dolan, 2000). These studies were mainly motivated by the desire to confirm the neural architecture of fear circuits established in animal research (see chap. 3, this volume) and have done much to delineate the neural bases of human fear.

Skeletal Nervous System Measures

The startle reflex has become increasingly popular as a probe for psychological processes over the last 20 years (for review, see M. E. Dawson, Schell, & Böhmelt, 1999). The use of the startle reflex in human fear learning is intended to extend work in animal conditioning in which fear-potentiated startle is well researched to the extent that the underlying neurobiology has been determined (P. J. Lang et al., 2000). Resembling results in animal research, startle reflexes in humans (for details, see Blumenthal et al., 2005), have been shown to be potentiated in anticipation of aversive, electrotactile USs (Hamm & Vaitl, 1996; Lipp et al., 1994). Moreover, relative to blinks elicited during neutral affective states, startle blinks elicited during aversive states—for instance, while watching aversive pictures—are facilitated, whereas blinks elicited during pleasant states are inhibited (P. J. Lang et al., 1990). Startle reflexes can be elicited at any time during the presentation of CSs and USs and thus permit the investigation of processes that occur during training or shortly after CS onset. Moreover, blink reflexes are outside conscious control. These advantages, however, are tempered by a number of issues that seem to limit the utility of the fear-potentiated startle paradigm in human fear conditioning.

Startle reflexes are elicited by medium- to high-intensity stimuli (e.g., 50-ms bursts of 100-dB(A) white noise), which themselves are regarded as aversive by participants. Thus, it is conceivable that the reflex-eliciting stimuli affect the emotional process under investigation. This potential confound can be limited by using lower intensity reflex-eliciting stimuli, albeit at the expense of reduced reflex amplitudes and probabilities, or by eliciting blinks with low-intensity air-puff stimuli, which seem subject to fear potentiation in the absence of an aversive reflex-eliciting stimulus (Lissek et al., 2005). Second, Cuthbert, Bradley, and Lang (1996) have shown that startle is potentiated during highly arousing aversive images but not during less arousing, but equally unpleasant, images. This prompted Vansteenwegen, Crombez, Baeyens, and Eelen (1998) to suggest that startle modulation may be a suitable measure of human fear conditioning during acquisition when CS arousal, as indexed by electrodermal responses, is high, but not during extinction, when CS arousal decreases. Thus, in an attempt to explain the retention of fear learning in verbal indices in the absence of reflex potentiation, these authors suggested that a failure to see fear-potentiated startle during extinction of human fear learning may reflect not a decline in conditioned fear but a decline in arousal. Alternatively, this discordance may reflect idiosyncrasies of verbal indices collected during a postextinction test rather than on the sensitivity of reflex probes. Third, recent work from our laboratory has provided evidence for startle potentiation in anticipation of a nonaversive US that did not affect the valence of the CS as indicated by verbal ratings (Lipp, Siddle, & Dall, 2003). These results suggest that, rather than emotional processes, blink facilitation in anticipation of a US in humans may reflect attentional processes. This interpretation is supported by findings of significant reflex facilitation in anticipation of pleasant and of unpleasant pictorial USs (Lipp et al., 2001).

However, research in the picture-viewing paradigm has clearly established the utility of blink startle as an index of stimulus valence by showing reflex facilitation during aversive stimuli and reflex inhibition during pleasant stimuli (Lang et al., 1990). In rodents, there is evidence for startle inhibition during appetitive conditioning (Schmid, Koch, & Schnitzler, 1995). A similar demonstration in humans that cannot be explained as reflecting attention is currently lacking, however.

Integrating Outcomes Across Response Systems

The previous sections provided a review of the various measures used to monitor experimentally induced fear in humans. These include measures predominately sensitive to the acquisition of contingency knowledge during paired presentations of CSs and USs (verbal ratings of US expectancy and contingency awareness, secondary task RT, autonomic physiological measures) as well as measures that reflect mainly the acquisition of fear (ratings of stimulus valence, affective priming or covert attention, blink-startle modulation). There is no strong separation between indices that track the acquisition of various components of conditioned responding, contingency knowledge, preferential attentional processing, or emotional responses. Rather, a single dependent measure may reflect a number of components. Blink startle, for instance, reflects the acquisition of an experimental contingency in absence of a change in CS valence (Lipp, Siddle, & Dall, 2003) as well as the acquisition of negative valence (Lipp et al., 1998).

Given the emphasis on a multisystem approach to measurement, the question arises regarding the extent to which measures from various response systems are related. This, in part, reflects on the various levels of specificity that indicators from different response systems offer and the extent to which they are subject to noise, that is, reflect other processes that are not the subject of investigation. Verbal report can be very specific with participants who are able to distinguish a number of emotional states. Physiological indices, however, are frequently less specific, but, as with electrodermal responses, for example, are sensitive to a number of psychological processes. Moreover, processes such as emotion, attention, or memory contribute to performance in a learning situation and their effect will become apparent in a nonspecific measure. Thus, finding low correlations across measures from different systems is not surprising. However, considerable progress has been made to delineate the physiological signatures, if not of discrete emotions, of pleasant and unpleasant states (M. M. Bradley, 2000). Recent work by Peter Lang and his colleagues has provided a set of indices from various response systems that can reflect the valence and arousal associated with discrete emotional responses (P. J. Lang et al., 1993).

A second problem associated with the use of measures from different response systems in the analysis of fear learning is the fact that indices differ in sensitivity. This difference in sensitivity can result in different results depending on the measure taken in a particular experiment. A recent study in our laboratory, for instance, used verbal ratings and affective priming to index the acquisition and extinction of negative stimulus valence. The measures provided parallel results after acquisition; both indicated that the CS+ was more negative than the CS– but differed after extinction. In a postextinction test session, CS+ and CS– did not lead to differential affective priming, whereas valence ratings continued to indicate differential evaluations (see also Vansteenwegen et al., 1998). The differential sensitivity of indices of fear learning remains even after exclusion of methodological confounds such as the direct comparison between measures taken during learning or after the completion of conditioning. Currently, it is not possible to generalize directly from studies using, for instance, verbal ratings to those that used blink-startle modulation or affective priming as an index of fear. This situation is likely to improve with the emergence of more studies that use an array of measures that will permit a more complete understanding of the fear-learning process.

CONCLUSION

Recent research on fear learning in neuroscience, animal behavior, and human conditioning has provided a number of exciting findings that should stimulate interest in the area of human fear learning (e.g., Ressler et al., 2004). Having at our disposal a better, more elaborate, and less confound-prone set of methodologies and measures and an improved knowledge of basic conditioning as informed by research in neuroscience and animal behavior, we are currently in a better position to understand the acquisition and maintenance of human fear than ever before. This will permit us to address the major challenges that face the field at present: (a) the integration of research findings that have emerged from basic neuroscience, behavioral studies in nonhuman animals, and studies in humans and the clarification of the extent to which these findings can inform application (Delamater, 2004), and (b) the development of a coherent theory of human fear learning that can resolve the current debates between single- and dual-process accounts of human conditioning (see chaps. 4, 5, and 6, this volume). Resolving these issues will increase our understanding of the acquisition and maintenance of fear as well as facilitate the development of more efficient interventions.

II

ACQUISITION AND MAINTENANCE OF FEAR

3

DEFENSES AND MEMORIES: FUNCTIONAL NEURAL CIRCUITRY OF FEAR AND CONDITIONAL RESPONDING

JENNIFER J. QUINN AND MICHAEL S. FANSELOW

From a neurobiological perspective, fear is the activation of the neural circuits that result in defensive behavior. Neurally, the circuits that normally mediate fear are well delineated, and this knowledge provides insight into how the brain translates environmental input to behavior. Biologically, we must recognize that the brain evolved these circuits because fear is adaptive and functional. Recognition of how these circuits act to fulfill fear's natural biological function provides clues to the understanding of anxiety disorders.

Over the past several decades, there has been a vast expansion in our understanding of the neurobiological bases of fear. The fear system is evolutionarily conserved across species, making investigations in animals relevant to human fear states. These investigations in animals, especially rodents, afford us the capability of direct experimental manipulation of this neurobiology that is not possible in humans. The use of specific brain lesions and genetic alterations as well as neuropharmacological manipulations and electrophysiological recordings have all contributed to our current knowledge regarding both innate and learned fear. Observations from human neuropsychological patients and functional imaging studies have generally corroborated the findings from animal experiments. Therefore, the elucidation of the neurobiological substrates, in addition to the learning and memory processes, that underlie fearful experiences are critical for a complete understanding of the pathophysiological conditions related to fear and anxiety as well as potential biologically based therapeutic interventions.

This chapter first provides brief overviews of the functional organization of defensive behavior and the neural circuits responsible for those behaviors. From this vantage, we can identify specific ways that functioning of the circuit can break down and result in inappropriate fear and anxiety. We hope this may begin to provide a coherent framework for conceptualizing the variety of anxiety disorders that afflict the human population.

WHAT IS FEAR?

Biologically, fear can be defined as a functional behavior system designed, through evolution, to allow an organism to defend against threats (e.g., predation). Such defensive behavior is designed to thwart a predator (D. C. Blanchard, Griebel, & R. J. Blanchard, 2001; Bolles, 1970; Edmunds, 1974). A predator may be averted at several points. For instance, if you are poisonous or foul tasting, you can prevent a predator from eating your relatives (Edmunds, 1974). Although such a behavior is a boon to your inclusive fitness (i.e., the ability of you and all your relatives to pass on their genes), doing something to prevent things from progressing to that stage has its obvious advantages on individual fitness (i.e., your own ability to pass on your genes).

As potential prey, we have evolved distinct stages of defense. Each stage is brought about by different stimulus conditions and results in distinct topographies of defensive behavior. The most systematic dissection of defensive behavior has been done in the rat, a heavily preyed on mammal that is sympatric with humans and, like humans, an opportunistic omnivore. We have argued that it is the prey's perception of the current level of risk that determines the stage of defense (Fanselow & Lester, 1988). The level of risk can be put on a continuum anchored at one end by complete safety and at the other by consumption by the predator (i.e., death; see Figure 3.1). We have termed this continuum the *predatory imminence continuum* because it refers more to the psychological perception of how imminent the end point is, rather than simply physical distance, time, or probability. Imminence is greater if the predator is 1 meter than 5 meters away, but it is also greater when you need to enter a foraging area that is often, as opposed to rarely, visited by a predator.

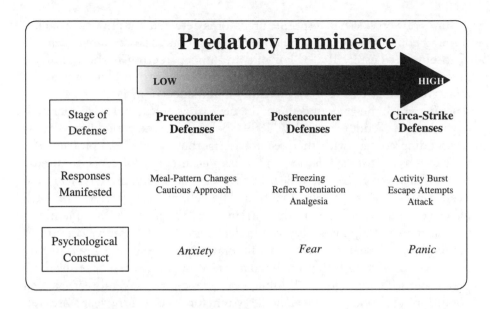

Figure 3.1. The predatory–imminence continuum. The level of perceived predatory threat is determined by the environmental stimulus conditions. These conditions invoke discrete stages of defense with adaptive responses appropriate to the level of threat. It is hypothesized that the psychological constructs of anxiety, fear, and panic exist along this continuum of predatory imminence. Anxiety, fear, and panic are adaptive when the responses that they engender are appropriate for the current situation. When a mismatch occurs between the level of threat and the response, the anxiety, fear, or panic observed is considered pathological.

Both the intensity and the topography of defensive behavior change with predatory imminence. For example, as risk of a mild electric shock in a rat's foraging area increases, the rat progressively alters its meal patterns to taking larger but less frequent meals, thereby reducing the number of trips to the foraging ground while maintaining total food intake (Fanselow, Lester, & Helmstetter, 1988). With greater increases in risk, however, that behavioral pattern suddenly breaks down: Food intake decreases and freezing begins to occur. Freezing is an innate response characterized by immobility concomitant with rigid muscle tone. Freezing increases with further increases in risk but is suddenly replaced by escape attempts when the rat receives shock (Fanselow, 1982).

Behaviors such as meal-pattern shifts (Fanselow et al., 1988) and stretched approach (D. C. Blanchard, R. J. Blanchard, Tom, & Rodgers, 1990), which occur in the initial part of this continuum in which predatory imminence is low but not nonexistent, are called *preencounter defenses*. These behaviors may correspond to the affective states of worry and anxiety. For example, stretched approach may have an information-gathering function (D. C. Blanchard et al., 1990) that may reflect the increased vigilance seen in states of worry. When a specific predator is detected but physical attack is not immediate or assured, we refer to the behaviors as *postencounter defenses* (Fanselow & Lester, 1988). For rats and mice, freezing is the dominant postencounter defense. Fear would seem the best way to characterize the affective state at this level of predatory imminence. This is the stage of defense for which the greatest detail of the neuroanatomical and molecular biology is known (Fendt & Fanselow, 1999). Behavior in the period immediately surrounding contact with the predator is vigorous, active, and protean. We refer to it as *circa-strike behavior,* and it has a clear correspondence to intense panic (Fanselow & Lester, 1988). In this schema, worry, anxiety, fear, and even panic have an adaptive function. The behaviors associated with each affective state are matched to the current demands of the environment.

Defensive responses observed under controlled laboratory conditions are similar to those in the organism's natural habitat. Defensive responses are also elicited by stimuli that predict danger. Many of the responses to these predictive stimuli are learned through experience. For several reasons, fear conditioning provides an ideal model system for investigating fear states relevant to humans. First, imaging studies have shown that brain regions known to be important for fear conditioning in animals (e.g., the amygdala and hippocampus) are the same regions implicated in human fear-conditioning studies (Büchel, Morris, Dolan, & Friston, 1998; Knight, Smith, Stein, & Helmstetter, 1999). In addition, deficits produced by selective lesions of these critical anatomical structures resemble those deficits seen in human pathological conditions resulting in damage to these same structures (e.g., Bechara et al., 1995; LaBar, LeDoux, Spencer, & Phelps, 1995). Second, fear is learned rapidly such that after only a single trial, animals show robust conditioned responses (CR; e.g., freezing; decreased pain sensitivity, termed *analgesia;* enhanced startle responses) to discrete cues (e.g., tone) and contexts that have been paired with shock. This is true in many instances of human fear conditioning as well. For instance, after a single attack by a stray dog, a person may show an intense fear response at the sight of a dog. Third, the fear memories for discrete stimuli as well as environmental contexts are stable over long time periods. Our laboratory has observed robust freezing without forgetting in rats to both tone and context for at least 16 months following training, a period that represents much of the animal's adult life span (Gale et al., 2004). For example, the person who was attacked by a dog as a child may show a fear response to dogs for the rest of his or her lifetime.

MEASUREMENT OF INNATE FEAR

An innate fear stimulus is one that produces a fear response in the absence of prior experience with that stimulus. Although this definition seems fairly straightforward, it is often difficult to characterize unambiguously fear stimuli as innate (as opposed to learned; Godsil, Tinsley, & Fanselow, 2003). Perhaps a fear stimulus can be considered innate when it produces a fear response following its first presentation? For instance, a cat may be considered an innate fear stimulus for rodents because it produces a robust fear response during the first encounter. By this account, the rodent's genome contains information regarding cats as innately fearful stimuli and adaptively shaped responses to such stimuli (D. C. Blanchard & R. J. Blanchard, 1972).

It is still possible, however, that some, if not all, defensive reactions observed in the presence of a cat are learned. For instance, it is possible that some aspect of the cat (e.g., its movements) serves as an aversive stimulus capable of supporting conditioning to other stimuli that are present. That is, the sight and smell of a cat may only evoke fear responses because they are paired with movement. Support for this comes from the observation that either a moving cat or inanimate object can evoke freezing in the rat, whereas presentation of the sight or smell of a dead cat does not (R. J. Blanchard, Mast, & D. C. Blanchard, 1975). Similarly, fear responses such as freezing, analgesia, and defecation are observed following the first presentation of footshock. This does not mean that footshock is an innately fearful stimulus that triggers such responses, however. In fact, we have shown that the freezing observed following footshock results from learning a predictive relationship between the contextual cues and footshock (Fanselow, 1980, 1986). That is, even after a single pairing of context with footshock, the context acquires the ability to predict the occurrence of footshock. Although these findings suggest that caution is warranted in concluding that a particular stimulus innately evokes fear, this does not mean that truly innate fear stimuli do not exist. Currently, studies using rodents are underway to clarify these issues using diverse stimuli that are putative innate fear stimuli ranging from the odor of fox feces to presentation of a cat (D. C. Blanchard et al., 2001; McGregor, Schrama, Ambermoon, Dielenberg, 2002; Rosen, 2004).

ACQUISITION AND MEASUREMENT OF LEARNED FEAR

Since Pavlov (1927), it has been known that an initially neutral conditioned stimulus (CS; e.g., bell) comes to elicit a CR (e.g., salivation) after it is paired with a biologically relevant unconditioned stimulus (US; e.g., food). In Pavlov's conditioning procedure, the CR was identical to the unconditioned response (UR) evoked by food delivery (i.e., salivation). It is not always the case that the CR and UR are identical, however. For example, in a typical fear-conditioning procedure, a tone is paired one or more times with a footshock. The footshock produces a robust activity-burst UR (Fanselow, 1982). Presentation of cues (discrete or contextual) that have previously been paired with footshock do not produce an activity burst; rather, the dominant behavioral CR to such cues is freezing (e.g., Bouton & Bolles, 1980; Fanselow,

1980). Freezing is defined as complete immobility except that needed for respiration while maintaining significant muscle tone (i.e., sleeping and paralysis do not constitute freezing behavior). In fact, even the freezing observed shortly following footshock presentation depends on conditioning to the context (Fanselow, 1980). Following fear conditioning, animals show an array of conditional fear responses to the contextual cues of the environment in which training occurred, as well as to discrete cues that predict the occurrence of footshock including: defensive freezing (e.g., Bouton & Bolles, 1980), autonomic arousal (e.g., Iwata & LeDoux, 1988), increased body temperature (e.g., Godsil, Quinn, & Fanselow, 2000), and decreased pain perception (e.g., Fanselow & Bolles, 1979).

In addition to measuring direct defensive reactions such as freezing or autonomic changes, the influence of conditional fear stimuli on the performance of other responses can be assessed. For instance, animals (including humans) show a reflexive startle response to the sudden onset of a loud auditory stimulus. Similarly, a blink of the eyelid is a natural, reflexive response to the presentation of a tactile stimulus (e.g., a puff of air) to the eye. When these reflexive responses are tested in the presence of a stimulus that predicts an aversive event, the magnitude of these responses is potentiated (J. S. Brown, Kalish, & Farber, 1951; M. Davis, 1986; Lindquist & Brown, 2004).

Additionally, conditional fear stimuli cause a pronounced suppression of the performance of ongoing goal-oriented (instrumental) behaviors. In a typical conditioned suppression procedure (e.g., Annau & Kamin, 1961; Estes & Skinner, 1941), an animal is first trained to perform an operant response (e.g., pressing a lever) to obtain a palatable outcome (e.g., sucrose pellet). Subsequently, the animal is fear conditioned with one or more Pavlovian CS–US pairings preferably in a separate, distinct context. During the test for conditioned suppression, the animal's instrumental response rates (i.e., lever pressing) are compared in the presence and absence of the fear CS. The magnitude of fear conditioning is inferred by the suppression of responding in the presence of the CS. In a similar procedure, Killcross, Robbins, and Everitt (1997) behaviorally and anatomically differentiated conditioned suppression and shifts in instrumental responding when a particular response results in an aversive consequence. It is important to recognize the precision with which behavioral changes must be assessed in such conditioned suppression procedures. It is probable, under certain circumstances, that suppression of ongoing instrumental behavior is a result of competing behavioral responses, such as freezing. That is, if the animal is freezing, it is incapable of pressing a lever for food.

NEURAL CIRCUITRY OF FEAR

The neural circuitry of Pavlovian fear conditioning to discrete unimodal cues (e.g., a tone) as well as more complex, polymodal cues (e.g., contexts) has been extensively examined using a variety of fear responses including freezing, autonomic changes, analgesia, fear-potentiated startle, and conditioned suppression (e.g., Fanselow & Poulos, 2005; Fendt & Fanselow, 1999). It is generally recognized that the amygdala plays a central role in fear conditioning (M. Davis, 1992a; see Figure 3.2). For instance, heightened activation of the amygdala occurs in patients experiencing specific phobias, as measured by positron emission tomography and functional magnetic resonance imaging (Birbaumer et al., 1998; Wik, Fredrikson, & Fischer, 1997).

The amygdala consists of a number of structurally and functionally heterogeneous nuclei within the medial temporal lobe. Among these nuclei, the lateral, basal, and central nuclei have been shown to contribute to learned fear (M. Davis, 1992a; Goosens & Maren, 2001; Nader, Majidishad, Amorapanth, & LeDoux, 2001). The lateral and basal nuclei constitute the frontotemporal amygdala (FTA; also referred to as the basolateral complex), given its extensive connections with the frontal and temporal cortices (Swanson, 2003). The FTA is critical for both the acquisition and expression of conditional fear (Maren, 2003). In fact, there is substantial evidence to suggest that the FTA is the site of storage for the direct Pavlovian association between the CS (both tone and context) and the US (footshock) in fear conditioning (Fanselow & LeDoux, 1999). Support for this comes from lesion (e.g., D. C. Blanchard & R. J. Blanchard, 1972; Campeau & Davis, 1995; Gale et al., 2004; Y. Lee, Walker, & Davis, 1996; Maren, 1998) and temporary inactivation (Helmstetter & Bellgowan, 1994; Muller, Corodimas, Fridel, & LeDoux, 1997; Wilensky, Schafe, & LeDoux, 1999) studies indicating that without a functioning FTA at the time of training or testing, the animal is incapable of learning or expressing fear memories when standard training parameters are used (but see Maren, 1999).

FTA Afferents

The FTA receives input from all sensory modalities including various brain regions responsible for processing nociceptive (i.e., pain) information (see Figure 3.2), thus making it a plausible site for the encoding of the CS–US associations underlying fear conditioning (Fendt & Fanselow, 1999). For instance, the FTA receives auditory information from the medial geniculate nucleus of the thalamus, as well as the auditory cortex. Romanski and LeDoux (1992) showed that auditory information reaching the FTA through either the thalamoamygdala or thalamocorticoamygdala pathway can result in normal fear conditioning to a tone paired with shock. Simultaneous removal of auditory information from both pathways disrupts fear conditioning to the tone, however. In addition, following auditory fear conditioning in control animals, there is an increase in the magnitude of FTA neuronal responses to the tone (Quirk, Repa, & LeDoux, 1995).

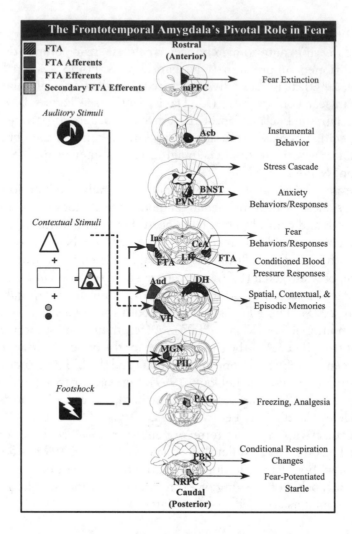

Figure 3.2. A simplified representation of the critical frontotemporal amygdala (FTA) circuitry that plays a central role in fear. The FTA receives abundant sensory inputs and projects to a number of output regions that are involved in the production of fear responses. Eight coronal sections throughout the rostra–caudal extent of the rat brain are shown. Different types of sensory information reach the FTA from a number of distinct brain regions. The FTA directly projects to a number of regions responsible for different aspects of the coordinated fear response. The central nucleus of the amygdala (CeA) and the bed nucleus of the stria terminalis (BNST) subsequently project to a number of brain regions that are responsible for the production of individual fear and anxiety responses, respectively. Acb = nucleus accumbens; Aud = auditory cortex; BNST = bed nucleus of the stria terminalis; CeA = central nucleus of the amygdala; DH = dorsal hippocampus; FTA = frontotemporal amygdala; Ins = insular cortex; LH = lateral hypothalamus; MGN = medial geniculate nucleus of the thalamus; mPFC = medial prefrontal cortex; NRPC = nucleus reticularis pontis caudalis; PAG = periaqueductal gray; PBN = parabrachial nucleus; PIL = posterior intralaminar nucleus; PVN = paraventricular nucleus of the hypothalamus; VH = ventral hippocampus. Brain slices taken from *The Rat Brain in Stereotoxic Coordinates*, by G. Paxinos and C. Watson, 1997. New York: Academic Press. Copyright 1997 by Elsevier. Reprinted with permission.

The hippocampus, which is important for processing contextual information (discussed subsequently), monosynaptically projects to the FTA through the ventral angular bundle (VAB; Ottersen, 1982; van Groen & Wyss, 1990), and through indirect projections through the subiculum and medial temporal cortices (Amaral & Witter, 1995). Stimulation of pathways from the medial temporal lobe results in long-term potentiation within the FTA (Maren & Fanselow, 1995; Yaniv, Schafe, LeDoux, & Richter-Levin, 2000), and contextual fear conditioning results in increased expression of immediate early genes within the FTA (Rosen, Fanselow, Young, Sitcoske, & Maren, 1998; Scicli, Petrovich, Swanson, & Thompson, 2004). Thus, the hippocampus is thought to process complex contextual information and transmit a representation of "context" to the FTA where it is then associated with footshock.

The pathways responsible for supplying US information to the FTA are not as well understood as the CS pathways discussed earlier (LeDoux, 2000). Investigations suggest, however, that multiple, parallel pathways are capable of providing such somatosensory information. These investigations have focused primarily on two regions: the posterior intralaminar nucleus of the thalamus (PIN) and the insular cortex (INS). The PIN receives somatic pain information from the spinal cord (LeDoux, Ruggiero, Forest, Stornetta, & Reis, 1987) and, in turn, projects to the FTA (Linke, Braune, & Schwegler, 2000). In addition, electrical stimulation of the PIN serves as an effective US capable of producing fear conditioning (Cruikshank, Edeline, & Weinberger, 1992). The INS also receives somatosensory information and subsequently projects to the FTA (Jasmin, Burkey, Granato, & Ohara, 2004; Shi & Cassell, 1998a, 1998b). Selective lesions of either the PIN or INS before conditioning do not disrupt fear conditioning, whereas combined lesions of the two regions do (Campeau & Davis, 1995; Shi & Davis, 1999). These data suggest that either the PIN or the INS is sufficient to provide US information in fear conditioning but that neither is necessary.

Further examination of these regions has compromised this interpretation. First, Brunzell and Kim (2001) showed that combined lesions of the PIN and INS disrupted tone, but not context, fear conditioning. Subsequently, Lanuza, Nader, and LeDoux (2004) showed that the combined PIN and INS lesion effects on fear conditioning described earlier are the result of fibers en route to the amygdala that pass through, but do not synapse in, the PIN. That is, the combined PIN and INS lesion is effective when electrolytic lesions of the PIN are used but not when axon-sparing excitotoxic PIN lesions are made. Altogether, these data suggest that multiple pathways mediate the transmission of US information to the FTA, with several being sufficient but no single pathway being necessary (see Fendt & Fanselow, 1999).

Thus, the FTA appears to have the requisite afferent projections necessary for processing convergent CS and US information in fear conditioning. In fact, there is evidence that such convergence occurs on single cells within the FTA. Romanski, Clugnet, Bordi, and LeDoux (1993) found that individual neurons within the lateral nucleus of the amygdala respond to both auditory (clicker) and somatosensory (footshock) stimuli.

FTA Efferents

The FTA subsequently projects to a variety of targets that are responsible for the production of the various components of a coordinated fear response (see Figure 3.2). One important FTA efferent is the central nucleus of the amygdala (CeA). The CeA itself has a variety of efferent targets (Petrovich & Swanson, 1997) that mediate autonomic and behavioral fear responses in rodents and primates (Fendt & Fanselow, 1999; Kalin, Shelton, & Davidson, 2004). For instance, the CeA sends discrete projections to both the lateral hypothalamus and periaqueductal gray (PAG) to mediate dissociable aspects of the integrated fear response. LeDoux, Iwata, Cicchetti, and Reis (1988) found that lesions of the lateral hypothalamus disrupt conditional changes in arterial pressure during presentation of an auditory stimulus that was previously paired with footshock but had no effect on conditional freezing. By contrast, lesions of the caudal region of the periaqueductal gray (PAG) disrupted conditional freezing behavior, while having no effect on arterial pressure (see also DeOca, DeCola, Maren, & Fanselow, 1998). In addition, the PAG mediates conditional analgesia (Helmstetter & Tershner, 1994). The analgesic response is mediated by endogenous opioids (i.e., endorphins), and it has two very important functions in fear (Bolles & Fanselow, 1980). First, it prevents pain of injuries from producing recuperative behavior that might disrupt defensive responses (Fanselow & Baackes, 1982). Second, it acts as a regulatory break on fear conditioning (S. L. Young & Fanselow, 1992). The CeA also projects to a number of other downstream nuclei to mediate various aspects of fear such as: The nucleus reticularis pontis caudalis to mediate fear enhancement of the startle response (Hitchcock & Davis, 1991; Rosen, Hitchcock, Sananes, Miserendino, & Davis, 1991); the parabrachial nucleus to mediate conditional changes in respiration; the paraventricular nucleus of the hypothalamus to initiate the release of stress hormones; the locus coeruleus and basal forebrain (either directly or indirectly) to mediate increased vigilance and attention (Cain, Kapp, & Puryear, 2002; M. Davis, 1992a).

The FTA also projects to the bed nucleus of the stria terminalis (BNST), which projects to many of the same regions as the CeA and mediates similar responses. The BNST, however, appears to mediate responses to different types of stimuli than fear CS, such as prolonged exposure to bright light (e.g., Lee & Davis, 1997; Walker & Davis, 1997). Additionally, intracerebroventricular infusion of corticotropin-releasing hormone (CRH), a neuropeptide critical for the activation of stress responses, similarly enhances the magnitude of the startle response to a loud noise. Lesions of the BNST disrupt the enhancement of startle using either of these procedures, whereas the potentiation of startle in the presence of a fear CS remains intact. Conversely, lesions of the CeA disrupt fear-potentiated startle but not light- or CRH-enhanced startle (Walker & Davis, 1997). Thus the CeA and BNST appear to be complementary outputs of the FTA that generate similar defensive behaviors but do so in response to different types of stimuli.

The aforementioned evidence supports the dominant view that the FTA stores the direct CS–US associations in Pavlovian fear conditioning. The very nature of a storage function makes it difficult to eliminate the possibility that the FTA is not involved in the storage of the CS–US association, however, and is instead strictly involved in modulating the acquisition and expression of the fear memory that is stored elsewhere. Given that FTA infusions of pharmacological agents that block the synaptic plasticity underlying long-term memory formation also disrupt later fear-conditioning performance tested in the absence of drugs (e.g., Bailey, Kim, Sun, Thompson, & Helmstetter, 1999; Fanselow & Kim, 1994; Huff & Rudy, 2004; Maren, Ferrario, Corcoran, Desmond, & Frey, 2003; Miserendino, Sananes, Melia, & Davis, 1990; Schafe & LeDoux, 2000), it seems likely that the FTA is storing something that contributes to fear memories. Granted, it may still be storing something other than the CS–US association that influences the expression of the CS–US association when it is retrieved from storage elsewhere (although to our knowledge, there is no data to suggest such an alternative region). This also seems unlikely given that FTA-specific pharmacological manipulations during fear conditioning completely block the expression of fear conditioning when tested off drug, and there is no indication of savings in these animals when compared with naïve control animals (Goosens & Maren, 2003). If the FTA were solely involved in modulating the acquisition and expression of fear memories stored elsewhere, some savings would be expected (i.e., faster rate of reacquisition compared with the rate observed in naïve control animals). Furthermore, the FTA is critical for the expression of both tone and context fear for at least 16 months following training (Gale et al., 2004; Maren, Aharonov, & Fanselow, 1996), suggesting that it is unlikely the FTA solely contributes to the consolidation of CS–US memory storage in another region.

In conclusion, the FTA provides a critical intersection between the sensory inputs and the behavioral and physiological outputs that constitute a highly regulated and adaptive system to subserve a coordinated fear response. It provides environmental cues with the ability to predict danger in advance, allowing an organism to respond appropriately to avoid or minimize injury or death.

HIPPOCAMPUS CONTRIBUTIONS TO PAVLOVIAN FEAR CONDITIONING

Although the neuroanatomical substrates previously discussed appear roughly to outline the basic system mediating Pavlovian fear conditioning, the hippocampus appears to play a role in at least some aspects of fear conditioning. The hippocampus is located within the medial portion of the medial temporal lobe. It consists of the dentate gyrus and cornis Ammonis subfields (CA1, CA2, and CA3). The major input to the hippocampus is provided by the adjacent entorhinal cortex, which receives much of its input from the surrounding medial temporal lobe cortices (perirhinal and postrhinal) and subiculum (Amaral & Witter, 1995). This input to the entorhinal cortex contains information from many sensory modalities including auditory, olfactory, visual, and somatosensory systems (Insausti, Herrero, & Witter, 1997; Majak & Pitkanen, 2003). Thus, the hippocampus is in a position to process multimodal information. In addition, the CA1 region of the ventral hippocampus communicates bidirectionally with the FTA (Amaral & Witter, 1995).

This general anatomical scheme for hippocampus information processing coordinates nicely with its proposed functional contributions to Pavlovian fear conditioning. Investigations of hippocampus involvement in fear conditioning have primarily elucidated a selective role for the hippocampus and adjacent medial temporal cortices in mediating contextual fear conditioning, although typically making no observable contributions to delay tone fear conditioning (e.g., Anagnostaras, Maren, & Fanselow, 1999; Burwell, Saddoris, Bucci, & Wiig, 2004; Kim & Fanselow, 1992; Phillips & LeDoux, 1992). In addition to these lesion experiments, pharmacological manipulations that disrupt normal hippocampus function during training (e.g., Bast, Zhang, & Feldon, 2003; Gale, Anagnostaras, & Fanselow, 2001; S. L. Young, Bohenek, & Fanselow, 1994) and hippocampus-specific genetic knockout manipulations (e.g., Shimizu, Tang, Rampon, & Tsien, 2000) disrupt contextual fear conditioning while leaving delay tone conditioning intact.

The hippocampus appears to process multimodal sensory information and configure the various environmental elements into a unified representation of context. Support for this comes from investigations of spatial learning showing that an intact hippocampus is necessary for the formation of integrated spatial maps (O'Keefe & Nadel, 1978). In addition, rodents show little fear conditioning to a context when very short context exposures are given prior to shock delivery. However, preexposure to the context alleviates this deficit (Fanselow, 1986, 1990; Wiltgen, Sanders, Behne, & Fanselow, 2001), presumably because the preexposure allows the animals ample time to form a configured context representation. The hippocampus is important for this configural processing during the preexposure phase (Barrientos, O'Reilly, & Rudy, 2002; Stote & Fanselow, 2004).

Damage to the hippocampus causes a selective loss of context fear, leaving fear to a discrete stimulus such as a tone intact (Kim & Fanselow, 1992; Phillips & LeDoux, 1992). An asymmetry exists, however, in the magnitude of memory loss for those memories acquired before and after the damage. Memory deficits for information acquired shortly before hippocampus insult (retrograde amnesia) are more pronounced than those for information acquired following hippocampus damage (anterograde amnesia). Although posttraining lesions of the hippocampus cause large deficits in context fear, pretraining effects are much less robust (Maren, Aharonov, & Fanselow, 1997). Therefore, it appears that the hippocampus normally mediates context fear but that other systems may compensate for the hippocampus in its absence (Wiltgen & Fanselow, 2003).

The involvement of the hippocampus in contextual fear conditioning is time-limited. That is, lesions made shortly after training (e.g., 1 day) severely attenuate freezing to a context that was previously paired with footshock, whereas lesions made long after training (e.g., 28–50 days) do not (Anagnostaras et al., 1999; Kim & Fanselow, 1992). The strongest evidence that the hippocampus is important for the consolidation of the unified, conjunctive context representation into a stable, long-term memory store outside of the hippocampus comes from two studies using context preexposure. If the hippocampus is critical for the consolidation of a unified context representation, then preexposure to the context (in the absence of footshock) long before context conditioning should alleviate the deficit produced by hippocampus lesions. This is precisely what was found for both anterograde (S. L. Young et al., 1994) and retrograde (Anagnostaras, Gale, & Fanselow, 2001) amnesia. Presumably, context preexposure long before training allowed for the formation and consolidation of a stable conjunctive context representation in some extrahippocampal structure. Thus, this nonhippocampal memory representation could be associated with the footshock at the time of training.

Investigations have begun to delineate a role for the hippocampus in cued fear conditioning as well. In general, these investigations fall into two categories. First, several investigators have shown that tone fear conditioning depends on an intact hippocampus when a "trace" conditioning procedure is used but not when a "delay" procedure is used (Huerta, Sun, Wilson, & Tonegawa, 2000; McEchron, Bouwmeester, Tseng, Weiss, & Disterhoft, 1998; McEchron, Tseng, & Disterhoft, 2000; Quinn, Oommen, Morrison, & Fanselow, 2002). Trace conditioning refers to a procedure in which presentation of the CS and US are temporally noncontiguous. That is, the CS is presented followed by some specified interval in which neither the CS nor US are presented, and then the US occurs. Delay conditioning refers to a procedure in which the CS and US are temporally contiguous. CS onset precedes US onset, and the two stimuli coterminate. Second, the ventral hippocampus appears to contribute to delay tone (and context) fear conditioning (Bast, Zhang, & Feldon, 2001; Zhang, Bast, & Feldon, 2001), whereas the dorsal hippocampus generally does not (but see Maren et al., 1997). Although an analysis of temporally graded retrograde amnesia for cued fear conditioning has not yet been conducted, evidence from trace eyeblink conditioning shows that the role of the hippocampus is time-limited (suggesting a role in consolidation) just as for contextual fear conditioning (Kim, Clark,

& Thompson, 1995; Takehara, Kawahara, & Kirino, 2003; Takehara, Kawahara, Takatsuki, & Kirino, 2002).

PLASTICITY IN FEAR CONDITIONING

At a systems level, it is clear that the FTA and its sensory input and response output regions perform differential functions in fear conditioning. It is important to understand how, at a cellular level, such learning might be acquired and expressed. Long-term potentiation (LTP) is a form of synaptic plasticity that leads to enduring increases in synaptic efficacy. LTP is artificially induced by brief, high-frequency stimulation of excitatory afferent projections. LTP was first demonstrated in the projections leading to the dentate gyrus region of the hippocampus (Bliss & Gardner-Medwin, 1973; Bliss & Lomo, 1973) but has since been shown within the CA1 and CA3 regions of the hippocampus (e.g., Alger & Teyler, 1976; Muller, Joly, & Lynch, 1988) as well as other brain structures, including the amygdala (e.g., Chapman, Kairiss, Keenan, & Brown, 1990; Clugnet & LeDoux, 1990; Maren & Fanselow, 1995), medial geniculate nucleus of the thalamus (e.g., Gerren & Weinberger, 1983), and neocortex (e.g., Lee, 1982).

The induction of LTP often depends on the N-methyl-D-aspartate (NMDA) type of excitatory amino acid receptors (Harris, Ganong, & Cotman, 1984; Malenka & Bear, 2004; Muller et al., 1988). As shown in Figure 3.3, opening of the NMDA receptor's ion channel requires that two events occur simultaneously: The neurotransmitter from the presynaptic neuron glutamate must bind to the postsynaptic NMDA receptor to activate the channel and the postsynaptic cell must be electrically depolarized (i.e., made more positive) to remove magnesium ions that would otherwise block the channel. When the channel opens because of the co-occurrence of these two events, there is an influx of calcium and sodium ions. Calcium influx into the postsynaptic cell triggers a subsequent cascade of events that mediates the long-term synaptic modifications responsible for LTP, such as increased glutamate release and postsynaptic AMPA (alpha-amino-3-hydroxy-5-methyl-4-isoxazole propionic acid) receptor density (e.g., Lynch, Larson, Kelso, Barrionuevo, & Schottler, 1983; Malenka & Bear, 2004; Malenka, Kauer, Zucker, & Nicoll, 1988). During high-frequency stimulation, NMDA receptor blockade, with the competitive antagonist DL-2-amino-5-phosphonovaleric acid (APV), completely blocks the induction of LTP both in vitro (Collingridge, Kehl, & McLennan, 1983; Harris et al., 1984) and in vivo (Morris, Anderson, Lynch, & Baudry, 1986). NMDA receptors are not necessary for the expression of LTP once it has been induced in the hippocampus, however (Muller et al., 1988). By contrast, NMDA receptors in the FTA are essential for both the induction and expression of LTP (Maren & Fanselow, 1995).

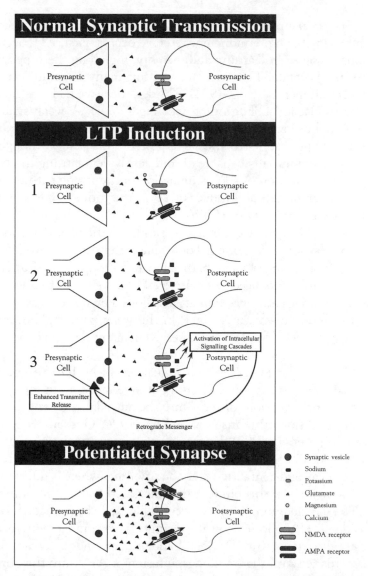

Figure 3.3. A simplified representation of N-methyl-D-aspartate (NMDA)-dependent long-term potentiation (LTP). During normal synaptic transmission, activation of a presynaptic cell results in glutamate release from synaptic vesicles. Glutamate binds to both NMDA and AMPA receptors. Although glutamate binding is sufficient to allow sodium and potassium ions to pass through the alpha-amino-3-hydroxy-5-methyl-4-isoxazole propionic acid (AMPA) receptor, it is not sufficient to allow ion flux through the NMDA receptor. The NMDA receptor is blocked by a magnesium ion that must be expelled. Depolarization of the postsynaptic cell removes the magnesium block, thereby allowing ion flux through the NMDA channel. Calcium is a critical initiator for the activation of multiple signaling cascades that ultimately lead to structural and functional changes at the synapse, such as increased transmitter release from the presynaptic cell and insertion of additional alpha-amino-3-hydroxy-5-methyl-4-isoxazole propionic acid receptors into the postsynaptic membrane. Both of these changes, in addition to the many other changes that occur, result in a greater response of the postsynaptic cell once stimulated.

For several reasons, it has been suggested that LTP may be a mechanism by which long-term memory storage occurs. First, LTP occurs in brain regions involved in learning and memory, including the hippocampus and amygdala. Second, LTP is persistent, lasting many weeks in control animals (Bliss & Gardner-Medwin, 1973). Third, associative LTP has characteristics similar to classical conditioning (see Figure 3.4). A weak synapse can be potentiated by pairing stimulation of this weak input with stimulation of a stronger input, leading to the same postsynaptic cell. Although the weak pathway is not initially capable of sufficiently depolarizing the postsynaptic cell for the induction of LTP, stimulation of the strong pathway depolarizes the postsynaptic cell and induces LTP at the formerly weak synapse. This "associativity" property of LTP is limited by temporal parameters (Levy & Steward, 1979) that are qualitatively similar to the temporal constraints imposed on classical conditioning. For instance, Kelso and Brown (1986) showed that forward pairing of weak pathway stimulation followed by strong pathway stimulation produced associative LTP in the weak pathway. Backward pairing of strong pathway stimulation followed by weak pathway stimulation failed to produce associative LTP in the weak pathway, however. This is similar to the behavioral results observed in many classical conditioning procedures.

At the behavioral level, manipulations of NMDA-receptor-mediated processing further support LTP as a putative mechanism for the storage of fear memories. Infusions of APV into the amygdala prevent the acquisition of fear conditioning (Fanselow & Kim, 1994; Goosens & Maren, 2003; Miserendino et al., 1990). Furthermore, intraamygdala infusion of arcaine, an antagonist at the polyamine regulatory site of the NMDA receptor, decreased delay and contextual fear conditioning, whereas infusion of spermidine, an agonist at this binding site, increased fear conditioning (Rubin et al., 2004). In addition, NMDA receptor blockade by intracerebroventricular infusion of APV prior to training disrupts long-term memory for contextual fear conditioning (Kim, DeCola, Landeira-Fernandez, & Fanselow, 1991). In accordance with these findings, infusion of APV into the dorsal hippocampus prior to training but not testing (Bast et al., 2003; Quinn, Loya, Ma, & Fanselow, 2005; S. L. Young et al., 1994) disrupts context conditioning. Additionally, genetic deletion of the NR1 subunit of the NMDA receptor in the CA1 region of the hippocampus disrupts context fear conditioning (Shimizu et al., 2000), whereas overexpression of the NR2B subunit of the NMDA receptor enhances contextual fear conditioning (Tang et al., 1999).

Investigations of hippocampus NMDA-receptor-mediated plasticity in fear conditioning to *discrete* stimuli are fewer. Huerta et al. (2000) showed that genetically engineered mice with a CA1-specific knockout of the NR1 subunit of the NMDA receptor had impaired trace, but not delay, fear conditioning compared with wildtype control mice. Quinn et al. (2005) showed that dorsal hippocampus infusions of APV disrupted the acquisition and ex-

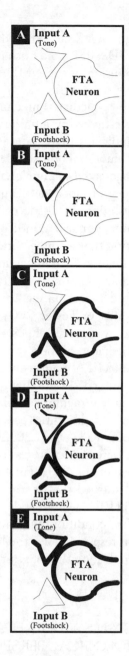

Figure 3.4. A simplified schematic of associative long-term potentiation (LTP) as a model of frontotemporal amygdala (FTA) plasticity underlying associative fear conditioning to a tone. Panel A = multiple sensory inputs (one activated by the tone and one by the footshock) synapse on a single FTA neuron. Panel B = initially, activation of the tone input alone is not strong enough to make the FTA neuron fire. Panel C = activation of the footshock input alone is sufficient to activate the FTA neuron. Panel D = if the tone and footshock inputs are activated simultaneously, synaptic modifications occur at the tone-FTA synapse (e.g., increased transmitter release and postsynaptic AMPA receptor density). Panel E = following these synaptic modifications, the tone input alone is capable of activating the FTA neuron.

pression of trace fear conditioning. Zhang et al. (2001) found that ventral hippocampus infusions of NMDA disrupted both delay tone and contextual fear conditioning, whereas infusion of the NMDA antagonist MK-801 disrupted only context fear.

Although NMDA-receptor-mediated mechanisms of synaptic plasticity have been extensively investigated in a variety of learning and memory procedures, some evidence indicates involvement of other mechanisms in the formation of long-term memories. For instance, an NMDA-independent form of LTP depends on voltage-gated calcium channels (VGCCs; Malenka, 1991). Although NMDA receptor blockade disrupts both short- and long-term memory for fear conditioning, blockade of VGCCs in the FTA disrupted only long-term memory for fear conditioning (Bauer, Schafe, & LeDoux, 2002). It is interesting that a similar finding was obtained using a spatial memory radial arm maze task. Systemic administration of the NMDA antagonist MK-801 impaired acquisition of the task, whereas verapamil, a VGCC antagonist, disrupted performance in a 10-day retention test (Woodside, Borroni, Hammonds, & Teyler, 2004). Future investigations of the molecular targets of these two sources of postsynaptic calcium may shed some light on the potential mediators of short- and long-term fear memories.

The influx of calcium into FTA neurons is crucially important for the activation of a number of signaling pathways that mediate the synaptic modifications underlying long-term fear memories. Inhibiting these downstream signaling molecules disrupts fear conditioning (e.g., Bourtchuladze et al., 1994; Goosens, Holt, & Maren, 2000; Kida et al., 2002; Schafe, Nadel, Sullivan, Harris, & LeDoux, 1999), whereas overexpression of these molecules enhances fear memories (Josselyn et al., 2001). Furthermore, Rumpel, LeDoux, Zador, and Malinow (2005) showed that fear conditioning drives AMPA receptors into the membrane of FTA neurons and that blockade of this AMPA receptor trafficking impairs fear conditioning. Thus, it appears that an LTP-like mechanism in the FTA is responsible for the long-term modifications at the cellular level that, in turn, lead to the long-term fear memories observed at the systems level.

ANXIETY DISORDERS FROM A NEUROBIOLOGICAL PERSPECTIVE

In this chapter, we have emphasized how fear and anxiety are adaptive when they play their natural biological roles. The defensive system is vital in curtailing dangerous behavior and replacing it with appropriate protective responses. To accomplish this, the type of defensive behavior must match the demands of the situation and the level of fear, anxiety, and even panic must be appropriate to the degree of threat in the situation. Anxiety disorders occur when there is a mismatch between defensive behavior and the demands of the situation or when the level of fear is not appropriately regulated. Rather than relying on *Diagnostic and Statistical Manual of Mental Disorders* categories, our intent here is to identify specific ways that this mismatch and dysregulation might occur.

Mismatch of defensive behaviors with the current environmental conditions is essentially a distortion of the predatory imminence continuum. If circa-strike behavior extends back from the extreme end of the predatory imminence continuum, we have panic disorder. If preencounter defenses invade nonthreatening environments, we have generalized anxiety disorder. Our analysis also suggests several conditions that could lead to such distortions.

Normally, fear is under control of negative feedback regulatory mechanisms imparted by the opioid analgesic CR mediated by the ventral PAG. This negative feedback circuit limits the level of fear and makes fear specific to the best predictors of threat (Fanselow, 1998). If these regulatory mechanisms fail, fear becomes inappropriate to the situation. A number of factors, including individual differences, might lead to diminished regulation of fear. For example, endogenous opioids are key components of this regulatory circuitry. This leads to a prediction that, as far as we know, has not been tested. People who have used opiates for either treatment or recreation are likely to be cross-tolerant to endogenous opioids (Lewis, Sherman, & Liebeskind, 1981) and therefore may be more prone to such dysregulation. That is, they may be more vulnerable to anxiety disorders.

We found that prior exposure to a series of electric shocks in one environment enhances the rate of acquisition of fear in a novel environment (Rau, DeCola, & Fanselow, 2005). We likened this effect to certain aspects of posttraumatic stress disorder (PTSD). Prior exposure to a traumatic stressor (the series of shocks) leads to a highly exaggerated fear response to a single shock that perhaps reminded the subject of the prior stress and also immediately established a new and overly strong phobia in the animals. This change in fear learning likely results from sensitization of the amygdala circuits that mediate conditional fear. It is interesting that the effect was resistant to behavioral extinction therapy. We completely extinguished fear of the context where the traumatic shock occurred, but this had no effect on the exaggerated impact of the later single shock. This suggests that some aspects of PTSD will survive exposure therapy because it represents a long-term sensitization of the fear system. We are currently trying to determine the molecular mechanisms of this sensitization in the hope that this will lead to useful adjuncts to the treatment of PTSD.

We provide these few examples of the relation between the neural systems mediating defense and anxiety disorders to illustrate a general direction we suggest for future research. We currently have a detailed understanding of the functional organization and neurobiology of fear and defensive behavior. It seems that now is the time to try to link psychopathology to specific alterations in the operation of what is normally a highly adaptive and regulated system.

In conclusion, fear, anxiety, and panic are components of a functional defensive behavior system that is critical to survival. Understanding how this system is built provides unique insights into the etiology of anxiety disorders, which we see as a dysregulation of this behavior system. Using this knowledge may help design new treatment strategies that target the specific components of the system that are inappropriately regulated in anxiety disorders.

4

CONTEMPORARY LEARNING THEORY PERSPECTIVES ON THE ETIOLOGY OF FEARS AND PHOBIAS

SUSAN MINEKA AND JON SUTTON

Clinical psychologists have long been interested in the causes of mental disorders and for years phobias seemed to have perhaps the most straightforward etiology. Watson and Rayner (1920) published the first human study of classical conditioning of fear in Little Albert. Although not initially afraid of white rats, Little Albert developed an intense phobic-like fear of white rats after he had been frightened by a loud gong several times in the presence of a rat. This idea that phobias are simply manifestations of intense classically conditioned fears became the dominant behaviorist view, and few psychologists today would dispute that classical conditioning can lead to the development of phobias. One of the major appeals of this early view was its simplicity. If people sometimes develop fears and phobias through simple classical conditioning (which can be very powerful, especially with highly traumatic events), why not hypothesize that this is the way that most people develop them? Moreover, myriad experiments on fear conditioning were conducted, and the phenomenon was found to be highly reliable and robust.

Yet with time it became clear that direct traumatic conditioning was neither necessary nor sufficient to explain the origins of all fears and phobias, and so a number of clinical scientists nearly abandoned this early conditioning view and ascribed to it at most an ancillary role. Nevertheless, as we attempt to demonstrate here, the reasons for this dismissal were mistaken. We present a new, revitalized associative account for the onset of fears and phobias. In particular, we illustrate some of the advances made by basic learning scientists that allow clinical scientists to have a more sophisticated and nuanced understanding of their origins.

One of the early criticisms of the early simple conditioning view was that many people with fears and phobias cannot recall a history of traumatic classical conditioning in the origins of their phobias, and thus the original behaviorist account certainly could not explain all cases. Although this could simply involve forgetting the original incident, it became clear that two other associative pathways were also involved in the acquisition of some fears and phobias (e.g., Mineka, 1985; Rachman, 1990). One is observational or vicarious conditioning. In this case, simple observation of someone else appearing frightened in the presence of an object or in a certain situation can result in the acquisition of a fear or phobia in the observer. Another is verbal or instructional learning. In this case, a person can acquire a fear simply through seeing, hearing, or reading frightening information about an object or a situation.

A second criticism was that not only are direct conditioning events unnecessary for the development of phobias, they are also insufficient. Specifically, critics of the early conditioning viewpoint noted that many individuals with histories of observational or direct conditioning do not develop fears or phobias (e.g., Rachman, 1990). What these researchers ignored, however, is the host of individual-difference variables that dramatically influence which individuals will develop a fear or phobia following a given event and which will show persistent fear over the course of time. Only by understanding this host of variables can we begin to make sense of why so many individuals who do have traumatic events do not develop fears or phobias (e.g., Mineka, 1985; Mineka & Zinbarg, 1996).

Finally, the early simple conditioning viewpoint ignored another variable affecting the outcome of a particular learning experience—that concerning the nature of the potentially phobic object itself. People are far more likely to develop fears and phobias for certain objects and situations than others. We seem to have a biologically based preparedness to most readily associate frightening outcomes with objects or situations that once posed a threat to our early ancestors (e.g., Öhman & Mineka, 2001; see also chap. 5, this volume).

OBSERVATIONAL AND INSTRUCTIONAL LEARNING OF FEARS AND PHOBIAS

As noted earlier, in addition to direct traumatic conditioning, two other associative pathways have been proposed: observational conditioning and instructional learning (Rachman, 1990). Anecdotal observations have long suggested that people can acquire intense fears or phobias simply by watching another individual behaving in a frightened manner in the presence of a potentially phobic object or situation. Retrospective studies of humans with phobias have confirmed these anecdotal observations for a small but significant proportion of those studied. For example, Öst and Hugdahl (1981) found that 17% of their sample of people with specific phobias reported vicarious conditioning experiences as being centrally involved in the origins of their phobias (40% for people with animal phobias). Also, Muris and Merckelbach (2001) reviewed eight studies on children with phobias and reported a wide range of estimates for modeling experiences as being at least partially responsible for the origins of the children's phobias (range 8%–73%).

Retrospective studies have enormous limitations, however, because they rely on people's fallible memories, often over long periods of time and under conditions that are likely to reduce rather than promote accurate recall (see the concluding section of this chapter). Thus, whenever available, it is preferable to rely on studies using experimental methodologies to show that such observational learning can occur. Indeed, many experiments have shown that individuals undergoing observational conditioning acquire conditioned responses (CRs; most often indexed by electrodermal responding) to previously neutral conditioned stimuli (CSs) after observing another individual who is ostensibly experiencing fear or pain from electric shocks in the presence of that CS (see Green & Osborne, 1985). Nevertheless, such studies are limited because, for ethical reasons, the "fears" conditioned cannot be intense and persistent phobic-like fears and thus cannot tell us whether these can be acquired through observation alone.

Fortunately studies involving nonhuman primates have helped to clarify the true potency of observational conditioning. In the 1980s, Mineka, M. Cook, and colleagues demonstrated that naïve laboratory-reared rhesus monkeys that were not initially afraid of snakes could readily acquire an intense phobic-like fear through vicarious learning. Nonfearful observer monkeys watched a related or an unrelated and unfamiliar wild-reared model monkey that had an intense phobic-like fear of snakes. The phobic monkey behaved fearfully in the presence of live and toy snakes and nonfearfully in the presence of neutral objects (e.g., M. Cook, Mineka, Wolkenstein, & Laitsch, 1985; Mineka, Davidson, Cook, & Keir, 1984). Moreover, this learning by observer monkeys occurred rapidly and was highly persistent, with no sign of diminution at the 3-month follow-up. Indeed, in one experiment, significant fear of snakes was acquired after only 4 minutes of exposure to a model behaving fearfully (Mineka & Cook, 1993). Furthermore, the maximum amount of exposure that any observer had to a model behaving fearfully with snakes was 24 minutes. The fear that the observer monkeys acquired was of comparable intensity to that of the model monkeys; the former observers could also serve as models for other unrelated observer monkeys, who in turn acquired an intense fear of snakes (M. Cook et al., 1985). Finally, observer monkeys also acquired an intense fear of snakes simply by watching videotapes of models behaving fearfully with snakes (M. Cook & Mineka, 1990).

Thus, this series of experiments with initially nonfearful monkeys clearly demonstrated that rapid observational conditioning of an intense and persistent fear of snakes can occur. This primate model has been considered by many to be powerful evidence that intense and persistent phobic-like fears can be learned by observation alone. Moreover, several other studies with children also support the influence of parental modeling on increasing children's fears, at least in the short term. For example, Gerull and Rapee (2002) studied 17-month-old children who watched their mothers display fear and disgust (with both facial expressions and negative verbalizations) to a rubber snake (or spider) for only 1 minute. These toddlers showed greater fear expressions and avoidance of that object up to 10 minutes later even though the mother changed and expressed neutral emotions to the snake (or spider) after the first minute. Unfortunately, there were no further tests to determine how long the influence of parental modeling lasted. This study nicely illustrates the important influence that even very brief displays of fear by parents can have on their children's fears, at least in the short term.

Much less evidence is available regarding the role of instructional or verbal learning in the origins of fears. Retrospective studies (with all their limitations) indicate that a small but significant number of people report that reading or hearing frightening information about some object or situation led to the development of their phobia (e.g., Öst & Hugdahl, 1981). There are, however, only a few actual demonstrations that fears can be learned this way in the laboratory, and even these studies document only that such learning can influence fear levels, leaving open the question of how these fears might develop into phobias.

In one such study, children aged between 7 and 9 years were presented with negative information from an adult in the form of a story about one toy monster and positive information about a different toy monster (Field & Lawson, 2003). Self-reported fear of the toy monster paired with the scary story increased, whereas self-reported fear of the toy monster paired with the pleasant story decreased. Moreover, the children also showed behavioral avoidance of the toy monster paired with the scary story, as well as a change in implicit attitudes toward the toy monster (using an implicit attitude task). Another study using children ranging in age from 4 to 12 years also found similar changes in self-reported fear up to 1 week following one pairing of an unknown dog-like animal called "the beast" with negative information in the form of a story (Muris, Bodden, Merckelbach, Ollendick, & King, 2003). Nevertheless, Muris et al. also acknowledged that mere exposure to negative information is unlikely to produce the severe fear and avoidance behavior that characterizes real clinical phobias. Instead, negative information may primarily set up negative expectancies that then potentiate the outcome of direct or observational conditioning episodes (e.g., Dadds, Davey, & Field, 2001).

In summary, there is much stronger evidence for the observational conditioning pathway to the origins of some phobic fears than for instructional learning. Nevertheless, instructional learning experiences may readily lead to the development of mild fears at least in children (although we do not know how transient such increases in fear may be). Moreover, these in turn may potentiate the outcome of direct or observational conditioning experiences.

INDIVIDUAL DIFFERENCES IN VULNERABILITY OR INVULNERABILITY TO FEARS AND PHOBIAS

As noted earlier, learning experiences are not always sufficient for the development of fears and phobias. Instead, there is a host of temperamental and experiential variables on which individuals differ that strongly affect the outcome of any of these learning experiences, with some increasing vulnerability and others decreasing vulnerability. Moreover, these variables can act singly or in combination to affect how much fear is experienced in any frightening situation, as well as how much fear is acquired and maintained into the future.

These variables were previously unrecognized because of a relatively systematic neglect by most researchers of the powerful effects that experiential variables, as well as temperamental and personality variables, play in understanding individual differences in the acquisition of fears. This occurred, in part, because of an overreliance on extrapolating from simple conditioning studies in which naïve animals were studied in isolated conditioning chambers, protected from all extraneous stimuli in the environment. Moreover, animals in a given experiment were all of the same strain (and therefore had similar "temperaments") and were all cage-reared, precluding examination of any individual differences in prior experiences with any of the stimuli used during conditioning. All these factors militated against finding individual differences in the outcome of conditioning.

Notably, individual difference variables mostly seemed like a nuisance factor to most conditioning researchers because they were interested in understanding the general principles of associative learning. Yet clinical scientists who extrapolated from such studies to what should occur in humans undergoing conditioning in the course of their everyday lives were shortsighted. Obviously, humans undergoing conditioning in their everyday lives are rarely naïve with respect to the stimuli encountered or isolated from extraneous variables that may affect the outcome of conditioning. Moreover, individuals undergoing the same experiences clearly have temperamental differences as well as differences in life experiences before, during, and after conditioning experiences.

Temperamental Variables

Pavlov (1927) initially made systematic observations that his dogs had different "temperaments" that affected the rapidity of forming excitatory and inhibitory CRs, as well as their stability once acquired. Later extensive research on rats also showed that there is a significant genetic or temperamental contribution to the formation of aversive associations in animals (cf. Gray, 1987, for a review). Similar differences also occur in humans (e.g., Levey & Martin, 1981; Zinbarg & Mohlman, 1998).

The longitudinal prospective studies initiated in the 1980s by Kagan and Biederman and colleagues provided important information on differences in the ease of acquiring fears in young children with behaviorally inhibited versus noninhibited temperaments. Children defined as behaviorally inhibited are timid, shy, and easily distressed, and this can be measured reliably at an early age. These investigators (e.g., Biederman et al., 1990) showed that children categorized as behaviorally inhibited at 21 months old were at higher risk for developing multiple specific phobias at 7 to 8 years old than were noninhibited children (32% vs. 5%). Furthermore, they also showed higher rates of generalized social anxiety by age 13 (e.g., Schwartz et al., 1999). Although this study did not show that the effects of behavioral inhibition on development of phobias are indeed mediated by differences in conditionability, this will be an important potential mediating mechanism to test in the future (e.g., Mineka & Zinbarg, 1996).

Experiential Variables

As noted earlier, humans undergoing conditioning in their everyday lives vary tremendously in terms of their prior experiences both with the CSs and unconditioned stimuli (USs) involved, as well in their general life experiences that may lead to a sense of mastery (or helplessness). Thus, they are not directly analogous to naïve animals undergoing conditioning procedures in isolated chambers in a laboratory, as we now illustrate.

Effects of Preexisting Individual Differences

The well-known phenomenon of *latent inhibition* (e.g., Lubow, 1998) clearly shows that an organism's prior exposure to a neutral CS before it is paired with an aversive US reduces the conditionability of that CS. Specifically, when people or animals have prior exposure to a CS before an aversive conditioning experience, the amount of fear conditioned is generally diminished relative to what happens with a truly novel CS. Several studies on phobias have reported results consistent with this phenomenon. For example, children who have had more previous nontraumatic encounters with a dentist are less likely to develop dental phobia if subsequently traumatized than are those with fewer previous nontraumatic encounters (e.g., Kent, 1997).

Even more powerful attenuation of conditioning may occur when an observer actually first sees another person behaving nonfearfully with a neutral CS (some object or situation) before having an aversive direct or observational experience with that CS. Mineka and Cook (1986) demonstrated this using their primate model of fear acquisition. Three groups of eight nonfearful monkeys each went through one of three pretreatments for six sessions. The *immunization* group first watched a nonfearful model monkey behaving nonfearfully with snakes and other objects; the *latent inhibition* group first had exposures by themselves to the snakes and other objects for the exact same amount of time that the immunization group did (but with no nonfearful models); and the *pseudoimmunization* control group first had exposures to nonfearful model monkeys behaving nonfearfully to neutral objects (but not to snakes). Subsequently, all three groups underwent the standard six-session observational conditioning protocol described earlier in which they all watched a fearful monkey behaving fearfully with snakes. As hypothesized, the immunization group showed no significant acquisition of snake fear, whereas the pseudoimmunization group showed strong and robust acquisition of snake fear. The latent inhibition group was intermediate: Members of this group showed significant acquisition of snake fear, but their level of fear did not differ significantly from the other two groups, quite likely because of limited statistical power.

Although we are not aware of any human study demonstrating this immunization phenomenon, it seems likely that children who have immunization experiences with a nonfearful parent (or perhaps a peer) behaving nonfearfully with the phobic object or situation feared by another parent or peer, will be immunized, either fully or partially, from any effects of later observing a fearful parent or peer behaving fearfully. Clinically, this would suggest that if phobic parents are concerned about passing on their own phobia to their children, they should make sure their children have plenty of exposure to someone behaving nonfearfully with their own phobic object before allowing their children to see them behaving fearfully with that object.

Latent inhibition and immunization both involve the effects of prior experiences with a potentially phobic object or situation before any aversive learning experiences. An individual's prior experiences with being able to control important aspects of his or her environment also have more general effects on fear and fear conditioning. Indeed, developmental psychologists interested in socioemotional development have long noted that infants and young children who are reared with a sense of mastery and control over important aspects of their environments have more secure attachment relationships and are less fearful and better able to cope with novel, frightening, and stressful situations (e.g., Chorpita, 2001; Watson, 1979). These ideas are necessarily based on the results of correlational studies, however, and are therefore not conclusive because environments that foster a sense of control and mastery usually have other correlated positive features that could actually be playing the critical causal role (e.g., Ainsworth, Blehar, Waters, & Wall, 1978).

Fortunately, experimental evidence for these conclusions derives from one longitudinal experimental study of infant peer-reared rhesus monkeys that were reared in controllable versus uncontrollable environments for the first year of life (Mineka, Gunnar, & Champoux, 1986). In the controllable environments, the two groups of four "master monkeys" each had levers to press and chains to pull to deliver food, water, and treats. In the uncontrollable environments, the two groups of four "yoked monkeys" each received access to the same food, water, and treats, but these were delivered uncontrollably whenever a master monkey earned a reinforcer (i.e., their manipulanda were inoperative). When tested in several frightening and novel situations between 7 and 11 months of age, the master monkeys reared with control adapted more quickly in several fear-provoking situations compared with the yoked monkeys reared without control. The master monkeys also showed more exploratory behavior when placed in a large unfamiliar primate playroom. Thus, early experience with control and mastery over positive reinforcers appears to affect the level of fear that novel and frightening events evoke, paralleling what is thought to occur in early human development. Thus, learning a sense of control or mastery may decrease the conditioning of fear either by decreasing the intensity of reactions to frightening events or by increasing the rate of habituation to them (or both). From a clinical standpoint, these results suggest that individuals reared with a sense of mastery over their environment may well show reduced susceptibility to developing fears, phobias, and certain other anxiety disorders (see also Chorpita, 2001; Mineka & Zinbarg, 1996).

Effects of Individual Differences in Experiences During a Learning Event

When an animal or person undergoes Pavlovian conditioning in an experimental setting, she or he has no control over the onset or offset of either the CS or the US because the conditioning events are all under experimental control. When Pavlovian conditioning occurs during our everyday lives, however, there is no experimenter controlling the timing of the CSs and USs, and frequently individuals do have some control over the US, such as when it will terminate. Having control over US offset has powerful effects on how much fear is conditioned. Indeed, the animal conditioning literature indicates that uncontrollable shock conditions anxiety to neutral CSs more powerfully than does the same amount of controllable shock (e.g., Mineka, Cook, & Miller, 1984; Mowrer & Viek, 1948). Indeed, Mineka, Cook, and Miller (1984) found that levels of anxiety conditioned with inescapable shock were twice as high as levels of anxiety conditioned with the exact same amount of escapable shock. Thus, the dynamics of Pavlovian conditioning are dramatically affected by the controllability of the US. What this means clinically is that humans undergoing traumatic conditioning experiences should acquire far less fear if they have some ability to escape that trauma (e.g., by running away) rather than having it terminate independently of their own responses (with amount of trauma exposure equated).

Effects of Individual Differences in What Occurs Following Conditioning

Once a certain level of fear is acquired through direct or vicarious conditioning, that level of fear is usually well maintained over time unless extinction trials occur. Nevertheless, the fear memory may be malleable (see Hendersen, 1985; Mineka & Zinbarg, 1996). For example, Rescorla (1974) discovered the *inflation effect* in which rats that were first conditioned to show a mild fear of a CS (by using a mild US) were later exposed to a stronger US presented randomly (not paired with the CS). When the rats were then tested with the CS, their level of fear was inflated as if the CS had actually been paired with the stronger US in the first place. Moreover, the stronger US does not need to be the same US that was used in conditioning initially. Thus, for example, a person who acquired a mild fear of automobiles following a minor accident might later show a more intense fear of automobiles if he or she were physically assaulted (see White & Davey, 1989). Hendersen (1985) also demonstrated that the longer the interval between when conditioning occurred and when exposure to the more intense US occurred, the greater the magnitude of the inflation effect. Hendersen noted that it is as if the organism has a representation in memory of the original US that can be altered through later experiences with more intense USs; moreover, the malleability of the fear memory increases with time since the original conditioning occurred.

More recently, Davey described a related phenomenon in humans called *US reevaluation* in which even socially transmitted information about the US acquired following conditioning can result in increased levels of fear (e.g., Dadds et al., 2001). So for example, if a person acquires verbal information that the US is actually more dangerous or traumatic than it had been during conditioning, this can be sufficient for his or her fear level to be inflated. Even mental rehearsal of CS–US pairings following conditioning can also enhance the strength of a mild CR conditioned in the laboratory (Davey & Matchett, 1994).

SELECTIVE ASSOCIATIONS AND THE NONRANDOM
DISTRIBUTION OF FEARS AND PHOBIAS

Another important variable affecting whether people will develop a fear or phobia concerns the nature of the CS that is present during learning. Seligman (1971) first systematized observations that fears and phobias seem to develop much more frequently to certain kinds of objects and situations than to others. For example, fears and phobias of snakes, spiders, heights, enclosed spaces, and water are far more common than for cars, bicycles, and guns, even though the latter may be at least as likely to be paired with trauma in contemporary society. Seligman hypothesized that this is because early in our evolutionary history, a selective advantage developed for animals that rapidly acquired intense fears of objects or situations that frequently were dangerous or posed a threat relative to animals that did not acquire these fears as readily. These early clinical observations regarding the nonrandom distribution of fears and phobias were systematized in several studies examining the content of the phobias of many individuals diagnosed with specific phobias (e.g., de Silva, Rachman, & Seligman, 1977; for a review, see Öhman & Mineka, 2001). Trained raters assessed the biological preparedness of the content of these phobias on a 1 to 5 scale. Ratings of 4 and 5 indicated that the phobic objects or situations were *probably* or *almost certainly* dangerous to pretechnological humans, whereas ratings of 1 and 2 indicated that these phobic objects or situations were probably or certainly not dangerous to pretechnological humans. As predicted, most of the phobias were rated in the 4 to 5 range.

Selective Associations

Experimental investigations provided even stronger support for many aspects of Seligman's preparedness theory of phobias. In the mid-1970s, Öhman and his colleagues in Sweden initiated a long series of human conditioning experiments on the selective associability of fear-relevant CSs with aversive USs. They compared conditioning when mild electric shock USs were paired with either CSs that were slides of fear-relevant stimuli (e.g., snakes, spiders, or angry faces) or CSs that were slides of fear-irrelevant stimuli (e.g., flowers, mushrooms, geometric figures, or happy faces). The most commonly used psychophysiological dependent variables were electrodermal responses, but sometimes other dependent variables were also measured, such as heart rate or corrugator responses (muscles controlling frowning seen when conditioning with facial stimuli). Numerous experiments found that CRs to the fear-relevant CSs were much more highly resistant to extinction than were CRs to the fear-irrelevant CSs (for review, see Öhman & Mineka, 2001). Moreover, one-trial conditioning only occurred with fear-relevant but not fear-irrelevant stimuli.

Subsequent research also demonstrated a qualitative difference in the nature of the CRs conditioned to fear-relevant versus fear-irrelevant CSs. For example, E. Cook, Hodes, and Lang (1986) reported that with fear-relevant CSs and heart rate as a dependent measure, the heart rate CRs showed a strong acceleratory component followed by a brief deceleratory component. In contrast, the heart rate CRs conditioned with fear-irrelevant CSs showed only a strong deceleratory component (as is typical in conditioning of heart rate using fear-irrelevant CSs). Similarly, Dimberg (1987) compared conditioning using angry versus happy faces as CSs, paired with mild electric shocks as USs. He found that the CRs to the angry faces (but not the happy faces) included corrugator activity, heart rate acceleration, and self-reported fear. As reviewed by Öhman and Mineka (2001), these and other results on qualitative differences in conditioning to fear-relevant versus fear-irrelevant CSs suggest that truly defensive responses, indicating active defense mobilization, are only conditioned with fear-relevant CSs. With fear-irrelevant CSs, the CRs are typically an enhanced orienting response.

Although this series of experiments provided strong support for the concept of selective associations, two major limitations prevented this line of work alone from serving as a compelling model for phobia acquisition. First, for ethical reasons, the fears conditioned in all these human experiments must necessarily be mild and transient, and we therefore cannot be certain that similar differences will occur in the conditioning of intense and long-lasting phobic level fears. Second, the humans in these experiments of course all have prior ontogenetically based associations to the fear-relevant and fear-irrelevant stimuli used as CSs. Thus, we cannot be confident that the different characteristics observed in conditioning to fear-relevant CSs really derive from phylogenetic or evolutionary (as opposed to ontogenetic or developmental) sources as preparedness theory maintains (see Mineka & Öhman, 2002a; Öhman & Mineka, 2001).

For these reasons, Mineka and M. Cook used their primate model to test whether similar effects would be observed in nonfearful observer monkeys exposed to fear-relevant versus fear-irrelevant objects. Their initial experiments reviewed earlier illustrated that rapid, robust, and long-lasting phobic fears of snakes can be acquired observationally, but they did not test whether similar learning would occur with fear-irrelevant objects. To do this, it was necessary to equate the exact level of fear shown by the models to the fear-relevant and fear-irrelevant stimuli. This was accomplished by using video-editing techniques. This way the model monkeys' actual fear-reactions to a live snake could be made to appear as if they had been exhibited to, for example, brightly colored flowers or a toy snake.

In one experiment, a group of observer monkeys (SN+/FL– group) watched a model monkey on videotape showing intense fear reactions to toy snakes (but not to flowers or neutral wood objects) (M. Cook & Mineka, 1990). The other FL+/ SN– group, by contrast, watched a model monkey on videotape showing the exact same intense fear reactions to brightly colored artificial flowers (but not to toy snakes or neutral objects). When later tested by themselves, the SN+/FL– group had clearly acquired a fear of snakes (but not flowers), but the FL+/SN– group had not acquired any fear of flowers (or snakes). Essentially identical results were obtained when observational conditioning to another fear-relevant stimulus (i.e., a toy crocodile) was compared with conditioning to another fear-irrelevant stimulus (i.e., a toy rabbit; M. Cook & Mineka, 1989).

In summary, these monkey experiments overcome the two limitations of the human prepared fear conditioning literature mentioned earlier. First, intense fears can be conditioned to fear-relevant (but not to fear-irrelevant) stimuli. Second, although these lab-reared monkeys had absolutely no prior exposure to any of the stimuli used in these videotape experiments (i.e., they had no ontogenetically based associations), they nonetheless showed major differences in the conditionability of fear-relevant versus fear-irrelevant stimuli.

Automaticity and Encapsulation

Further work by Öhman and his colleagues revealed other important differences in the characteristics of conditioning to fear-relevant CSs. One series of studies demonstrated the automaticity of processing of fear-relevant (but not fear-irrelevant) stimuli. In one experiment, Öhman and Soares (1994) showed that participants who were already fearful of spiders or snakes (but not both) showed nonconscious activation of their fear responses when presented with subliminal presentations of their feared objects (but not their nonfeared objects). In another experiment, they showed that CRs to supraliminal fear-relevant CSs were maintained during an extinction procedure in which the CSs were presented subliminally. That is, even though subjects could no longer identify the stimulus to which they were responding, they continued to show CRs to fear-relevant but not fear-irrelevant CSs (e.g., Öhman & Soares, 1993). Finally, they also showed that conditioning could even occur to subliminal fear-relevant (but not fear-irrelevant) CSs paired with shocks. That is, subjects acquired CRs to fear-relevant CSs that they could not even identify during conditioning (e.g., Öhman & Soares, 1998). Thus, only fear-relevant CSs gain preferential access to preconscious attentional mechanisms. Such results may help explain why phobic fears can sometimes be elicited with great speed even with minimal stimulus input (e.g., reacting to a snake in the grass long before there is any conscious recognition that a snake is there; see Öhman & Mineka, 2001).

Another important aspect of this line of work on prepared fear conditioning is that CRs to fear-relevant stimuli seem to be especially resistant to conscious cognitive control. For example, several experiments found that when subjects were told they would no longer be shocked at the end of conditioning, those conditioned with fear-irrelevant stimuli showed immediate extinction of their CR, but those conditioned with fear-relevant stimuli continued to show electrodermal CRs (e.g., Soares & Öhman, 1993). Moreover, Schell, Dawson, and Marinkovic (1991) measured subjects' expectancies for when USs would occur, as well as their electrodermal responses during conditioning and extinction. Subjects conditioned with fear-relevant (but not fear-irrelevant) CSs continued to show electrodermal CRs well after their expectancies that they would be shocked had extinguished. Thus, knowledge that USs will no longer be forthcoming has little if any impact on CRs to fear-relevant CSs.

The Concept of an Evolved Fear Module

Öhman and Mineka (2001; Mineka & Öhman, 2002a) proposed an evolved behavioral module for fear learning to best explain the complex pattern of results that has emerged over the past 30 years. Borrowing the concept of an evolved behavioral module from Tooby and Cosmides (e.g., 1992), they argued that the fear module is a relatively independent mental, behavioral, and neural system that was tailored by evolutionary pressures to help solve problems of adapting to dangerous and potentially life-threatening situations that were encountered in the environments of our very early ancestors. The fear module, like other evolutionarily shaped behavioral systems, shows four distinctive characteristics.

First, it shows relative selectivity with respect to the input it accepts, with the system being especially sensitive to certain stimuli that provided recurrent survival threats to our early evolutionary ancestors. This is consistent with evidence reviewed earlier that fear learning is especially robust with fear-relevant CSs in both monkeys and humans. Moreover, the nature of the CR is often qualitatively different (indeed, truly defensive) with fear-relevant CSs.

Second, behavioral systems with deep evolutionary origins are typically not under conscious control but instead are directly and rapidly activated by stimuli whether we want it or not because these brain systems evolved in animals with much more primitive brains than ours well before the emergence of language and thought. Such effects are illustrated by Öhman and colleagues' experiments showing automatic activation and conditioning of CRs with subliminal fear-relevant CSs.

Third, Öhman and Mineka (2001) also argued that such behavioral systems are typically encapsulated from higher cognitive influences, again having evolved in animals with much more primitive brains. This was illustrated in experiments showing that conditioning with fear-relevant CSs is not affected by direct information that shocks will no longer occur, as well as in experiments showing that fear responding with fear-relevant CSs continues after extinction of expectancies (see chap. 6, this volume; Lovibond & Shanks, 2002, for an alternative point of view; see Wiens & Öhman, 2002, for a reply).

Fourth, Öhman and Mineka (2001) also noted that such evolutionarily shaped behavioral systems usually have some dedicated neural circuitry, which in the case of fear and fear learning is centered in the amygdala.

Thus, the primary characteristics of the fear module include selectivity with regard to input, automaticity with regard to activation, encapsulation from higher cognitive influences, and a dedicated neural circuitry. In this way, the fear module concept integrates many diverse findings about fear and fear learning from different domains (e.g., clinical, cognitive, learning, neurobiological). Moreover, the fear module concept also sets an agenda for future research that may improve understanding of both basic and clinical aspects of fear and anxiety.

Thus far, we have reviewed evidence from animal and human studies supporting Rachman's idea of three associative pathways being involved in the development of fears and phobias: direct, vicarious, and instructional learning. We have also demonstrated that more traditional conditioning models were vastly oversimplistic and how contemporary models need to take into account the wide range of temperamental, experiential, and evolutionary variables that affect how much fear is acquired and maintained.

In the past 25 years, a small group of researchers has sought to verify that these associative pathways are indeed involved in the ways strongly suggested by the research reviewed here. Typically, these several dozen studies have simply asked people about what they believe had caused the development of their fears and phobias (usually with structured questionnaires to assess various kinds of learning experiences). Some of these studies have raised doubts about how often these associative pathways are actually involved, with some suggestions that certain fears and phobias are innate. We now review the foundations of this nonassociative account. Finally, we critically evaluate the soundness of this new approach that relies on the reliability and validity of the retrospective recall method used in these studies.

THE NONASSOCIATIVE ACCOUNT OF FEAR ACQUISITION

In the literature investigating the origins of phobias through self-report, many studies have found a subset of participants who either cannot recall the onset of their phobia or report having always been fearful. One hypothesized explanation for these reports is that participants simply cannot recall experiences that actually occurred (e.g., caused by forgetting or childhood amnesia; see the final section of this chapter). Another postulated explanation, which we focus on first, however, is provided by a new nonassociative account (e.g., Menzies & Clarke, 1995a; Poulton & Menzies, 2002a, 2002b). This account stipulates that for certain *evolutionarily* relevant dangers, fears are innate, developing without any negative experiences with the stimuli. This is in contrast to the position of Öhman and Mineka (2001), who specified that evolutionarily relevant fears require at least a small amount of experiential input to emerge. The nonassociative account acknowledges the importance of conditioning pathways in the acquisition of "evolutionarily neutral" (e.g., dental) fears and, in some cases, of certain evolutionarily relevant fears.

Both the prepared conditioning and nonassociative accounts have noted that the fear and avoidance of certain historically dangerous stimuli or situations is under partial genetic control and has served a survival benefit to the species. Moreover, Menzies and Clarke (1995a) also stated "(a)ccording to this [nonassociative] view, then, given maturational processes and normal background experiences . . . most members of the species will show fear to a set of evolutionary stimuli on their *first* encounter" (p. 42). Included in this evolutionarily relevant group are four fears in particular: fear of strangers, heights, early separation, and water (see Menzies & Harris, 2001).

The nonassociative account draws greatly from developmental and cross-cultural work demonstrating that most infants experience normative developmental fears to the four stimuli just mentioned. For example, Menzies and Harris (2001) cited primate and cross-cultural research in support of infants' fear of strangers and separation anxiety. They also reviewed the work of Gibson and Walk (1960) who found that infants' avoidance of the visual cliff was a developmentally normative reaction. Finally, for water fear Graham and Gaffan (1997) found that about 50% of mothers whose children were currently or previously afraid of water reported that this fear was present at the child's first contact. We are not aware of any careful cross-cultural or developmental work showing that water fear is innate, however.

If the development of these four fears is normative, why do a minority of people continue to have severe fears and phobias beyond childhood, whereas the majority of people do not? First, the nonassociative account acknowledges significant genetically based variability in the fear reactions of different individuals even during an initial encounter (e.g., Menzies & Harris, 2001). Thus, even at initial contact, people's fear responses vary from mild to more pronounced.

Second, in addressing the issue that these fears are usually transient and restricted to an early developmental stage, the nonassociative account invokes the process of habituation (Menzies & Clarke, 1995a). That is, over time, most children have repeated exposures to their feared situation without significant negative experiences, and thus the fear habituates. Yet if habituation is so common, why do any adults manifest these innate (nonassociative) fears (Menzies & Harris, 2001)? Menzies and Clarke hypothesized three reasons why fear may continue, or reappear if it once habituated: lack of safe exposures, innately based poor habituation, and nonspecific stress. Lack of safe exposures can occur because of practical limitations in opportunities for exposure or because of self- or parental-chosen avoidance of the situation. In the case of poor habituation, the nonassociative account posits genetically based individual differences in rates of habituation such that certain individuals need much larger amounts of exposure before habituation occurs (Menzies & Harris, 2001). Notably, however, even the proponents of this nonassociative account have acknowledged a dearth of supportive data for this second hypothesized mechanism (Poulton, Waldie, Craske, Menzies, & McGee, 2000).

Third and finally, the nonassociative account hypothesizes that high levels of general stress may result in the reemergence of a previously habituated evolutionarily relevant fear. Poulton and colleagues (2000) cited as evidence animal work conducted by Groves and Thompson (1970) demonstrating dishabituation when a novel, sensitizing stimulus is presented close in time to the presentation of a previously habituated stimulus. Poulton and colleagues claimed support for this hypothesis when they found that, for children who were not fearful at age 11, nonspecific stress between ages 14 and 15 predicted height phobia at age 18 but not the evolutionary neutral dental phobia.

Several methodological issues seriously qualify the conclusions that can be drawn from this study, however. Specifically, fears and phobias were only measured at ages 11 and 18, stressful life events were assessed only between ages 14 and 15, and diagnostic interviews at age 18 only inquired about fear in the past year. Thus, many stressful events and several fear or phobia onsets and remissions could have taken place during the other 6 years for which there is no information. More substantive support for the dishabituation account would require a study implementing frequent assessments of both life stress and fear or phobic outcomes to more clearly elucidate temporal relationships and developmental trajectories.

An interesting point of overlap between the associative and nonassociative explanations of fear or phobia onset is that both seem to address the finding that many participants who do have a history of aversive or traumatic experiences do not develop fears or phobias of those stimuli. In a study using retrospective recall, Menzies and Parker (2001) found that participants with a fear of heights did not differ significantly from nonfearful control participants on the proportion reporting direct or indirect conditioning experiences, age during conditioning experiences, or self-reported fear level prior to reported conditioning experiences. Moreover, the nonfearful control participants recalled higher levels of fear and pain during their direct conditioning experiences than did their counterparts with fear of heights. These authors concluded that this latter finding accords with the nonassociative account: Individuals who have always had a fear of heights (one of their innate fears) would probably engage in less dangerous acts and therefore be subjected to less pain because of their concerns or avoidance. Although this line of thinking may seem plausible, the results of Menzies and Parker actually did not adequately test or confirm this hypothesis because both their fearful and nonfearful participants reported low and comparable levels of height fear prior to putative conditioning events. Yet their theory presupposes lower levels of fear prior to conditioning events in those participants who do not develop significant fear. Thus, their results are actually not consistent with their hypotheses.

It is interesting that the associative account seems to provide a better potential explanation of these particular findings by Menzies and Parker (2001). As reviewed earlier in this chapter and by Mineka and Öhman (2002b), a host of temperamental and experiential differences (e.g., latent inhibition and perceptions of control) lead to differences in how much fear is acquired during traumatic experiences and how much fear is maintained into the future. Moreover, children with relatively fearless and outgoing temperaments, particularly if they have a sense of learned mastery over their environment, will be more likely to engage in risky activities that could lead to the occurrence of aversive experiences with certain stimuli, which nevertheless would not lead to fear acquisition because of these temperamental or experiential variables.

It is beyond the scope of this chapter to flesh out a full critique of the nonassociative account. The interested reader is directed to a special issue of *Behaviour Research and Therapy* (2002, pp. 121–208), which includes articles by Poulton and Menzies (2002a, 2002b), Mineka and Öhman (2002b), and a number of other researchers. Particular points of contention involve defining evolutionary relevance, the amount of genetic contribution to specific phobias, the role of individual personality and experiential factors, and explication of the complexities of contemporary conditioning theory (which are discussed in this chapter). We also raise the issue here that even if particular mild or moderate fears are innate, phobias probably require experiential input. Furthermore, the nonassociative account does not address the issue of how a normative height fear in infancy transitions into height phobia, nor does it address the developmental trajectories of the normative fears of strangers and separation as they pertain to childhood and adult anxiety disorders (e.g., Mineka & Öhman, 2002b). This area of substantial debate has significant implications for theory and research on the etiology of phobias.

RELIABILITY OF RETROSPECTIVE RECALL

It is vital for researchers positing both associative and nonassociative accounts to be aware of the serious limitations and implications of drawing conclusions from this corpus of work based on retrospective studies. Although the temporal gaps between fear or phobia onset and time of recall have shortened in some recent retrospective studies of college students and children (e.g., Menzies & Parker, 2001) relative to earlier investigations in adult populations, even the more recent investigations have entailed recall over many years. Furthermore, even prospective work often becomes dependent on substantial retrospective recall. For example, the Dunedin Multidisciplinary Health and Developmental Study, used extensively in studies by Poulton, Menzies, and colleagues, followed an entire birth cohort with multifaceted interviews and measures obtained at birth and ages 3, 5, 7, 9, 11, 13, 15, 18,

21, and 26 (see Poulton & Menzies, 2002a, for relevant methods and findings). Each follow-up period thus had at least a 2-year gap, and phobias were assessed only at ages 3, 11, 18, and 21. As we review here, even 2-year gaps allow substantial room for errors in recall.

Accuracy of Recall for Childhood Events

The first issue to be addressed is the accuracy of human memory for early events, given that many studies investigating self-reports of fear and phobia onset assume that college students and adult participants can accurately recall events that often occurred during childhood. One review of available evidence concluded that autobiographical recall for childhood events is often quite accurate (Brewin, Andrews, & Gotlib, 1993), especially for central features of childhood events that were unique, consequential, and unexpected. One study investigating the memories of college students for significant early childhood events (e.g., a sibling birth before the participants' sixth birthday), found that parents validated about 60% of participants' early memories and denied less than 15% of the students' reports (Usher & Neisser, 1993). Researchers have also noted several caveats regarding the veracity of recall for childhood events, however. For example, Henry, Moffitt, Caspi, Langley, and Silva (1994) reported that validity was suspect for recall of subjective states (e.g., anxiety) and cautioned that retrospective reports are less reliable for testing hypotheses that require precise estimation of event dates and frequencies. Furthermore, Brewin and colleagues (1993) also cautioned that unless there are clear anchor points, people may forget the exact timing and sequencing of events as well as their emotional reactions during them.

Accurate recall of temporal sequencing and emotional states is essential for connecting possible associative learning experiences with fear or phobia onset. Several factors pose a particular challenge to veridical reporting. One factor discussed by Hyman and Loftus (1998) is the concept of *time-slice errors*, which occur when an accurately recalled event is not the one that was actually asked about. In the case of fear, these errors may occur because the person does not associate an earlier event with fear onset or because a given event may be one of several that ultimately resulted in the development of a phobia. They also discussed the possibility that a person may be unable to recall an event because of childhood amnesia (discussed later). A third factor raised by Kendler, Myers, and Prescott (2002) involves possible false-positive endorsement of events related to onset of fears and phobias. These authors speculated that events may be endorsed as part of a search for meaning or may mark the first memorable experience with an already feared stimulus. Fourth, Hyman and Loftus (1998) concluded that "people reconstruct their past attitudes and mental states based on their current ones adjusted by their implicit theories concerning constancy and change during the intervening time period" (p. 943). Fifth, Bradburn, Rips, and Shevell

(1987) reported that when recall of an event is challenging, people might use their inferences to conclude that an event was infrequent, distant, or never happened. Thus, people's own theories about memory itself can affect recall.

Reliability Checks on Recall

Several investigations have implemented reliability checks for participants' recall. Overall, the results have been troubling with regard to validating retrospective reports about fear and phobia onset. One relevant study of people with spider phobias did offer strong support for recall reliability in that parental confirmation of children's reports of direct conditioning or having always been fearful yielded kappa values greater than .8 (Merckelbach, Muris, & van Schouten, 1996).

In contrast, three other studies raise serious doubts about the reliability of retrospective recall. For example, Henry et al. (1994) asked participants for the number of serious injuries in the 2 years before assessments at ages 9, 11, 13, and 15. They compared this total with participants' recall at age 18 for all injuries that occurred between ages 7 and 15. They found only modest agreement ($r = .42$, $\kappa = .34$). This result is particularly relevant and troubling because injuries are one common US involved in the onset of a number of phobias.

A second study relevant to fear onset also found significant levels of disagreement. Kheriaty, Kleinknecht, and Hyman (1999) investigated dog or blood and injury fearful students on the origins of their fear as well as the timing of its onset. Parents were also contacted to confirm their child's account, with 55 of 80 returning questionnaires. Among the offspring of these 55 parents, 42 students recalled some associative pathway related to fear onset; parents validated this onset pathway in 26 cases (62%). Parents named an earlier and different event than the student had named in 9 cases (21%), and 7 parents (17%) did not know how their child acquired the fear. It is important that for the remaining 13 student participants who reported no recall of fear origin, 8 parents (62%) identified a specific event related to the onset of the student's fear. Finally, for the 28 cases in which the age of fear onset was recalled by both parents and children, children reported fear onset nearly 3 years later than parents did.

A third study conducted by Taylor, Deane, and Podd (1999) also yielded disturbing results. These investigators asked a sample of adults with driving fear to ascribe a cause for the onset of their fear at two time points, 1 year apart. Strikingly, only 54% of attributions remained the same at these two points. In addition, of the 11 people (13% of the sample) initially endorsing "cannot remember," only 2 continued to say "cannot remember" at follow-up. Nearly one quarter (6 of 23) of those who said "always been this way" changed at Time 2.

In summary, studies implementing reliability checks have highlighted the problems with relying on retrospective studies that only use self-report. We also note that studies implementing reliability checks using parental reports are also problematic because they tend to make the rather dubious assumption that parental recall is always more accurate than participant recall.

Childhood Amnesia

One additional explanation for the findings that certain participants (e.g., Kheriaty et al., 1999; Öst & Hugdahl, 1981) have no recall for fear or phobia onset is that it may have occurred during a period of childhood amnesia. Essentially, there is an early period of life during which children will not form enduring memories. For example, Usher and Neisser (1993) identified students using a screening questionnaire to determine who knew that they had experienced one of four childhood events before age 6 (birth of a sibling, hospitalization, a family move, or death of a family member). They then investigated students' recall of these experiences. Aspects of the birth of a sibling and a hospitalization could be recalled by more than half the sample 2 to 3 years of age at the time of the event. For the other two events (i.e., family move, death of a parent), it was not until age 4 that more than half the sample met the recall criterion. The authors concluded that the effects of childhood amnesia are not the same for all events, and at ages 3 and 4 only certain exceptional experiences will be available for recall in adulthood.

In a related finding, Pillemer (1998) noted that adults asked to date their earliest memory on average cite 3 to 4 years old and that there is a marked decrease in the amount and complexity of memories acquired before the early school years. Neisser (2004) also offered the caution that even when people can recall a particular early event, this does not mean that the critical age for remembering other types of events has been reached; different criteria will yield different estimates. In sum, when people report having always been fearful, especially without external corroborating sources, phobia etiology could be the consequence of associative learning that occurred before the age of accessible verbal memory.

Forgetting

Another reason many participants may not recall conditioning experiences is because they are simply forgotten. That is, to the degree that direct conditioning events may not always be severe or that indirect encounters may not be unique or consequential, these experiences may simply not be encoded well in memory or are forgotten over time. Using a general life events inventory, Monroe (1982) reported that adult participants asked to recall events over a 2-year period endorsed an average of seven events for the more recent year but only three for the previous year, suggesting a substantial drop-off in recall over just a 2-year period. Monroe then conducted a prospective investigation of recall of life events in which these same participants were given monthly assessments at the end of each of 4 consecutive months. Monroe totaled the number of negative events reported in these 4 monthly assessments and compared it with the total number of negative events recalled over the most recent 4-month period in the 2-year retrospective investigation. He found a significant decrease (2.25 vs. 0.97 events) in the average number of negative events reported using the longer recall period (but for severe events, see G. W. Brown & Harris, 1982, who found higher levels of reliable recall).

Furthermore, concerns have been raised about the memorability of indirect experiences that are less unique, consequential, surprising, and perhaps less emotionally potent than direct experiences (Field, Argyris, & Knowles, 2001). For example, Withers and Deane (1995) found that participants with memories of direct conditioning were more confident in their recall than those endorsing indirect conditioning.

In summary, event properties, time sequencing, memory biases, and inferences about memory are integral facets of the retrieval process. Thus, there is substantial reason for concern when examining retrospective studies of the experiences most relevant to the etiology of fears and phobias. As Kleinknecht (2002) cogently noted, because of these factors, "without corroboration retrospective accounts should be viewed at best as suggestive and hypothesis generating rather than hypothesis supporting or disconfirming" (p. 160).

At present, one conclusion that can be drawn from this literature is that a failure to endorse an associative pathway is not the same as confirming the absence of associative learning. Conversely, another conclusion is that endorsement by a research participant of an associative pathway is not tantamount to confirming that the recalled associative experiences actually played a causal role. Even with corroboration, the problem of failure to endorse an associative pathway is even more serious than the problem of concluding that an associative experience that is recalled actually played a causal role. This is because concluding with confidence that something did not happen is similar to the problem of trying to prove the null hypothesis (see Mineka & Öhman, 2002b).

How could such studies be more useful? Two obvious improvements would be the consistent inclusion of corroborating sources as well as a prospective methodology with frequent monitoring. Ideally such a study design would need to include a large number of participants assessed prospectively over at least the first 20 years of life. Specifically, infants, children, and parents would need to be assessed at least several times a year both for their fears of a wide range of commonly feared stimuli or situations and for the occurrence of relevant events (and personality factors) that could contribute to developing vulnerabilities, invulnerabilities, or fears. Unfortunately, although the Dunedin Study is excellent for many purposes, it cannot be used in a convincing manner for testing theories of fears and phobias because it was not designed for this purpose. Assessments were spaced too far apart, and inadequate information was provided about a range of relevant events and personality vulnerabilities.

CONCLUSIONS

We have reviewed evidence from several research traditions, both historical and contemporary, that is relevant to understanding the etiology of fears and phobias. First, we reviewed evidence regarding Rachman's (1990) three pathways etiological model that emphasizes a variety of associative factors. In doing so, we showed how traditional behavioral models fell short because they ignored the important role that temperamental and experiential individual differences play in the outcome of any learning experiences (see also Mineka, 1985; Mineka & Zinbarg 1996). By attending to the wide range of individual difference factors that play a role, a picture begins to emerge of the many interacting vulnerability (and invulnerability) variables that are important in the search for the etiology of fears and phobias.

Our review focused special attention on studies using the two kinds of complementary and synergistic research strategies that have historically been the cornerstone of work on this topic. Specifically, we discussed experimental animal research in which potent and long-lasting fears can be experimentally induced and manipulated, as well as human experimental research in which mild and transient analogue fears can also be induced and manipulated. Evidence for any given risk factor is often considered strongest when it has been demonstrated using both research strategies, although this is not always feasible (e.g., because of limitations in our ability to measure and manipulate cognitions in animals and because of ethical limitations that disallow certain kinds of questions to be addressed in human studies). Notably, when the complementary strategies have both been used, the results have almost always led to similar conclusions.

Next, we focused our attention on a more recently developed strategy in which researchers rely on individuals' retrospective recall for events that they believe were involved in the origins of their fears and phobias (e.g., Öst & Hugdahl, 1981; Poulton & Menzies, 2002a, 2002b). Some have proposed that the results of many of these studies raise doubts about the conclusions drawn from the experimental research tradition reviewed initially because their findings often reveal a significant proportion of people who do not recall an associative mode of onset or who state that they have always had this fear or phobia. Moreover, these researchers have also found that a significant number of people without fears and phobias do recall prior putative conditioning events that did not lead to the development of fear. We also reviewed considerable evidence, however, that gives serious reason to doubt the validity of these studies as well as the conclusions drawn from them. In particular, there are large problems both with the accuracy of recall of emotional events (and with their sequencing) that often happened many years earlier and with the soundness of attributing causality to events that happened long ago even if they are accurately recalled. Indeed, we find it somewhat surprising that so much attention has been devoted to the nonassociative account given that it relies solely on studies using retrospective recall and yet lacks adequate experimental support of the studies' validity.

In conclusion, we suggest that it would be more prudent to incorporate the findings from experimental animal research, analog human experiments, and the few corroborated self-reported retrospective studies and conclude that a contemporary associative account of persistent fear and phobia acquisition is the most validated, comprehensive, and plausible theory. As noted earlier, the most stringent test of the ecological validity of our account will come from future investigations using a longitudinal, prospective methodology with frequent assessments of potentially relevant learning experiences and fear and phobia onset, as well as occasional assessments of other variables such as temperament and perceptions of control.

5

COGNITIVE MECHANISMS IN FEAR ACQUISITION AND MAINTENANCE

GRAHAM C. L. DAVEY

Fear, an important component of any organism's survival repertoire, primes the organism for rapid defensive action and activates a range of evolved prewired defensive reactions that facilitate survival in threatening situations. Because to survive organisms need to react rapidly and appropriately to the presence of threat, traditional models of fear and anxiety have tended to emphasize the reflexive and noncognitive nature of the systems involved (e.g., evolved natural defensive reactions to potential danger cues such as rapid movement in one's direction, Ball & Tronick, 1971; looming shadows, Hayes & Saiff, 1967; and sudden, jerky movements, Scarr & Salapatek, 1970). Such evolved, built-in reactions to potential threat make evolutionary sense and have played a prominent role in a number of accounts of human fear responding (e.g., Mineka & Öhman, 2002b; Öhman & Mineka, 2001). This approach to understanding fear was also extended to circumstances in which an individual needs to learn about new environmental threat stimuli during its own lifetime to facilitate survival. Early models of acquired fear emphasized the "noncognitive" and relatively reflexive aspects of the processes thought to be involved. For example, classical conditioning was the mechanism of choice for learning about events that predicted threat; early conditioning studies of pioneers such as Watson and Rayner (1920) did little to dispel the view that fear learning was acquired through associative learning processes that were involuntary and reflexive in nature.

Nevertheless, in the latter part of the 20th century, psychology underwent a so-called cognitive revolution. Fostered by the development of new inferential techniques, researchers began to find ways of describing the cognitive mechanisms that mediated basic psychological processes (e.g., associative learning, Davey, 1992a; Rescorla, 1980) and more general psychopathological states such as depression (Abramson, Seligman, & Teasdale, 1978; Beck, 1987) and anxiety (Clark, 1986; Mathews & MacLeod, 1994).

In two broad sections, this chapter describes how our knowledge of the cognitive factors involved in human fear and anxiety has developed over recent years. The first section describes the nature of the information-processing systems involved in processing threat and how these systems are affected by fear-related states such as anxiety. The second section describes how acquired knowledge affects the way an individual reacts to potentially threatening stimuli and events. It also covers the role of acquired beliefs and expectancies in the acquisition and maintenance of fear and anxiety. Finally, the chapter considers how these cognitive factors interact to form the cognitive network underlying fear responding, and the chapter concludes by discussing the various therapeutic implications of this network.

INFORMATION PROCESSING, FEAR, AND ANXIETY

Reactions to a potentially fear-evoking or threatening stimulus are determined by a number of important cognitive factors. These include attentional factors that select the stimulus for processing; interpretational factors, which allow rapid judgments to be made about the nature and intensity of the threat posed by the stimulus; and memory factors that prioritize potential threats for storage and retrieval at a later date. These three factors are discussed here.

Attentional Factors

It makes sense for organisms to prioritize potential threatening stimuli for rapid processing. Evolution has tended to optimize this prioritization by selecting for prewired, defensive reactions that are automatically triggered by potential survival-threatening cues (e.g., looming shadows, rapid movement toward one). These prewired responses alone are not usually sufficient to guard against the range of threats that an organism may encounter in its lifetime, however; organisms must often learn to identify threats and process this threat information rapidly. Thus, it makes sense from a survival standpoint that when the organism perceives itself to be in danger it selectively and rapidly processes anything that might be threatening.

Such information-processing biases have been found extensively in anxious humans, whether anxiety is a general trait of the individual or has been acutely induced (Mathews, 1990; Mathews & MacLeod, 1994). In particular, anxious individuals have been shown to preferentially allocate attention to threatening stimuli and threatening information (Eysenck, 1997; Mathews & MacLeod, 1994; Mogg & Bradley, 1998) and, in some circumstances, to have difficulty disengaging attention from threatening stimuli (Fox, Russo, Bowles, & Dutton, 2001). This information-processing bias appears to maintain hypervigilance for threat and maintain the anxious state.

Two particular procedures have been important in identifying this information-processing bias: the emotional Stroop procedure (e.g., Mathews & MacLeod, 1985; Watts, McKenna, Sharrock, & Trezise, 1986) and the attentional probe task (e.g., MacLeod, Mathews, & Tata, 1986). In the former procedure, participants are presented with individual words, either threat relevant (e.g., *death*) or emotionally neutral (e.g., *carpet*), in colored ink. The participant names the ink color as rapidly as possible. Most Stroop studies indicate that anxious individuals take longer to name the color of threat-relevant words than do nonanxious individuals, suggesting that their attention has been biased toward processing the threatening word rather than its color (for a review, see Mathews & MacLeod, 1994). In the attentional probe task, participants are simultaneously presented with a threat word and a neutral word on a computer screen. A probe stimulus then appears in the location formerly occupied by one of the words, and the participant has to detect the probe as rapidly as possible. Highly anxious participants detect more rapidly the probes in the location previously occupied by the threat word, suggesting that their attention had been selectively biased toward the threat word (e.g., B. P. Bradley, Mogg, White, Groom, & de Bono, 1999; Bryant & Harvey, 1997).

These types of studies have indicated that (a) this preferential allocation of attention to threatening stimuli occurs preattentively (i.e., prior to conscious awareness of the word's meaning; Mogg, Bradley, & Halliwell, 1994; Mogg, Bradley, Williams, & Mathews, 1993); (b) it occurs with both verbal and nonverbal (emotional faces) stimuli (B. P. Bradley, Mogg, Falla, & Hamilton, 1998; B. P. Bradley et al., 1997); and (c) anxious individuals attend to threatening stimuli, whereas nonanxious individuals shift attention away from threatening stimuli (B. P. Bradley et al., 1999; Mogg & Bradley, 1998). Current theories of attentional biases in anxiety differ as to their theoretical interpretation of these findings. The two most prominent theories are the *biased attentional direction* account and the *shifted attentional function* account (E. Wilson & MacLeod, 2003).

The biased attentional direction account posits that high- and low-anxious individuals differ in the direction of their processing bias to threatening information; furthermore, as the intensity of the threatening stimulus increases, anxious individuals will increasingly orient attention toward that stimulus, and nonanxious individuals will increasingly orient away (Eysenck, 1997; J. M. G. Williams, Watts, MacLeod, & Mathews, 1997). Alternatively, the shifted attentional function account argues that both high- and low-anxious individuals orient away from mildly threatening stimuli and toward highly threatening stimuli but that high-anxious individuals will also orient toward stimuli of intermediate threat intensity (Mathews & Mackintosh, 1998; Mogg & Bradley, 1998). Studies that have investigated attentional biases to threat stimuli using stimuli from a range of intensities have tended to support the shifted attentional function account (e.g., E. Wilson & MacLeod, 2003), indicating that high-anxious individuals may differ from low-anxious individuals primarily in their appraisal of threat intensity rather than in the direction of their attentional orientation to threat.

Interpretational and Judgmental Biases

Given that early studies of anxious individuals' attentional styles indicated a bias toward prioritizing threatening information, other processing biases were soon investigated. Subsequent studies indicated that anxious individuals also exhibited strong interpretational biases. For example, when presented with ambiguous information that can be interpreted positively, neutrally, or negatively (e.g., "I was surprised to be called to see my boss today."), high-anxious individuals will regularly endorse a threatening or negative interpretation (Davey, Hampton, Farrell, & Davidson, 1992; MacLeod & Cohen, 1993; Mathews, Richards, & Eysenck, 1989). It is easy to conceive of ways in which this interpretational bias might maintain fear and anxiety by maintaining the range of potential threats the individual perceives. Other studies suggest that for anxious individuals, threat-related interpretations of events are either more readily available or more easily constructed than their benign alternatives. For example, Cavanagh and Davey (2004) found that individuals who were afraid of spiders could generate more reasons that spiders would be harmful and fewer why they might be safe compared with nonfearful individuals.

Making judgments about whether stimuli or events are threatening, and assessing how threatening they might be is a process that probably has ramifications across many, if not all, of the information-processing biases we see in anxious or fearful individuals. For example, as already stated, current theories of attentional bias such as the shifted attentional function account (Mogg & Bradley, 1998) imply that attentional biases will be determined by the individual's appraisal of threat intensity (E. Wilson & MacLeod, 2003), thus processes that contribute to the individual's judgments of threat severity will also feed into other potential cognitive biases.

A study by Halberstadt and Niedenthal (1997) suggests that participants in an emotional state will tend toward making judgments about stimuli on emotive rather than nonemotive dimensions, thus increasing the ability to discriminate on those dimensions and resulting in a conceptual "stretching" of them. Cavanagh and Davey (2001) found that anxious individuals gave priority to processing stimuli on threat–safety dimensions compared with other dimensions (e.g., color). As a result, anxious individuals rated fear-relevant (FR) stimuli (e.g., spider, snake) as significantly more threatening than did nonanxious individuals but conversely rated fear-irrelevant (FI) stimuli (e.g., rabbit, kitten) as significantly safer than nonanxious individuals. This suggests that their prioritized use of this dimension had indeed caused it to be "stretched" relative to nonanxious individuals. This prioritized dimensional processing provides a mechanism by which anxious individuals can exhibit what initially appear to be paradoxical tendencies to give priority to both threat and safety information (e.g., Cavanagh & Davey, 2001; Thorpe & Salkovskis, 1998). It also provides a possible explanation for why anxious individuals appraise stimuli of intermediate threat intensity as more threatening than do nonanxious individuals.

Memory

If avoiding danger is an urgent business, then we would expect memory processes to perform optimally to enable individuals who are fearful, anxious, or under threat to identify and avoid those dangers—in both the present and the future. Yet the large research literature covering the effect of fear and anxiety on memory is equivocal, difficult to interpret, and contains as many failures to find effects of fear and anxiety on memory as it does successes (Coles & Heimberg, 2002). Intuitively, memory processes might aid the survival of individuals under threat through (a) deep encoding of stimuli associated with threat or danger so that there are strong retrievable memories of threat-relevant information for future use and (b) rapidly facilitated retrieval of threat-related information when under threat. Some early models of information processing and emotion were consistent with these intuitive hypotheses. Beck, Emery, and Greenberg (1985) argued that the cognitive schemata of anxious individuals would be biased toward focusing on danger and vulnerability; thus, when anxious schema are activated, the encoding and recall of anxiety- or mood-congruent information (e.g., threat) will be facilitated. Evidence supporting this hypothesis is equivocal. Whereas some studies find evidence for enhanced encoding and recall of threat-relevant information in anxious or fearful individuals, just as many studies have failed to find such effects (cf. Coles & Heimberg, 2002; Rusting, 1998).

Coles and Heimberg (2002) listed a number of possible reasons for these ambiguous results. First, memory biases may depend not only on anxiety, but also on how anxiety manifests itself; for example, studies have been significantly more successful at finding memory biases in individuals experiencing panic disorder, posttraumatic stress disorder, and obsessive–compulsive disorder than in those individuals experiencing generalized anxiety disorder or social phobia. Second, the expression of memory biases may be affected by the broad range of procedures that have been used across studies. Third, most memory studies ask fearful or anxious individuals to recall stimuli that they fear; studies may fail to find memory biases because such individuals are reluctant to focus on their feared stimuli. This last point is reflected in the views of both J. M. G. Williams and colleagues (1997) and Mogg, Mathews, and Weinman (1989), who have argued that the memory and emotion literature is best understood by assuming that both encoding and retrieval of threat-related material involves both automatic and strategic components and that anxiety could have separate effects on these different components. Specifically, in the early stages of threat processing, anxious individuals' attention is drawn toward such information, increasing the possibility of its priming and successful encoding. In subsequent stages of processing when the elaboration of the material becomes more strategic, anxious individuals will orient away from or avoid threat-relevant information and thus compromise its retrieval.

The preceding discussion indicates how difficult it is at present to assess the role of memory biases in fearful responding. Our intuitive beliefs that memory processes ought to play an adaptive role in protecting the organism when it is in a threatened or fearful state have yet to be convincingly endorsed by the evidence. Coles and Heimberg (2002) suggested that current inconsistencies in this literature could be addressed by (a) considering variables that may moderate memory biases (e.g., hemispheric laterality effects), (b) conducting studies to disentangle the relative contributions of encoding and retrieval processes in memory biases, and (c) investigating the developmental aspects of memory biases in anxious or fearful children to shed light on how any putative memory bias might develop in vulnerable children.

BELIEFS AND EXPECTANCIES

The previous sections describe how being in a fearful or anxious state can influence the way an individual processes information related to threat. Fear responding can also be influenced, however, by the beliefs and expectancies that individuals have acquired about FR stimuli and threatening outcomes. Evidence suggests that these beliefs and expectancies play an important role in maintaining fear-based responding, motivate avoidance responding, and are resistant to disconfirmation.

Outcome Expectancy Beliefs

For many years it had been assumed that the persistent and so-called irrational nature of fearful or phobic responding meant that it was not amenable to control by strategic cognitive processes (e.g., Seligman, 1971). More recent studies investigating the nature of phobic beliefs, however, suggest that those with phobias do indeed possess a cognitive network of beliefs related to possible threatening outcomes associated with their phobia and that the accessibility of these beliefs form the basis for outcome expectancy judgments. Studies of individuals with spider and height phobias suggest that these people possess a range of specific and articulate beliefs about how dangerous contact with their phobic situation might be (Menzies & Clarke, 1995b; Thorpe & Salkovskis, 1995, 1997) and that these beliefs are differentially accessed when assessing whether a situation associated with their phobia is likely to be harmful or safe (Cavanagh & Davey, 2004). For example, Cavanagh and Davey have shown that estimates of negative outcome expectancy in a simulated conditioning experiment (cf. McNally & Heatherton, 1993) covary with the number of reasons that individuals with phobias could generate as to why their phobic stimulus might be harmful or dangerous and are inversely related to the number of reasons why it might be safe. These findings are consistent with the processes found in simulation heuristics (Tversky & Kahneman, 1973) in which probability judgments are determined by the ease with which causal explanations can be constructed or retrieved from memory. Thus, the outcome expectancy bias found in those with phobias appears to covary with the development of accessible beliefs about the threatening or harmful nature of the phobic situation.

Conditioning studies of fearful responding also have demonstrated that individuals both with and without phobias appear to possess outcome expectancy biases to certain FR stimuli that they can verbalize and that these biases facilitate the acquisition of fear responding and retard extinction of the response. For example, using a threat-conditioning procedure in which participants were warned that they might receive aversive outcomes (unconditioned stimuli [USs]) following certain conditioned stimuli (CSs) but in fact receive none, Davey (1992b) found that participants began the conditioning procedure with a significantly higher expectancy of aversive outcomes following FR stimuli (e.g., pictures of snakes and spiders) than FI stimuli (e.g., pictures of kittens and pigeons). This expectancy bias dissipated with continued nonreinforcement but could be reinstated by a single CS–US pairing. This a priori expectancy bias can be found with both phylogenetic and ontogenetic FR stimuli (Honeybourne, Matchett, & Davey, 1993; McNally & Heatherton, 1993) and may well explain many of the rapid learning effects previously ascribed to biological preparedness (Davey, 1995). Further studies have indicated that this preconditioning expectancy bias appears to be determined by a number of judgments that an individual makes about the CS or threat cue, including how dangerous or harmful it might be (Davey & Craigie, 1997; Davey & Dixon, 1996), how many characteristics the CS shares with the potential aversive US (Davey & Dixon, 1996), and how much the CS is currently feared by the individual (Davey & Dixon, 1996; Diamond, Matchett, & Davey, 1995).

As might be expected, participants with phobias exhibit a significantly greater US expectancy bias than those without phobias when the CS is their

phobic stimulus. When presenting participants with and without spider phobias with slides of either spiders or kittens (CSs), Diamond and colleagues
(1995) found a main effect for spiders at the outset of the procedure (i.e., participants gave higher US expectancy ratings to spider slides regardless of whether
they were phobic or not) and a significant picture–phobia interaction in which
participants with phobias receiving spider slides gave higher US expectancy
ratings than the control participants receiving spider slides. Findings such as
these have been replicated in both conditioning procedures and covariation
assessment procedures in which participants are asked to make a posteriori
judgments about the covariation between phobic stimuli and aversive events
(Davey & Dixon, 1996; de Jong, Merckelbach, Arntz, & Nijman, 1992). Although these expectancy biases can be reliably detected and measured, it is still
unclear how they originate. Attempts have been made to address this issue in
terms ranging from the biological prewiring of associative predispositions (preparedness theory, cf. Öhman, 1997; Öhman, Dimberg, & Öst, 1985; Seligman,
1971; see also chap. 4, this volume) to the determination of expectancy biases
through the cultural communication of fear relevance (cf. Davey, 1994b, 1995).
Nevertheless, the issue in this context is not how such biases are determined
but that they exist and are exaggerated in individuals with phobias.

Consistent with the results of laboratory-based conditioning and
covariation assessment studies are findings on the overestimation of fear in
people with clinically diagnosed phobias. Compared with those without phobias, individuals with phobias overestimate the level of consequential danger
associated with their phobic stimulus. This has been shown to be the case for
those with spider (Arntz, Lavy, van den Berg, & van Rijsoort, 1993), snake
(Taylor & Rachman, 1994), height (Menzies & Clarke, 1995b), and social
phobias (Lucock & Salkovskis, 1988), as well as for individuals with claustrophobia (Telch, Valentiner, & Bolte, 1994) and agoraphobia (van Hout &
Emmelkamp, 1994). In addition, path models and structural equation modeling have indicated that the overprediction of aversive consequences in individuals with phobias arises from the overprediction of danger elements of
the phobic stimulus and the underprediction of available safety resources
(e.g., escape routes; Arntz, Hildebrand, & van den Hout, 1994; Taylor &
Rachman, 1994).

These findings are consistent with those from laboratory-based studies
indicating that (a) individuals with clinical phobias have heightened expectancy of aversive outcomes following encounters with their phobic stimulus
when compared with those without phobias and (b) danger assessments may
be a significant contributor to this expectancy bias.

Outcome Expectancy Beliefs as Determinants of Fearful Responding

Considerable evidence suggests that outcome expectancy biases are
causal elements in developing and maintaining a variety of aspects of phobic

responding. First, in laboratory-based aversive autonomic conditioning studies, verbal statements of US expectancy correspond closely to changes in differential autonomic conditioned responses (CRs) indicative of conditioned fear. For example, participants only exhibit a differential autonomic CR when they are able to verbalize the CS–US contingency (cf. Dawson & Schell, 1987). Even when the CS is presented subliminally, discriminative conditioned responding appears to be differentially associated with greater US expectancy ratings (Öhman & Soares, 1998). Similarly, when measured on a trial-by-trial basis, differential conditioning only appears after the emergence of contingency awareness (Biferno & Dawson, 1977; Dawson, Schell, & Tweddle-Banis, 1986), and participants regularly fail to exhibit differential responding in studies that have deliberately attempted to mask the CS–US relationship (Dawson, 1973; Dawson, Catania, Schell, & Grings, 1979). This correlation between self-report of US expectancy and differential CRs does not appear to be the result of a post hoc attribution resulting from the individual observing changes in the strength and probability of the CRs they emit. For example, studies that have adopted online measurement of both US expectancy and CR magnitude during the acquisition phase of aversive conditioning have shown that changes in verbal reports of US expectancy reliably precede predicted changes in differential CRs indicating conditioned fear (Biferno & Dawson, 1977; Dawson et al., 1986; Öhman, Ellstrom, & Bjorkstrand, 1976).

Second, in studies investigating phobic overestimation of fear, estimates of the dangerous outcomes associated with a phobic stimulus are inversely associated with the level of approach behavior shown by those with phobias in behavioral avoidance tasks (BATs; e.g., Kirsch, Tennen, Wickless, Saccone, & Cody, 1983; Valentiner, Telch, Petruzzi, & Bolte, 1996), suggesting that outcome expectancies are associated not only with physiological indices of fear and anxiety but also with behavioral avoidance.

Third, studies have shown that the overestimation of fear in people with phobias existing at the height of the phobia tends to disappear following successful therapy (e.g., Adler, Craske, Kirshenbaum, & Barlow, 1989; Williams, Kinney, & Falbo, 1989). This is also true of a posteriori covariation biases; those with phobias show a significant a posteriori covariation bias to their phobic stimulus before successful treatment, but this bias reverts to normal levels following treatment (e.g., de Jong et al., 1992).

Fourth, when individuals with spider phobias are tested both before and after treatment for the phobia, they show significant decreases in the endorsement of spider-relevant threat beliefs compared with appropriate nontreatment control participants (Thorpe & Salkovskis, 1997). This suggests that successful treatment is accompanied by a significant decrease in beliefs about the threatening consequences of encountering spiders.

In summary, this evidence strongly indicates that (a) the development of outcome expectancies in aversive conditioning studies precedes the development of differential physiological CRs indicative of fear, (b) an outcome expectancy bias is associated with both physiological and behavioral indices of the phobia, and (c) outcome expectancy biases and associated threat beliefs are significantly reduced following successful treatment of the phobia.

Outcome Expectancy Beliefs and Reasoning Biases

A perplexing feature of fear-based disorders such as specific phobias is that fear-based beliefs and expectancies associated with such conditions are extraordinarily resistant to disconfirmation. Part of the reason for this can be traced to the robust avoidance behaviors exhibited by individuals who are phobic or fearful. Taking pains to avoid any possible contact with their phobic stimulus or situation means that those with phobias rarely put themselves into physical contact with the stimulus in a way that will disconfirm their exaggerated negative outcome beliefs.

In addition to avoidance responding, fearful and phobic individuals also exhibit reasoning biases that act to maintain their dysfunctional outcome beliefs. For example, a number of studies have shown that individuals with phobias are characterized by a strong tendency to confirm rather than falsify prior beliefs. That is, they possess a reasoning bias that is demonstrated in a tendency to endorse logical syllogisms that are consistent with their phobic beliefs regardless of their logical status (de Jong, Haenen, Schmidt, & Mayer, 1998; de Jong, Weertman, Horselenberg, & van den Hout, 1997). In fact, individuals with phobias will selectively search for threat-confirming information when asked to judge the validity of logical syllogisms related to their individual fears (Smeets, de Jong, & Mayer, 2000).

Another reasoning bias that acts to maintain FR beliefs is ex consequentia reasoning (Arntz, Rauner, & van den Hout, 1995), in which individuals with phobias infer danger not only based on objective danger information but also on their perception of their own fear or anxiety (i.e., "If I feel anxious, there must be danger"). A number of fear-conditioning studies have investigated the effect of giving participants false auditory feedback suggesting that they are still showing physiological signs of fear during a CS even when they are not (Davey, 1987, 1988; Russell & Davey, 1991). This has the effect of (a) retarding extinction of the conditioned fear response, (b) strengthening the participant's belief that the aversive US will be presented again in the future, and (c) inflating the participant's rating of the US's aversiveness. Such findings suggest that when individuals perceive that they may be anxious or fearful, this information reinforces and even inflates existing beliefs about danger and threat. Subsequent studies have suggested that this reasoning error may be a traitlike information-processing bias that might render individuals vulnerable to anxiety disorders (Arntz et al., 1995), and the tendency to use anxiety response information as a heuristic for reinforcing existing danger beliefs is directly related to existing levels of trait anxiety (Muris, Merckelbach, & van Spauwen, 2003).

Thus, in addition to possessing strong outcome expectancy beliefs that maintain fear and trigger avoidance strategies, fearful individuals also possess reasoning biases that lead them toward using evidence to verify rather than disconfirm these beliefs. This may seem paradoxical given the distress that these beliefs and their outcomes entail, but given the importance of survival, it seems that cognitive processes that maintain vigilance for and avoidance of threat are likely to be preferentially selected. Hence, the processes that influence the strength and validity of beliefs about threat are likely to adopt a "better safe than sorry" strategy.

Factors Affecting the Evaluation of Outcome Expectancy Beliefs

Encoded in the outcome expectancy beliefs possessed by people who are fearful or phobic is not only information about the specific nature of the outcomes expected with the threatening stimulus or event (e.g., "If I encounter a spider, I will come to physical harm") but also information about how frightening and aversive the individual will find this outcome experience (Davey, 1989, 1992a, 1993a; Thorpe & Salkovskis, 1995). This is important because evidence from human and animal conditioning studies suggests that the strength of the conditioned fear response will be determined by how aversive the organism evaluates the outcome to be (Cracknell & Davey, 1988; Davey, 1992a; Davey & Matchett, 1994; Rescorla, 1980).

Studies from the conditioning literature suggest that a number of cognitive processes can lead one to reevaluate the potential aversiveness of a threatening outcome (or aversive US); these are called US revaluation processes (Davey, 1989, 1992a, 1997). These processes can act either to devalue or to inflate the aversive evaluation of the expected outcome. Although the animal conditioning literature has identified processes by which a US can be revalued (see Davey, 1992a; Rescorla, 1980), the human ability to represent symbolically and communicate complex information means that there are many more ways in which US revaluation can take place in humans; some of these are described in the following sections.

Experience With the Outcome–US Alone

Postconditioning experiences with the US, in the absence of the CS, can lead to revaluation of the US if these experiences lead one to perceive the US as either more or less aversive than it was during the conditioning episode (Davey & McKenna, 1983; White & Davey, 1989). Davey, de Jong, and Tallis (1993) described a number of cases in which a fear or anxiety reaction was significantly affected by experiences that led an individual to revalue the potential aversiveness of the threatening outcome. For example,

L.L. was not anxious in social situations, despite having always associated them with internal physical symptoms. Subsequently, L.L. was alone at home when similar physical symptoms preceded an uncontrollable attack of diarrhea. This increased L.L.'s aversive evaluation of those physical symptoms, and from then on, L.L. became extremely anxious in social situations and developed severe agoraphobic symptoms. Thus, although L.L. had never experienced trauma in a social setting prior to his onset of anxiety, the experience of internal physical symptoms followed by a bout of diarrhea significantly inflated the aversive evaluation of the internal cues he experienced in those settings.

Socially and Verbally Transmitted Information About the Outcome–US

Having already acquired a set of outcome expectancy beliefs, individuals may receive either socially or verbally communicated information about those outcomes–USs that leads them to reassess their evaluation of it. If this reassessment increases their aversive evaluation of the US, the next presentation of the threat situation or CS will evoke a stronger fear response. Davey and colleagues (1993) provided the example of M.F., a bank employee who was threatened with a gun during a robbery. He returned to work the next day without complaining of any residual fear symptoms. During a police interview 10 days after the robbery, however, he was informed that the bank robber was very dangerous and had killed several people. From then on, M.F. was unable to return to work and developed severe anxiety problems. Such examples demonstrate how socially transmitted information can lead one to inflate the aversive or threatening nature of the outcome to the point at which fearful or phobic responding is triggered.

More recent studies have shown that verbally communicated fear information is important in the development of fears and phobias in children. Specifically, these studies have shown that negative information about a novel toy or animal can lead to the establishment of fear beliefs that determine the child's rating of how frightening that toy or animal is and the degree of behavioral avoidance they will exhibit toward them (Field et al., 2001; Field & Lawson, 2003).

Interpretation of Interoceptive Cues

This chapter has already covered how an individual's evaluation of his or her own fearful reactions to a stimulus can verify existing phobic beliefs and maintain fearful responding (i.e., ex consequentia reasoning, Arntz et al., 1995). In addition, many anxious individuals attend to their own bodily sensations and use these stimuli as information about possible threatening events or to assess the aversive nature of potentially threatening outcomes (cf. Davey, 1988; Valins, 1966). Fear-conditioning studies have demonstrated that when participants believe they are emitting a strong fear CR (e.g., in a false feedback study), they emit a stronger differential CR and exhibit a resistance to extinction compared with control participants (Davey, 1987; Russell & Davey, 1991). Subsequent studies have suggested that individuals may perceive what they believe to be a strong CR and attribute this to the fact that they must still be anxious or frightened by the forthcoming US; this inflates the aversive evaluation of the US, which in turn triggers a stronger CR on subsequent trials (Davey & Matchett, 1996).

Cognitive Rehearsal of the Outcome–US

Another important feature of anxiety-based disorders such as phobias is the rehearsal of possible aversive outcomes in which those with phobias indulge (Marks, 1987). Laboratory fear-conditioning studies have demonstrated that when participants are asked to rehearse features of the US following conditioning, the fear CR subsequently increases in strength and becomes more resistant to extinction (Davey & Matchett, 1994; T. Jones & Davey, 1990). In particular, cognitively rehearsing the US appears to inflate the perceived aversiveness of the US and, in anxious individuals, produces sequential increments in anxious responding that are typical of clinical incubation (Davey & Matchett, 1994; Eysenck, 1979). This US inflation during rumination is potentially caused by two processes. First, ruminating about the US in an anxious state is likely to lead to selective processing of the US's emotional or threatening features (Mathews & MacLeod, 1985, 1994) or facilitate the recall of relevant anxiety-related information in memory (Bower, 1981); laboratory-based studies indicate that US rehearsal fear enhancement is significantly facilitated when rehearsal takes place in the context of an anxious mood (Davey & Matchett, 1994). Second, perseverative US rumination may be associated with the worry-related phenomenon of catastrophizing (Davey & Levy, 1998; Vasey & Borkovec, 1992). Catastrophizing is a process by which individuals begin thinking about a specific threat topic and proceed through a series of possible catastrophic steps, perceiving the threat as increasingly worse (higher probability of occurrence and causing greater emotional discomfort) with each step (Vasey & Borkovec, 1992).

Coping Strategies That Devalue the Outcome–US

One reason many individuals have traumatic experiences but do not develop phobic responding is because they adopt coping strategies that allow them to devalue the stressful meaning of the trauma. Such processes are characteristic of appraisal strategies used to assess the threatening meaning of a stressor (Lazarus & Folkman, 1984). These include downward comparison (e.g., "other people are worse off than me"; Wills, 1981), positive reappraisal (e.g., "in every problem there is something good"; Davey, 1993a), threat devaluation (e.g., "these problems simply aren't important enough to get upset about"; Davey, 1993a), optimism (e.g., "everything will work itself out"; Scheier & Carver, 1992), and denial (e.g., "I refuse to believe this is happening"; Breznitz, 1983). Some evidence suggests that individuals who are able to devalue either the impact of trauma or the aversiveness of threatening outcomes are less likely to develop phobic symptoms. Davey, Burgess, and Rashes (1995) compared the coping strategies of people with simple phobias, panic disorder patients, and normal control participants. They found that both those with simple phobias and panic disorder patients reported significantly less use of threat devaluation strategies than control participants. They also found that reported use of threat devaluation strategies was inversely related to levels of some specific phobias.

To summarize, fearful responding can be affected by the individual's evaluation of the potential aversive outcome (US), but this evaluation can be affected by a range of processes that can either devalue or inflate the perceived aversiveness of that outcome.

CONCLUSIONS AND CLINICAL APPLICATIONS

This chapter has discussed evidence for the involvement of a variety of cognitive processes in fear responding. Some are information-processing mechanisms that bias the individual to allocating attentional resources to threat and can operate at preattentive levels. Other processes involve higher order beliefs about threat that mediate and maintain the fear response. Additional factors represent appraisal processes that can influence attentional resourcing (threat appraisal), the evaluation of threat cues (availability heuristics; prioritized processing of threat and safety dimensions) and potential aversive outcomes (US revaluation processes), and the insulation of fear beliefs from disconfirmation (e.g., phobic reasoning biases).

Figure 5.1 provides a schematic representation of the way in which these various processes may operate and contribute to the avoidance and physiological fear responses that are the end product of this cognitive network. The model illustrates that cognitive factors can have either a direct effect on fear responding by contributing to the activation and strength of the fear response (fear triggers) or an indirect effect by acting to modulate the nature of the information on which these triggers depend (appraisal processes). The model also emphasizes the importance of cognitive processes that act to maintain phobic beliefs (reasoning biases) despite disconfirmatory evidence; this demonstrates how belief systems associated with fear and phobia use a variety of processes to insulate them from change.

Figure 5.1 indicates that individuals with exaggerated and distressing fear and anxiety responses of the kind experienced in many anxiety disorders will possess several of the following characteristics: (a) exaggerated attentional and interpretive biases for threat, (b) a tendency to judge potentially threatening events as more threatening than nonfearful individuals, (c) a core set

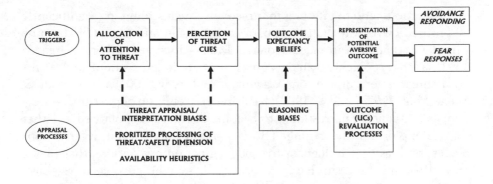

Figure 5.1. A schematic representation of processes directly involved in triggering fear (fear triggers) and factors that indirectly act to modulate the nature of the information on which these triggers depend (appraisal processes). UCs = unconditioned stimuli.

of phobic outcome beliefs or fear schema that link their feared stimuli with potentially aversive outcomes, (d) a set of reasoning biases that insulate these core beliefs from disconfirmation, and (e) a set of outcome appraisal processes that either maintain or inflate the aversive evaluation of the outcome rather than devalue it (US revaluation processes). All these factors could be addressed in treatment to ameliorate fearful responding.

Although there is considerable evidence that fearful or anxious individuals possess a bias toward the allocation of attention to threatening stimuli (Mogg & Bradley, 1998; J. M. G. Williams et al., 1997), it has not been clear whether this bias is a cause of anxiety or a consequence of experiencing anxiety. If it is a cause, then finding practical ways to disrupt or attenuate this bias should have beneficial effects on the experience of anxiety. Studies have suggested that attentional and interpretative biases for threat may have a causal effect on experienced anxiety and the processing of future information (Mathews & MacLeod, 2002). These studies have shown that experimentally induced processing biases for threat not only will cause congruent changes in state anxiety but also tend the individual toward interpreting new information in a threatening way (Hertel, Mathews, Peterson, & Kintner, 2003; Mathews & Mackintosh, 2000; Mathews & MacLeod, 2002). One implication of this research is that the construction of suitable training programs to alleviate attentional and interpretive biases could have a beneficial effect on anxiety experienced by individuals with phobias and fears. To date, however, studies have only been conducted on analog, nonclinical populations; it remains to be seen whether attentional training is successful with pathologically anxious individuals.

One factor that appears to influence individuals' tendency to allocate attention preferentially to threat is their appraisal of threat intensity (Mogg & Bradley, 1998; E. Wilson & MacLeod, 2003). That is, individuals who are highly anxious tend to interpret intermediate threat stimuli in a significantly more threatening way than nonanxious individuals, and this will determine whether a stimulus is attended to or avoided. As discussed earlier, one reason for this is that people with anxiety give priority to judging stimuli and events on a threat–safety dimension (Cavanagh & Davey, 2001; Halberstadt & Niedenthal, 1997; Landau, 1980), resulting in stretching of the threat–safety dimension, which causes stimuli to become distinct and polarized as either threatening or nonthreatening. This is a good example of an information-processing bias that influences the judgments and evaluations that play a critical role in the cognitive fear network; it may be possible to establish training procedures for anxious individuals to diminish their dependence on the threat–safety dimension when making judgments about stimuli. Such procedures might be based on similarity judgment tasks (Cavanagh & Davey, 2001; Halberstadt & Niedenthal, 1997) but with a procedure that forces people to judge stimuli on the basis of dimensions other than threat–safety (e.g., color, size, inanimate, or animate).

One of the most significant and durable aspects of phobic and anxious responding is the set of phobic or outcome beliefs that anxious individuals hold. These beliefs appear to play a significant role in motivating avoidance responses and generating fearful responding (McNally & Steketee, 1985; Thorpe & Salkovskis, 1995). Such beliefs are hypothesized to be part of a larger maladaptive fear schema that consists of a series of interconnected memory associations that maintain anxiety, avoidance, and the saliency of perceived threats (Beck & Clark, 1997; Beck et al., 1985; J. E. Young, 1999). As noted earlier, such maladaptive beliefs are insulated from disconfirmation by both the avoidance responses they generate (which prevent the individual from encountering disconfirming evidence) and the reasoning biases that tend anxious individuals toward using evidence to verify rather than disconfirm these beliefs. Therefore, any procedure that challenges these maladaptive outcome beliefs and overcomes the inherent processes designed to protect them ought to have therapeutic benefits.

Intuitively, one might suspect that either cognitive therapy (used to challenge and restructure maladaptive beliefs) or exposure therapy (used to confront the individual with disconfirming evidence) might be successful in changing such beliefs. Indeed, evidence suggests that these approaches would be successful in modifying maladaptive outcome expectancy beliefs. First, when individuals with spider phobia were tested both before and after cognitive therapy for their phobia, they showed a significant decrease in the endorsement of spider-relevant threat beliefs compared with nontreatment control participants (Thorpe & Salkovskis, 1997). Second, a study by Teachman and Woody (2003) suggests that exposure therapy is also successful in changing maladaptive belief systems. Following group-based exposure therapy, they found that implicit associations linking the words *afraid* and *disgusting* with spiders were significantly reduced, and these changes were maintained

2 months following treatment. These findings provide support for the fact that outcome expectancy beliefs linking stimuli (e.g., spiders) with aversive outcomes (e.g., fear, disgust) in fear schemas can be changed over the course of exposure therapy and modified by experience.

This chapter has identified two particular reasoning biases that maintain maladaptive fear beliefs (ex consequentia reasoning and the tendency to endorse logical syllogisms that are consistent with existing fear beliefs). It remains unclear whether these reasoning biases are a premorbid trait, a vulnerability factor for anxiety disorders, or a consequence of having acquired fear beliefs. Although people with phobias do exhibit an enhanced reasoning bias compared with control participants, they also show these reasoning biases in areas unrelated to their phobias, suggesting that it is a general characteristic of anxious or fearful individuals (de Jong et al., 1997). Although exaggerated reasoning biases could be addressed in structured cognitive therapy, it would be useful to have more evidence on whether these biases were indeed a vulnerability factor for anxiety disorders or whether they could be reduced with successful therapy.

The outcome (US) revaluation processes is another area that may lead to therapeutic applications of knowledge. The anxious individual's fear schema contains associations between stimuli or events and potentially aversive outcomes; and how the individual evaluates the aversiveness of these outcomes will determine the strength of the fear response (Davey, 1992a; Davey, 1997). This chapter has reviewed a number of processes that can influence the aversive evaluation of the outcome (US), by either inflating or devaluing its aversiveness. Using these processes to devalue the aversiveness of the outcome would seem to have therapeutic advantages. Most of the US revaluation processes discussed earlier are already used in many treatment programs. For example, devaluation of expected outcomes through habituation with repeated exposure is a standard consequence of exposure therapies, as are attempts to influence the evaluation of outcomes by verbally or socially transmitted information in most forms of psychotherapy. Unfortunately, it is significantly easier to inflate the aversiveness of a feared outcome than it is to devalue it (Davey, 1997), and given the urgency of survival, this may well represent the "better safe than sorry" strategy that immunizes fear learning and its supporting cognitive schemas from rapid change. It may nonetheless be possible to protect individuals against the acquisition of fear-based disorders by training them to adopt coping strategies that would automatically act to devalue threatening or stressful events. A number of these cognitive appraisal strategies were discussed earlier in the chapter (see Davey & McDonald, 2000); they represent ways of cognitively evaluating threats in a way that devalues their potential aversive impact (e.g., downward comparison, positive reappraisal, optimism, cognitive disengagement) and moderating the effect of outcome expectancy beliefs. Such appraisal strategies have already been found to be used less regularly by people with anxiety disorders (Davey et al., 1995), and their adoption can successfully reduce symptoms in disorders such as PTSD (Foa, Steketee, & Rothbaum, 1989; Veronen & Kilpatrick, 1983). It is clear that training individuals to use such coping strategies could provide transferable immunization across a range of anxiety disorders.

6

FEAR AND AVOIDANCE: AN INTEGRATED EXPECTANCY MODEL

PETER LOVIBOND

Avoidance is a prominent feature of both normal and abnormal fear and anxiety reactions. It is normal and indeed adaptive for people to avoid situations that pose a genuine threat to their physical or social well-being—for example, walking through a minefield or criticizing their boss. By contrast, it is maladaptive to avoid situations that are objectively nonthreatening, such as when a person experiencing social phobia refuses a social invitation or a person with obsessive–compulsive disorder washes for hours each day. Although such unnecessary avoidance may reduce anxiety symptoms in the short term, it is in itself a form of impairment because it prevents the person from attaining positive goals. Moreover, there is good evidence that avoidance acts to preserve anxiety reactions in the longer term. For all of these reasons, clinicians have been concerned to find methods for controlling avoidance, and laboratory researchers have been interested in understanding the mechanisms underlying the development and maintenance of avoidance.

Basic research in avoidance learning has focused on a number of key questions. First, like any other form of learning, researchers have attempted

Preparation of this chapter was supported by Grants A10007156 and DP 0346379 from the Australian Research Council. I thank Fred Westbrook for helpful discussions related to this chapter.

to define the conditions under which avoidance is learned, the content of what is learned, and the mechanisms by which learning generates avoidance behavior. Second, researchers have aimed to define and account for the relationship between anxiety and avoidance. Finally, researchers have tried to understand how avoidance is extinguished, and thereby to define optimal methods for its elimination. In this chapter, I review traditional accounts of avoidance, more recent accounts arising from clinical research, and selected experimental data from both animal and human studies. I then describe an integrated cognitive model, centered on the concept of expectancy, and explore its empirical and clinical implications. In this chapter, I use the terms *fear* and *anxiety* interchangeably.

EARLY FINDINGS AND TWO-FACTOR THEORY

A great deal of basic research on avoidance learning has been carried out in laboratory settings, much of it with animal subjects. In a typical animal avoidance experiment, a warning stimulus such as a light or tone is followed by an aversive stimulus such as electric shock, unless the animal makes a designated avoidance response ("signaled avoidance"). The response might be running from one side of a chamber to the other, jumping a hurdle, turning a running wheel, or pressing a lever. Typically, performance of the response not only cancels the shock, but also terminates the warning stimulus. In unsignaled avoidance, there is no specific warning stimulus, but shock is presented on a regular schedule unless the response is made, in which case shock is withheld for a designated period of time.

Early work on avoidance learning treated it as a variant of Pavlovian conditioning, but it soon became clear that there were greater similarities with instrumental learning such as the positive reinforcement procedures studied by Thorndike and Skinner. The avoidance response was determined by the experimenter, not by the unconditioned stimulus (US) as in Pavlovian conditioning, and omission of the electric shock was a plausible source of reinforcement. Yet in the stimulus–response (S–R) climate of the mid-20th century, how could the absence of an event serve as a reinforcer? A solution to this problem was proposed by Mowrer (1947) in the form of two-factor theory. Mowrer recognized that there are two separate learning processes involved in an avoidance experiment. First, there is Pavlovian conditioning of fear to the warning stimulus (which serves as a conditioned stimulus [CS]), resulting from its initial pairings with shock (US). Subsequently, there is an instrumental conditioning process in which the animal learns to perform the particular response designated by the experimenter. Yet rather than explaining this response learning in terms of avoidance of future shock, Mowrer suggested that the response is in fact reinforced by escape from the warning stimulus—that is, by the immediate reduction of the fear elicited by the warning stimulus. This account was consistent with the drive reduction theories of the time and became the dominant account of avoidance learning by which all subsequent theories have been judged. It is important to note that it was the prevailing theoretical model when the behavior therapy movement began in the 1960s and is still cited as an account of the highly successful behavioral procedures of exposure and response prevention.

Despite its popularity, however, it has long been recognized that two-factor theory has difficulty explaining a number of established features of avoidance (e.g., Herrnstein, 1969). For example, avoidance responses can still be learned even if the response does not terminate the warning signal, as long as it prevents the subsequent shock. According to two-factor theory, instrumental learning should not proceed if there is no source of fear reduction. Perhaps most important for clinical applications, the degree of fear elicited by the warning stimulus has been shown to decline across the course of avoidance learning. Well-trained animals perform the avoidance response reliably but with little apparent fear reaction to the appearance of the warning stimulus. Two-factor theory can in principle account for the reduction in fear by pointing out that once the animal is responding consistently, the warning stimulus is no longer followed by shock, leading to extinction of fear. Two problems relate to this account, however. First, Mineka has shown that the amount of fear reduction observed during avoidance training is greater than can be attributed to Pavlovian extinction alone (Mineka & Gino, 1980; Starr & Mineka, 1977). Second, if fear was extinguished, why does the animal continue to respond? Two-factor theory relies on fear to promote avoidance responding and fear reduction to reinforce it.

Not only do animals continue to respond despite a reduction in fear levels, but also they will sometimes do so for hundreds of trials, even though the experimenter has switched off the shock generator. The situation changes dramatically, however, if the experimenter alters the apparatus to prevent the avoidance response from being performed. First, the animal shows a return of the strong fear reactions it had shown to the warning stimulus early in training (Baum, 1970; Solomon, Kamin, & Wynne, 1953). Second, as long as no shock is presented, the avoidance response rapidly extinguishes, as demonstrated by reintroducing availability of the response. Two-factor theory can account for the return of fear by arguing that Pavlovian conditioning of fear to the later portions of the warning stimulus has not been extinguished because the animal has always responded before the end of the stimulus. However, the theory has no ready explanation for why response prevention is so effective in eliminating avoidance responding. Response prevention may well allow Pavlovian extinction of fear to later portions of the warning stimulus, but why should this weaken avoidance responding when loss of fear to the more critical earlier portions failed to do so? Furthermore, empirically, avoidance responding often extinguishes well before Pavlovian fear extinction (see Mineka, 1979). Thus, even though two-factor theory is often credited with providing a theoretical justification for the clinical procedure of exposure combined with response prevention, it cannot readily do so.

Clinical research has also raised several difficulties for the original Mowrer two-factor theory. Just as in the laboratory, fear and avoidance in patients are often dissociated from each other (Rachman, 1976). Tests of the specific hypothesis that avoidance is based on escape from fear have also been negative. For example, Rachman and colleagues (1986) showed that during exposure therapy, agoraphobic patients who were instructed to leave the fear-evoking situation when their fear reached a given level improved as much as patients given standard instructions to try to remain in the situation until their fear subsided. In addition, patients often report beliefs about danger and safety that are outside the scope of two-factor theory—for example, a conviction of their own imminent death in the case of panic disorder—and they report basing their behaviors on these beliefs. These observations do not, of course, invalidate the theory, but they do suggest that other factors might play a causal role in regulating fear and avoidance in patients. In historical context, the crucial contribution of Mowrer's (1947) two-factor theory has been the insight that there are two learning processes involved in avoidance: Pavlovian learning of fear and instrumental learning of avoidance behavior. Alternative theoretical models of these two core processes have been developed to better account for the empirical evidence.

INFORMATIONAL FACTORS IN CONDITIONING

During the 1960s and 1970s, a new approach to Pavlovian conditioning was developed that promised a solution to some of the problems encountered by two-factor theory. This new approach emphasized the informational or signal value of a stimulus with respect to predicting the future occurrence of biologically significant events. In particular, Rescorla and LoLordo (1965), Seligman (1968), and others extended the seminal work by Pavlov (1927) and Konorski (1967) concerning the phenomenon of conditioned inhibition. They confirmed that a stimulus with a negative relationship to a significant event would acquire properties opposite to those of a stimulus with a positive association to that event. That is, a stimulus that predicted the absence of shock (a "safety signal") would acquire the ability to reduce fear.

During the same period, groundbreaking research by Kamin (1969), Rescorla (1967), and Wagner (1969) led to a much better understanding of the conditions under which learning occurs. Many of these new findings were captured in the highly influential Rescorla–Wagner model (Rescorla & Wagner, 1972; Wagner & Rescorla, 1972). The essential premise of this model is that learning is a function of the discrepancy between what is predicted by all stimuli present on a given trial and what actually occurs on that trial. If, for example, a shock occurs that is not predicted, it will lead to excitatory (fear) learning. If, however, shock is predicted by stimuli present but does not actually occur, this will lead to inhibitory (safety) learning. The model may be illustrated by applying it to the procedure of conditioned inhibition, a powerful method for establishing inhibitory learning. On one type of trial, a certain stimulus (e.g., a tone) is paired with electric shock to establish it as a conditioned excitor of fear. On intermixed trials, the tone is presented in compound with a second stimulus, say, a light, and followed by no outcome. According to the Rescorla–Wagner model, on compound trials the shock is predicted by the tone but does not occur, thus leading to a negative discrepancy and the development of inhibitory learning to the light.

It was soon realized that avoidance learning is functionally highly similar to Pavlovian conditioned inhibition. On some trials (those on which the avoidance response is not made), the warning stimulus is presented and followed by shock. On the remaining trials, the same stimulus is accompanied by the avoidance response and followed by no shock. Thus the avoidance response stands in the same relationship to shock as a Pavlovian conditioned inhibitor (safety signal). This parallel was investigated directly by Morris (1975), who carried out regular avoidance learning with one group of animals but also included a control group in which each animal was "yoked" to a partner animal in the avoidance group. Whenever the avoidance animal received the warning stimulus or shock, so did the yoked control animal. The yoked group did not have access to the avoidance response, however. Instead, whenever the avoidance animal made a response, the yoked animal received an exteroceptive stimulus (a light). When the yoked animals were subsequently trained in the shock avoidance procedure, they learned much faster when their responses were followed by the light, suggesting that the light had acquired reinforcing properties. Starr and Mineka (1977) used a similar yoking procedure to show that an exteroceptive stimulus yoked to avoidance responding acquired the capacity to inhibit fear.

Safety Signal Account

The parallel between avoidance and Pavlovian conditioned inhibition led some researchers to propose a safety signal account of avoidance learning (e.g., Weisman & Litner, 1972). This account relies on the idea that avoidance responding almost always leads to feedback stimuli of some sort—for example, tactile and proprioceptive stimulation in the case of lever pressing or a change in contextual cues in the case of running to the other end of a shuttle box. As described earlier, such feedback stimuli may become learned safety signals, which could serve as an alternative source of (positive) reinforcement for avoidance responding.

The safety signal formulation has several advantages over two-factor theory. First, it can account for avoidance learning that occurs without termination of the warning stimulus. Second, it can account for the reduction in fear that occurs during the course of avoidance learning by active inhibition from feedback stimuli. Third, by appealing to the phenomenon of "protection from extinction" (Soltysik, Wolfe, Nicholas, Wilson, & Garcia-Sanchez, 1983), the safety signal theory can explain preservation of fear to the warning stimulus despite many trials without shock. In terms of Rescorla and Wagner's (1972) model, protection from extinction occurs because there is no discrepancy between what is predicted to occur and what actually occurs. On avoidance trials the feedback stimuli counteract the warning stimulus, leading to a net prediction of no outcome—this is exactly what occurs, so there is no new learning, that is, no extinction. If the avoidance response is prevented, however, the excitatory properties of the warning stimulus are revealed and fear returns; there is now a discrepancy between what is predicted (shock) and what occurs (nothing), so extinction proceeds.

Some theorists have referred to the safety signal theory of avoidance as a variant of two-factor theory (e.g., Gray, 1975; Mineka, 1979). Although it retains the two processes of Pavlovian and instrumental learning, it does in fact represent a substantial theoretical shift from the original two-factor position. In particular, it accepts the idea that two-factor theory was designed to circumvent, namely, that the absence of an event can generate learning (see Gray, 1975, pp. 319–321). In the safety signal model, it is the absence of shock that generates Pavlovian conditioned inhibition to feedback stimuli. In turn, acceptance that the absence of an event can generate learning implies acceptance of some version of the construct of expectancy because it is hard to see how the omission of a stimulus can cause learning unless it was expected in some sense of the term. This is the core idea underpinning the Rescorla–Wagner account of inhibitory learning. By contrast, safety signal theorists appear to have retained a fairly traditional view of instrumental learning because they speak in terms of positive reinforcement by feedback stimuli rather than in terms of contingency learning or expectancy processes.

Thus, the safety signal theory of avoidance is probably best regarded as a hybrid theoretical model in that it combines a modern informational view of Pavlovian conditioning with a traditional reinforcement view of instrumental conditioning. It is this feature that leads the model to share one of the limitations of Mowrer's (1947) two-factor theory, namely, the difficulty in explaining why response prevention should eliminate avoidance responding. Even if response prevention extinguishes Pavlovian fear to the early portions of the warning stimulus, the safety signal model fails to explain why this should undermine the acquired reinforcing properties of the feedback stimuli or the relationship between the instrumental response and reinforcement because neither the response nor its feedback stimuli are present during response prevention.

Seligman and Johnston's Theory

Another influential hybrid model of avoidance was proposed by Seligman and Johnston (1973). It is interesting that they adopted the opposite strategy to safety signal theorists; they combined a highly cognitive, expectancy-based mechanism for instrumental learning with a traditional reflexive account of Pavlovian conditioning. Seligman and Johnston accepted not only that avoidance responses predict the absence of an otherwise expected aversive event, but also that subjects (both animal and human) directly learn that relationship. They argued that subjects learn the outcome of responding and of not responding and then make a decision whether to respond or withhold responding on the basis of a comparison between the two expected outcomes. However, despite their emphasis on expectancy in the instrumental component, Seligman and Johnston did not grant expectancy a causal role in Pavlovian conditioning and hence in fear and anxiety. Instead they preferred to take a traditional view of Pavlovian conditioning as reflexive and noncognitive (although they did foreshadow the possibility that expectancy could play a role in Pavlovian responding; see Seligman & Johnston, 1973, footnote 9).

Seligman and Johnston's (1973) model can readily account for the persistence of avoidance responding despite shock being switched off because the expectation of shock in the absence of responding is never tested and is therefore unchanged. Similarly, the model can account for the effectiveness of response prevention in eliminating avoidance performance because this manipulation clearly does contradict the expectancy. That is, response prevention allows participants to learn that responding is unnecessary because shock will not occur anyway. The model does not make strong predictions concerning the relationship between fear and avoidance responding, however; there is no common link between the Pavlovian and instrumental components. Thus, the model fails to account directly for the decline in fear observed during avoidance training (over and above what can be attributed to Pavlovian extinction) and also for the return of fear when the avoidance response is prevented (although it could appeal to the preservation of fear to the later portions of the warning stimulus).

HUMAN ASSOCIATIVE LEARNING

A second stream of research that has far-reaching implications for our understanding of avoidance is human conditioning. Historically, the empirical and conceptual analysis of associative learning has been based primarily on animal research. The underlying justification for this approach has been the idea that animal research is concerned with "fundamental" conditioning processes that have been preserved across evolution and are also present in humans. In support of this assumption, there has been a close parallel between empirical findings in animal and human conditioning. Furthermore, models developed to account for animal conditioning have been applied successfully to other forms of learning in humans, including contingency learning and causal judgment (Dickinson, 2001). The question of how to conceptualize this close empirical relationship is quite a contentious one, however.

It has typically been assumed that conditioning processes in humans are quite distinct from "cognitive" processes, such as language, reasoning, and consciousness. Conditioning is seen as the formation of associations that regulate the transmission of activation in a mechanistic fashion, whereas the cognitive system is seen as acquiring, storing, and operating on symbolic or propositional representations of the environment. Of course such a representational system is itself quite capable of learning associative relationships and indeed in laboratory studies human participants can typically provide a verbal description of the relationships they have learned. Accordingly, it has generally been accepted that there are two competing systems operating in humans exposed to associative relationships: an automatic, mechanistic conditioning system and an effortful, representational cognitive system (e.g., Razran, 1955; Squire, 1994). Although often implicit rather than explicit, this "levels of learning" view is almost universally accepted in psychology. Yet it is interesting that laboratory research on associative learning in humans does not fit well with this view at all.

The majority of this research has been carried out with Pavlovian procedures, for example, electrodermal conditioning in which a neutral CS is paired with an electric shock US or eyeblink conditioning in which a CS is paired with an air-puff US. Typically, one stimulus (CS+) is paired with the US while a control stimulus (CS−) is not. Using these procedures, it has been difficult to find evidence for a separate, reflexive conditioning system (for reviews, see Dawson & Schell, 1985; Lovibond & Shanks, 2002). For example, there is a close correspondence between development of conditioned responses (CRs) and self-reported expectancy of the US. Participants classified as unaware of the relationship between the stimuli and the US on the basis of a postexperimental interview fail to show differential CRs to CS+ and CS−. Explicit attempts to distract or overload the cognitive system using a masking task successfully prevent conscious learning, but they also eliminate differential conditioned responding. Responding is strongly influenced by verbal instructions, and there is growing evidence for the role of reasoning in more complex conditioning procedures such as blocking and retrospective revaluation (Lovibond, 2003; Mitchell & Lovibond, 2002).

This research suggests that (a) knowledge derived from conditioning experiences is encoded in propositional form, such that it can be integrated with knowledge acquired symbolically, and (b) elicitation of behavior is tied to the outcome of propositional analysis rather than to earlier or lower level cognitive processes. Although the majority of research has come from Pavlovian conditioning, a similar conclusion has been reached in reviews of other forms of learning in humans, including instrumental conditioning (e.g., Brewer, 1974; Williams & Roberts, 1988) and implicit learning (Shanks & St. John, 1994). These findings make it difficult to defend a strong version of the traditional conceptualization of conditioning as automatic, unconscious, and compartmentalized from higher order cognition (although this is a matter of ongoing debate; see final section of this chapter). It is therefore of interest to consider the implications of the propositional view for avoidance learning in humans. Before doing so, however, it is useful to consider recent cognitive models of fear and avoidance in humans that have emerged from clinical research rather than from the laboratory.

COGNITIVE MODELS OF CLINICAL ANXIETY AND FEAR

A number of cognitive models of anxiety disorders and associated therapeutic strategies have been developed in clinical psychology (e.g., Beck & Emery, 1985; Clark, 1986). These models treat clinical anxiety as involving irrational or excessive threat appraisal, resulting in exaggerated beliefs about the probability or cost of potential negative outcomes. For example, Clark (1986) argued that panic patients misinterpret their own bodily symptoms of arousal as signifying a catastrophic outcome such as a heart attack, thus triggering a positive feedback loop resulting in a panic attack. According to cognitive models, exposure therapy works by contradicting the irrational threat beliefs held by patients.

Researchers working within this cognitive approach have more recently identified a mechanism that shares many features with avoidance learning. Salkovskis, Wells, and colleagues (e.g., Salkovskis, Clark, & Gelder, 1996; Wells et al., 1995) have introduced the notion of "within situation safety behaviors" to explain resistance to exposure therapy in panic disorder and social phobia. According to this analysis, during exposure to fear-provoking stimuli patients carry out subtle safety behaviors that are specifically intended to avert harmful outcomes (e.g., fainting or heart attack in the case of panic). These behaviors act to prevent the disconfirmation of inappropriate danger beliefs concerning the fear-provoking stimuli, because the absence of harm is instead attributed to the safety behaviors. The notion of safety behaviors is strikingly consistent with a safety signal model of avoidance derived from animal research, in which safety information (a predictor of shock omission) serves to protect a danger cue from extinction (Soltysik et al., 1983; Wagner & Rescorla, 1972). Clinical researchers have couched their explanation in terms of a reasoning process based on consciously accessible propositional beliefs about danger, however. This explanation is highly concordant with the propositional view of associative learning that has emerged from laboratory studies with human participants.

AN INTEGRATED EXPECTANCY-BASED MODEL

I have organized the preceding material so that the reader will appreciate the opportunity to define a model of avoidance that takes advantage of recent developments in animal conditioning, human conditioning, and clinical psychology. I have recently developed such an integrated model, based on the concept of expectancy (see also Lovibond, Saunders, Brady, & Mitchell, in press). This model is intended to apply directly to human avoidance learning, but it is consistent with the position I have argued elsewhere (Lovibond & Shanks, 2002) that there is a continuity in the evolution of the mechanisms underlying associative learning from animals to humans. In this section, I outline the key features of the model and describe preliminary research designed to test the model, and in the following section, I highlight alternative views and future directions for research and application.

Overview

The essential features of the expectancy model are as follows:

1. Pavlovian conditioning of fear is based on learning of the relationship between the warning signal and an aversive outcome. Presentation of the warning stimulus elicits an expectancy of the aversive outcome, which generates anxiety or fear (cf. Lovibond & Shanks, 2002; Reiss, 1991).
2. Instrumental learning of the designated avoidance response is based on learning of the relationship between the response and the omission of the expected aversive event. Performance of the response derives from a comparison process based on the expected outcome of responding and not responding.
3. Both of the previously mentioned forms of learning are represented as propositional knowledge, are available for self-report, and are subject to reasoning processes.
4. Avoidance interacts with anxiety through the mediating process of expectancy of the aversive outcome.

The expectancy model follows Mowrer's (1947) classic distinction between Pavlovian and instrumental learning processes. The model is similar to Seligman and Johnston's (1973) account with respect to the instrumental learning component. It is also similar to the safety signal model with respect to its emphasis on inhibitory learning. It assumes, however, that omission of the expected aversive event is directly associated with a central representation of the avoidance response, rather than with feedback stimuli from the response. The common element of expectancy allows the model to make clear predictions concerning the interplay between avoidance and anxiety. By assuming that learning is represented symbolically, the model also makes clear predictions regarding self-reported contingency knowledge and expectancy, for both laboratory participants and anxious patients.

Laboratory Research and the Expectancy Model

The expectancy model can deal with the primary findings in the animal literature on avoidance learning. For example, it correctly anticipates the reduction in anxiety that occurs once the avoidance response has been learned through inhibition of shock expectancy by availability of the avoidance response. Like Seligman and Johnston's (1973) model, the expectancy model accounts for the persistence of avoidance despite discontinuation of shock on the basis that the expected outcome of not responding (i.e., shock) is never tested and hence is preserved. Similarly, it accounts for the effectiveness of response prevention in eliminating avoidance responding because the absence of shock directly disconfirms this expectancy. Finally, the expectancy model predicts a complete return of fear or anxiety when the avoidance response is made unavailable (Baum, 1970; Solomon et al., 1953). The expectancy account attributes the modulation of anxiety directly to the central decision to make the avoidance response rather than to an indirect Pavlovian process based on response feedback. In this respect, it is compatible with prevailing cognitive theories of coping, such as Lazarus and Folkman's (1984) model in which coping appraisal directly attenuates threat appraisal and hence anxiety.

Relatively little systematic research has been conducted on avoidance learning in humans, particularly with aversive stimuli capable of inducing some degree of anxiety. In our laboratory, we have therefore developed a procedure based on Pavlovian autonomic conditioning, designed to allow testing of the expectancy model (Lovibond et al., in press). The basic procedure is shown in Figure 6.1. Each trial starts with presentation of a warning stimulus (CS), typically for 5 seconds. During the CS, participants may choose to press one of four response buttons. Response availability is signaled by illumination of individual buttons. Regardless of whether the designated correct button is pressed, the CS always has the same duration. Similarly, there is a fixed delay, typically 5 to 10 seconds, between offset of the CS and the point at which the US shock may be delivered. During the delay, participants are asked to indicate their expectancy of shock using a 180-degree rotary pointer labeled "certain no shock" at the left extreme and "certain shock" at the right extreme.

In this procedure, shock is presented or not presented as a function of the nature of the CS (danger or safety cue) and the response made, if available. For example, if a safe CS is presented, no shock will occur, regardless of which buttons are illuminated or whether any particular response is made. If a shock CS is presented and the correct avoidance response is either unavailable (button not illuminated) or it is available but not chosen, then shock

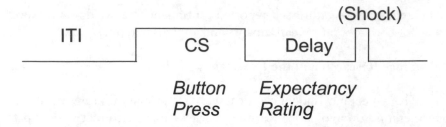

Figure 6.1. Schematic of trial procedure used for human avoidance learning. CS = conditioned stimulus; ITI = intertrial interval.

will occur. If a shock CS is presented and the correct response is both available and chosen by the participant, then no shock will occur. After the end of the trial, there is an interval of approximately 30 to 50 seconds before the next trial commences.

In our initial studies with this procedure, we contrasted unavoidable trials (shock CS with no buttons illuminated) with avoidable trials (shock CS with all four buttons illuminated). Participants soon learned the correct response, and their expectancy of shock declined over repeated avoidable trials. However, electrodermal responding, our physiological index of anxious arousal, was greater on avoidable than unavoidable trials, contrary to the predictions of expectancy theory. We reasoned that electrodermal responding may have been elevated by arousal because participants had to choose a response—for example, performance or social anxiety driven by fear of making an error or looking foolish. To control for this source of arousal, we introduced a procedure in which participants were required to make a response on every trial. With this methodological refinement, electrodermal responding was lower on avoidable trials than on unavoidable trials by the end of training, just as for the expectancy measure. We also showed that making the correct response unavailable led to an immediate restoration of both shock expectancy and electrodermal responding, as predicted by the expectancy model (Lovibond et al., in press). The within-session recording of anxiety is preferable to the more common procedure of testing off-baseline (e.g., Starr & Mineka, 1977) because there is no change in context and response availability can be controlled.

We have also obtained data that support the prediction shared by the safety signal model and the expectancy model that a source of safety can protect a Pavlovian fear CS from extinction. First, using a purely Pavlovian procedure, we have shown that a stimulus present during nonshocked exposure to a target CS previously paired with shock can interfere with the extinction of the target CS that would normally occur. This interference was demonstrated by testing the target CS alone, which revealed that relative to a control CS the target CS had retained its ability to elicit shock expectancy and arouse fear (Lovibond, Davis, & O'Flaherty, 2000). More recently, we have shown the same protection from extinction effect using an avoidance response. A response that had been effective in preventing shock signaled by one CS was made available during extinction of a second shock CS, and when that CS was tested alone, it showed the same pattern of return of fear on both the electrodermal and expectancy measures (Lovibond, Mitchell, Minard, & Brady, 2005). The latter demonstration that an avoidance response can interfere with extinction of fear to a Pavlovian CS is directly analogous to the process postulated by Salkovskis and colleagues (e.g., Salkovskis et al., 1996) when safety behaviors are performed during exposure therapy. The parallel results for expectancy and electrodermal responding support the assumption of the expectancy model that these measures are driven by a single (propositional) process.

Clinical Implications of the Expectancy Model

One of the most important predictions of the expectancy model is that the associative learning underlying avoidance is encoded in a propositional form that makes it available for self-report. Thus patients should be able to articulate both threat beliefs (e.g., estimated probability and cost of harmful outcomes) and beliefs regarding the consequences of their own actions. Anxiety should closely track the joint outcome of these two types of belief. This view is highly congruent with the assumptions of classic cognitive therapy for anxiety disorders (e.g., Beck & Emery, 1985; Hawton, Salkovskis, Kirk, & Clark, 1989) but is incompatible with cognitive models that also postulate separate unconscious learning processes such as situationally accessible knowledge (Brewin, Dalgleish, & Joseph, 1996). Laboratory research has so far failed to find good evidence for unconscious learning of this type, but it remains to be seen whether extreme events such as trauma might lead to such learning as some authors have suggested (see Brewin & Holmes, 2003).

Leaving aside the possibility of unconscious learning, the expectancy model supports the use of both "behavioral" techniques, such as exposure and response prevention, and "cognitive" techniques, such as identifying and challenging dysfunctional threat beliefs and preventing safety behaviors. Critically, the expectancy model provides a unifying theoretical framework for combining these techniques. Behavioral and cognitive therapies originated from distinct theoretical positions and are often combined on the assumption that they operate on different underlying mechanisms. The expectancy model suggests that gains can be made by recognizing the common mechanisms and combining techniques in a synergistic way. For example, the model suggests that exposure and response prevention should be closely integrated with verbal and cognitive strategies to draw the patient's attention to the contradictions between their experience and their threat beliefs (see also Lovibond, 1993; Zinbarg, 1990). An important task for future clinical research is to determine the optimal combination of language and experience for various anxiety disorders and to test the assumption of a common mechanism.

The expectancy model also suggests novel clinical interventions. For example, laboratory research has shown that humans can change their associative knowledge about a target stimulus retrospectively and that such changes can be induced by language as well as by experience (Lovibond, 2003). This research suggests that verbal techniques may be effective in providing new attributions for past events such as traumatic experiences. For example, it may be possible for a therapist to reduce the strength of a patient's maladaptive attribution for a traumatic event (e.g., blaming oneself for an assault) by providing an alternative "scapegoat" attribution (e.g., to some specific or unstable feature present at the time). The expectancy model also predicts that any intervention that successfully reduces the perceived cost of an expected outcome should undermine both anxiety and avoidance behavior. Davey (1989) has shown that such "reinforcer devaluation" can reduce anxiety in the laboratory, and has discussed clinical applications of this procedure (Davey et al., 1993). It would be interesting to test whether this type of manipulation in itself reduces avoidance behavior, or whether these behaviors need to be targeted directly, as some animal research suggests (e.g., Colwill & Rescorla, 1990). Finally, the expectancy model provides strong support for ongoing animal research on fear conditioning and avoidance because it points to a continuity in the underlying associative mechanisms and provides a conceptual framework for linking animal research not only to human conditioning, but also to the broader domain of human learning, memory, and reasoning.

ONGOING DEBATES AND FUTURE DIRECTIONS

One of the most contentious aspects of the expectancy model presented here is the idea that associative learning—Pavlovian and instrumental conditioning—is based on the same cognitive processes that are involved in higher order reasoning tasks, not on a separate, lower level system. The levels of learning position is strongly entrenched in virtually every domain of psychology, and not surprisingly vigorous defenses of this position have been offered (e.g., Manns, Clark, & Squire, 2002; Martin & Levey, 1989; Wiens & Öhman, 2002). Even proponents of the cognitive position concede that there are some empirical results that support the levels of learning position (see Lovibond & Shanks, 2002; Shanks & Lovibond, 2002). This debate is certain to continue and to generate new results to help distinguish among the rival positions. In the anxiety literature, an example of a model that denies a cognitive basis to conditioning is the "neo-conditioning" account of panic proposed by Bouton and colleagues (2001). These researchers have summarized evidence in support of a traditional unconscious view of conditioning in the etiology of panic, and it will be interesting to see how well this model competes with cognitive models in accounting for new data on panic.

A further important literature concerns associatively based changes in valence. Research on so-called evaluative conditioning suggests that pairing an initially neutral stimulus with a pleasant or unpleasant stimulus can lead to changes in the affective valence (like–dislike) of the target stimulus (see De Houwer, Baeyens, & Field, 2005). Under some circumstances, these affective changes appear to be resistant to informational manipulations such as extinction. One strong interpretation of these findings is that evaluative conditioning involves a separate, nonanticipatory learning system (e.g., Baeyens & De Houwer, 1995), a position similar to the levels of learning model discussed earlier. An interesting alternative possibility is that like–dislike reactions are based on the same associative learning mechanism as classic anticipatory CR measures but that they involve a different mode of accessing the underlying memory representation—for example, activation of affective aspects of the US memory (Konorski, 1967) without the establishment of a clear sensory expectancy of future US occurrence. Considerable controversy exists concerning the similarities and differences between evaluative conditioning and other forms of conditioning (e.g., De Houwer et al., 2005; Lipp & Purkis, 2005), and this will be a fertile field for future research. In the present context, one critical issue that needs to be addressed is the relative role of evaluative–affective reactions and expectancy-based reactions in fear and anxiety.

Within the specific domain of avoidance learning, a contrary position to the cognitive model presented here has been put forward and supported by new evidence over a number of years by Donald Levis and his colleagues (e.g., Levis & Levin, 1972; Unger, Evans, Rourke, & Levis, 2003). Levis has argued that traditional two-factor theory provides a better account of avoidance data than subsequent models such as the safety signal model and Seligman and Johnston's (1973) model. We have argued against Levis's position elsewhere (Lovibond et al., in press), but the important point for present purposes is that there is no consensual view in the literature concerning the processes underlying avoidance learning. Given the clinical importance of avoidance, it is clear that additional laboratory research, particularly with human participants, would be extremely useful. In this respect, an interesting development is an expectancy-based model proposed by De Houwer, Crombez, and Baeyens (2005) in which the avoidance response serves not as a conditioned inhibitor but as a negative occasion setter for the warning stimulus–unconditioned stimulus relationship. According to this model, the avoidance response does not inhibit fear directly but does so indirectly by modulating the strength of the association between the warning stimulus and the aversive outcome. It remains to be seen whether this model can be developed to account for performance of the avoidance response itself and whether the role of the response is better conceptualized as inhibition or occasion setting.

Several theoretical and applied issues would be useful for researchers of all theoretical persuasions to address in future research. One of these is how to conceptualize secondary avoidance. In many clinical disorders, patients not only engage in within-situation avoidance behaviors like those discussed by Salkovskis and colleagues (e.g., Salkovskis et al., 1996), but also, when possible, they avoid the threatening situation altogether. All theories of avoidance predict that such secondary avoidance will prevent extinction of fear simply because the threatening stimulus is unavailable for relearning. Exposure therapy necessarily overcomes secondary (CS) avoidance but does not in itself prevent primary (US) avoidance. In addition, it remains to be determined how primary avoidance interacts with secondary avoidance.

A second important issue is how pharmacological interventions such as anxiolytic drugs interact with anxiety and avoidance. Much is already known about drug interactions with Pavlovian fear conditioning (e.g., Harris & Westbrook, 1999), but extension of this research to avoidance learning would have important theoretical and clinical implications. For example, drugs may operate directly by influencing the brain processes involved in avoidance learning. However, they may also operate by establishing a state or context that has stimulus properties and acts to modulate learning or to protect danger cues from extinction. Finally, it would be useful to examine whether covert strategies, such as the cognitive rituals that some patients with obsessive–compulsive disorder report, can be understood as avoidance responses. These internal processes pose a challenge in terms of both measurement and achieving response prevention.

CONCLUSION

Converging evidence is mounting for an integrated, expectancy-based model of avoidance and anxiety. This model accounts for much existing data and provides a framework for understanding the effectiveness of current clinical interventions for avoidance and anxiety, and points to ways of improving these interventions. The model gives particular emphasis to patients' expectancies regarding threat and strategies for reducing threat and to the search for both experience-based and verbal interventions to target maladaptive expectancies. The model also denies the existence of a separate unconscious learning system for anxiety. At the same time, competing theoretical models make different clinical predictions. The empirical study of avoidance has languished over the past 30 years, but the stage is set for a renewed research effort, both in the laboratory and in the clinic, to understand better the processes underlying avoidance and its role in anxiety.

7

FEAR CONDITIONING IN AN EMOTION REGULATION CONTEXT: A FRESH PERSPECTIVE ON THE ORIGINS OF ANXIETY DISORDERS

JOHN P. FORSYTH, GEORG H. EIFERT, AND VELMA BARRIOS

> Clinical experience has shown that, ironically, it is often the patient's very attempts to solve the problem that, in fact, maintains it. The attempted solution becomes the true problem.
> —Nardone and Watzlawick (1993, p. 54)

For fear-conditioning research and theory to have any appreciable impact on clinical practice, it must explain how Pavlovian fear conditioning can account for disordered experiences of anxiety and fear. That is, it must show how fear conditioning—a ubiquitous and adaptive form of learning—can become disordered or maladaptive, resulting in human suffering and an anxiety disorder. To date, it has not done so.

The purpose of this chapter is to outline theory and research that may help explain how fear-conditioning processes become clinically disordered. Taking into account prior discussions of critical individual difference variables (e.g., Craske, 2003), we will restrict the focus here to psychological and experiential variables and processes that are considered crucial in explaining the genesis, maintenance, and alleviation of anxiety disorders rather than anxiety per se (Barlow, 2002; Barlow, Allen, & Choate, 2004). One such process is *emotion regulation*, a heterogeneous set of human actions for managing the experience and expression of emotion.

Emotion regulation processes—the tendency to avoid, suppress, or escape from aversive emotional states and the contexts or cues that may evoke them—characterizes virtually all anxiety disorders (Barlow, 2002; Barlow et al., 2004). The field of emotion regulation suggests that the tendency to regulate emotion is dependent on verbal–cognitive processes and that individuals differ in how they regulate emotions. This work also suggests that emotion regulation may do more harm than good when applied to aversive emotional states, and may function to transform normal anxiety and fear into disordered anxiety and fear. Inflexible forms of emotion regulation, when juxtaposed with fear learning and competing approach contingencies, are likely predispositions for the development and maintenance of disordered fear and functional impairment typical of those with anxiety disorders. Our intent is to show how this work may complement and advance fear-conditioning accounts of anxiety disorders.

FROM NORMAL FEAR AND CONDITIONING TO ANXIETY DISORDERS: A FRESH PERSPECTIVE

Although the clinical relevance of fear-conditioning research as a model of anxiety disorders has been criticized (e.g., Menzies & Clarke, 1995a; Rachman, 1991), these criticisms do not hold up in light of contemporary learning theory (Bouton et al., 2001; Forsyth & Eifert, 1996a, 1996b, 1998; Mineka & Zinbarg, 1996). That is, all but one. The challenge facing Pavlovian conditioning research is explaining how a functional and ubiquitous learning process (conditioning) coupled with equally functional and ubiquitous emotional responses (fear and anxiety) would lead to anxiety disorders for some individuals but not others.

This issue is a bit different than asking whether individual differences moderate fear learning (Eysenck, 1976; Mineka & Zinbarg, 1996). Given the right combination of experiential, contextual, and biological individual difference factors, fear learning may be potentiated or depotentiated. From this perspective, the problematic features of fear conditioning have to do with its potentiation, a term that means to endow with power or potency so as to make something (in this case, an anxiety disorder) possible (Oxford English Dictionary, 1989). Individual differences that endow fear conditioning with power (i.e., potentiate it) make fear learning problematic and contribute to the development, maintenance, and persistence of anxiety disorders. This is the core message underlying most individual differences accounts of Pavlovian fear conditioning and the anxiety disorders.

This work highlights the complexity of Pavlovian learning. Yet acknowledging that fear learning is complex does not mean that it is problematic simply because individual differences affect fear-learning processes. In our view, the challenge facing this line of research and theory is to explain how and why potentiated fear conditioning is problematic and capable of yielding an anxiety disorder. Neither potentiated fear (e.g., Rosen & Schulkin, 1998) nor fear learning itself nor individual differences that potentiate both explain how an anxiety disorder develops.

When fear is evoked, the typical acute consequence is disruption and narrowing of ongoing behavior. Such disruptions ready organisms to take immediate action to prepare for, escape from, or avoid threat. It makes evolutionary sense to learn to fear stimuli that have been associated with aversive consequences. Mammals learn to respond appropriately to threat or danger by actively avoiding stimuli that predict aversive responses, in part because it makes adaptive sense to do so. Our challenge, then, is to explain the parameters and processes that transform fear from being adaptive in some contexts to maladaptive or dysfunctional in others. This is the more general aim of this chapter.

This chapter addresses how fear conditioning, in the context of emotion regulatory processes, can yield an anxiety disorder and not simply conditioned fear, anxiety, or avoidance experienced by most humans at some point in their lives. We suggest that fear conditioning can become problematic when individuals act to down-regulate (i.e., struggle with, control, suppress, avoid, escape) the effects of fear learning (e.g., contexts, antecedents, and consequences) in a rigid fashion. Such down-regulation endows fear-conditioning processes with power and potency and interferes with meaningful life activities, thus fostering functional impairment in those with anxiety disorders.

What Makes Fear Learning a Clinical Problem?

Classical fear conditioning emerged as a model of anxiety disorders largely because of Watson and Rayner's (1920) demonstration of fear acquisition in Little Albert. The correspondence between Albert's behavior and anxiety problems led to the recognition of a process by which fears could be acquired (e.g., Eysenck, 1976; Wolpe, 1958). Yet this does not mean that fear learning itself is problematic or that fear learning is an adequate analog of phobias or anxiety disorders. Albert behaved in accord with his history; there were no costs associated with his conditioned fear or avoidance. The same is true of most analog conditioning research. By contrast, fear learning and avoidance across the anxiety disorders are typically associated with costs because such behaviors are set within a context of competing approach contingencies (cf. Hayes, 1976). Such competing contingencies are reflected in the reasons anxious clients seek treatment (e.g., "My fear of driving is driving my husband crazy" or "I can't drive to work because I might panic").

This dual-component view (Hayes, 1976) suggests that fear learning becomes problematic only when it (a) removes access to reinforcing events or (b) puts the individual in contact with aversive events. The resulting avoidance is disruptive when competing contingencies supporting *a* or *b* (or both) are present. A pedestrian who hears the horn blare of an oncoming car and jumps out of the way would likely experience intense fear, some conditioning, and clearly demonstrates avoidance. Yet this person would not be considered phobic, in part because there are few or no approach contingencies (Hayes, 1976). In fact, approach (running into the street) would be extremely punishing. This situation is analogous to avoidance learning paradigms in which a signal is followed by the emission of an avoidance response or else the onset of an aversive stimulus. Such behaviors are not phobic because there is no competing approach element in the situation. Whereas etiologically all phobic behavior is avoidance behavior, not all avoidance behavior is phobic behavior (see Hayes, 1976), nor is all fear learning phobic learning.

From a functional process-oriented perspective, classical fear conditioning is recognized as a means to alter the functions of events and direct behavior as a consequence. Yet such learning cannot account for the development of an anxiety disorder. If there are no approach contingencies in the situation (i.e., approach–avoidance conflict), then fear learning is just fear learning and avoidance is simply avoidance, not an anxiety disorder. Implications of this account have yet to be fully tested in human fear conditioning analogs but have been demonstrated in animals (e.g., see Hayes, Lattal, & Myerson, 1979). Such tests in humans are a challenge because humans can expand the scope of approach–avoidance contingencies through language and verbal behavior.

The Role of Language in Disordered Fear

Humans can respond to approach–avoidance contingencies verbally and symbolically without confronting the actual contingencies directly. Thus, a person who learns that fear is bad and must be managed before doing important tasks (e.g., attend a child's school play) may struggle to manage the emotional response first before engaging in important and valued actions second. This type of learning makes the approach–avoidance conflict more complex and requires consideration of how humans manage emotions. This difference between animals and humans is accounted for by social contingencies and the human capacity to engage in complex verbally mediated relations. Both elements allow humans to engage in self- and emotion-regulatory actions that are not possible to the same degree in nonverbal organisms, such as primates.

Despite ample evidence (e.g., Suomi, 1999) that primates experience and express pain and chronic states of anxious arousal, there is no indication that they suffer about the experience of having pain and anxiety. Rhesus monkeys exposed to uncontrollable and unpredictable aversive stimulation experience alarm responses followed by long-term anxious arousal. They will learn to avoid the source and context of aversive stimulation, but as best we can tell, they do not act deliberately to regulate their emotional experience. Humans, by contrast, can and do suffer about their own emotional pain and histories by responding to conditioned responses (CRs) with evaluative verbal behavior and thinking (e.g., "God, this is awful," "I'm going to pass out") and by engaging in efforts to suppress, avoid, or escape emotional pain and related thoughts. Thus, humans can become fearful of fear, depressed about anxiety, worried about the future, agonize about the past, and struggle to avoid or escape from unpleasant thoughts, feelings, behavioral tendencies, and the circumstances that have evoked them or may evoke them in the future. The capacity of language, coupled with social contingencies regarding the experience and expression of emotion, make this possible.

Emotions, and the implications of regulating emotional experience for personal happiness (Hayes, Strosahl, & Wilson, 1999), are largely shaped by social and cultural conventions and contact with other human beings. Much of this learning is dependent on complex forms of relational learning entailed in language and verbal–symbolic behavior (Forsyth & Eifert, 1996b). Language provides humans with emotional experiences without exposure to physical stimuli or events that ordinarily elicit those responses (Forsyth & Eifert, 1996b). For instance, suppose a person has learned to associate fear with "danger" and "sudden quick movements" and with actions such as "running away." Despite having no negative history with snakes, if a person hears someone say "snakes make sudden quick movements," they may now derive that snakes are dangerous and something to be afraid of.

Verbal–relational tendencies are socialized, emerge by age 2 under most circumstances, and are built into human language and cognition (for a detailed account of relational processes, see Hayes, Barnes-Holmes, & Roche, 2001). Such learning begins with an extensive history of reinforcement for relating many stimuli in different ways based largely on their formal stimulus properties (e.g., beach ball is a ball, basketball is a ball), and thereafter through more indirect relations (e.g., spoken word "ball" is the same as written word ball). Such a history makes it possible for humans to relate novel stimuli in numerous ways without being taught to do so. Thus, the person described in the earlier example may avoid going into the woods after hearing someone say, "I saw a snake in the woods." The woods may become a dangerous place that evokes fear. Learning, in this example, was established almost entirely through arbitrary verbal relations, arbitrary meaning that new relations are not dependent on physical stimulus properties (e.g., the woods are not more or less snaky) but rather established by social convention.

Language Entangles Humans in Struggle With Emotions

Language-based capacities to evaluate and respond relationally to evaluations, thoughts, and feelings with more evaluations enable humans to struggle with their own emotions while acting not to have them. One can try to run away from the experience of fear and its arbitrarily related events without being taught to do so. That is, the experience of fear can be established through derived relations with other events, including those that entail strong approach contingencies.

Several studies have shown transfer of fear, avoidance, and other stimulus functions after a history of learning relations between arbitrary stimuli. Equivalence represents one form of relational learning in which humans learn that otherwise arbitrary stimuli are similar or interchangeable with one another (e.g., A = B = C stimuli are treated as part of the same class; Augustson & Dougher, 1997). This work is important in showing how contextual factors can establish arbitrary verbal relations between events that are not taught directly and how a range of emotive and psychological functions may transfer through such networks. For instance, if painful shock is associated with C, it is likely that A and B will also evoke CRs. This has been demonstrated with several functions (including fear); complex relations (e.g., same–opposite; larger–smaller); and classes involving more than three members (Hayes et al., 2001).

This work points to the kinds of histories that may transform the experience of a sudden quick movement of the heart into "this is dangerous" and "I might be dying" without contacting the aversive contingency (i.e., death). It also points to how language may fuse verbal processes with formal properties of private and public events. Such fusion means that the stimulus properties of actual events become mutually entailed (fused) with the words used to describe them, and thus humans can respond to words about some event as if responding to the actual event. Consequently, humans can establish contingencies almost entirely through verbal processes. For instance, a child might hear an adult say, "don't touch the hot stove or you'll get burned." Later in life, this same person might hear a friend say, "I got burned by trusting that guy." Such a history, in turn, can lead an individual to respond to those verbal constructions as being the same as the actual events (the word *burned* is the same as being physically burned), even when faced with powerful contradictory contingencies (e.g., "I might get 'burned' if I trust that person in a relationship;" *burned* meaning *hurt*).

Unlike humans, nonverbal organisms are unable to make complex relational responses (e.g., pick the scariest object from a picture of the moon, a tree, and a small wasp). A nonverbal animal would not respond above chance, whereas a verbally sophisticated human would likely choose the wasp. Here "scary" is not a formal stimulus property but rather a stimulus property that has been given arbitrary social significance. Verbal–relational processes not only make it possible for humans to regulate aversive emotional experience so as to suppress, control, avoid, or escape it but also can expand the scope of limited fear-learning experiences. Both point to the role of socially mediated contingencies in shaping the experience and expression of emotion. When such contingencies are juxtaposed with classical conditioning contingencies, otherwise adaptive fear learning can lead some individuals down the path toward an anxiety disorder.

EMOTION REGULATION AND THE ANXIETY DISORDERS

Several accounts explain the shift from normal to clinically disordered fear. Most share two notions. First, fear and anxiety are somehow dysregulated, such that either emotional response occurs too frequently, too intensely, or for too long. Second, anxiety and fear are evoked by cues that do not demand such responses. That is, fear and anxiety are evoked in the absence of real threat. The combination of dysregulated emotion occurring in contexts that do not call for an anxious response may result in functional impairment.

The Nature of Emotion Regulation

Emotion regulation refers to heterogeneous actions designed to influence "which emotions we have, when we have them, and how we experience and express them" (Gross, 2002, p. 282). Such actions include reappraisal, distraction, avoidance, escape, suppression, emotion and problem-focused coping, and use of substances to enhance or blunt emotional experience. These actions can be applied to both positive and negative emotional states.

In the context of aversive states, emotion regulatory processes share a common functional goal: to minimize the frequency, intensity, duration, or situational occurrence of internal feeling states (e.g., fear and anxiety), associated thoughts, and physiological reactions. Some regulatory processes are habitual, occurring in or outside of awareness (e.g., selective attention), whereas others are more purposeful (e.g., blame, rumination, avoidance). Most processes, however, involve altering the form or frequency of events that precede an emotional response or the consequences of emotional responding, including the emotional response itself. The former is termed *antecedent-focused* emotion regulation, whereas the latter refers to *response-focused* emotion regulation (Gross, 1998).

Emotion regulation research and theory aims to bring together processes involved in the experience, expression, and modulation of emotion, including the positive and negative consequences of emotion regulation itself (e.g., achievement of goals, restriction in life functioning). That is, emotion regulation characterizes a range of psychological phenomena that have been shown to influence the experience and expression of emotion. This volume includes several chapters outlining how emotion regulatory processes (e.g., re-appraisal, avoidance) influence, or occur as a consequence of, fear learning (e.g., see chaps. 8 and 9, this volume). Although emotion regulation is not a dysfunctional process, it can become dysfunctional when emotions cannot and need not be regulated and when the very act of emotion regulation gets in the way of meaningful life activities (i.e., regulation that competes with powerful approach contingencies; see Hayes, 1976). It is for these reasons that emotion regulation is gaining currency in psychopathology research (Eifert & Forsyth, 2005) and mental health care (Gross & Muñoz, 1995).

Figure 7.1 illustrates the typical points where emotional experience tends to be regulated. In a simplified manner, this model suggests that humans may regulate the antecedents and consequences of emotions. For anxiety disorders, antecedents may include situations in which fear is likely to occur, bodily and environmental cues that evoke such reactions, whether emotionally relevant information is attended to, and how such information is evaluated (e.g., "I can't get through this"). In Pavlovian conditioning terms, the relevant antecedents would be conditioned stimuli (CSs) and possibly unconditioned stimuli (USs) and the contexts in which both may occur. Front-end regulatory strategies are important because how one responds to emotional inputs, and particularly the verbal evaluation of those inputs (i.e., this is dangerous, awful), affect the emotional consequences that may follow (Gross, 1998). Thus, escalation of the emotional sequence can be attenuated or avoided depending on how one manages the antecedents that may evoke or occasion emotional experience.

Once the emotion occurs, regulation efforts tend to focus on the intensity, duration, and general quality of the emotional response and its consequences. Such response-focused regulation strategies may involve taking a break, relaxing, deep breathing, seeking distraction, affiliating with others, or doing something pleasant. There is nothing disordered about emotional regulation when applied in a context sensitive and flexible manner. Indeed, such strategies are often taught to patients in therapy with positive results, particularly when patients are instructed to use them flexibly. Problems may arise when persons make rigid efforts to down-regulate the cognitive, physiological, or behavioral components of negative emotions when such efforts are unnecessary to engage competing approach contingencies. Such down-regulation strategies are often subtle in those experiencing anxiety disorders and usually take the form of suppression, control, avoidance, or escape (Barlow, 2002).

Healthy and Unhealthy Forms of Emotion Regulation

Historically the field of emotion regulation research and theory has been agnostic with regard to the positive and negative consequences of emotion regulation strategies for psychological health and wellness. Increasingly, however, we are learning that certain forms of emotion regulation may be healthier than others and that some may produce human suffering. We briefly summarize findings from this literature that are relevant to a better under-

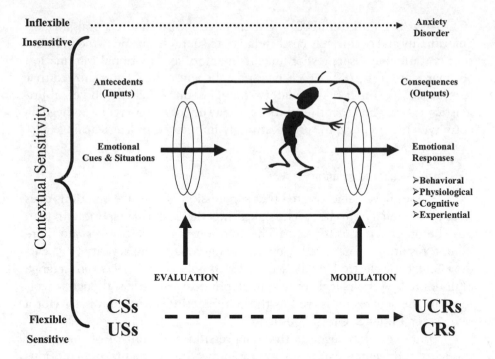

Figure 7.1. A consensual model of emotion regulation in a fear-learning context. CSs = conditioned stimuli; USs = unconditioned stimuli; UCRs = unconditioned responses; CRs = conditioned responses. Adapted from "Antecedent and Response-Focused Emotion Regulation," by J. J. Gross, 1998, *Journal of Personality and Social Psychology, 74*, p. 226. Copyright 1998 by the American Psychological Association.

standing of how emotion regulation may make fear and fear learning problematic.

Antecedent-Focused Regulation

Antecedent forms of emotion regulation characterize actions occurring before emotional response tendencies are fully engaged. The most studied strategy, reappraisal, refers to verbal–linguistic actions that change the meaning of an emotion-eliciting situation for better or worse (Lazarus & Alfert, 1964). Research suggests that positive reappraisal is a flexible and effective means of minimizing negative impact of an aversive event (Gross, 1998, 2002). This strategy subsumes numerous actions (e.g., sense making, acceptance) with the goal of reframing an emotion-eliciting situation in less emotional terms. Less functional antecedent strategies include avoidance, distraction, suppression, and escape.

Studies suggest that positive reappraisal strategies are less likely to be used by depressed and anxious persons relative to healthy control participants (Garnefski et al., 2002) and that infrequent use of reappraisal is associated with more depressive and anxious symptoms in healthy adolescents

(Garnefski & Spinhoven, 2001). Others have shown that reappraisal is less emotionally and cognitively costly relative to suppression and avoidance and that chronic use of suppression impairs memory for emotional information (Richards & Gross, 2000). Ochsner and colleagues (2004) also showed that reappraisal, like other self-regulatory strategies, draws heavily on verbal linguistic processes and that these processes may up- or down-regulate amygdala activity. This circuitry, in turn, is strongly implicated in fear learning (e.g., LeDoux, 2000).

Response-Focused Regulation

Studies have demonstrated that suppression of aversive emotions does not provide relief from the psychological experience of that emotion. In fact, just the opposite tends to occur: The emotion becomes stronger and more salient, resulting in increased sympathetic nervous system activity (e.g., cardiovascular and electrodermal response; Gross & Levenson, 1997) and a range of undesired psychological content (e.g., physical sensations, thoughts, feelings) in the suppressor as well as those interacting with him or her (for a review, see Butler & Gross, 2004).

Other research suggests that suppression and control of unwanted thoughts and feelings can result in more unwanted thoughts and emotions (Wegner, 1994; for a review, see Purdon, 1999). Moreover, emotion suppression has been shown to contribute to suffering and pain (Hayes et al., 1999), distress and restriction in life functioning (Marx & Sloan, 2002), diminished contact with meaningful and valued life activities, and poorer overall quality of life (Hayes, 2004a; Hayes et al., 2004; Hayes, Wilson, Gifford, Follette, & Strosahl, 1996). Individuals who chronically engage in suppression also tend to report more negative experiences and fewer positive ones (Gross & John, 2003; Kashdan, Barrios, Forsyth, & Steger, in press). Such relations appear to be completely mediated by inauthenticity (John & Gross, 2004), a construct similar to nonacceptance (Hayes et al., 1999).

The emerging consensus is that response-focused emotion regulation requires effort, only works to a point, and is counterproductive when emotions are intense and aversive. Thus, reacting to our own reactions can actually amplify those reactions in a vicious self-perpetuating cycle, resulting in an increase of the undesired emotion, particularly in contexts in which the regulation of emotion would be most desired (Craske, Miller, Rotunda, & Barlow, 1990).

The Importance of Being Flexible

From a functional view, the utility of emotion regulation depends on whether it achieves desired outcomes and can be flexibly applied depending on context. That is, because emotion regulation characterizes socially acquired behaviors (not immutable traits), it ought to be sensitive to contextual determinants. For instance, although positive reappraisal is often a useful strategy for minimizing the impact of an aversive emotion, it should not be uniformly applied. It does not seem advantageous to remain in a highly aversive situation using positive reappraisal when other options are more viable. Flexibility, or the ability to discriminate between a range of stimuli in and outside a context, is crucial for the functional utility of emotion regulation strategies (Bonanno, Papa, LaLande, Westphal, & Coifman, 2004). In fact, discrimination failure, or regulating emotions indiscriminately in a trait-like fashion, is emerging as a core theme that distinguishes problematic from functional emotion regulation (John & Gross, 2004).

Language processes can facilitate or interfere with discrimination and contingency shaped responding (see Hayes, 2004b, for a detailed account). For instance, rules can make learning contingencies more rapid, or they can interfere with learning contingency relations (e.g., Hayes, Brownstein, Zettle, Rosenfarb, & Korn, 1986). The behavioral account of human inflexibility has focused on how language processes diminish contact with approach contingencies by establishing patterns of self- and emotion regulation as prerequisites for effective action (Zettle & Hayes, 1982). Experiential avoidance, a recent term used to describe this tendency, refers to behaviors to alter the frequency, duration, or form of unwanted private events (i.e., thoughts, feelings, and physical sensations) and the cues and situations that occasion them (Hayes et al., 1999). Experiential avoidance characterizes a set of actions that tend to be more rule governed than contingency shaped. Thus, it yields behaviors that appear more rigid than circumstances warrant.

Because experiential avoidance entails the same set of processes that can make emotion and thought regulation problematic, it is thought to contribute to numerous problems associated with unwanted psychological and emotional content (Hayes et al., 1996). In fact, persons so predisposed will likely experience approach–avoidance conflicts across numerous situations for the simple reason that experiential avoidance is rigidly and inflexibly applied and is thus pitted up against numerous life contingencies (verbally and nonverbally derived) that demand approach (e.g., going to work, running errands, taking a vacation, being with people).

For instance, persons who use chronic suppression tend to report feeling a sense of incongruence between the private and outer behavior, fear being accepted by others, and thus use suppression in relationships they care about and are afraid to lose (for a review, see John & Gross, 2004). This example illustrates how emotion regulation interfaces with several verbally derived approach–avoidance conflicts. It also suggests how this tendency may be a potentially self-destructive process that is associated with significant costs and a range of negative outcomes, including functional impairment in interpersonal, social, and occupational domains; overall poorer quality of life (Gross, 1998; Hayes et al., 1996; Quilty, Van Ameringen, Mancini, Oakman, & Farvolden, 2003); and even illness and greater mortality risk (Denollet et al., 1996).

The question, then, is why do we avoid feelings and thoughts as if they were the enemy? From an emotion regulation perspective, social learning creates a context in which forms of experiential avoidance and nonacceptance can thrive (Hayes et al., 1999). Emotion regulation is used as evidence of maturity, emotional stability, health and wellness, success, fulfillment, and happiness. We typically do not question what life might be like if unpleasant emotions and thoughts were treated simply as events to be experienced as part of being fully human, not as events that must be managed and controlled (cf. Blackledge & Hayes, 2001). We do not question the cultural mandate that equates failures of emotion regulation with suffering and misery and connects "positive" thoughts and feelings with an ability to engage life to its fullest. In this cultural context, anxious thoughts and feelings become obstacles to living and the achievement of valued goals. They are reasonable justifications for inaction and are quite often fused with a sense of self-worth (e.g., "I'm not good enough," "I am broken"). It follows that unwanted feelings and thoughts must be managed and controlled (e.g., "I need to be fixed before I can do what matters to me"), even at significant cost to the individual.

Paradoxically, the first step toward healthy emotion regulation may involve fostering greater discrimination and less rule-governed behavior, particularly as applied to regulating unwanted emotional experiences. Evidence suggests that this stance puts humans (and most nonverbal organisms) in a better position to exert control when they have it, namely, in responding to natural contingencies. We expand on this later by showing how experiential avoidance functions to maintain disordered experiences of anxiety and fear and serves as a risk factor for the development and maintenance of anxiety disorders.

Experiential Avoidance: A Potentially Toxic Form of Emotion Regulation

Experiential avoidance is thought to function as a psychological diathesis underlying the development and maintenance of anxiety disorders and several other forms of psychopathology (Blackledge & Hayes, 2001; Hayes et al., 1996). It is a process related to how we influence our emotions, when we have them, and how we experience and express them. As such, experiential avoidance is an overarching emotion regulation strategy (see Gross, 1998) that differs from largely inherited biological individual differences that may make persons more vulnerable to developing an anxiety disorder (e.g., behavioral inhibition, Gray, 1990; temperament, Kagan, 1989; neuroticism, Eysenck, 1976).

Although Gray (1990) and Kagan and Snidman (1999) readily acknowledged the importance of environmental variation in activating and modulating the influence of behavioral inhibition and temperament, they also emphasized the strong heritable components and identified a number of associated brain structures and neurophysiological correlates (for a review, see Fox, Henderson, Marshall, Nichols, & Ghera, 2005). Neuroticism is likewise thought of as an important individual difference predisposition—a proxy for biological dysregulation—that covaries with the tendency to be more or less emotionally reactive (Eysenck, 1976; Flint, 2004; Gross, Sutton, & Ketelaar, 1998; Larsen & Ketelaar, 1989; Tellegen, 1985). Such tendencies describe emotionality, whereas emotion regulation describes how and why emotions direct or disrupt a range of psychological, physiological, and sociobehavioral processes (cf. Blair, Denham, Kochanoff, & Whipple, 2004).

Temperament and other biological individual differences are important in conferring risk for anxiety pathology. Yet it is important to recognize that the tendency to be more or less emotional is not necessarily problematic, unless one is willing to claim that emotions are somehow problematic. Indeed, the tendency to regulate emotions is only modestly related with baseline individual difference domains such as neuroticism (e.g., $r = .03$; see Gross & John, 2003). Such weak relations suggest that the tendency to suppress, and to engage in experiential avoidance more generally, does not occur simply because persons experience more negative affect or negative emotions that need to be regulated. Estimates of the additive and nonadditive heritability of neuroticism are low and comparable to other complex human traits (27%–31% and 14%–17%, respectively; see Flint, 2004, for a review). Nonetheless, it remains to be seen whether temperamental factors (e.g., neuroticism) interface with (a) contingencies that help establish less functional forms of emotion regulation (e.g., rigid use of avoidance-oriented coping strategies; cf. Leen-Feldner, Zvolensky, Feldner, & Lejuez, 2004) and (b) concomitant strong approach contingencies that may make emotion and its regulation problematic.

Evidence Supporting Experiential Avoidance as a Toxic Diathesis

To show that emotional avoidance functions as a behavioral diathesis and risk factor for anxiety-related pathology, it is important to demonstrate that this predisposition functions to exacerbate aversive emotional responding in individuals with no known history of psychopathology. Consistent with this view, our lab has shown that greater predispositions toward emotional avoidance (as assessed using the Acceptance and Action Questionnaire; Hayes et al., 2004), including the deliberate application of instructed emotion regulation strategies (i.e., suppression), results in more acute emotional distress but not greater autonomic reactivity (Feldner, Zvolensky, Eifert, & Spira, 2003). This study is important, for it is the first to show that emotional avoidance and emotion regulation strategies potentiate experimentally induced acute episodes of emotional distress using panicogenic inhalations of 20% CO_2-enriched air. Most notably, such effects were shown in healthy individuals with no known psychopathology.

We have since replicated these findings and found that emotional avoidance, but not other psychological risk factors for panic (e.g., anxiety sensitivity), tends to covary with more severe panic response, even in healthy individuals (Karekla, Forsyth, & Kelly, 2004; see also Spira, Zvolensky, Eifert, & Feldner, 2004). After several trials of inhaling CO_2-enriched air, individuals high in experiential avoidance endorsed more panic symptoms, more severe cognitive symptoms, and more fear, panic, and uncontrollability than their less avoidant counterparts. As with all of our previous studies, magnitude of autonomic responses failed to discriminate between groups.

The work discussed here as well as other related studies (e.g., Sloan, 2004) suggest that emotional avoidance may constitute an important psychological diathesis and risk factor for the development, maintenance, and potential exacerbation of anxiety-related problems (for reviews, see Feldner, Zvolensky, & Leen-Feldner, 2004; Hayes et al., 1996). For this reason, emotion regulation has increasingly become a primary treatment target in newer behavior therapies.

Broadband Nonregulatory Strategies: An Example of Experiential Acceptance

There have been efforts to test alternative strategies designed to undo excessive emotion regulation and thus foster greater discrimination and willingness to stay in contact with aversive private experiences without acting on them or because of them. For instance, we compared the effects of an acceptance versus an emotion regulation context on avoidance behavior and reported fear in women high in anxiety sensitivity (Eifert & Heffner, 2003). All women were asked to participate in a CO_2-enriched air challenge procedure that reliably produces physiological sensations similar to those experienced by people during panic attacks (Forsyth & Eifert, 1998). Prior to the challenge, half of the women were taught how to accept and make space for their reactions, whereas the remaining half was taught a breathing skill to regulate their reactions. Nearly half of those instructed to regulate their fear worried that they would lose control, and quite a few of them (20%) actually did—in fact, they dropped out of the study. In contrast, participants taught to accept their reactions reported less intense fear and fewer catastrophic thoughts and were less avoidant behaviorally (0% dropout rate).

Our results were replicated in a study of the effects of accepting versus suppressing the effects of CO_2 challenge in persons with panic disorder (Levitt, Brown, Orsillo, & Barlow, 2004). Participants were instructed either to accept or to suppress their responses to the CO_2. The acceptance group was significantly less anxious and less avoidant than the suppression or no-instruction control participants. Yet the groups did not differ in terms of self-reported panic symptoms or physiological responses. People in these studies had no choice about experiencing the physical sensations; people cannot choose not to have emotions such as fear and anxiety in such a context, and likewise they may not have such a choice in other fear-conditioning episodes. They can, however, choose to act to regulate fear and anxiety when it occurs or not.

Clinical studies also suggest that attempts to control anxiety may have negative effects. For example, Wegner (1994) found that efforts to control anxiety in the face of ongoing stress tends to exacerbate physiological arousal. Additional work confirms that the tendency to suppress thoughts is strongly related to extent of anxiety, obsessive–compulsive disorder (OCD) complaints, and depression in healthy persons and those with OCD (McLaren & Crowe, 2003). Healthy individuals who suppress personally relevant intrusive thoughts experience more depression, obsessionality, and anxiety compared with persons who tend to accept such thoughts (Marcks & Woods, 2005). Additionally, Craske, Rowe, Lewin, and Noriega-Dimitri (1997) showed that adding diaphragmatic breathing does not increase the effectiveness of interoceptive exposure treatment for panic disorder. In fact, breathing retraining, a form of emotion regulation, can lead to poorer outcomes than treatment without such training (Schmidt et al., 2000).

In a more general way, coping efforts to minimize anxiety may (paradoxically and unintentionally) maintain pathological anxiety and increase the anxiogenic effects of interoceptive stimulation (Craske, Street, & Barlow, 1989). For instance, Spira and colleagues (2004) found that avoidant coping strategies (e.g., denial, substance abuse) predicted more frequent and intense CO_2-induced physical and cognitive panic symptoms than acceptance-based coping strategies. These findings are consistent with studies showing that attempts to avoid aversive private events are ineffective and may be counterproductive (McLaren & Crowe, 2003).

Overall, this work suggests that purposefully trying to control anxious feelings may increase the very anxiety one wants to control (Gross & Levenson, 1997), while increasing the probability of future occurrences of unwanted emotional responses (Hayes et al., 1996, 1999). Worse yet, anxiety suppression and control efforts can also decrease positive emotional experiences (Gross, 2002), resulting in more anxiety, which will likely be followed by more effort to control the anxiety in a self-perpetuating cycle.

FEAR LEARNING IN AN EMOTION REGULATION CONTEXT

As described earlier, fear learning provides an important experiential foundation for stimuli to acquire aversive functions. Verbal processes, in turn, can expand the range of events that may evoke fear and avoidance, following aversive learning. Thus, any point in the emotion generative process could be a target of regulation in a fear-learning context (see Figure 7.1). For instance, persons may act to avoid antecedents that evoke or occasion fearful responding (i.e., CSs); aversive stimuli that may evoke fear (i.e., USs); or contexts that may reliably predict a relation between CSs and the emotion of fear (i.e., CRs). Persons may also act to avoid or escape from the experience of fear itself and accompanying thoughts, sensations, or behaviors.

We propose that emotion regulation strategies may shift fear and fear learning from being a normative process to a disordered process when persons (a) do not accept that they will experience certain emotions, thoughts, memories, or physical sensations they do not like; (b) are unwilling to be in contact with them as they are; (c) take deliberate steps to alter their form, frequency, or circumstances that occasion those experiences; and (d) do so rigidly and inflexibly even at significant personal cost (Hayes et al., 1996). These behavioral predispositions, and the verbal–cognitive processes that guide them, are central to understanding the development and maintenance of anxiety disorders and figure prominently in contemporary behavioral approaches to treatment such as acceptance and commitment therapy, dialectical behavior therapy, functional analytic psychotherapy, integrative behavioral couples therapy, and mindfulness-based cognitive therapy (see Hayes, 2004a, for an overview).

An important element of this model is the idea that rigid emotion regulation (i.e., control, avoidance) may emerge as a consequence of fear learning. Another is that language may transform fear learning into anxiety pathology. The processes that establish and shape emotion regulation may function as important predispositions for fear and fear learning to become problematic. There are at least two ways this could happen. First, verbal processes can expand the range of stimuli relevant to previous (adaptive) learning, including logically related events (e.g., "I was afraid in the mall," "I felt trapped," "I could be trapped in an elevator or an open field or a marriage,"), imagined futures, or fear itself. Second, language can create self-amplifying loops (e.g., rules about how not to think of fearful things, which when followed evoke thinking about fearful things). Language also provides many strong approach contingencies. Thus, persons can follow the same relational repertoire that simultaneously expands fear learning and amplifies it through rule-governed and contingency-based behavioral regulatory processes. Experiential avoidance is a life-constricting behavior because humans cannot avoid their psychological experience of the world while engaging powerful approach contingencies in that world.

This account points to several processes that may turn emotional and psychological pain into suffering. One process is the tendency to self-regulate unpleasant emotions. Another points to the role of language in maintaining such regulation tendencies. Verbal relational learning is additive (Hayes et al., 2001) and thus can function to expand the range of events (a) that evoke fear based on limited learning and (b) for which emotion regulation is applied. These processes bring behavior under aversive control and can turn emotional pain into suffering because successful emotion regulation—itself a form of avoidance—becomes a prerequisite for effective action (i.e., approach).

Often such relations take the form of rules such as, "I can't fly in a plane because I will have a panic attack" or "I don't want to go out because I'm depressed." These examples hint at the kinds of approach–avoidance relations described earlier. Contrast these with "I can fly and may have a panic attack," and "I will go out along with my depression." These examples include only approach–approach contingencies and show how excessive emotion regulation may act to turn fear learning into disordered fear and fear learning. Emotion regulation can be successfully targeted in prevention and intervention efforts when taught flexibly. Fear, fear learning, and approach contingencies are facts of life, however, that need not and often cannot be changed or avoided. Teaching acceptance may be critical in protecting people experiencing fear and anxiety from developing anxiety disorders.

Basic and Applied Implications of an Emotion Regulation Account

This chapter has provided an outline for conceptualizing fear learning in an emotion regulation context. This perspective does not diminish work regarding the nature of fear learning, including work showing how individual differences occurring before, during, and following fear conditioning can potentiate or depotentiate the likelihood, strength, and persistence of fear-learning processes (e.g., Mineka & Zinbarg, 1996). Rather, this view suggests that it is critical to evaluate what people do about fear-learning processes when developing clinically relevant conditioning accounts of anxiety disorders. This section briefly highlights basic and applied implications of an emotion regulation account for fear-conditioning research.

Research Implications

Certain forms of emotion regulation can exacerbate fearful and anxious responding. Thus, a person in a fear-learning experience with a greater tendency toward experiential avoidance ought to (a) be more likely to respond to that experience negatively, (b) show greater efforts to escape from experiential and psychological aspects of that experience, (c) show greater disruptions in ongoing behavior, and consequently (d) act to avoid similar kinds of experiences to a greater degree than individuals who are not so predisposed. This process may increase the likelihood of negative emotional learning and promote resistance to extinction.

Second, conditioning arrangements could be juxtaposed with emotion regulation processes that are selected for (i.e., individual difference) or manipulated directly (e.g., training to suppress, express, accept the antecedents and consequences of fear learning). Regardless of the strategy used, it is important to develop experimental preparations that more closely resemble the kinds of contingencies humans might confront in the natural environment. In the natural environment, for instance, it would be unusual for a CS to appear, then disappear, and then be followed by a US. Yet this is precisely the kind of contingency used in trace and some forms of delay conditioning. Whereas such contingencies yield more reliable conditioning in the lab, in the natural environment the CS and US occur closely together, at times simultaneously, because the CS often delivers the US.

Third, conditioning in language-able humans is far from noncognitive. Verbal–symbolic processes are often embedded with human experience and allow for complex forms of relational responding that cannot be explained by invoking stimulus generalization, higher order conditioning, or mediated generalization. Networks of verbal relations are expansive and contextually situated, as are the functions that transfer through such relations. As networks expand, functions that transfer do not degrade in the same way responding may degrade across a stimulus generalization gradient or through second- or third-order conditioned relations (Hayes et al., 2001). This means that there is probably no such thing as a purely nonverbal conditioning event in verbally able humans, in part because the experience of human emotion is psychological, relational, and verbal. It also means that fear conditioning in humans likely involves a complex interaction of classical and operant (e.g., verbal behavior, emotion regulation) learning processes.

Fourth, ethical constraints and practical considerations have made it difficult to model fearful emotional responding in human conditioning research. For instance, fearful responding in the natural environment is rarely approximated in the laboratory, the exception being studies using panicogenic challenge agents as USs. This must change if we are to develop more ecologically valid models of human fear learning. Also, allowing participants to set the intensity of aversive USs is far different from how fear learning occurs in the natural environment.

Fifth, human fear-learning research tends to occur in relative isolation from competing environmental demands. Participants sit idly and are typically presented with aversive contingencies that have no costs associated with them. In the natural environment, such learning typically occurs in the context of competing approach contingencies and ongoing actions. For instance, a rat will cease bar pressing for food in the presence of a CS that has been reliably paired with shock. Likewise, in the natural environment, most humans will show disruption and narrowing of behavior when afraid. Eventually, however, the rat will return to bar pressing at CS offset, and most humans will also return to doing what was important to them.

Experiential avoidance, by contrast, can result in less flexible behavior, keeping people off track and miserable long after threat has passed. In this context, experiencing anxiety is not merely a bump in the road but is psychologically costly because emotion regulation sets up anxiety as a barrier to be overcome to live a vital life. Persons who engage in experiential avoidance often build their lives around not experiencing fear and anxiety. These actions keep people stuck and are disruptive because they are unnecessary, contextually insensitive, and get in the way of meaningful life activities. That is, approach–avoidance contingencies best characterize problematic experiences of fear and fear learning in the natural environment.

Human fear-learning research needs to attend to competing approach–avoidance contingencies, rather than just aversive ones. Such work may include study of how emotion regulation potentiates or depotentiates fear learning and how the consequences of fear learning and its regulation disrupt meaningful goal-directed actions. Although a challenge, modeling such contingencies in the laboratory with humans must be done. The same is true of work evaluating how experiential avoidance functions as a predisposition for, and how it may emerge as a consequence of, fear learning. Numerous emotion regulatory processes could be studied, either alone or in combination with other behavioral processes. Knowing that such regulatory tendencies account for much human suffering and are salient targets for treatment are two good reasons that such work ought to make its way into fear-conditioning research. This view is making its way into mainstream cognitive–behavioral therapies for anxiety disorders, resulting in a rethinking of the symptom-focused mastery and control agenda (Barlow et al., 2004).

Clinical Implications

Lastly, the literature on emotion regulation and experiential avoidance suggests clinical strategies that target emotion regulation and the verbal processes supporting it (e.g., Eifert & Forsyth, 2005; Hayes et al., 1999). For instance, experiential exercises based on metaphor and paradox may be used to teach clients how to experience anxious thoughts and feelings from a detached, observer perspective (e.g., noticing thoughts as thoughts) with the aim of fostering greater experiential openness, psychological flexibility, and less rule-governed behavior. By weakening verbally regulated avoidance contingencies that might set up approach–avoidance conflicts in the natural environment, an acceptance posture may help clients to transform problematic fear and anxiety into just fear and anxiety. If true, this would suggest that interventions that defuse regulation may result in more approach–approach relations in a client's natural environment and a broader range of functioning. It also suggests that therapists should attend to approach–avoidance contingencies, not simply aversive or avoidance contingencies (for a treatment guide, see Eifert & Forsyth, 2005).

The extant literature suggests that the verbal–relational properties entailed in language and emotion regulation are additive, expansive, and dependent on context (Hayes et al., 2001). Also, it is becoming increasingly clear that contextual factors are important in fear renewal and relapse (see chaps. 9, 10, and 11, this volume). Language processes serve as an important context that may function to occasion fear relapse and renewal. For instance, suppose a person has learned that panic attacks, elevators, and avoidance belong in the same relational class. These relations are evoked in the context of going to work (approach contingency) and other activities that involve closed spaces. Interoceptive and exteroceptive exposure may be successful in altering such relations, including altering the functions of other events that might be part of this network. Yet a broad transformation across the network may be incomplete, meaning that unchecked elements of the network may function to reactivate previously altered relations, including emotion regulation itself. For example, suppose this person later finds herself in a relationship and feels "trapped." This feeling may evoke panic and avoidance; because both were previously related to closed spaces, this feeling may evoke renewal of fear to elevators and other closed spaces. Unfortunately, we know little about how verbal processes function in exposure therapy and fear renewal. Yet research on verbal processes suggests that such outcomes are likely and may be difficult to prevent (Hayes et al., 2001). This highlights why disrupting emotion regulation may be critical, in part, because it helps hold together and make toxic aversive emotional states in the context of competing environmental demands.

CONCLUSION

The success of behavior therapy is based in large part on the principle of conducting clinical science with an eye on practical utility. The utility of fear-conditioning accounts of anxiety-related suffering is a good news–bad news story. The good news is that conditioning research and theory has helped elucidate mechanisms and processes that underlie behavioral accounts of the origins, maintenance, and amelioration of anxiety disorders. The bad news is that early behavior therapists represented classical conditioning and problematic psychological content as sufficient models for the development and maintenance of anxiety disorders. This led to the notion that anxiety-related suffering is about excessive physiological responding or other psychological content, including avoidance.

This chapter introduced the idea that fear and its conditioned basis are not disordered processes per se but become so when humans act on them and because of them so as to alter their form, frequency, or occurrence. When people respond to fear and fear learning so as not to experience them and devote increasingly large amounts of time and energy to that goal, one has the seeds of a problem with fear and fear learning. Without emotion regulation, under most circumstances, fear learning can be potentiated or depotentiated by numerous individual difference factors (Mineka & Zinbarg, 1996) in the same way that appetitive and other forms of learning (operant conditioning) can be potentiated or depotentiated by factors occurring before, during, and following learning. Potentiated fear learning may be unpleasant and temporarily disrupt behavior, yet it would not necessarily yield an anxiety disorder unless fear conditioning itself is viewed as a problem.

By contrast, rigid and excessive efforts to down-regulate fearful respond-ing can result in behavioral impairment because the very agenda of success-ful down-regulation becomes a prerequisite for effective action. Although the regulation of anxiety and fear may result in temporary relief (e.g., anxiety reduction through negative reinforcement), the cumulative effect of such actions over time is life constriction and long-term suffering. As outlined in this chapter, emotion regulatory actions, when inflexibly applied, can take over a person's life and turn the experience of fear and the effects of fear learning into an emotional experience that is a problem, not simply a painful experience. The emerging consensus is that such regulation (a) is learned and can be learned independently of fear-conditioning experiences (e.g., as a generalized operant), (b) tends to make aversive emotions more intense and more likely to occur ("if you don't want it, you've got it"), and (c) gets in the way of meaningful life activities. Functional impairment, therefore, is viewed as a consequence of inflexible emotion regulation efforts. These and other outcomes of anxiety regulation, when coupled with powerful approach con-tingencies, may function as predisposing and maintaining factors for anxiety pathology.

III

EXTINCTION, RENEWAL, AND REINSTATEMENT OF FEAR

8

ANATOMICAL, MOLECULAR, AND CELLULAR SUBSTRATES OF FEAR EXTINCTION

MARK BARAD

BEHAVIORAL ANALYSIS OF FEAR AND EXTINCTION

Extinction, the progressive reduction in the response to a feared stimulus when it is repeatedly presented without any adverse consequence, is a crucial model of behavior therapy for human anxiety disorders. Much progress has been made toward understanding the anatomical and physiological basis of fear and its extinction through studies in rodent models. This chapter reviews the considerable neurobiological literature of extinction. Although some background in neuropsychology or neuroscience may be necessary to grasp fully the many technical aspects of this review, even without such a background, readers can gain a solid foundation by reading the introductory paragraphs of each section and trusting that the data in the following paragraphs support the syntheses presented.

As described in some detail in previous chapters, much fear is learned through Pavlovian, or classical, conditioning; elements in the environment of an aversive experience become associated with that unpleasantness and thereby elicit much of the defensive response to the aversive experience itself. Such fear conditioning has long served as a model for the pathogenesis of human anxiety (Eysenck, 1979; Watson & Rayner, 1920; Wolpe & Rowan, 1988). In experimental classical conditioning, an initially neutral stimulus, called the conditioned stimulus (CS), elicits a conditioned fear response (CR), after temporal pairing with an intrinsically aversive stimulus, such as a shock, called the unconditioned stimulus (US). Robust fear conditioning can be generated with even a single such pairing and can persist for months (Fanselow, 1990). After CS–US pairing, the CS comes to elicit a coordinated fear response that includes physiological and behavioral responses; increases in heart rate and blood pressure; changes in respiration, avoidance, potentiation of the startle response, and freezing (remaining motionless except for breathing; Blanchard & Blanchard, 1969; Bolles & Fanselow, 1980; M. Davis, 1992a; LeDoux, 2000). Most data on fear in rodents come from behavioral measures because of their noninvasive nature and the difficulty and expense of performing invasive physiological monitoring.

Extinction of fear also uses a Pavlovian model; the feared stimulus is repeatedly presented in the absence of adverse consequences. The result of such a procedure is the progressive reduction of the fear response. The initial work on the psychology of fear extinction began in the 1920s and has accelerated enormously, particularly in the past 5 years. This chapter first explains the support for the contention that extinction is new inhibitory learning and not erasure. Next, it reviews data implicating basolateral amygdala, infralimbic prefrontal cortex, and hippocampus in the acquisition and expression of fear extinction learning. Next, it reviews a variety of drug targets in extinction learning. These experiments have led to identification of drugs that accelerate extinction and therefore may become important adjuncts to facilitate the speed and efficacy of behavior therapy of human anxiety disorders. The chapter ends by presenting a testable model for the learning and expression of extinction within simple cellular circuits in the amygdala.

Extinction Is New Learning, Not Erasure of the Original Memory

Extinction has several meanings. First, it refers to presenting the CS repeatedly after conditioning in the absence of the US. Second, it refers to the result of that procedure: a progressive weakening of the CR. Finally, it describes the presumptive learning process underlying that weakening, which is hypothesized to be a form of learned inhibition. Pavlov made the original observation that extinction effectively reduced the CR in his experiments with conditioned salivation in dogs (Pavlov, 1927). He also concluded that extinction resulted from new inhibitory learning rather than erasure of the original conditioned association. Evidence for the preservation of the original fear learning is reviewed extensively elsewhere in this book, but in outline it consists of the observation that even after fear extinction, the original fear can return without further training (CS–US pairing) by a variety of experimental manipulations. For example, even completely extinguished fear can return spontaneously after the passage of time (Baum, 1988) or be "reinstated" by US presentations (Rescorla & Heth, 1975) or other stressful circumstances. Conditioned fear can be "renewed" when the CS is presented in a context different from that in which extinction took place (Bouton & King, 1983). Although some evidence has emerged to challenge this view (Lin, Lee, & Gean, 2003; Lin, Yeh, Leu, et al., 2003; Lin, Yeh, Lu, & Gean, 2003), the preponderance of evidence continues to support it, and it remains the consensus that extinction is new inhibitory learning.

Stages of Extinction Learning

Like other learning, extinction learning has identifiable stages that may involve separate anatomical and cellular mechanisms and alterations of synaptic strength. Learning has been thoroughly studied in behavioral models of excitatory conditioning, usually involving spatial learning or fear acquisition learning. In both types of protocols, experiments have linked learning to changes in synaptic strength. Increases and decreases in synaptic strength can be modeled, in turn, using artificial protocols of synaptic stimulation *in vivo* and *in vitro* in slices of brain and are termed *long-term potentiation* (LTP) and *long-term depression* (LTD). Much research demonstrates that the same molecules necessary for generating these models of synaptic change are equally necessary for generating behavioral learning (Blair, Schafe, Bauer, Rodrigues, & LeDoux, 2001; Morris et al., 2003). Furthermore, the stages of synaptic plasticity also map on the stages of behavioral learning. In general, these stages can be separated into the induction, consolidation, and expression (or retrieval) stages (Morris et al., 2003).

Induction is the first stage of learning, when synaptic and behavioral changes are initiated in response to environmental information. Induction seems to depend on calcium entry into cells in response to relevant stimuli. In many forms of learning, including fear conditioning, calcium must enter through the N-methyl-D-aspartate (NMDA) type of glutamate receptor (NMDAr) for induction, although, as discussed subsequently, this may not be true for extinction learning. *Consolidation* is the second stage of learning, when early reversible behavioral and synaptic changes become permanent. Evidence for consolidation came first from experiments demonstrating that over time, new memories became resistant to disruption by electroconvulsive stimulation. Since then, multiple experiments have elucidated a variety of mechanisms involved in consolidation, including modulatory neurotransmission; second messengers within the cell; translation (the synthesis of new proteins); and transcription (the synthesis of new messenger RNAs from DNA). *Expression* describes the demonstration of a memory by the behavioral response to a cue. The ability to express a response depends on prior learning stages but often not on the same molecules involved in those stages.

For example, induction and expression of spatial memory depend on different classes of glutamate receptors (Massicotte & Baudry, 2004).

Glutamate, the major excitatory neurotransmitter in the brain, has two classes of receptors that allow ion fluxes when activated. The NMDA type requires two simultaneous signals to open: glutamate and depolarization of the postsynaptic cell. Thus, it is an ideal molecule to generate associative learning and does so by allowing calcium into the cell, in which it initiates a variety of changes that alter the strength of the stimulated synapse. Consistent with this, NMDA receptor antagonists block the induction of spatial learning. In response to the calcium influx, AMPA (alpha-Amino-3-hydroxy-5-methyl-4-isoxazole propionic acid) type glutamate receptors increase at the synapse, permitting greater synaptic transmission, which is believed to mediate behavioral memory (Massicotte & Baudry, 2004).

Extinction Training Evokes Opposing Responses to the Conditioned Stimulus

Behavioral data indicate that extinction differs from the best studied forms of learning. Extinction requires more trials than acquisition learning and is more efficient with temporally massed than with temporally spaced presentations in mice. During extinction training, CS-alone presentations appear to evoke two responses: "incubation," which tends to increase responding to the CS, and "extinction," which weakens it. It appears that massed training helps initiate extinction by overcoming the incubation response. This leads to the hypothesis that incubation acts to constrain extinction until the CS presentations clearly violate the animals' "expectation" of US occurrence.

Not only is extinction more reversible than other forms of learning by phenomena such as reinstatement and renewal, but also its induction appears to follow an unusual learning rule that suggests two opposing mechanisms may be involved. A widely replicated learning rule is that temporally spaced training trials result in stronger learning than temporally massed trials (Barela, 1999; Carew & Kandel, 1973; Ebbinghaus, 1885/1913; Fanselow, DeCola, & Young, 1993; Fanselow & Tighe, 1988; Freudenthal et al., 1998; Gibbon, 1977; Humphreys, 1940; Jenkins, Barnes, & Barrera, 1981; Josselyn et al., 2001; Kogan et al., 1997; Scharf et al., 2002; Terrace, Gibbon, Farrell, & Baldock, 1975; Tully, Preat, Boynton, & Del Vecchio, 1994). Nevertheless, this does not seem to be the case for extinction learning.

Experiments in our laboratory have shown that extinction learning in mice is less effective for temporally spaced than for massed CS presentations. Mice were fear conditioned with footshock as the US. A day later, we presented 20 CSs alone at different intervals using behavioral freezing as an index of fear. Whereas CS presentations separated by 6 seconds or 60 seconds yield both short- and long-term extinction of fear, presentations with intertrial intervals of 10 minutes or more generate neither short- nor long-term extinction. Although these findings might suggest that massed training is better than spaced for extinction, the situation is more complicated. For example, when extinction CS presentations are spaced 20 minutes apart, freezing increases. This increase does not carry over to the test of fear on the next day, but no extinction learning occurs. This strengthening or "incubation" mechanism has been observed by others (Cain, Blouin, & Barad, 2003; Rohrbaugh & Riccio, 1970; Silvestri, Rohrbaugh, & Riccio, 1970), but not consistently. This observation led us to hypothesize that unpaired CS presentations can elicit two learning mechanisms: a weakening mechanism of extinction learning and a mechanism that tends to strengthen the memory, acting as a brake on extinction learning. The incubation process may be related to reconsolidation, in which memories reactivated by CS presentation require additional protein-synthesis-dependent consolidation to avoid erasure (Nader, Schafe, & LeDoux, 2000; Suzuki et al., 2004). We further hypothesize that massing facilitates extinction in mice because it overcomes the strengthening effect. As one test of this hypothesis, we used spaced blocks of massed CS presentations, which proved significantly more effective in generating extinction learning than a single massed block of the same total number of CSs (Cain, Blouin, & Barad, 2003).

Trial spacing effects in extinction remains an area of study with many inconsistent results (see chap. 9, this volume). Such inconsistency suggests that the specifics of protocol or preparation may play important roles in the outcome of extinction procedures. For example, there may be differences in rules governing fear extinction compared with appetitive extinction. It is easy to imagine the evolutionary consequences of losing a fear response prematurely being more severe than those of losing a little bit of food. Important species differences may exist as well. For instance, it generally requires more CS presentations to extinguish fear in a mouse than in a rat. Perhaps this is because mice have more predators. Therefore, trial spacing in extinction may translate poorly from any one animal model to humans. The phenomenology of fear extinction in mice points to an important concept deserving of further elucidation: the concept of expectation. Animals extinguish when CSs are not paired with USs, that is, when the expectation of shock is violated. Yet when and how does the animal (or human) "know" that the expectation has been violated? One piece of information may be encoded in the temporal spacing of CS presentations.

The following sections outline the neural basis of extinction learning, beginning with studies of the anatomical basis of fear extinction learning in the brain and followed by a summary of data from pharmacological and genetic studies. Local infusion of pharmacological agents has significantly enhanced our understanding of the contributions that different areas make to fear extinction and to the molecular bases of extinction. Notably, extinction affects many learned behaviors, and the neural basis of extinction of these different behaviors may well differ both in anatomical location and in molecular mechanism from fear aquisition. After covering the anatomical and physiological basis of fear extinction, the chapter concludes with potential clinical implications and applications of the growing understanding of the neural basis of fear extinction.

THE ANATOMICAL BASIS OF FEAR EXTINCTION LEARNING

Three anatomical areas are strongly implicated in the extinction of conditioned fear. The strongest data on this subject indicate that the basolateral amygdala (BLA) plays a crucial role in extinction learning, just as it does in fear learning itself. The colocalization of fear learning and extinction learning suggests that local circuits play a crucial role in fear extinction. Distinct structures also play a role in extinction, however. Infralimbic prefrontal cortex provides crucial modulatory input during extinction learning, the nature of which remains to be completely defined. It is not apparent that the hippocampus plays an essential role in the learning of extinction itself, but it clearly provides important information permissive for the expression of extinction in appropriate contexts.

Amygdala

The amygdala appears to be the central anatomical location for processing fearful stimuli into fearful emotions and behaviors. It contains many identified nuclei, of which the BLA complex (comprising lateral, basolateral, and basal nuclei) appears to process incoming sensory stimuli. The output of these nuclei goes to the central nucleus of the amygdala, which, in turn, orchestrates the various behaviors that characterize fearful responding (e.g., changes in heart rate, blood pressure, startle, and freezing; M. Davis, 1992b; LeDoux, 1993). Because the amygdala is necessary for the expression of conditioned fear and it is not possible to study extinction of fear that is no longer expressed, amygdala lesion and inactivation studies are not useful for studying fear extinction. Instead, data implicating the amygdala in extinction of conditioned fear come from methods that do not interfere with the expression of conditioned fear: stereotaxic infusions of drugs into the amygdala or from electrophysiological studies.

In vivo electrophysiological data implicate the lateral amygdala in acquisition and extinction of conditioned fear. Extracellular responses in the amygdala increase in slope and amplitude during fear acquisition and decrease during extinction (Rogan, Staubli, & LeDoux, 1997). Similarly, increased firing early after a CS increases during fear conditioning and disappears during extinction (Quirk et al., 1995). These results demonstrate that lateral amygdala cells report extinction by decreased responses, but they cannot localize the mechanism of that decrease, which could be occurring either in the responding lateral amygdala cells themselves or in cells that drive their responses.

Data derived from the stereotaxic infusion of drugs into the amygdala also provide evidence that the mechanisms interfered with are occurring in the amygdala; these experiments have less anatomical specificity than electrophysiological experiments, however. Because drugs track back along the infusion cannula and also diffuse in unpredictable ways, it is difficult to claim localization to the small individual amygdaloid nuclei, and such results are reported by the overall target of infusion, usually the BLA. Many drug infusion experiments have implicated BLA in extinction because infusions in the BLA of the NMDA receptor inhibitor 2-amino-5-phosphonovalerate (APV) prevent extinction (Falls, Miserendino, & Davis, 1992): the mitogen-activated protein (MAP) kinase (MEK) inhibitors PD98059 (Lu, Walker, & Davis, 2001) and U0126 (Lin, Yeh, Lu, et al., 2003); the PI3 kinase inhibitor wortmannin (Lin, Yeh, Lu, et al., 2003); the protein synthesis inhibitor anisomycin (Lin, Yeh, Lu, et al., 2003), the calcineurin inhibitors FK506 and cyclosporin A (Lin, Yeh, Lu, et al., 2003) and the L-type voltage-gated calcium channel (LVGCC) antagonist; nimodipine (Cain, Jami, Ponnusamy, & Barad, 2005). Conversely, extinction can be facilitated by infusions of the NMDA receptor agonist d-cycloserine (Walker, Ressler, Lu, & Davis, 2002) or the LVGCC agonist BayK8644 into the BLA (Cain et al., 2005). Thus abundant evidence indicates that the BLA plays an essential role in the learning of extinction.

Infralimbic Prefrontal Cortex

A series of experiments has demonstrated an important role for infralimbic prefrontal cortex (ILPFC) in extinction learning. Early conflicting reports indicated that lesions of medial prefrontal cortex prevented extinction of conditioned fear (Morgan, Romanski, & LeDoux, 1993) or had no effect (Gewirtz, Falls, & Davis, 1997). Two important findings clarified the role of infralimbic prefrontal cortex: First, lesions that spared the caudal part of the infralimbic cortex had no effect on extinction; second, even properly placed lesions did not affect extinction acutely but had an effect on the retention of that extinction at 24 hours (Quirk, Russo, Barron, & Lebron, 2000). Thus, the ILPFC seems to be particularly important for the consolidated memory of extinction. Consistent with this interpretation, in vivo recordings of thalamomedial prefrontal responses show depression during extinction training, followed by potentiation 1 day later (Herry & Garcia, 2002); ILPFC cell firing shows no response to CS presentations during extinction but increases in response to CS presentations on the day after extinction (Milad & Quirk, 2002); and, most dramatically, brief electrical stimulation of the ILPFC during unextinguished CS presentations in a pattern designed to mimic naturally occurring responses after extinction decreased fear responses and accelerated extinction (Milad & Quirk, 2002). Consistent with an important role for the prefrontal cortex in extinction learning, dopamine depletion in the prefrontal cortex by 6-hydroxy dopamine (Fernandez Espejo, 2003) and antagonism of protein synthesis by anisomycin (Santini, Ge, Ren, Pena de Ortiz, & Quirk, 2004) both block extinction. Thus, ample evidence suggests that the medial prefrontal cortex makes a substantial contribution to extinction learning. The prefrontal contribution to extinction is not a necessity, however; with enough CS presentations, extinction is delayed but still occurs in ILPFC-lesioned animals (Lebron, Milad, & Quirk, 2004).

Hippocampus

Although no evidence implicates the hippocampus in cue fear extinction learning, there are data indicating that it plays an important role in extinction of context fear (Fischer, Sananbenesi, Schrick, Spiess, & Radulovic, 2004; Vianna, Szapiro, McGaugh, Medina, & Izquierdo, 2001). It is not clear, however, how specific this is to extinction learning itself and how important it is to learning new information about context (Phillips & LeDoux, 1992) because this structure plays an important role in learning about complex configural information, including context information. What is clearer is that the hippocampus is essential for providing much of the information underlying the context dependence of cue fear extinction. Context dependence is described at length in chapter 9 of this volume, in which the authors describe renewal, in which fear extinguished in one context returns, or is "renewed," when the CS is presented in a context different from that of extinction (Bouton & King, 1983).

Permanent lesions of the fornix or of the hippocampus itself abolish reinstatement of fear by presentations of the US alone, but the same lesions have no effect on context-dependent renewal effects (Frohardt, Guarraci, & Bouton, 2000; A. Wilson, Brooks, & Bouton, 1995). Reversible inactivation of the dorsal hippocampus using muscimol, an agonist of inhibitory $GABA_A$ receptors, prevents context-dependent renewal, however (Corcoran & Maren, 2001). It is unclear why these results are inconsistent, but inactivation during the expression of extinction alone is a superior paradigm because it eliminates problems associated with the effect of lesions on fear conditioning and extinction, which may allow the brain to recruit other systems to use discrete cues instead of context in these protocols.

NEUROTRANSMITTERS, RECEPTORS, CHANNELS, AND INTRACELLULAR MOLECULES

This section presents data on the cell biological mechanisms of extinction. Much of the data already cited to support localization of extinction learning also indicate the involvement of specific cellular mechanisms. In addition to infusion experiments, systemic drug treatments provide data supporting a variety of cellular mechanisms. Consistent with the idea that extinction is a form of new inhibitory learning rather than erasure, fear extinction shares many molecular mechanisms with other forms of learning, such as the NMDA receptors, second messengers (intracellular signaling molecules), and protein synthesis. In addition, unlike fear acquisition, fear extinction is dependent on an unusual mechanism for learning-related calcium entry, LVGCCs, and on changes in inhibitory, γ-aminobutyric acid (GABA) transmission through $GABA_A$ receptors. There has also been a rapid elucidation of the roles of modulatory neurotransmitter systems in the acquisition, consolidation, and expression of extinction, implicating noradrenaline, dopamine, endocannibinoids, and acetylcholine in aspects of the acquisition, consolidation, or expression of extinction learning. These discoveries may soon yield new medications to use as adjuncts to exposure-based therapies for human anxiety disorders.

Channels

NMDA Receptors

An abundance of evidence demonstrates that calcium entry into neurons at postsynaptic sites is crucial to the synaptic plasticity that underlies learning (Stanton, 1996). One of the strongest molecular indications that extinction is a form of learning has been its dependence on the NMDA type of glutamate receptor, like so many other forms of associative learning, including fear conditioning itself (Kim, DeCola, Landeira-Fernandez, & Fanselow, 1991; Miserendino et al., 1990). The NMDA receptor is a calcium channel that requires two simultaneous signals to open, the release of glutamate from presynaptic terminals and the depolarization of the postsynaptic cell, which relieves a magnesium-mediated blockade of the channel pore. Pharmacological evidence for extinction's dependence on the NMDA receptor comes from both infusion of the NMDA receptor antagonist APV directly into the amygdala (Falls et al., 1992) and from systemic treatments with NMDA receptor antagonists including MK-801 (Baker & Azorlosa, 1996) and 3-(R)-2-carboxypiperazin-4-propyl-1-phosphonic acid (CPP; Santini, Muller, & Quirk, 2001). All of these treatments prevent long-term extinction learning. Consistent with these results, a transgenic mouse engineered to overexpress the NMDAR2b subunit, which shows increased NMDA-receptor-dependent signaling, also shows improved learning of both fear acquisition and fear extinction (Tang et al., 1999).

It is interesting that NMDA receptor activity may not be essential for the induction of fear extinction but only for its consolidation. Extinction induction proceeds identically after systemic injections of the NMDA antagonist CPP or of a vehicle (the liquid used to dissolve the active drug) alone (Santini et al., 2001). No persistent extinction is present 24 hours later in those animals treated with CPP during extinction, however, although substantial extinction remains in vehicle-treated animals.

A dramatic demonstration of the importance of NMDA receptor activity in consolidated extinction learning comes from the effect of d-cycloserine, an agonist at the modulatory glycine-binding site on the NR1 subunit of the NMDA receptor (Bowery, 1987; Scatton, 1993). This drug significantly accelerates the extinction of fear-potentiated startle in rats when given either systemically or directly into the BLA (Ledgerwood, Richardson, & Cranney, 2003, 2004; Walker et al., 2002). A pilot clinical trial has already shown that treatment with d-cycloserine in combination with a virtual-reality behavior therapy regime accelerates desensitization of fear of heights in subjects with acrophobia (Ressler et al., 2004) Thus, NMDA receptor activity is both necessary and sufficient for the consolidation of extinction memory, although it does not mediate the induction of extinction learning.

LVGCCs

LVGCCs may be crucial to the induction of fear extinction. Systemic injections of LVGCC antagonists nifedipine and nimodipine block extinction both during induction and on long-term retention testing 24 hours later (Cain, Blouin, & Barad, 2002; Lin, Lee, et al., 2003; Suzuki et al., 2004). More recently, we have shown that nimodipine infused directly into the BLA also prevents both induction and long-term retention of extinction, suggesting that LVGCCs s act in the amygdala during extinction induction (Cain et al., 2005). These data support the claim that the amygdala contributes essential plasticity (cellular or synaptic) to extinction learning, and they demonstrate an essential role for LVGCCs in the earliest stages of extinction learning.

In summary, calcium entry is crucial in both the acquisition and the consolidation of extinction learning. It appears that entry through LVGCCs is particularly important during the induction stage of extinction learning, whereas NMDA receptors are crucial for extinction consolidation.

$GABA_A$

GABA is the predominant inhibitory neurotransmitter in the adult brain. Benzodiazepines act as agonists at an auxiliary site of the $GABA_A$ receptor and are frequently used to treat symptoms of anxiety in humans. Inhibitory learning, including extinction, does not have to depend on inhibitory neurotransmission, but there is evidence that benzodiazepines and other $GABA_A$ agents have substantial effects on the learning and expression of extinction. For example, infusing the $GABA_A$ antagonist picrotoxin into the BLA immediately after extinction of conditioned fear increased the amount of extinction measured drug free 1 day later (McGaugh, Castellano, & Brioni, 1990). Conversely, injecting rats with $GABA_A$ agonists before entry into a context prevented extinction of context fear (Bouton, Kenney, & Rosengard, 1990). Together, these findings suggest that GABA acting at $GABA_A$ receptors contributes to extinction learning. An alternative explanation for the second set of results is state-dependent learning (Overton & Winter, 1974). When rats were treated with the drug during extinction training and then tested drug free, they showed substantial freezing (i.e., blockade of extinction), but when treated with the drug both before extinction and before testing, they demonstrated even better extinction than animals extinguished after vehicle injections (Bouton et al., 1990). This suggests that extinction learning was not prevented by the presence of benzodiazepines. Instead, extinction learning occurred but could only be expressed in the presence of the internal context provided by the drug injection.

Evidence that $GABA_A$ receptors play a role in the expression of extinction is more compelling. As noted, rats treated with a benzodiazepine before both extinction training and testing for extinction (1 day later) showed more extinction than animals trained with a vehicle and tested with either drug or vehicle (Bouton et al., 1990). These data weakly suggest that a $GABA_A$ agonist can improve the expression of extinction. In a stronger demonstration, injection of a partial inverse agonist of $GABA_A$ receptors, FG7142, before the final test of extinction of freezing in rats blocked the expression of extinction of cue and context fear (J. A. Harris & Westbrook, 1998). A limitation of this experiment is that nonextinguished control rats were freezing near ceiling, which might have obscured any general effect of FG7142 in increasing freezing independently of extinction. To control for this, the experiment was replicated and extended (Jami & Barad, 2005). Mice were fear conditioned with different levels of footshock, either moderately high (0.7 mA) or low (0.4 mA). Groups that had the CS paired with high shock were extinguished by 20 CS presentations in a novel context, and those that had the CS paired with low shock spent equal time in the novel context without CS presentations. Thus, all groups of mice had identical freezing to the CS, although only some had been extinguished. Subgroups of both groups were injected with vehicle or increasing doses of FG7142 before testing with three CS presentations. Animals treated with vehicle showed equal freezing. FG7142 caused a dose-dependent reversal of extinction in the extinguished group without increasing freezing in nonextinguished animals trained with low shock. These results indicate that the increase in freezing caused by FG7142 was specific to extinction and not to a general effect on the freezing response. This experiment was repeated using infusion of a $GABA_A$ antagonist picrotoxin directly into the BLA of mice. Again, in a dose-dependent fashion, picrotoxin blocked extinction expression without affecting nonextinguished fear. These data indicate that extinction expression is strongly dependent on specific increases in $GABA_A$ neurotransmission in BLA. Consistent with these results, $GABA_A$ binding sites increase in the lateral amygdala after fear extinction in rats (Chhatwal, Myers, Ressler,

& Davis, 2005). These results together support the hypothesis that inhibitory learning, at least in the case of extinction, is, in fact, mediated by inhibitory neurotransmission.

Modulatory Neurotransmission

A variety of modulatory neurotransmitters and their receptors play important roles in extinction, particularly in its consolidation and expression. The adrenergic, dopaminergic, and cannabinoidergic systems all appear to act to modulate extinction learning, rather than being essential for it because enough CS presentations can overcome their influence on extinction memory. The dopaminergic system appears exclusively to affect the consolidation phase of extinction learning, whereas the adrenergic and cannabinoidergic systems show effects during the acquisition phase as well. In addition, muscarinic acetylcholine neurotransmission appears to be essential for the expression of extinction learning.

Noradrenergic Neurotransmission

The noradrenergic system was one of the first modulatory neurotransmitter systems implicated in extinction learning (Mason, 1983). Lesions of the locus coeruleus and of the dorsal noradrenergic bundle cause substantial (95%) depletion of noradrenaline in the forebrain. Mason and his colleagues demonstrated that such lesions have no effect on the acquisition or retention of a variety of tasks, including those motivated by fear. Extinction of these tasks is substantially slowed in lesioned animals, however, suggesting that noradrenergic neurotransmission is essential for extinction learning to take place.

Studies using systemic injections of drugs that affect noradrenergic neurotransmission have partially confirmed and extended the conclusions of the earlier lesion studies. Yohimbine, an alpha2 adrenergic antagonist, accelerates extinction of cue and context conditioned fear in mice by about sixfold (Cain, Blouin, & Barad, 2004). Yohimbine-treated mice showed significant extinction during spaced exposures, whereas those treated with propranolol showed significant day-to-day incubation, or increases in fear (Cain et al., 2004). Propranolol, an antagonist of postsynaptic beta receptors that reduces noradrenergic activation of cells that carry these receptors, shows only the barest trend toward slowing extinction in mice (Cain et al., 2004). In fear extinction of mice, the role of the noradrenergic system is modulatory. When enough CSs are presented during extinction training, conditioned fear extinguishes identically in mice treated with vehicle, yohimbine, or with propranolol (Cain et al., 2004). It is interesting that yohimbine by itself has well-known anxiogenic effects in human patients. It induces panic attacks in those with panic disorder and both panic attacks and flashbacks in patients with posttraumatic stress disorder (Charney, Woods, Krystal, Nagy, & Heninger, 1992; Southwick et al., 1993).

Despite having little effect on slowing extinction, propranolol did have an effect on the response to spaced CS presentations during extinction training (Cain et al., 2004). As described earlier, temporally spaced CS presentations yield acute increases in fear during CS-only exposures and result in no extinction at all the next day (Cain et al., 2004). Yohimbine-treated mice showed significant extinction during spaced exposures, however, whereas those treated with propranolol showed significant day-to-day incubation, or increases in fear (Cain et al., 2004). These results appear to support the hypothesis that CS-alone presentations evoke both a response-weakening mechanism and a response-strengthening mechanism that acts to prevent extinction learning. Both beta-adrenergic neurotransmission and massing of CS presentations help to overcome an inhibitory constraint on extinction learning. Adrenergic transmission may act to weaken or strengthen this inhibitory mechanism. More practically, a drug like yohimbine might serve as a useful pharmacological adjunct to accelerate behavior therapy of human anxiety disorders, even though by itself, it is anxiogenic.

Dopaminergic Neurotransmission

A number of experiments have implicated dopaminergic neurotransmission in extinction. Cocaine, amphetamine, and the dopamine D1 agonist SKF 38393 all block extinction of fear-potentiated startle when injected before CS presentations to induce extinction learning (Borowski & Kokkinidis, 1998; Willick & Kokkinidis, 1995). Noncontingent administration of cocaine or SKF 38393 also reversed extinction of fear, however, suggesting that it was acting as a reinstating stimulus and leaving the direct effects of D1 receptors on extinction learning itself unclear (Borowski & Kokkinidis, 1998). Consistent with a role in promoting, rather than blocking, extinction learning, dopamine depletion in the prefrontal cortex using 6-hydoxydopamine infusion or genetic knockout of the D1 receptor both delay extinction of conditioned contextual fear, without affecting either its acquisition or expression (El-Ghundi, O'Dowd, & George, 2001; Fernandez Espejo, 2003). These data implicate D1 activity in promoting the extinction of fear but not its acquisition.

However, the dopamine D2 agonist quinpirole prevents extinction of cue-conditioned fear in rats (Nader & LeDoux, 1999), again without affecting acquisition or expression of conditioned fear itself. These authors argued that it did so by interfering with the ability to recall the CS–US association, perhaps reducing D1-dependent neurotransmission. On the basis of these results, the D2 antagonists, sulpiride and quinpirole, were tested in massed and spaced extinction protocols (Ponnusamy, Nissim, & Barad, 2005). Sulpiride potentiated extinction in both protocols, but the role of D2 receptor activity in inhibiting extinction was shown to be only modulatory because the blockade of extinction by quinpirole (as well as its facilitation by sulpiride) disappeared with enough CS presentations.

Cholinergic Neurotransmission

Several investigators argue that muscarinic acetylcholine receptors are important for extinction learning (Prado-Alcala, Haiek, Rivas, Roldan-Roldan, & Quirarte, 1994). After passive avoidance training, rats were extinguished by weekly returns to the training chamber for 8 weeks. Maximum time for each exposure was 10 minutes, but trials were terminated as soon as the rat crossed into the shock compartment (although no shocks were given). Before the seventh weekly trial, half of the rats were injected with a vehicle and half with scopolamine. The eighth and final trial was again drug free. Although all animals showed gradual declines in avoidance over the first six trials, animals treated with scopolamine showed reversal of their extinction after scopolamine injection. Extinction returned for the last drug-free trial, indicating that, like $GABA_A$ receptors, muscarinic acetylcholine receptors are particularly important for the expression of extinction. Because of the experiment's design, nothing can be said about whether these receptors are necessary for extinction learning. We tested whether scopolamine has an effect on extinction learning when injected before CS exposures (Ponnusamy & Barad, 2005). No defect in extinction was observed when animals were tested, drug-free, 1 day after extinction training. These results support the idea that muscarinic neurotransmission does not directly affect extinction learning but only its expression.

Cannabinoidergic Neurotransmission

Recently, cannabinoidergic neurotransmission has garnered considerable interest in the field of learning research after endogenous cannabinoids were shown to modulate LTP in the hippocampus (R. I. Wilson & Nicoll, 2002). It is interesting that mice carrying a genetic deletion of the CB1 receptor exhibited slowed extinction of fear (Marsicano et al., 2002), although their acquisition and expression of auditory fear conditioning was not affected. This effect was replicated using acute injections of the CB1 inhibitor SR141716A (Marsicano et al., 2002; Suzuki et al., 2004). Furthermore, extinction training elevated endocannabinoid levels in the basolateral complex of the amygdala, suggesting that endocannabinoids may affect extinction in that structure (Marsicano et al., 2002). This finding has been exploited to accelerate extinction of fear-potentiated startle using systemic injections of AM404, an inhibitor of the catabolism and reuptake of endogenous cannabinoids (Chhatwal, Davis, Maguschak, & Ressler, 2005).

Intracellular Molecules

As might be expected for any learning phenomenon, and particularly one subject to so many modulatory influences, a variety of intracellular molecules play important roles in extinction. Intracellular molecules include second messengers, that is, kinases (enzymes that modify the activity of other proteins by adding phosphates to specific amino acids) and phosphatases (which remove those phosphates, cyclic nucleotides, and other molecules whose activity is controlled directly by neurotransmitters binding to their receptors or by the influx of ions through channels that may or may not be receptors). This category also includes the protein synthetic machinery, which has proven crucial to many forms of long-term learning and LTP, including extinction learning.

Second Messengers

The MAP kinase pathway in the BLA was the first second-messenger system identified as crucial to extinction (Lu et al., 2001). Calcineurin has been implicated in extinction learning and in depotentiation of fear-potentiated startle in BLA (Lin, Lee, et al., 2003; Lin, Yeh, Leu, et al., 2003; Lin, Yeh, Lu, et al., 2003). Extinction was blocked by two calcineurin inhibitors. One of these studies showed that a PI-3 kinase inhibitor, wortmannin, also blocked extinction learning (Lin, Yeh, Lu, et al., 2003). Much more remains to be learned about the roles of second messenger systems in extinction learning and memory.

Protein Synthesis

Many forms of long-term learning are dependent on protein synthesis (reviewed in Barondes, 1970; H. P. Davis & Squire, 1984). Extinction learning also seems to depend on protein synthesis in more than one location. One group of researchers has shown that anisomycin infusion into BLA prevents extinction (Lin, Yeh, Lu, et al., 2003); another group has shown that anisomycin infusion into infralimbic prefrontal cortex prevents extinction learning (Santini et al., 2004).

CLINICAL IMPLICATIONS

Because extinction has been such a fruitful model for behavior therapy, many of the identified neural bases of fear extinction described in this chapter may yield clinical applications. In fact, several systemic drugs have been shown to accelerate extinction learning in animals including d-cycloserine (Walker et al., 2002), yohimbine (Cain et al., 2004), sulpiride (Ponnusamy et al., 2005), and AM 404 (Chhatwal, Davis, et al., 2005). Other pathways have clear potential for the discovery of other drugs that may do the same.

Such facilitation of extinction in animals predicts that drugs like these may prove to be useful as adjuncts to exposure-based psychotherapy for human anxiety disorders. This kind of approach represents a new paradigm for the treatment of anxiety disorders: not the either–or of drugs or therapy but using drugs to improve the efficiency of behavior therapy and giving them not chronically but only in association with therapy sessions. M. Davis and his colleagues have already supplied clinical proof of this principle (Ressler et al., 2004). These investigators administered d-cycloserine or placebo to participants with acrophobia just before each of two virtual-reality exposure therapy sessions. The groups did not differ in their reported anxiety during the first therapy session. This is consistent with evidence for the lack of a role for NMDA receptors during the acute induction of extinction. When tested at 2-week follow-up, however, the d-cycloserine-treated patients showed significantly greater decreases in fear than placebo-treated patients. In summary, this clinical trial demonstrates that medications can be used not to treat a phobia directly but to facilitate psychotherapy. In addition, it shows that facilitation of extinction in laboratory rodents can effectively predict facilitation of exposure-based therapy of human anxiety.

GENERAL CONCLUSIONS

This chapter has reviewed the growing body of literature on the neurobiological basis of fear extinction in rodents. That literature supports the hypothesis that extinction is not erasure of original memory but a learned inhibition of the expression of that memory. Anatomically, the basolateral amygdala makes a crucial contribution to fear extinction, as it does to fear conditioning. In addition, other areas of the brain make important contributions to extinction: The infralimbic prefrontal cortex makes an important contribution to the induction of fear extinction, perhaps by storing part of the memory of extinction or by transmitting information about the contrast between expected and actual outcomes of the CS; the hippocampus plays a crucial role in controlling when and where extinction memory is expressed.

At the level of neurotransmitters, channels, and intracellular mechanisms, a great deal of evidence demonstrates that extinction shares many molecules with other forms of learning. There are also molecules specific to extinction learning, however. For example, extinction learning may depend on L-type voltage calcium channels. Also, the D2 receptor blockade interferes with acquisition of associations, and it also facilitates the extinction of fear. Most strikingly, analysis of certain molecules has already yielded multiple ways to facilitate extinction learning. Extinction might be easier to improve because it is not erasure of the original memory but coexists with it in a delicate balance that can easily be disrupted by changes of time, context, or unrelated stressors. In such a balanced situation, relatively weak molecular interventions can make a substantial difference in outcome. Original learning lacks such characteristics, and the system for acquiring new information may already be closer to its optimal efficiency. The lack of efficiency and permanence of extinction may account for many of the limitations of exposure-based therapy, but it also allows for interventions to facilitate both extinction and therapy, as evidenced by the elegant demonstration that d-cy-closerine, given in conjunction with therapy sessions, can facilitate the treatment of acrophobia (Ressler et al., 2004).

Studies of the basic neurobiology of extinction in rodents have yielded a new and exciting paradigm of psychiatric and psychological treatment: the use of medications as adjuncts to facilitate psychotherapy. Drugs can powerfully affect cell biological processes, and therapy can direct those effects to the specific pathways requiring modification. This paradigm may well play a rapidly expanding role in psychotherapy in coming years, starting with the treatment of anxiety disorders but perhaps reaching into other areas of psychotherapy as well.

9

COUNTERACTING THE CONTEXT-DEPENDENCE OF EXTINCTION: RELAPSE AND TESTS OF SOME RELAPSE PREVENTION METHODS

MARK E. BOUTON, AMANDA M. WOODS, ERIK W. MOODY,
CEYHUN SUNSAY, AND ANA GARCÍA-GUTIÉRREZ

It is reasonably well established that extinction involves new learning rather than merely destruction of the old (e.g., Bouton, 2002, 2004; Myers & Davis, 2002), and several chapters in this book further attest to this (chaps. 8, 10, 11, this volume). In the animal laboratory, after tone–shock pairings have caused the tone to evoke fear, repeated presentations of the tone alone can eliminate that fear. Although fear behavior goes away, the result does not imply that extinction has destroyed the original learning, which remains in the memory system and brain, ready to return to performance under the right conditions. The fact that the original performance can recover after extinction may be an important insight into understanding relapse after therapy (e.g., Bouton, 1988, 1991b, 2000, 2002; Kehoe & Macrae, 1997).

Preparation of this chapter and the new research reported here was supported by Grant RO1 MH64847 from the National Institute of Mental Health to Mark E. Bouton.

Another important insight into relapse is that the new learning involved in extinction seems especially dependent on the context for retrieval. This means that many manipulations of the context can cause an extinguished fear (or, indeed, any extinguished behavior) to recover or return (e.g., Bouton, 2002, 2004). The first part of this chapter provides a brief summary of findings from the animal learning laboratory that support this view. The main focus of the chapter, however, extends beyond this point. Given that extinction is at least partly context-dependent new learning, are there ways to take advantage of this fact and prevent relapse? This question has recently been a focus of research in our laboratory, and the major intent of this chapter is to summarize some of that research. The overarching theme is that as far as we have been able to determine, extinction can often remain sensitive to the context (and responding thus susceptible to relapse) even after extinction procedures that have been designed to optimize the new learning. Instead, the treatments that are most effective at preventing postextinction recovery effects may be those that provide a specific "bridge" between the extinction context and the contexts in which relapse will be most harmful if it occurs.

FOUR RELAPSE EFFECTS

We have previously summarized a number of extinction phenomena suggesting that extinction is a context-specific form of new learning (e.g., Bouton, 1988, 1991b, 2002, 2004). Perhaps the most fundamental of these is the *renewal effect* in which extinguished responding to the tone (the conditioned stimulus [CS]) returns if the context is changed after extinction. Renewal has been observed in every conditioning preparation in which we have studied it, including fear conditioning and appetitive conditioning, in which the tone is paired with food rather than footshock in rats (e.g., see Bouton, 2002). (It is worth noting that we have found many strong parallels between fear conditioning and appetitive conditioning.) In most of our research, *context* is defined as the chamber or Skinner box in which a rat receives the tones and shocks. Renewal occurs in at least three experimental designs (e.g., see Bouton, 2002). In *ABA renewal*, conditioning (e.g., tone–shock pairings) occurs in Context A, and then extinction trials (tone-alone trials) are presented in a second context, Context B, until fear of the CS has disappeared. In a final test, the animal is returned to the original conditioning context (Context A) and merely presented with the tone. At this point, conditioned responding (e.g., fear of the tone) returns. *ABC renewal* also occurs: Here the rat receives conditioning in Context A, extinction in Context B, and then testing in a third (neutral) context (Context C). *AAB renewal* has also been observed: In this case conditioning and extinction both occur in Context A and then the final test occurs in a second (neutral) context (Context B).

All examples of renewal illustrate that extinction does not destroy the original learning and that the response triggered by the extinguished CS depends on the current context. ABC and AAB renewal further suggest that what is learned in extinction is more context-dependent then what is learned during conditioning. That is because in both cases, the animal shows performance that is more consistent with conditioning than with extinction when the tone is tested in a new context. In addition, a context switch after extinction has a more profound effect on responding to the CS than a similar switch after conditioning in many preparations (e.g., Bouton, 2002).

Two further features of renewal are worth mentioning. First, it occurs after fairly extensive extinction. For example, several investigators have found renewal when a few trials of fear conditioning are followed by 100 extinction trials or more (e.g., Gunther, Denniston, & Miller, 1998; Rauhut, Thomas, & Ayres, 2001; Tamai & Nakajima, 2000), although "massive" extinction (800 trials) might eliminate it (Denniston, Chang, & Miller, 2003). Second, we find renewal when we manipulate many kinds of contexts. Most often, we have manipulated the physical conditioning chamber, which is analogous to the room context manipulated in human memory research (being in the same room during learning and testing similarly promotes memory retrieval, e.g., Smith & Vela, 2001). Renewal also occurs when we manipulate the interoceptive context created by ingestion of drugs. For instance, renewal occurs when fear is extinguished under the influence of a benzodiazepine tranquilizer and then tested in the sober state (Bouton, Kenney, & Rosengard, 1990; for results with alcohol, see Cunningham, 1979). "Contexts" may also be provided by other background cues including hormonal state, mood state, and the memory of recent events (e.g., see Bouton, 2000).

Still another kind of context may be provided by the passage of time. That is, as time elapses, internal and external stimuli that correlate with it may change. Just as extinction may be specific to its physical or drug context, it may also be specific to its temporal context. This is our explanation of *spontaneous recovery* (e.g., Pavlov, 1927) in which extinguished responding recovers when a temporal interval (a retention interval) is introduced between extinction and testing. Although other explanations are available (e.g., Rescorla, 2004), one of the most reasonable is that spontaneous recovery is the renewal effect that occurs when the CS is tested outside the temporal extinction context.

A third relapse effect is *reinstatement*. Operationally, reinstatement occurs when the organism is exposed to the unconditioned stimulus (US; e.g., the footshock), again after extinction. When the CS is presented afterward, it evokes responding again. Our research indicates that the effect depends substantially on context conditioning. When the US is presented, it becomes associated with the contemporary context. Reinstatement then occurs when the extinguished CS is presented in that context. Contextual conditioning creates a kind of context-specific anticipation of the US, and this triggers extinguished responding to the CS. For example, the US must be presented in the context in which the CS is tested if reinstatement is to occur (e.g., Bouton, 1984; for more discussion, see Bouton, 2002, 2004). Because of the role of context conditioning, we think of reinstatement not as a phenomenon that depends on recent reexposure to the US but rather on presenting the extinguished CS in a context that arouses an active anticipation of the US.

A final relapse effect is *rapid reacquisition*. In this phenomenon, if CS–US pairings are resumed after extinction has taken place, the conditioned response may be reacquired rapidly, suggesting (again) that conditioning is saved after extinction (e.g., Bouton, 1993; Kehoe & Macrae, 1997). As we show later, rapid reacquisition may occur because it is another form of ABA renewal (Bouton, Woods, & Pineño, 2004; Ricker & Bouton, 1996) in which the organism is returned to the original conditioning "context" provided by recent conditioning trials. Thus, by, for example, the third reacquisition trial, the previous conditioning trials have returned a part of the context that was present during original conditioning. Once again, extinction does not destroy the original learning but leaves it ready to return to performance with the right manipulation of the context, broadly defined.

On the contextual view, lapses and relapses are seen as an almost inevitable concomitant of behavior change. The findings seem consistent with the clinical literature. For example, Solomon, Garb, Bleich, and Grupper (1987) studied combat stress reaction in Israeli veterans of the 1973 Yom Kippur War who were later also engaged in the 1982 Lebanon war. In an analog of the renewal effect, several veterans who were "cured" of combat stress reaction after 1973 had it renew in 1982 when they were exposed to contextual cues that were similar to those that had surrounded impactful episodes in the original war. In addition, in a potential analog of reinstatement, simple anticipatory anxiety created by being recalled to service in 1982 caused a return of the stress reaction in other cases (see also, e.g., Toren, Wolmer, Weizman, Magal-Vardi, & Laor, 2002). Other examples of renewal have been observed in studies of the extinction of spider fear and responses to alcohol cues in undergraduates (see chap. 11, this volume; Collins & Brandon, 2002). There are therefore grounds for thinking that initial learning in the real lives of humans might also be hard to erase—and relatively susceptible to relapse with manipulations of the context.

HOW CAN RELAPSE BE PREVENTED?

As A. J. Lang, Craske, and Bjork (1999) have recognized, if extinction and therapy are examples of new learning rather than unlearning, then it is reasonable to ask whether there are ways to enhance the new learning to prevent relapse. One way to address this question is to investigate methods that might attenuate relapse as it is represented in the effects just described.

In what follows, we discuss two general strategies. First, we consider several ways in which one might strengthen or "optimize" extinction learning. This strategy assumes that stronger extinction learning might be less vulnerable to relapse. Second, we consider a strategy that accepts the inherent context-specificity of extinction and attempts to build "bridges" between the extinction context and other possible contexts in which lapse and relapse might occur. To date, our research suggests that the latter approach might be especially efficient and effective.

Optimizing Extinction Learning

Counterconditioning Instead of Extinction

Wolpe (1958) suggested that a "counterconditioning" procedure that actively connects a new relaxation response to the phobic CS might be more effective than simple extinction. Partly because of this idea, we have studied counterconditioning in rats in a method in which a CS is paired with footshock in the first phase (causing the CS to evoke fear) and then with food in the second phase (which replaces fear behavior with appetitive behavior). We discovered that counterconditioning, like extinction, can still leave the original fear susceptible to renewal, spontaneous recovery, and reinstatement (Bouton & Peck, 1992; Brooks, Hale, Nelson, & Bouton, 1995; Peck & Bouton, 1990). Counterconditioning does not necessarily abolish the original learning and thus does not guarantee protection from relapse.

Trial Spacing Effects: Conditioning

It is widely known that learning can be better if trials are spaced rather than massed in time (e.g., Spence & Norris, 1950). This sort of observation has led Craske and her colleagues to investigate the effects of spaced exposures in exposure therapy (e.g., A. J. Lang et al., 1999; Tsao & Craske, 2000; chap. 11, this volume). Most of the conditioning research on trial spacing has focused on the acquisition of the conditioned response, however, rather than extinction, and not all of the mechanisms that explain trial spacing in acquisition predict that trial spacing will also facilitate extinction (discussed subsequently).

We have studied the effects of trial spacing on appetitive conditioning (Bouton & Sunsay, 2003; Sunsay, Stetson, & Bouton, 2004; Sunsay & Bouton, 2006). Our research has identified at least three mechanisms that contribute to it. First, with very short intertrial intervals (ITIs), responding is suppressed by a short-term habituation process in which the recent trial reduces responding on the next trial (Bouton & Sunsay, 2003; Sunsay et al., 2004). One of the main candidates for this effect is the self-generated priming mechanism in Wagner's "sometimes opponent process" ("SOP") model of conditioning (Wagner, 1981; Wagner & Brandon, 1989, 2001). According to this model, presentation of a stimulus (e.g., a CS) activates ("primes") its representation in short-term memory. The representation persists temporarily in that state, making the stimulus less surprising on the next trial. Priming of the CS in short-term memory has two consequences. First, it may make the CS less able to control performance when it is presented again. Second, it may make it more difficult to learn about the CS. We have obtained evidence that priming is important in our conditioning preparation when the interval between trials is under 4 minutes (Bouton & Sunsay, 2003; Sunsay et al., 2004).

Note, however, that an effect that disappears when trials are spaced by 4 minutes cannot explain examples of trial spacing effects that occur with longer intervals. It is important to note that conditioning in this preparation still proceeds better with ITIs longer than 4 minutes (Sunsay & Bouton, 2006). Accordingly, we have identified two other mechanisms that account for the longer term trial-spacing effect. The first is "blocking" by the context. According to this mechanism, the context also becomes associated with the US, and this competes with conditioning to the CS (e.g., Pearce & Hall, 1980; Rescorla & Wagner, 1972; Wagner, 1981). With long ITIs, context conditioning has more opportunity to extinguish between trials, and the context is therefore less effective at competing with the CS. We confirmed a role for context blocking in an experiment in which we removed the rats from the context during the long ITI (cf. Barela, 1999). Removing rats from the context should spare the context from extinction and thus allow it to compete better with the CS. Consistent with this prediction, removing the rats from the context during a long (24-minute) ITI reduced the advantage this ITI had over conditioning with a 4-minute ITI (Sunsay & Bouton, 2006).

Another experiment still found a trial spacing effect in a within-subject design that controlled for context blocking, however. Two CSs (A and B) were conditioned over a series of trials that had a sequence that can be summarized as ABBA. (The actual trial sequence was somewhat more complicated.) Each trial always followed the preceding trial (and presentation of the US) by an interval of 5.5 minutes. Because consecutive trials were spaced equally, the associative strength of the context was equal when A and B were reinforced, and there should have been equivalent context blocking. Nonetheless, presentations of CS (A) were relatively spaced in time, and conditioning with the spaced CS (A) was better than conditioning with the massed CS (B).

The results, therefore, suggest that time may play a third role that goes beyond the context blocking and priming mechanisms. One possible explanation is the "stimulus fluctuation" mechanism proposed by Estes (1955a, 1955b) and since accepted by other memory models (e.g., Bjork & Bjork, 1992; A. J. Lang et al., 1999). On this view, many stimulus elements are present in the background, and these fluctuate in and out of an available state over time. Conditioning with spaced trials allows a large amount of fluctuation between trials, and numerous different elements therefore become connected with reinforcement. Because conditioning with massed trials does not allow as much stimulus fluctuation between trials, fewer elements become associated with reinforcement, and there is less overall learning in the long run. In the short run, however, there should be an advantage to massed trials: After the first few trials, the massed CS is presented with elements that have just been conditioned, whereas the spaced CS is not. Unfortunately, this prediction is not consistent with the conditioning literature. In classical conditioning experiments, spaced trials yield better conditioning from the start.

Trial Spacing Effects: Extinction

As we noted earlier, not all of the mechanisms that contribute to trial spacing in conditioning have implications for extinction. The context blocking mechanism, for example, describes the effects of spaced USs, which are unique to acquisition. Nonetheless, the CS priming mechanism and the effect of longer intervals that is not reducible to context blocking could influence extinction. We have therefore run experiments examining the effects of comparable ITIs in extinction (Moody, Sunsay, & Bouton, in press).

According to the CS priming mechanism, when trials are sufficiently massed in time, all but the first CS presentation occur when the CS has been primed. When applied to extinction, SOP theory (e.g., Wagner, 1981) makes two separate and equally interesting predictions. First, massed presentations should result in less responding to the CS than spaced trials during extinction. That is, during the extinction phase, the model predicts a *performance* effect: There should be a more rapid loss of responding to the CS with massed trials than with spaced. The model also predicts, however, that massed presentations will result in less learning about the CS; when the CS is already primed in short-term memory at the start of a trial, it will not be surprising enough to allow much learning. The model thus also predicts a *learning* effect: Massed trials should allow less extinction learning and thus perhaps provide even less protection than usual against relapse effects such as spontaneous recovery and reinstatement. It is interesting that the stimulus fluctuation mechanism (Estes, 1955a, 1955b) makes similar predictions. Massed trials will allow less stimulus fluctuation between trials than spaced trials, and because the stimuli are similar from trial to trial, they will generate a relatively rapid loss of responding in extinction. Because fewer fluctuating elements become connected with extinction, however, there is less overall extinction learning and hence less protection from relapse effects like spontaneous recovery. Clinically speaking, both theories suggest that although spaced extinction trials might cause a slower loss of responding during therapy, their effect might be more permanent in the long run.

Moody et al. (in press) therefore investigated the effects of ITI during extinction using the methods used in our acquisition research (Bouton & Sunsay, 2003; Sunsay & Bouton, 2006; Sunsay et al., 2004). We began by comparing the effects of 1-minute and 4-minute ITIs in extinction, intervals that had previously suggested a short-term CS priming effect in conditioning. In the extinction experiments, all rats first received repeated CS–US (tone–food) pairings with intermixed ITIs of 1, 4, and 16 minute (+25%). This method gave the subjects experience with the different ITIs. After conditioning was complete, different groups received a single extinction session with either a variable 1-minute or a 4-minute ITI (+25%). Seventy-two hours later, all subjects then received a spontaneous recovery test in which the CS was presented alone with an ITI averaging 2 minutes (the geometric mean of 1 and 4 extinction values, which should generalize equivalently from the extinction it is; see Church & Deluty, 1977). The same 10-second CS was used in all groups and all phases. The findings are summarized in Figure 9.1. As the upper panel (Moody et al., in press, Experiment 2) shows, the 1-minute ITI produced a more rapid loss of responding than the 4-minute ITI, a finding that is consistent with our results with the same ITIs in acquisition. As seen in the lower left panel, however, the ITI had no apparent impact on responding during the spontaneous recovery test. Extinction with either ITI allowed spontaneous recovery, and to a statistically indistinguishable extent. Thus, the short ITI affected extinction performance but not extinction learning as it was represented in the strength of spontaneous recovery.

A separate experiment tested groups extinguished with 1- and 4-minute ITIs for reinstatement (Moody et al., in press, Experiment 4b). At the end of the extinction session, all rats received four unsignaled USs and then testing of the CS alone (with a 2-minute ITI) beginning 2 minutes later. As shown in the lower right panel of Figure 9.1, extinction with the two ITIs had no differential impact on reinstatement. The results do not seem consistent with the predictions of either SOP (e.g., Wagner, 1981) or the stimulus fluctuation model (e.g., Estes, 1955a, 1955b). We observed a *performance* effect on trial massing during extinction but no effect on extinction *learning* as it might be represented in spontaneous recovery and reinstatement tests. Our priming effects (Bouton & Sunsay, 2003; Sunsay et al., 2004; Moody et al., in press) may thus reflect a short-term effect on performance more than a long-term effect on learning.

As we have already noted, trial spacing still influences acquisition when we extend the ITI beyond the apparent upper limit of this short-term process. Moody et al. (in press) therefore also compared the effects of extinction with 4-minute and 16-minute ITIs. The results of these experiments are summarized in Figure 9.2. As the top panel suggests, there were no differences in extinction performance with these two ITIs. The lower panels summarize tests of spontaneous recovery and reinstatement. As before, there was no effect of extinction ITI on spontaneous recovery when tested 72 hours after extinction (lower left). The reinstatement results (lower right) were more interesting. Here, the 16-minute ITI did have an advantage: It led to less reinstatement than the 4-minute ITI. This result has been replicated in at least one other experiment, and observation of the rats in the 16-minute

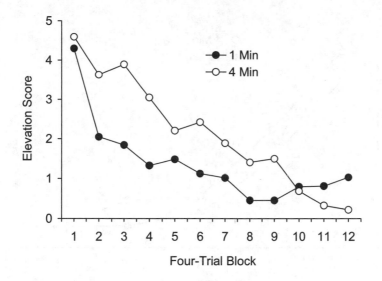

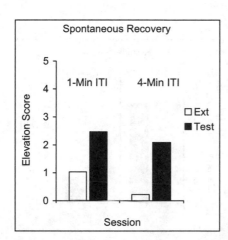
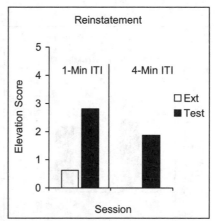

Figure 9.1. Mean elevation scores during four-trial blocks of extinction (Ext) with intertrial intervals (ITIs) of either 1 minute or 4 minutes (upper panel) and during subsequent tests for spontaneous recovery (lower left) or reinstatement (lower right). From "Printing and Trial Spacing in Extinction: Effects on Extinction Performance, Spontaneous Recovery, and Reinstatement in Appetitive Conditioning," by E. W. Moody, C. Sunsay, and M. E. Bouton, in press, *The Quarterly Journal of Experimental Psychology*. Copyright 2006 by the Experimental Psychology Society. Reprinted with permission.

condition indicated that they were awake and responsive to the food pellets during the reinstatement test, despite a relatively lengthy extinction session necessitated by the long ITI.

It is possible that the reinstatement results indicate that the 16-minute ITI caused better extinction learning. The fact that it did not reduce sponta-

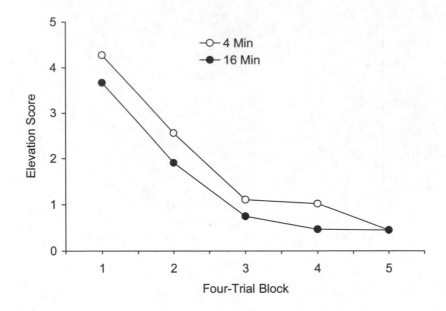

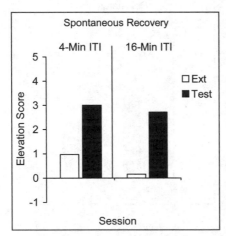

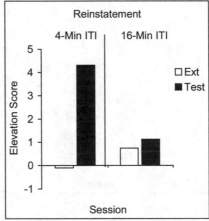

Figure 9.2. Mean elevation scores during four-trial blocks of extinction (Ext) with intertrial intervals (ITIs) of either 4 minutes or 16 minutes (upper panel) and during subsequent tests for spontaneous recovery (lower left) or reinstatement (lower right). From "Printing and Trial Spacing in Extinction: Effects on Extinction Performance, Spontaneous Recovery, and Reinstatement in Appetitive Conditioning," by E. W. Moody, C. Sunsay, and M. E. Bouton, in press, *The Quarterly Journal of Experimental Psychology*. Copyright 2006 by the Experimental Psychology Society. Reprinted with permission.

neous recovery raises doubts about this idea, however. The difference between the effect on spontaneous recovery and reinstatement is also consistent with the fact that spontaneous recovery and reinstatement are themselves supported by different mechanisms. For example, as we have noted, reinstatement (but not spontaneous recovery) depends on context conditioning; although spontaneous recovery is a "temporal context" effect (e.g., Bouton, 1993), reinstatement uniquely depends on the acquisition of a direct context–US association created by presentation of the US. The 16-minute ITI might simply interfere with the learning of the context–US association. The 16-minute ITI entailed a large amount of exposure to the context, which could make context conditioning difficult (e.g., extensive exposure to a cue can reduce its readiness to enter into an association—"latent inhibition"). Thus, it is possible to account for the results without claiming that the 16-minute ITI causes better long-term extinction learning about the CS.

The results of our tests of the effects of ITI in extinction suggest a number of conclusions. First, they suggest a dissociation between the effects of ITI on extinction performance and extinction learning as inferred by our spontaneous recovery and reinstatement tests: The 1-minute interval suppressed performance in extinction but had no discernible impact on behavior in the relapse tests. Second, because of this, SOP theory and the stimulus fluctuation mechanism do not necessarily capture the effects of trial spacing quite right. Third, the fact that trial spacing caused differences in extinction performance without affecting long-term extinction learning is inconsistent with the idea that higher levels of responding during extinction might make extinction learning more effective in the long run (e.g., Bjork & Bjork, 1992; A. J. Lang et al., 1999; see also Rescorla, 2001). In fact, correlations between individual rats' performance during extinction and during spontaneous recovery testing were usually positive, not negative. Long-term extinction learning is thus not a simple reflection of the strength of responding in extinction.

It is worth observing that the small literature on trial spacing effects in extinction has produced many conflicting results. For example, in flavor aversion learning, Westbrook, Smith, and Charnock (1985) found better extinction learning when two extinction trials were spaced (separated by 24 hours) rather than massed (separated by 0.5 hours). (Long-term learning was tested 48 hours after Trial 2.) Unfortunately, there was no test of the shorter-term effect on performance during extinction because it was experimentally advantageous to limit the rats' consumption of the flavored-water CS on the extinction trials. More recent fear conditioning results from the same laboratory also suggest that two extinction trials separated by long ITIs (12 hours or 24 hours) produce better long-term extinction than a short 2-minute ITI when testing occurred 12 hours or 24 hours after the second extinction trial (Morris, Furlong, & Westbrook, 2005). There was no priming effect on performance in extinction like the one we have reported (e.g., Moody et al., in press). The total pattern, however, is again not consistent with SOP or stimulus sampling theory.

In a fear-conditioning procedure with mice, Cain, Blouin, and Barad (2003) have produced still another wrinkle. They found that extinction with massed trials caused a more rapid loss of fear, but better long-term protection against spontaneous recovery than extinction with spaced trials. For example, extinction with an extremely brief 6-second ITI caused a more rapid loss of freezing than 60-second or 600-second ITIs, but less freezing in tests conducted 24 hours or 192 hours later. Cain et al. (2003) suggested that massed trials might be more effective at "inducing" a biological process necessary for extinction. They also suggested that spaced inductions are especially effective: When chunks of five trials with the 6-second ITI were separated by 20-minute interchunk intervals, there was even better protection against spontaneous recovery. Unfortunately, we have not been able to produce analogous findings in our appetitive method (Moody et al., in press). At this point in time, it is not clear which aspect of Cain et al.'s procedure produced their findings, although Rescorla and Durlach (1987) have also reported more enduring effects of massed (10-second ITI) than spaced (2-minute ITI) extinction trials in the autoshaping preparation in which pigeons peck at illuminated disks associated with food.

This leads to the fourth and final implication of our work to date on ITI effects on extinction. Although effects of extinction ITI have been reported in the literature, their effects on the "relapse" phenomena of interest here have been strikingly inconsistent. More basic research will be needed to untangle the complexities. It is therefore worth considering other manipulations that might optimize the long-term effectiveness of extinction.

Extinction in Multiple Contexts

Another approach to optimizing extinction learning is to provide extinction in multiple contexts. On the basis of the human memory literature, which suggests that learning word lists in multiple contexts can improve memory transfer to still other contexts (e.g., Smith, 1982), Bouton (1991b) suggested that extinction conducted in several contexts might also make extinction generalize better across contexts. For example, if an individual context is made up of multiple elements, then extinction in multiple contexts might increase the overall number of elements that are connected with extinction. This might decrease the likelihood of renewal after a final context switch, because it is more likely that some of the contextual elements connected with extinction might be similar to some present in the new context.

Gunther et al. (1998) reported supporting evidence. Rats that received fear conditioning in Context A were subsequently given extinction treatments in a single context (Context B) or in multiple contexts (Contexts B, C, D). Forty-eight hours following extinction, all subjects were tested in yet another context (Context E). The multiple-context procedure reduced renewal relative to that observed after extinction with the same number of trials in a single context, although the authors suggested that it did not abolish it. Chelonis, Calton, Hart, and Schachtman (1999) reported compatible results in a flavor-aversion procedure. Rats received a pairing of a sucrose solution and illness in Context A and then received extinction trials in either Context B or in Contexts B, C, and D. Renewal testing occurred in Context A 24 hours later. The results again suggested that extinction in multiple contexts causes less renewal than extinction in a single context. In the current volume, Vansteenwegen et al. report new data suggesting that exposure to a spider in multiple contexts can reduce a renewal of electrodermal responding that occurs when the spider is presented in a new location (analogous to ABC renewal). Extinction in multiple contexts might thus protect against either ABC or ABA renewal.

None of the aforementioned studies tested the theoretical mechanisms behind the multiple context extinction effect. Although extinction in multiple contexts might enhance generalization by connecting extinction with a wider variety of contextual elements, there are other possibilities. For example, when all the extinction trials occur in one context, inhibition that is potentially learned during extinction (e.g., Rescorla & Wagner, 1972) would be associated with the one context; if the extinction trials were distributed over several contexts, there would be less inhibition learned in any one of them. Inhibition in a context might "protect" the CS from total associative loss (e.g., Rescorla, 2003; see also Thomas & Ayres, 2004) and thus leave a basis for relapse; reduced contextual inhibition would reduce any protection from extinction. Alternatively, in the multiple-context procedure, each context switch during extinction would cause a renewal of responding. This means that the multiple context group would respond more (on average) in extinction. Rescorla (e.g., 2001) has suggested that extinction learning may be enhanced if there is ample responding to the CS during extinction. No data are available, however, to know whether response level contributed to the effect of extinction in multiple contexts. Gunther and colleagues did not measure behavior during extinction, Vansteenwegen et al. (this volume) do not report data from extinction, and although Chelonis and colleagues did report such data, they did not find more responding in the multiple-context group than the single-context group. There is much we do not know about extinction in multiple contexts.

Bouton, García-Gutiérrez, Zilski, and Moody (in press) therefore extended these findings using the fear-conditioning method that we use extensively in our laboratory (conditioned suppression; e.g., Estes & Skinner, 1941). Rats were initially trained to lever press for food reinforcement on a variable interval (VI)-90 schedule in four counterbalanced contexts (B, C, D, and E). This was followed by fear conditioning (several tone–shock pairings) in a fifth context, Context A. Following conditioning, the rats received three daily sessions of extinction, each of which contained four presentations of the CS without shock (each presented while the rats were lever pressing for food). One group received the three sessions in Context B, whereas the other group received them in Contexts B, C, and D. Twenty-four hours later, both groups were tested with the CS in yet another context (Context E). Fear of the CS was measured through the suppression of lever pressing during the CS relative to response rates in a comparable period prior to the CS.

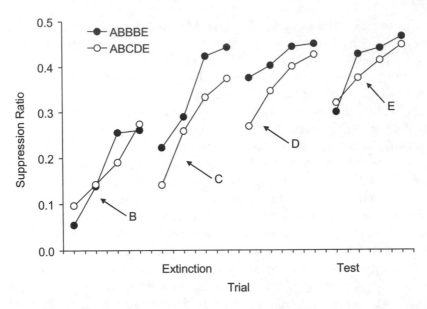

Figure 9.3. Mean suppression ratio during each trial of extinction and the final renewal test. Group ABBBE received extinction in only one context: B. Whereas Group ABCDE received extinction in multiple contexts: B, C, and D; both groups were tested for renewal in a different context: E. 0 indicates complete suppression and 0.5 indicates a lack of suppression. From "Extinction in Multiple Contexts Does Not Necessarily Make Extinction Less Vulnerable," by M. E. Bouton, A. García-Gutiérrez, J. Zilski, and E. W. Moody, in press, *Behaviour Research and Therapy*. Copyright 2006 by Elsevier. Reprinted with permission.

The results of that study are presented in Figure 9.3, which shows fear of the CS during each extinction and renewal test trial. The measure of fear is the standard suppression ratio, which is the ratio of the number of bar presses in the CS divided by the total bar presses in the CS and in the 1-minute "pre-CS" period before each trial; a ratio of 0 indicates maximal suppression, and a ratio of 0.5 indicates none. During extinction, Group ABCDE showed more suppression than Group ABBBE because the context switches between Extinction Sessions 1 and 2 and between 2 and 3 caused renewal effects. The results thus confirm that the rats discriminated among various contexts and that the multiple-context manipulation was effective. As shown at right in the figure, however, when the groups were tested in Context E during the final renewal test, both exhibited a significant, and statistically indistinguishable, renewal of fear of the CS. Extinction in multiple contexts thus had no impact on the strength of the final renewal effect.

These findings were replicated in other experiments, including one that did not involve lever-press training in Contexts B, C, and D (which might have encouraged more generalization between the contexts; cf. Honey & Hall, 1989). Once again, the single- and multiple-context groups showed the same final renewal effect. Another experiment explored the effects of multiple-context extinction on ABA renewal (as opposed to "ABC" renewal).

Again, there was similar final renewal in groups given extinction training in one context or in multiple contexts. Neither ABC nor ABA renewal is reduced by extinction in multiple contexts in the fear-conditioning method we have used extensively in our laboratory.

The results suggest that there are important variables that modulate the positive impact of extinction in multiple contexts (Chelonis et al., 1999; Gunther et al., 1998; chap. 10, this volume). In fact, we already knew that there were such variables. Chelonis and colleagues (1999, Experiment 2) failed to replicate their attenuation of renewal by extinction in multiple contexts when the rats were given equivalent exposure to all the experimental contexts in extinction. (Our experiments deliberately avoided equating context exposure in an attempt to optimize conditions for producing the effect.) Moreover, Gunther and colleagues (1998) found that the advantage of extinction in multiple contexts is undone if fear conditioning is *likewise* first conducted in multiple contexts. Thus, the overall pattern across laboratories indicates that extinction in multiple contexts is no "magic bullet" that prevents the renewal effect.

From a theoretical perspective, the results are puzzling. The fact that the multiple-context group showed more fear during extinction is consistent with the idea that there was less contextual inhibition present to protect the CS from extinction (Rescorla, 2003), more fear responding in extinction to learn the inhibition of (cf. Rescorla, 2001), or both. Extinction learning in either the one-context or multiple-context condition was still surprisingly context-specific. Yet the results of our multiple-context experiments are consistent with our investigations of extinction ITI (Moody et al., in press). Specifically, manipulations that might optimize extinction learning and demonstrably affect performance in extinction provide surprisingly little protection against relapse, and the level of responding in extinction may be a misleading predictor of the long-term success of extinction. Regardless of our ITI and multiple-context manipulations, extinction remained remarkably dependent on its temporal and physical context.

Other Methods for Optimizing Extinction Learning

Other behavioral techniques might improve extinction learning. As mentioned earlier, Denniston et al. (2003) found that a "massive" extinction treatment (800 extinction trials) abolished the renewal effect. Perhaps truly prolonged extinction therapy might help provide a hedge against relapse. In another method, Thomas and Ayres (2004) found that extinguishing several separately conditioned fear CSs together in a compound reduced the amount of renewal to each compared with a condition in which each CS was extinguished separately. Stimulus compounding should theoretically increase the trial-by-trial rate of associative change in extinction (Rescorla & Wagner, 1972; see also Rescorla, 2000), although it is not clear why it would make extinction less context-specific and less vulnerable to renewal. Both the stimulus compounding and massed extinction methods deserve follow-up. For example, we do not know whether their effects are general across the various relapse effects or are unique at preventing renewal.

Chemical Adjuncts To Extinction

Another line of research suggests that certain drugs might enhance the effects of exposure therapy. If extinction generates new learning, then substances that facilitate the brain substrates of learning may also facilitate extinction. There is evidence that fear extinction is mediated in part by N-methyl-D-aspartate (NMDA) receptors in the amygdala (see chap. 8, this volume). The involvement of NMDA receptors in extinction is interesting because they have been implicated in several other forms of learning and in long-term potentiation, a model of learning at the level of the synapse (e.g., Fanselow, 1993). More important, new evidence suggests that the administration of d-cycloserine (DCS), a partial agonist of the NMDA receptor, can facilitate fear extinction learning: When a few extinction trials are given, rats administered DCS during extinction show less evidence of fear than control animals during a test without the drug (e.g., Ledgerwood et al., 2003; Walker et al., 2002). Extending the work to humans, Ressler et al. (2004) found that individuals with acrophobia given DCS during brief exposure to heights in a virtual-reality setting showed facilitated extinction in that setting when it was tested 1 week and 3 months later. The results thus suggest that DCS may be a promising adjunct to extinction and exposure therapies.

Although DCS appears to increase the effectiveness of a small number of extinction trials that do not cause complete extinction, little is known about how the drug affects extinction learning. Is it merely facilitating the rate of "normal" extinction learning, which continues to be vulnerable to relapse? Or is it doing something different and somehow protecting against relapse effects? In this regard, Ledgerwood and colleagues' (2004) finding that extinction with DCS weakens reinstatement created by exposure to the US after extinction is especially important. At the present time, however, we do not know whether the drug reduced reinstatement by causing deeper extinction learning or by interfering with the process that causes reinstatement. For example, if DCS works by facilitating inhibitory conditioning of the extinction context, it might uniquely interfere with reinstatement (by making it more difficult to create context conditioning) but have less impact on other relapse effects. Although chemical adjuncts may facilitate extinction learning, truly effective adjuncts will be ones that also decrease the vulnerability to relapse.

Bridging Between the Extinction Context and Possible Relapse Contexts

Retrieval Cues For Extinction

If extinction procedures that should optimize extinction learning are somewhat ineffective at preventing relapse, then we may wish to consider another strategy. One rule of thumb is that conducting extinction in the context in which relapse will be most problematic for the client should always be a good treatment option. That is, exposure treatments that are conducted in the contexts in which the CS is likely to be encountered in real life and relapse is a clear danger will presumably be an effective extinction procedure. This idea also leads to the prediction that there may be less relapse when treatments are designed to provide a specific "bridge" between the extinction context and possible relapse contexts.

One technique that attenuates renewal and spontaneous recovery is presenting a retrieval cue for extinction at the time of the test. An extinction cue is a stimulus that is presented occasionally during extinction; if it is also presented just before testing, it can attenuate or completely prevent renewal or spontaneous recovery of extinguished appetitive conditioning (e.g., Brooks & Bouton, 1993, 1994). A similar effect on spontaneous recovery has been found in taste aversion (Brooks, Palmatier, Garcia, & Johnson, 1999) and in conditioned tolerance with ethanol (Brooks, Vaughn, Freeman, & Woods, 2004). Extinction cues seem to function as negative occasion setters or as part of the extinction context (e.g., Brooks, 2000). In other words, when an extinction cue is presented, it retrieves extinction or functionally informs the subject that extinction is in effect. It thus provides a bridge between the extinction and test contexts.

The effects of extinction cues have been demonstrated in humans. In one experiment (Collins & Brandon, 2002), social drinkers received extinction exposure to alcohol cues that had presumably been conditioned in the natural environment. The dependent measures were the weight of saliva elicited by exposure to the alcohol cues and the self-reported urge to drink. To extinguish reactivity to alcohol cues, the participants received several visual and olfactory exposures (trials) to beer, after which they completed urge rating forms. During extinction, they also received an extinction retrieval cue that consisted of a unique pencil and eraser along with a neon-colored clipboard; these were used to complete the forms. The participants were then tested for a renewal of alcohol reactivity in a context that was either the same as or different from the extinction context. During the renewal test, only some of the participants received the extinction cue. Consistent with the animal literature, (a) responding was renewed when the context was switched after extinction, but (b) this effect was reduced by presentation of the extinction cue (see also Vansteenwegen et al., this volume).

A related finding has been reported in spider fear in humans (see chap. 11, this volume). Mystkowski, Craske, and Echiverri (2002) found that spider fear that had been reduced through an exposure treatment in one context (a room or a patio outdoors) returned to some extent when the spider was then tested in the other context. Mystkowski, Echiverri, Labus, and Craske (in press) further found, however, that fear that was renewed this way was reduced in participants who mentally reinstated the treatment context (e.g., by recalling the physical surroundings in which the treatment occurred) before being tested in the new context (cf. Smith, 1979). Mental reinstatement of the extinction context might work like an extinction cue; mental operations, like explicit retrieval cues, can help bridge the extinction treatment from one context to another. There is thus a value in using retrieval cues, such as occasional mailings or telephone calls, as well as training retrieval strategies that might help patients remember extinction and thus reduce relapse (see Brandon, Collins, Juliano, & Lazev, 2000; Hiss, Foa, & Kozak, 1994).

Extinction in the Potential Problem Context

The most straightforward bridging treatment, however, may be to conduct therapy in the presence of contextual cues that the therapist knows are likely to cause relapse. We have obtained further evidence supporting this point in rapid reacquisition. As discussed earlier, when the CS and US are paired again after extinction, conditioned responding can return rapidly. We have suggested that when CS–US pairings are resumed after extinction, they constitute a return of the subject to the context of conditioning and therefore produce an ABA renewal effect (Ricker & Bouton, 1996). This "trial signaling view" is consistent with Capaldi's (e.g., 1994) sequential learning theory, which would predict that during conditioning, reinforced trials might come to signal other reinforced trials; during extinction, nonreinforced trials might likewise come to signal other nonreinforced trials. The idea suggests that rapid reacquisition is especially likely when there have been many conditioning trials and thus ample opportunity to learn trial signaling (e.g., Napier, Macrae, & Kehoe, 1992; see also Ricker & Bouton, 1996).

One implication is that we should be able to slow down the rate of reacquisition by interfering with trial signaling (Bouton, 2000). One way to weaken a reinforced trial's tendency to signal other reinforced trials is to use a procedure that includes occasional reinforced trials among the extinction trials. Such a procedure would allow reinforced trials to become associated with both conditioning and extinction. Thus, a partial reinforcement (PRF) procedure in extinction should theoretically protect against rapid reacquisition, because it would reduce the renewal effect ordinarily cued by a few reinforced trials.

We have investigated these ideas in appetitive conditioning (Bouton et al., 2004). The critical manipulation took place during extinction. One group received a traditional CS-alone extinction procedure, whereas another group received a partial reinforcement procedure in which the CS was usually presented alone but occasionally paired with the US. Not surprisingly, the PRF procedure slowed down the loss of responding during extinction, but it also had an impact on reacquisition. The results of the reacquisition phase in one experiment (Bouton et al., 2004, Experiment 2) are presented in Figure 9.4. Rapid reacquisition was evident: Rats that had received simple ex-

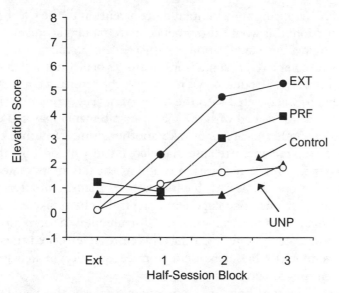

Figure 9.4. Mean elevation scores during half-session blocks of two reacquisition sessions that occurred after subjects were given different response-elimination techniques. The first block represents eight initial nonreinforced trials. See text for further explanation. EXT = extinction; PRF = partial reinforcement; UNP = unpaired conditioned stimulus and unconditioned stimulus. From "Occasional Reinforced Trials During the Extinction Can Slow the Rate of Rapid Reaquisition," by M. E. Bouton, A. M. Woods, and O. Pineño, 2004, *Learning and Motivation, 35*, pp. 371–390. Copyright 2004 by Elsevier. Reprinted with permisison.

tinction developed conditioned responding more rapidly than a control group that was receiving CS–US pairings for the first time. Most important, however, the PRF group showed slower reacquisition. It is worth noting that this slowing of the rapid reacquisition effect was not as profound as that in another group that received the same number of CSs and USs in extinction, but in an unpaired manner (Frey & Butler, 1977; Rauhut et al., 2001). Although the CS–US unpaired extinction procedure was the most effective at slowing down rapid reacquisition, it might be difficult to implement such a procedure outside the laboratory. The new, most surprising, and most clinically applicable result is that partial reinforcement in extinction can indeed slow the rapid reacquisition effect.

These results are consistent with the trial-signaling view (Ricker & Bouton, 1996). They are surprising because other theories suggest precisely the opposite outcome. For instance, the idea that the rate of reacquisition simply reflects the strength of the CS–US association remaining after extinction (e.g., Kehoe, 1988; Kehoe & Macrae, 1997) cannot explain it, because the PRF group had received many more conditioning trials, and if anything a stronger CS–US association, than the other groups. The conditioning model of Pearce and Hall (1980) also predicts more rapid reacquisition in the PRF condition. In their view, the occasional reinforced trials in extinction would be surprising and maintain more attention to the CS than would simple extinction; this would also produce more rapid reacquisition.

The findings have implications for the prevention relapse. For a smoker or drinker who completely abstains from cigarettes or alcohol, a "lapse" caused by the passage of time (spontaneous recovery), the return of contextual conditions previously associated with the habit (renewal), or merely entering a context strongly associated with the US (reinstatement) may cause the client to smoke another cigarette or take another drink. Whether this lapse leads to a more permanent relapse may depend in part on how the client responds after that first reacquisition trial; has the client associated having one cigarette or one drink with having more of them soon afterward? We have introduced an operant component here. If the client takes a cigarette or a drink, he or she is using a voluntary or "instrumental" action. More recent research (Woods & Bouton, 2006) has therefore investigated the effects of occasional reinforced trials in extinction on reacquisition in an instrumental (operant) learning situation.

Renewal, reinstatement, and spontaneous recovery have all been demonstrated in operant conditioning (e.g., see Bouton, 2002; Bouton & Swartzentruber, 1991), but there is relatively little previous research on rapid reacquisition. In one of our experiments, different groups of rats received lever-press training on a VI-30 second schedule of reinforcement in which responses were reinforced on the average of every 30 seconds. Two of the groups then received a typical response–no outcome extinction procedure, whereas two other groups received a PRF procedure during extinction in which lever presses were occasionally reinforced. To reduce responding, the PRF procedure was made gradually leaner throughout the 8-day extinction phase (from VI-4 minute to VI-32 minute). The test for reacquisition involved placing the rats on either a VI-2 minute or a VI-8 minute schedule and allowing them to experience the response–outcome contingency. The question was whether extinction with occasional reinforcement for responding (the lean VI schedules) would slow the expected rapid reacquisition.

The results of this experiment are summarized in Figure 9.5, which shows the response rate of the groups during training, response elimination, and reacquisition testing at the left, center, and right. Similar to the Pavlovian conditioning findings (Bouton et al., 2004), the PRF procedure again slowed the rate at which responding was eliminated; in fact, the animals in the PRF groups were still responding a bit at the end of the response–elimination phase. The PRF procedure was nonetheless effective at slowing the rate of reacquisition on either the VI 2-minute or VI 8-minute reinforcement schedule introduced at the end of the experiment. Further work suggests that the PRF procedure mainly affects how the animal responds soon after each new response–reinforcer pairing. After extinction, responding returns quickly, but after the PRF procedure, responding remains at a slower and steadier rate. The implication of these results for substance abuse treatment is that an oc-

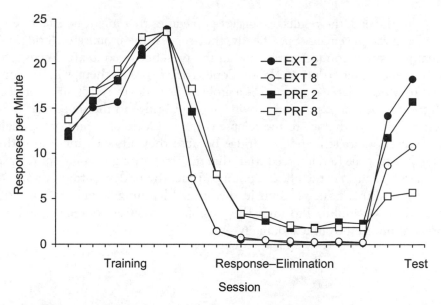

Figure 9.5. Mean number of lever-press responses during each session of training, response–elimination (extinction or partial reinforcement), and reacquisition testing on either a variable interval VI-2 minute or a VI-8 minute schedule of reinforcement. EXT = extinction; PRF = partial reinforcement.

casional taste of a cigarette or drug without a binge may help break the connection between a lapse and full-blown relapse (e.g., Bouton, 2000). The principle is also relevant when thinking about aversive learning situations, because the conditioning of a fear or anxiety may sometimes involve many trials. For example, an overweight child might be repeatedly teased by other children. To combat the anxiety, the child might undergo therapy and even move to a new school. The occurrence of a subsequent tease might signal additional teasing, however, thereby causing a full return of the child's anxiety. An occasional tease during treatment (i.e., a partial reinforcement extinction procedure) could teach the child that one tease does not necessarily lead to another and thus help prevent future relapse.

FINAL THOUGHTS AND COMMENTS

Research in the animal laboratory suggests that extinction can be remarkably context-specific. It cannot be assumed to destroy the original learning. The research reviewed in this chapter suggests that this may be true even when we try to optimize extinction learning by adding an incompatible US (counterconditioning), by spacing the extinction trials, or by conducting extinction in multiple contexts. To date, our attempts to optimize extinction learning have still left extinction surprisingly specific to its context—and therefore subject to relapse.

In the end, the results do suggest procedures that might be effective in reducing relapse effects. Specifically, they suggest the promise of "bridging" treatments that conduct extinction in the presence of contextual cues that will be encountered during relapse. Conducting exposure therapy in the context in which relapse is going to be a problem provides the most direct bridge. Retrieval cues for extinction provide another bridge in the sense that they bring a piece of therapy to the relapse context. Occasional reinforced trials in extinction are still another bridge because they allow extinction in the presence of a cue (a reinforced trial) that may be a strong stimulus for relapse in many clients. At the present point in time, the bridging strategy appears most promising. Basic research in the animal learning laboratory may still provide a powerful tool to study the possible mechanisms of relapse, and its prevention, in the clinical domain.

10

RENEWAL AND REINSTATEMENT OF FEAR: EVIDENCE FROM HUMAN CONDITIONING RESEARCH

DEBORA VANSTEENWEGEN, TRINETTE DIRIKX, DIRK HERMANS, BRAM VERVLIET, AND PAUL EELEN

A 32-year-old woman experiencing panic attacks was successfully treated by a cognitive–behavioral therapist. Some time after completing therapy, she wrote the following to a newsgroup:

> Hi, I have been having panic attacks for the past 6 years. They came on right about the time I was getting a much-desired promotion at my job. For 3 years I thought I had asthma. I knew nothing of panic attacks at the time. After a horrible panic attack that led to a visit to the emergency room and some intravenous valium, I finally knew.
>
> I completed cognitive–behavioral therapy for the panic attacks, and it did help. But I'm still struggling to get through every day. I blame a lot on my career since that is where they began. I know I felt normal for all my life prior to beginning my career. So I pray I can feel normal again. Several things worry me now. One is that I plan to quit my job for good and get pregnant and the very idea of leaving this job gives me hope, but

Debora Vansteenwegen is postdoctoral researcher of the fund for Scientific Research Vlaanderen (FWO-Vlaanderen).

I worry that being cooped up in the house will distort reality and my panic will increase . . .

Do you think that her worries are justified? Clinical practitioners report that relapse is not at all rare, yet it is not easy to predict relapse for this particular woman or, indeed, any particular person who has completed therapy. However, we can ask this: What are the determinants of relapse?

Psychologists who systematically investigate relapse began by evaluating the effectiveness of their therapy not only at the end of treatment but also at different moments later on. First, in an attempt to achieve a better understanding of this clinical phenomenon, Rachman (1989) developed the concept of "return of fear," which he described as the reappearance of fear that has undergone partial or complete extinction. He described several studies in which a specific data pattern of a decline in fear (or some of its symptoms) was followed by an interval without relearning, at the end of which a return of the original fear (or fear symptoms) was observed. This return does not have to be a complete return to the original level of fear, but might be partial as well.

Inspired by Rachman, other researchers continued systematic analyses of the conditions for return of fear. Some of them focused on individual differences that are predictive for the amount of return of fear (e.g., Wood & McGlynn, 2000). Others described the situations in which the return takes place. For example, return of fear can be influenced by factors that are present before (e.g., initial level of fear), during (e.g., the speed of fear reduction, the hierarchy of exposure material), and after treatment (e.g., a confrontation with a stressful life event; Jacobs & Nadel, 1985).

The questions posed by the newsgroup user at the beginning of this chapter concern in part the possible impact of posttreatment changes in life on the return of fear. Indeed, several clinical examples show that episodes of return of fear do often co-occur with major changes in life or other stressful events (Jacobs & Nadel, 1985). In line with these observations, animal conditioning research demonstrated that changes in context (physical–external or internal) or unpredicted confrontations with the original fear-eliciting stimulus after extinction can restore at least part of the original fears after extinction (for a review, see Bouton, 2000; see also chap. 9, this volume). In the classical conditioning literature, these observations stimulated the development of new theories about extinction.

The focus of this chapter is exposure and the phenomenon of return of fear based on theory and research about extinction in classical conditioning literature. First, we describe in detail how recent theoretical developments about extinction helps to understand better the phenomenon of return of fear. Second, we argue how human conditioning research is an essential step in relating animal conditioning findings to the clinical setting. Third, we focus on two specific posttreatment manipulations in more detail, namely, renewal (changing the context after extinction) and reinstatement (the presentation of unpredicted unconditioned stimuli [USs] after extinction). We present an overview of the available evidence in this regard and describe how a better understanding of the underlying mechanisms of these two phenomena has implications for the clinical study of return of fear. It also provides a gateway for clinical application of this research in the prevention of reoccurrence of fear.

EXPOSURE AND EXTINCTION

Most often the behavioral treatment of anxiety disorders (e.g., specific phobias and panic disorder) involves repeated and systematic exposure to the fear-provoking stimulus (e.g., Öst, 1997). Although such exposure-based treatment is highly effective in reducing immediate symptoms of fear, there is substantial evidence that fear may return with the passage of time (Rachman, 1989). It is assumed that exposure therapy involves processes analogous to extinction. During an extinction procedure, the conditioned stimulus (CS) is repeatedly presented without the US and this most often leads to a decrease in conditioned responding. During exposure therapy, the patient is repeatedly exposed to the object of fear (CS), and generally a decrease in fear is observed. Hence, classical conditioning theory and, more specifically, recent theoretical developments about extinction have implications for exposure treatment.

Theories about extinction (for a review, see Rescorla, 2001) suggest that extinction of conditioned responding should not be equated with unlearning. Instead, extinction involves additional learning. After an acquisition period during which the CS was associated with a US, new information is provided about the CS. During acquisition, the CS becomes a good predictor of the US; during extinction this acquisition information needs correction because the CS is no longer a good predictor. This correction or new information does not remove the older association between the CS and the US, but it masks or inhibits what was learned during acquisition so that two associations coexist: a CS–US association or excitatory link and a CS–no-US association or inhibitory link. In chapter 9 of this volume, Bouton and colleagues describe evidence from the animal conditioning literature that supports the idea that an extinction procedure does not render the CS neutral. Four postextinction restoration phenomena are described to demonstrate that extinction cannot be defined as unlearning: spontaneous recovery (return after the mere passage of time), disinhibition (return after the presentation of a novel stimulus), reinstatement (return after reexposure to the US), and renewal (return after a context change).

Translated to the clinical situation, this suggests that even if a therapeutic procedure is effective in reducing fear, the fear-arousing association to the object of fear is not erased and hence, given certain conditions, it can be expressed in fear responses again. Reexposure to the US, a context change, the presentation of a new stimulus or even the mere passage of time, may reactivate the "hidden" association and lead to (partial) return of fear. Apparently, the best conceptualization is that exposure treatment temporarily or contextually masks the fear-arousing association but does not erase it.

UNDERLYING MECHANISMS OF EXTINCTION

The focus of this chapter is on the underlying mechanisms in extinction and their repercussions for clinical practice. To the extent that extinction and exposure share the same mechanism, the study of the underlying mechanisms helps to evaluate which interventions are beneficial in reducing the impact of postextinction factors and hence help to increase the stability and permanence for the exposure effects obtained in therapy. The majority of knowledge about the underlying mechanisms comes from animal studies. It cannot be unconditionally accepted, however, that similar mechanisms will be obtained in human studies. Similar results and procedures do not necessarily also indicate similar processes. Although in general mechanisms can be formulated on the basis of the procedures independently of the paradigm by which they are investigated (see, for example, predictions of the Rescorla & Wagner [1972] model), it is quite often observed that although procedures are similar, different mechanisms play a role depending on the paradigm used. For example, in their overview on behavioral and neurological extinction, Myers and Davis (2002) argue that the underlying mechanism for extinction can be different depending on the type of animal conditioning paradigm that is used. Within the animal conditioning literature, different mechanisms can be found even when similar procedures are used; thus it comes as no surprise that differences can be observed between animal and human conditioning research.

One solution is to bridge the gap, carefully and systematically, between animal conditioning studies and studies with (sub)clinical populations. These two types of research differ in the subjects under investigation, but they also differ in the extent of experimental control over different aspects of the procedure. In an animal conditioning study, acquisition as well as extinction is under full experimental control. In a clinical context, there is obviously no experimental control over the acquisition of fear. The specific circumstances of fear acquisition are often unknown. When exactly did acquisition happen? Was it one-trial learning or a repeated experience? What were the physical, internal, and emotional contexts of which it happened? Moreover, the exposure itself, although more or less under the control of the therapist, is often not process-pure. That is, treatment involves much more than a simple extinction procedure, such as modeling, counterconditioning, and social reinforcement. As described later, to differentiate mechanisms responsible for extinction, exact information about the circumstances of acquisition and extinction is of crucial importance.

One solution is laboratory-based studies in which fear is established before it is extinguished. Despite the loss of ecological validity, the strength of conditioning studies is that they distill the theoretical assumptions to their essence and allow study of the phenomenon under strictly controlled circumstances, thereby permitting better analysis of the underlying mechanisms. Hence human conditioning studies are most promising to fill the gap between animal conditioning research and studies with clinical populations. Furthermore, to draw conclusions about the specific emotion of fear, a paradigm is used that experimentally induces fear in humans (within ethical constraints) or that at least includes an aversive learning situation. Of the different human conditioning paradigms, the human fear-conditioning paradigm (e.g., Hamm & Vaitl, 1996; Lipp et al., 1994; Lovibond et al., 2000) most closely resembles a real-life fear situation.

HUMAN FEAR CONDITIONING

In the conditioning paradigm as it is used in our lab, neutral visual stimuli (i.e., pictures of human faces without expression, black-and-white pictorial drawings, geometric figures) are used as CS and either an electrocutaneous stimulus that is idiosyncratically selected as "not painful but asking some effort to tolerate" or a loud aversive noise is used as US. Both USs are rated as clearly unpleasant, intense, and startling. We use a differential conditioning procedure in which during acquisition one of two visual stimuli (CS+) is systematically followed by the US and the other visual stimulus (CS–) is not. During extinction, both stimuli are again presented in a semi-randomized order, but the US is no longer presented. In almost all experiments, instructions are given at the beginning of the experiment that participants should focus on the US and try to predict its occurrence. Depending on the experiment, acquisition consists of 4, 8, or 10 conditioning trials for each CS. During extinction, both the CS+ and CS– are presented, but the CS+ is no longer followed by the US. In all experiments, the extinction phase consists of at least as many extinction trials as acquisition trials. In experiments with a small number of acquisition trials (e.g., four), the number of extinction trials is up to 2 times the number of acquisition trials. Associative learning effects (i.e., acquisition and extinction effects) are measured by an increase or decrease in differential responding to the CS+ and CS–.

Because emotions are latent constructs that can only be measured indirectly through verbal, behavioral, or psychophysiological indices (Öhman, 1987), we included the measurement of these indices of emotional change in our procedure. Often the correlations among the indices are low, partly because physiological, behavioral, and verbal responses provide unique contributions to the construct of fear. That is, whereas introspection from verbal indices reveals valuable information, bodily responses and indirect behavioral measures provide additional information that may not always be accessible through language-based processes. The verbal ratings within this paradigm are usually taken retrospectively at the end of each conditioning phase. Participants have to indicate to what extent they expected the US to occur when the CS+ or CS– was presented. They are also asked to indicate how pleasant or unpleasant, fearful, and aroused they felt when watching the last CS+ or CS–. The advantage of the psychophysiological indices is that they can be taken online without being obtrusive. Skin conductance, considered as an index of orienting, anticipation, and US expectancy (e.g., Dawson & Furedy, 1976; Hamm & Vaitl, 1996; Lovibond et al., 2000); and startle modulation, best considered as an index of fear—sensitive to both arousal and valence of the stimulus (e.g., Cuthbert et al., 1996; Hamm & Vaitl, 1996; chap. 2, this volume)—are taken as physiological indices.

The behavioral indices used are affective priming and the secondary reaction time task. The latter task involves the presentation of unpredictable tones during the CS+, the CS–, and the intertrial intervals. Participants are instructed to press a button as soon as they hear the tone. An increase in reaction times for tones presented during one stimulus over another is traditionally interpreted as an indication for more attentional resource allocation toward the former stimulus, and therefore reaction times are expected to be slower during CS+ than CS– presentations. Hence, the reaction times can be registered online as well. Finally, the affective priming task serves as an indirect measure of valence. The CS+ and the CS– are used as primes and precede positive and negative target words within a very short interstimulus interval (300 ms). Participants are asked to categorize the target words as quickly as possible as positive or negative. This categorization is typically faster when the valence of the prime and the target are congruent (positive–positive or negative–negative) than when the valences are incongruent (positive–negative). Hence, when responses for negative target words that follow the CS+ stimulus are faster than responses for words that follow the CS–, then the CS+ is indirectly and automatically evaluated more negatively than the CS– (Hermans, Spruyt, & Eelen, 2003; see chap.2, this volume, for extensive discussion of the various indices).

Although not all indices are included in all studies, the series of studies conducted in our lab systematically show that after acquisition, the CS+, in contrast to the CS–, is verbally rated as more negative (valence), more arousing, and more fearful (Dirikx et al., 2004; Hermans, Vansteenwegen, Crombez, Baeyens, & Eelen, 2002) and becomes a better predictor for the US (US expectancy ratings; Hermans, Vansteenwegen, et al., 2002; Vansteenwegen et al., 2005; Vervliet, Vansteenwegen, Baeyens, Hermans, & Eelen, 2005; Vervliet, Vansteenwegen, & Eelen, 2004). The CS+ elicits more electrodermal responding (Vansteenwegen et al., 2005; Vervliet et al., 2005; Vervliet et al., 2004) and more eyeblink startle potentiation (Vansteenwegen et al., 1998). The secondary reaction-time task shows slower reactions when a tone is presented during the CS+ than when the tone is presented during the CS– (Dirikx et al., 2004). Also, the affective priming task showed a systematic differentiation between CS+ and CS– after acquisition in the expected direction (Hermans, Spruyt, et al., 2003; Hermans, Crombez, Vansteenwegen, Baeyens, & Eelen, 2002; Hermans, Vansteenwegen, et al., 2002; Vansteenwegen, Francken, Vervliet, Declerq, & Eelen, in press). On the basis of this verbal, physiological, and behavioral evidence, we are confident that the CS+ after acquisition has become a fearful stimulus, as defined by properties of negative valence: high arousal (P. J. Lang, Bradley, & Cuthbert, 1997) and US expectation (e.g., Davey, 1994a).

The extinction data from our paradigm can be summarized as follows. Conditioned online verbal US expectancy, electrodermal responding (Vansteenwegen et al., 1998, 2005; Vansteenwegen, Francken, et al., in press), eyeblink startle modulation responses (Vansteenwegen et al., 1998), and differential reaction times in a secondary reaction-time task decrease over extinction trials (Dirikx et al., 2004; Hermans, Dirikx, Vansteenwegen, Baeyens, & Eelen, 2005). Using these measures in a procedure with an equal number of trials in extinction as in acquisition, almost always the differentiation between CS+ and CS– has disappeared at the end of extinction. In contrast, the affective priming data still show an equally large CS+ to CS– differentiation at the end of extinction than at the end of acquisition (Hermans, Crombez, et al., 2002; for a demonstration with an extinction procedure with 3 times the number of acquisition trials, see Vansteenwegen, Francken, et al., in press). Finally, verbal valence, arousal, and fear ratings significantly decrease (e.g., Hermans, Crombez, et al., 2002), although some differentiation between CS+ and CS– usually persists at the end of extinction.

In sum, we can conclude that the CS+ in our paradigm becomes a fearful stimulus after acquisition, and that at the end of a standard extinction procedure, the CS+ has lost at least one essential aspect of fear, namely, US expectancy. However, it seems to be more difficult to change the valence aspect of the CS+ through the extinction procedure (as predicted by evaluative conditioning theory; for a review, see De Houwer, Thomas, & Baeyens, 2001). Next, we focus on the phenomena of renewal and reinstatement. Following a short overview of existing evidence from the animal conditioning literature, evidence for these phenomena obtained in our laboratory and an analysis of the underlying mechanisms are presented.

RENEWAL OF FEAR

Renewal is defined as the return of extinguished conditioned responses caused by changes in the contextual cues that were present during extinction. The observation most frequently reported is ABA renewal. Bouton and colleagues (e.g., Bouton & Bolles, 1979; Bouton & King, 1983) demonstrated that conditioned responding is renewed when animals are tested in the original acquisition context after extinction in a different context. Renewal effects are also obtained when, after extinction in a different context, transfer of extinction is tested in a third context (ABC renewal; Bouton & Brooks, 1993). Finally, AAB renewal was demonstrated in animals (Bouton & Ricker, 1994). In such a procedure, acquisition and extinction take place in an identical context, but testing is executed in a new context. This type of renewal is not as robust as the other types, but the observation itself has nevertheless important theoretical and clinical implications (for discussion, see Thomas, Larsen, & Ayres, 2003; Vervliet, 2004).

Evidence in the clinical literature stresses the importance of the context in exposure therapy as well. Mineka, Mystkowski, Hladek, and Rodriguez (1999) showed a return of self-reported fear 1 week after a single-session exposure-based treatment when treated participants with spider phobia were tested in a different room. Rodriguez, Craske, Mineka, and Hladek (1999) showed a return in the level of heart rate responding for one specific stimulus 2 weeks after exposure treatment when the incidental (room) and meaningful (therapist) context were changed. Finally, Mystkowski, Craske, and Echiverri (2002) manipulated the contexts in a more naturalistic way and used an inside and an outside context. They showed a clear return of fear in self-report data 1 week after a single-session exposure-based therapy when participants were tested in the other context. These clinical studies can best be compared with an ABC type of renewal: Exposure therapy probably takes place in a context different from the original acquisition context, and return of fear occurs in a new, third context. Furthermore, there is some clinical evidence that a return of fear in those with spider phobia is observed not only when the context has been changed but also when a new spider is presented that is not similar to the spiders used in therapy (Rowe & Craske, 1998b). This suggests that exposure effects are not only restricted to the exposure context but also to the specific stimuli used during exposure.

Renewal demonstrations in the human conditioning literature are scarce. There are some demonstrations of renewal in human contingency learning (García-Gutiérrez & Rosas, 2003a; Rosas, Vila, Lugo, & Lopez, 2001; Vervliet, Vansteenwegen, & Eelen, in press). In our laboratory, renewal was demonstrated in a human fear-conditioning paradigm with skin conductance and retrospective US expectancy ratings as indices of learning. Contexts were manipulated by turning the central lighting of the experimental room on or off. In the first experiment (Vansteenwegen et al., 2005) two groups were compared: an ABA renewal group and an AAA control group. The renewal group received acquisition in one context, extinction in the opposite context, and was tested again for the CSs in the original acquisition context. In the control group, all phases were executed in the same context. Although no change in differential electrodermal responding was observed when switching the context after acquisition, there was a clear return of conditioned responding with the context change after extinction. No such return was observed in the control group. The retrospective US expectancy ratings confirmed this data pattern. Thus, in line with animal research, we demonstrated in our human fear-conditioning paradigm that although acquisition easily generalizes to a new context, extinction does not.

In a second experiment, we tested an AAB renewal group using the same procedure except that acquisition and extinction took place in one context and testing took place in another (unpublished results). We did not obtain renewal in this design. Both the CS+ as well as the CS– elicited more conditioned responding because of the change in context, indicating that the context shift did not go unnoticed but that the CS+ did not elicit more expectancy than the CS–. Hence, when using a context change that was similar to the context change in the ABA design, we did not obtain an AAB renewal effect.

In a second line of research, we investigated whether differences in generalization between acquisition and extinction could also be observed when stimuli rather than contexts were manipulated. As mentioned earlier, this may have implications for the clinical practice. For example, a person bitten by a dog may easily develop a general fear of dogs (generalization of acquisition). When systematically exposed to a different dog, will this exposure effect then generalize as easily to a general nonfear of dogs? Is what has been acquired during extinction confined to the specific stimuli used, or does it generalize toward similar but not identical stimuli?

To investigate this question, in a first experiment (Vervliet et al., 2005) with skin conductance and retrospective US expectancy ratings, an AaA group was compared with an AAA control group. After normal acquisition, the AaA group received extinction with similar but not identical stimuli and was then tested again with the original acquisition stimuli. For the AAA control group, acquisition, extinction, and testing were executed with the same stimuli. Although differential acquisition effects generalized substantially to the extinction stimuli in the AaA group, the participants hardly generalized from what was learned with the extinction stimuli to the original acquisition stimuli after extinction. In a second experiment (Vervliet et al., 2004), the equivalent of an AAB renewal design was tested. In one group (AAa), acquisition and extinction were executed with identical stimuli, but testing after extinction took place with similar but not identical stimuli. An AaA control group using the same stimuli but in different phases replicated the return as observed in the previous study. In the AAa group, however, no return was observed despite the fact that postexperimental interviews indicated the stimulus change had been detected.

In sum, in the fear-conditioning paradigm, evidence was obtained that extinction in a context different from the acquisition context or with a stimulus that differs from the acquisition stimulus can cause a return of fear. Because no generalization decrement was observed after acquisition, these ABA renewal effects suggest that generalization of acquisition is much easier than generalization of extinction. However, this asymmetry between the generalization of acquisition and extinction was not observed in an AAB renewal design in which acquisition and extinction took place in the same context.

MECHANISMS OF RENEWAL AND CLINICAL IMPLICATIONS

Inspired by several postextinction restoration effects observed in their animal conditioning laboratory, Bouton and his colleagues developed a contextual theory about extinction (see chap. 9, this volume) stating that it would typically involve acquisition of new context-specific information (Bouton, 1988, 2000). The extinction context acquires a modulatory role and helps to disambiguate the old knowledge (CS–US association and acquisition) and the new knowledge (CS–no US association or extinction). Renewal is observed as a consequence of leaving the extinction context. By consequence, the extinction information is made less available.

Translating this idea to clinical practice suggests that, during exposure, the association of the fearful object with negative consequences is not subjected to change. Rather, one learns that under certain circumstances, this association does not apply. Typically, these circumstances are defined by context factors. The extinction information is only effective in the presence of the exposure-therapy context. According to this approach, exposure effects will always be context- (and by extension, stimulus-) specific, and hence expectations with regard to the generality and permanence of the effects of exposure are pessimistic.

Two alternative mechanisms are traditionally used to explain the context-specificity of extinction (see Lovibond, Preston, & Mackintosh, 1984). The first mechanism includes the formation of a direct inhibitory association between the extinction context and the US. Hence, the extinction context directly predicts the nonoccurrence of the US and as such protects the CS from extinction (Lovibond et al., 2000). Translated to clinical practice, a patient learns that the therapy context is safe (safety signal hypothesis). When leaving the therapy context, the inhibitory power of the context and therapist is no longer present, and because the objects of fear were protected from extinction, fear returns. Following the second alternative mechanism, the fearful object is perceived as a partially different stimulus in the exposure context than in the acquisition context. In this respect, exposure might have involved a (partially) "wrong" stimulus, and fear returns when the original acquisition stimulus is presented. In the animal conditioning literature, this mechanism is called *generalization decrement*. Note that our demonstration of restricted generalization in the ABA and the AaA designs goes beyond simple generalization. Participants showed no loss of generalization after acquisition, whereas they did after extinction. Hence, the perceptual differences between the stimuli by themselves can not be held responsible for the observed differences.

Bouton and his colleagues demonstrated, however, that in their animal conditioning preparations, the context did not become inhibitory during extinction (e.g., Bouton & King, 1983), and showed no generalization decrement between acquisition and extinction. Hence, they made a strong case in favor of the modulatory mechanism in their preparation.

However, as discussed earlier, arguing on the basis of this evidence that similar mechanisms are at play in our human fear-conditioning experiments is not justified. What can we tell about the mechanisms on the basis of our own data? First of all, we did obtain return of fear in an ABA design, with contexts as well as stimuli. In both experiments, the context and stimulus changes clearly had an impact on extinction performance. Second, to the extent that there was no decrement in conditioning when changing from acquisition to extinction, a simple explanation on the basis of generalization decrement is discarded. Third, we did not obtain evidence for a return in the AAB designs using similar context and stimulus changes as in the successful ABA designs. In human contingency learning paradigms, however, we did obtain evidence for AAB renewal (Vervliet et al., in press). In the animal conditioning literature, there are similar reports about difficulties obtaining AAB as well (e.g., Bouton & King, 1983; Bouton & Swartzentruber, 1989). Moreover, Thomas et al. (2003) demonstrated in a systematic study that AAB effects are weaker compared with ABA effects. Therefore, it would not be fair to argue here that demonstrating AAB renewal in our paradigm would be impossible; indeed arguing the nonexistence of something is by itself impossible. We can conclude, however, that AAB renewal is at least more difficult to obtain than ABA renewal.

The modulatory mechanism can explain our findings, although it cannot explain why our AAB effects are less easily obtained than the ABA effects without taking into account some additional explanations. As long as no AAB effects are demonstrated, the directly inhibitory context–US association can also explain our results. When asked to formulate the learning rule of the experiment, participants often simply reported that one context seemed to be safe. Hence, they do not specify spontaneously a modulatory relationship but rather describe the context as a safety signal. Of course, this may be caused by a lack of verbally expressed precision or specificity rather than by the absence of the modulatory mechanism itself. A third possibility is that both mechanisms operate at the same time in our ABA design and that some participants behave following the former and others the latter. Further research will address this issue.

For clinical practice, the general conclusion that AAB effects are weaker than ABA effects as well as the possibility of the formation of a direct inhibitory context–US association, suggest that it might be helpful to imitate the original acquisition situation whenever possible during treatment. Unfortunately, the exact circumstances of acquisition are often not traceable; even if traceable, there would always be differences between the exposure and the acquisition context that cannot be excluded because of practical and ethical considerations. For example, the presence of the therapist is an essential part of the exposure context. The therapist must always be aware that she or he can become a safety signal and hence prevents fear of the objects to extinguish. Also, when the extinction information is always bound to the stimuli and contexts of the exposure training, one might want to focus on the explicit training of the transfer to other contexts (and generalization to other stimuli) as a strategy to reduce renewal effects.

PREVENTION OF RENEWAL

In the animal conditioning literature, two strategies are suggested to prevent renewal and to stimulate transfer to other contexts. The first one is the use of retrieval cues (Brooks & Bouton, 1994). These cues are stimuli that can be carried from the extinction context toward the test context and retrieve the information from the extinction–exposure episode. Brooks and Bouton (1994) demonstrated in an ABA renewal design that testing with cues that were also present throughout extinction reduced the renewal effect. The second method is extinction in multiple contexts. Although not all researchers find a reduction of renewal when using this method (see chap. 9, this volume), there are at least two clear demonstrations of a reduction when using multiple contexts. Gunther, Denniston, and Miller (1998) showed that rats that received extinction in three contexts compared with those that received extinction in only one context showed less return of conditioned suppression in a fourth context. Chelonis, Calton, Hart, and Schachtman (1999) demonstrated in a conditioned taste-aversion procedure that after exposure in three contexts, the test in the original acquisition context produced less renewal than when exposure took place in one and the same context.

In the clinical literature, there are parallel lines of evidence. Rowe and Craske (1998b) showed a return of fear toward a new type of stimulus after exposure with one and the same stimulus. This return was reduced when multiple stimulus examples were used during exposure. Evidence for the effectiveness of the retrieval cue method was presented by Collins and Brandon (2002). They showed that the return of alcohol cue reactivity after extinction caused by a context change could be reduced by the use of retrieval cues that were present during extinction.

In a differential human contingency learning experiment (Marescau, Vansteenwegen, Vervliet, & Eelen, 2006), we demonstrated the effectiveness of retrieval cues in reducing the renewal effect. In this task, participants predicted the occurrence of a sign (US) on the back of a card. On the front, one of two neutral pictures was presented. During acquisition, one of the pictures was paired systematically with the US, whereas the other picture was not. Before participants received feedback about the presence of the US, they were asked to indicate on every trial to what extent they expected that the US would be present. Contexts were manipulated by changing the background color of the cards, and the retrieval cue was a small black cross that preceded 75% of the CSs during extinction. Three groups were created. Two groups (ABA and ABA retrieval) received acquisition and testing in the same context and extinction in a different context; the third group received no change of contexts (AAA). In contrast with the AAA group, a stronger renewal effect was obtained in the ABA group; however, the ABA retrieval group tested with cues showed less return of US expectancy than the ABA group tested without cues.

This experiment replicated the findings from Brooks and Bouton (1994) and showed that discrete cues previously presented during extinction can attenuate renewal when presented in the test context. It cannot be considered a demonstration of return of fear, however, because no emotional learning was involved. In a first attempt to demonstrate the effect of retrieval cues in the ABA renewal design in our human fear-conditioning paradigm, we conducted a study with skin conductance and retrospective US expectancy ratings as indices of learning (Vansteenwegen et al., in press). Participants who received acquisition in one context (dark–light manipulation, discussed earlier) and extinction in the opposite context were tested in the original acquisition context, either with a retrieval cue that was presented during extinction or with a cue that was presented during acquisition. This acquisition cue was equally familiar as the extinction cue but was supposed to activate the acquisition information instead of the extinction information. The data showed that in comparison to the acquisition cue group, the extinction cue group showed less recovery of conditioned electrodermal responding and retrospective US expectancy after extinction. Thus, the procedure used to create the retrieval cues was effective, and research that analyzes whether the retrieval cues effectively reduce renewal can begin.

In a second line of research, we aimed to replicate promising findings with the multiple-context method in a clinical analog experiment with students with spider anxiety (Vansteenwegen, Vervliet, Hermans, Baeyens, & Van den Bergh, 2006). Although we did not experimentally induce fear in this study, we strictly controlled the extinction phase in the sense that the only differences between groups concerned manipulations of the contexts. We included three groups: a single-context group, a multiple-context group, and an extinction control group. The single context group watched a videotape that repeatedly showed a crouching spider in a specific location of a house; participants were then tested with a tape with the same spider in a new location. A multiple-context group was treated similarly but watched video fragments of the same spider in different locations. In the control group, a videotape was presented with an equal number of fragments with locations of a house without the spider. After exposure, all three groups were tested for the spider in a new context. Electrodermal responding and ratings of the fragments showed a decrease over trials only in the extinction groups (multiple and single) and not in the control group. More important, presenting the spider in a new context revealed a return of the responses in the single-context group, and as expected, this return was significantly less in the multiple-context group. Hence, within this line of research, we demonstrated that manipulating the contexts effectively reduces the return of fear of spiders in students with fear of spiders. To our knowledge, this is the first demonstration of the effectiveness of this method in a controlled human fear experiment. In the future, we plan to study the effectiveness of this multiple-context method in our conditioning paradigm as well.

MECHANISMS THAT PREVENT RENEWAL OF FEAR AND THEIR IMPLICATIONS

We propose that two mechanisms are important to explain renewal: the modulatory mechanism in which the context modulates the relation between the CS and the US and the direct inhibitory association between the context and the US. As long as retrieval cues contribute to the retrieval of the extinction context, they may be helpful in preventing return of fear regardless of the underlying mechanism. Either they will partially activate the representation of the context that has a direct inhibitory association with the US or they will reactivate the context that is necessary to activate the context-dependent inhibitory CS–US association. Only empirical evidence is available, however, for the effectiveness of the retrieval cues in a paradigm in which the context has a modulatory function (Brooks & Bouton, 1994). Future research could address whether retrieval cues are effective when renewal is caused by a direct context–US inhibitory association.

In the case of the direct inhibitory association model, using multiple contexts increases the number of safe contexts that develop an inhibitory association with the US. Because there will be more similarities between the new context and the exposure contexts, generalization toward a new context will be easier. Whether the exposure in multiple contexts will finally "unprotect" the CS from extinction and change the affective meaning of the CS is not clear. Similar reasoning can be applied to the modulatory mechanism; the number of contexts in which the CS is no longer followed by the US increases. Because of enhanced encoding variability or increased similarities between exposure and test contexts (or both), generalization to a new context will be easier. It is not clear whether these multiple exposures will break down the original CS–US association, however.

The retrieval cue method does not change what is actually learned during exposure; the CS–US association is still context-dependent or the extinction context still protects the CS from extinction during exposure. In contrast, the multiple-context method effectively increases the number of contexts that might have an impact on what is learned and therefore might have the potential of changing the original CS–US acquisition rule. Intuitively, it seems possible that increasing the number of exceptions (in Context 1, the CS is no longer followed by the US; in Context 2, the CS is no longer followed by the US, etc.) will help to change the general acquisition rule (i.e., CS predicts the US) into a new general CS–no US rule (the CS does not predict the US). From a theoretical point of view, however, it is not immediately clear how this process of generalization would develop. Further research is needed to clarify the underlying mechanisms of these methods.

REINSTATEMENT OF FEAR

Reinstatement is defined as the return of extinguished conditioned responses caused by the experience of one or more US-only presentations after extinction. A typical reinstatement experiment first involves acquisition of conditioned responses through the contingent presentation of a CS and a US. Next, a series of unreinforced CSs is presented, resulting in the extinction of conditioned responding. After extinction, the crucial reinstatement phase follows during which one or more US presentations are administered in the absence of the CS. In contrast to a control group that does not receive the additional US-only trials, a (partial) return of fear is typically observed when the CS is tested.

Reinstatement has been studied extensively in the animal laboratory and seems to be a robust phenomenon. In addition to studies that use an aversive Pavlovian procedure (e.g., Bouton, 1984), reinstatement has also been shown in appetitive preparations (e.g., Delamater, 1997) and instrumental conditioning procedures (e.g., Baker, Steinwald, & Bouton, 1991). Over the years, different theoretical accounts of postextinction reinstatement have been developed. Rescorla and Heth (1975) suggested that the additional US presentations after extinction restore the US representation that had been depressed across extinction. This account did not support the growing evidence that the reinstatement context was of crucial importance, however. Bouton and Bolles (1979) convincingly showed that conditioned contextual stimuli are necessary to obtain reinstatement (but see Richardson, Duffield, Bailey, & Westbrook, 1999, for an example of counterevidence). To deal with this context-dependency observation, the context–CS summation view was formulated. During the reinstatement phase, the reinstatement context becomes excitatory, and this contextual conditioning is assumed to summate with the residual associative strength of the CS after extinction. On the basis of the observation that contextual excitation not always summates with CSs, Bouton and colleagues formulated a third account (e.g., Bouton & King, 1986). In this view, reinstatement is interpreted as a special form of occasion setting by contextual cues. US-only presentations in the test context restore conditioned fear to the context and make it more difficult to retrieve the extinction information. Note the parallel here with Bouton's modulatory account for renewal. Leaving the extinction context makes it more difficult to retrieve the CS–no US association.

Contrary to the extensive amount of research in animals, reinstatement studies with humans are rare. Several experiments have been conducted on reinstatement in human contingency learning experiments (García-Gutiérrez & Rosas, 2003a, 2003b; Vila & Rosas, 2001). These studies provide interesting information on the mechanisms of reinstatement. As already noted, however, it remains questionable whether the causal judgment task reveals the same mechanisms as the ones that operate in aversive conditioning procedures.

We have been studying reinstatement using the differential fear-conditioning paradigm with verbal US expectancy, fear, and valence ratings at the end of each phase and an online secondary reaction-time task as an index of learning. In the three reinstatement studies discussed here, acquisition and extinction proceeded uneventfully. After extinction, the crucial reinstatement manipulation was implemented. Both the reinstatement group and the control group watched the black background of a computer screen during the reinstatement phase. No pictures were presented. Participants in the reinstatement group received a limited number of US-only presentations (usually two or four). In the control group, no USs were administered. Next, all participants were tested for a return of conditioned responding under conditions of extinction.

In the first reinstatement study (Hermans et al., 2005) a significant reinstatement effect was obtained. The extinguished US expectancy associated with the CS+ reappeared selectively in the reinstatement group, but this return of conditioned responses was not observed in the control group. A similar pattern was observed in the fear ratings. In the second study (Dirikx, Hermans, Vansteenwegen, Baeyens, & Eelen, in press), the reinstatement effect in the US expectancy ratings was successfully replicated.

One limitation of these first two studies, however, was that the secondary reaction time task did not corroborate the reinstatement effects. In this sense, one could still argue that these results were (partially) caused by demand effects. In a third study (Dirikx et al., 2004), this possibility was ruled out. In addition to reinstatement in the fear ratings, a significant reinstatement effect was established in the secondary reaction time task. After the US-only presentations, a differential slowing in reaction times reappeared in the reinstatement group, whereas no changes were observed in the control group. These experiments illustrate that when studied in humans, the confrontation with unpredicted USs after extinction can restore (part of) the original fear. To our knowledge, these are the first demonstrations of reinstatement of fear responses in a human population.

MECHANISMS OF REINSTATEMENT AND CLINICAL IMPLICATIONS

The fear-conditioning paradigm allows for the manipulation of several variables that may elucidate the mechanisms that drive reinstatement. Unraveling this phenomenon may lead to a better knowledge of clinical relapse and to concrete guidelines for treatment and prevention of relapse. An important question is, for example, whether the reinstating US needs to be the same US as the one during acquisition. In the animal laboratory (Rescorla & Heth, 1975) as well as in human contingency learning studies (García-Gutiérrez & Rosas, 2003b), reinstatement has been found with a reinstating US that differed from the US that was paired with the CS+ during acquisition. García-Gutiérrez and Rosas (2003b) concluded from these findings that their reinstatement observation probably depended on a change from the interference context that is induced by presenting an outcome on its own and that reinstatement can therefore be considered as a special form of renewal. If these findings prove to be replicable in human fear conditioning (i.e., reinstatement with a US different from the US during acquisition), this would dramatically increase the circumstances in which a return of fear would be possible because any context changes might elicit reinstatement. In addition, if it is true that reinstatement can, to a certain extent, be considered a special case of renewal, this would suggest that methods available to reduce renewal may be applicable to attenuate reinstatement as well.

Given that Rescorla and Heth (1975) observed reinstatement in rats with a reinstating US that was qualitatively different from the one used during acquisition but had the same affective properties (i.e., aversive) as the original US, it remains unclear whether reinstatement in human fear-conditioning preparations requires the presentation of a stimulus that shares affective properties with the acquisition US. If the US indeed needs to be aversive but may nonetheless be qualitatively different from the original US, an explanation of fear reinstatement as a special form of renewal does not seem to be sufficient, and to some extent the affective congruency should be accounted for in what is learned during reinstatement. An account that takes into consideration the formation of an association between the US and the reinstatement context is needed.

Also, further research that manipulates the reinstatement and test context might reveal the conditions under which reinstatement occurs, as well as the mechanisms that drive reinstatement. For instance, it has been repeatedly shown that reinstatement can be reduced by exposure to the reinstatement context after the presentation of the reinstating USs (e.g., Richardson et al., 1999). This finding has been interpreted as evidence for context conditioning of the US as a mechanism that drives reinstatement (Bouton, 1991a). Replicating this finding within the human fear-conditioning preparation would further validate this theory. Debate about the underlying mechanisms responsible for reinstatement in the animal conditioning literature continues (for further discussion, see Delamater, 1997; Richardson et al., 1999). Future conditioning research that disentangles the mechanisms is needed before advice for clinical practice can be formulated.

The reinstatement studies described here illustrate that the CS–US relationship is not abolished by the extinction procedure. Nevertheless, most responses seemed to decrease readily during the extinction phase. An interesting exception is the valence response. By the end of our extinction procedure, the CS is no longer a fearful stimulus because the expectancy of the US is extinguished, but it might still have an unpleasant connotation because of its previous history. In clinical practice, this might lead to the situation in which after exposure therapy the patient no longer fears the CS (e.g., open spaces, elevators) and no longer actively expects the CS to be followed by a US (e.g., a panic attack) but retains a strong dislike for the CS. Hermans, Vansteenwegen, and colleagues (2002) suggested that the remaining negative valence of the CS+ after extinction might function as an affective motivational source for the reemergence of conditioned fear responses. We consider the role of stimulus valence in return of fear as complementary to the role of context conditioning of the US during reinstatement. In our view, stimulus valence might account for individual differences in the strength of the reinstatement effect because in all three reinstatement studies from our laboratory, the more negative the CS+ (or the affective difference between CS+ and CS–) after extinction, the stronger the reinstatement that was observed. These findings yield concrete starting points for the prevention of reinstatement by acting on the negative valence of the phobic object in addition to the reduction of arousal and expectancies.

CONCLUSIONS

This chapter provided an overview of the evidence related to renewal and reinstatement in human associative learning. Together with clinical and human contingency learning paradigm demonstrations, initial evidence for these phenomena in human fear-conditioning experiments has been established. This line of research might play an important role in future work because it fills in the gap between animal findings and clinical studies and allows study of the underlying mechanisms responsible for the return of fear. In this way, it may lead to a better understanding of the circumstances that elicit a return of fear. A logical first step will be to disentangle the mechanisms responsible. We can then try to manipulate these mechanisms to allow systematic study and, it is hoped, eventually prevent return of fear following extinction.

11

EXPOSURE THERAPY AND EXTINCTION: CLINICAL STUDIES

MICHELLE G. CRASKE AND JAYSON L. MYSTKOWSKI

Repeated, nonreinforced exposure is a core component of treatment for phobias and anxiety disorders, and exposure therapy is considered "well established" or "probably efficacious," according to stringent outcome evaluation criteria, for almost all anxiety disorders (Chambless et al., 1996). Not every recipient of exposure therapy benefits, however (nonresponse rates roughly vary from 10%–30% depending on the anxiety disorder; see Craske, 1999). Also, with the possible exception of specific phobias, those who do benefit do not typically achieve complete fear reduction, and some respondents, including those with specific phobias, experience a subsequent return of fear (e.g., Rachman, 1989). Hence, investigations aiming to improve the efficacy of exposure therapy are warranted and, we propose, will proceed most effectively if guided by learning theory.

Extinction learning served as the explicit model of behavior therapy (see chap. 10, this volume). Extinction processes continue to be emphasized in models of therapeutic change such as emotional processing theory (Foa & Kozak, 1986). It is now well understood that rather than a passive process, extinction is an inhibitory but active form of learning (Bouton, 1993; Miller & Matzel, 1988). Thus, even though extinction can eliminate fearful responding with enough unpaired conditioned stimulus (CS) exposures, retention of the original association can be uncovered by various procedures including changing the test context (renewal; Bouton, 1993), presenting unsignaled unconditioned stimuli (USs; reinstatement; Rescorla & Heth, 1975), or simply allowing time to pass (spontaneous recovery; Baum, 1988). Thus, clinical models of therapeutic change have been revised accordingly to suggest that exposure therapy generates a new, nonpathological fear structure that "overrides" the intact, pathological fear structure (Foa & McNally, 1996).

Despite this revision, models of mechanisms and implementation of exposure therapy have failed to keep up with advances in extinction theory and research. Translation of advances in learning and extinction theory may result in improved outcomes from exposure therapy. The purpose of this chapter is to review advances in the translation from basic extinction theory to the clinical application of exposure and outline areas in need of future research.

RETURN OF FEAR

The inhibitory nature of extinction may explain a phenomenon known as *return of fear*, which was first documented as the reemergence of fear following systematic desensitization and was attributed to spontaneous recovery of conditional fear following extinction (e.g., Rachman, 1966). Return of fear does not refer to the development of new fears or the relearning of existing fears. Instead, the sequence involves a decline in fear followed by a period devoid of relearning or reexposure to the "treated" stimulus, at the end of which fear resurges at a level higher than was seen at the end of the decline. Thus, return of fear looks like the renewal of a previously weakened or extinguished fear (Rachman, 1989). Importantly, return of fear does not refer to clinical relapse—a much broader process that occurs in relation to an array of stimuli and involves protracted distress and impairment in functioning—because return of fear is measured in response to a single presentation of a target stimulus.

Return of fear has been observed following treatment of specific phobias (e.g., Salkovskis & Mills, 1994; Shafran, Booth, & Rachman, 1993), obsessive–compulsive disorder (e.g., Likierman & Rachman, 1980), agoraphobia (Craske, Sanderson, & Barlow, 1987), and performance anxieties (Craske & Rachman, 1987). Return of fear is assessed between sessions (from the end of one session to the start of the next) and over follow-up intervals (from the end of treatment to follow-up retesting). These are referred to as between-session or short-term, and long-term return of fear, respectively. Between-session return of fear tends to lessen with repeated exposure sessions (e.g., Philips, 1985). The proportion of people who experience long-term return of fear ranges from 19% to 62%, depending on population, intervals, and operationalization of return of fear (e.g., Craske, 1999). Although the average amount of fear that returns is relatively small, the phenomenon provides a window for studying mechanisms of exposure therapy.

Various attempts have been made to isolate the variables responsible for return of fear, although surprisingly few of them have been from a solid theoretical framework of extinction theory. Because return of fear resembles dishabituation and because highly aroused conditions contribute to dishabituation (Groves & Thompson, 1970), various studies have examined the relationship between return of fear and arousal (i.e., heart rate). Several post hoc analyses have indicated a positive association between initial heart rate and long-term return of fear (e.g., Rachman & Lopatka, 1988), whereas others have yielded contradictory results (e.g., Shafran et al., 1993). The only study to evaluate heart rate a priori (in a quasi-experimental design) observed more return of fear in those participants with the highest heart rate in anticipation of the target stimulus (Craske & Rachman, 1987). If return of fear is truly representative of dishabituation, however, then it would be strongly mediated by state arousal at the time of retesting, and yet direct attempts to potentiate return of fear through inductions of state arousal have failed (Rachman & Whittal, 1989a). Thus, dishabituation remains a nonviable explanation of return of fear.

Others have emphasized danger-laden beliefs to explain return of fear. Specifically, Booth and Rachman (1992) reported that claustrophobic participants whose beliefs in their fearful cognitions increased just before reassessment showed more return of fear. In another study, the number and believability of negative cognitions, which reduced during treatment, increased for those who showed return of fear (Shafran et al., 1993). It is nonetheless difficult to discern whether phobic thoughts were the cause or the consequence of the observed return of fear in these studies. The study of depressed mood as another variable that may contribute to return of fear again has yielded contradictory results (e.g., Salkovskis & Mills, 1994, vs. Rachman & Whittal, 1989a).

Others have evaluated exposure process variables in relation to return of fear. Rachman and Whittal (1989b) observed a link between slow fear reduction and increased return of fear in post hoc analyses. Slower fear reduction was attributed to trial-and-error learning, whereas abrupt fear reduction was attributed to insight and reasoning that was considered more generalizable and longer lasting. These findings were not replicated in other studies (e.g., Rose & McGlynn, 1997), however, and all of the findings were limited by their post hoc nature. Findings pertaining to intensity of exposure similarly are mixed (Sartory, Rachman, & Grey, 1982, vs. Grey, Rachman, & Sartory, 1981). Even the end point of exposure does not relate consistently to return of fear. In one study, participants whose exposure continued until fear reduced 100% from baseline values reported significantly more return of fear on average than those whose exposure was discontinued when their fear reached a reduction of 50% of baseline values (Rachman, Robinson, & Lopatka, 1987). These results were limited by statistical regression artifacts and different durations of exposure (18 minutes vs. 33 minutes), however, and were not replicated (Rachman & Lopatka, 1988). A recent extension of overlearning trials by 200% of the number of trials to reach fear reduction again did not affect rates of return of fear (Farchione, 2002).

Certain applications of learning theory have provided the most consistent set of results pertaining to return of fear thus far. These include experimental investigations of posttreatment variables that have found support for the role of reinstatement effects (e.g., exposure to stressful events after treatment) in return of fear (e.g., Hermans, Dirikx, Vansteenwegen, Baeyens, Van den Bergh, & Eelen, 2005), described by Vansteenwegen et al. in chapter 10 of this volume. The second application is the experimental investigation of context shift and renewal effects, described next.

CONTEXT RENEWAL AND RETURN OF FEAR

Bouton and colleagues (e.g., Bouton & Nelson, 1998) have shown that partial fear recovery occurs in rats when a CS is extinguished or counterconditioned in one context (other than the one in which acquisition occurred) and is later presented in a different recovery context (see chap. 9, this volume). Having similarity across extinction and recovery contexts, however, prevents or minimizes a fear recovery effect (Bouton & King, 1983). It is presumed that contexts that are novel or different from the one encountered during fear extinction cause reliance on associations of fear acquisition rather than fear extinction, leading to fear renewal (Bouton, 1993). The context specificity of extinction suggests a continued effort for the expression of new learning (or exposure treatment gains) to be maintained against the backdrop of older, fearful learning. Thus, return of fear may reflect maintenance of original conditioning events in memory that are reactivated by a relevant context. Contexts associated with successful exposure treatment will activate nonfearful memories, whereas contexts associated with original fear acquisition will elicit fearful memories, causing return of fear.

In the first experimental manipulation in individuals with phobias, Rodriguez, Craske, Mineka, and Hladek (1999) found only weak support for the influence of context on return of fear. We administered one session of graded exposure trials, with participant modeling, to individuals fearful of spiders in one of two experimental settings (i.e., Context A or B), and reassessed 2 weeks later in either the same or a different experimental context. Dependent measures included self-reported fear as well as behavioral avoidance and heart rate, measured during an approach task to a live spider. A context-based return of fear was detected with heart rate and, to some extent, with behavioral avoidance measures, but not with self-report measures. There were two methodological confounds that may have contributed to the weak effects. Specifically, all participants had some exposure to both experimental contexts, with the tarantula present, before the treatment phase. These exposures may have served as extinction trials that minimized differences between later context shifts. Also, the two contexts were treatment rooms with different physical dimensions and appearances, but they were not dramatically different and were part of the same laboratory. The lack of a salient context manipulation, even though participants were aware of the differences between contexts, may have minimized the chance of observing contextual effects on the return of fear.

Given these two methodological limitations, Mineka, Mystkowski, Hladek, and Rodriguez (1999) replicated the Rodriguez and colleagues study without exposure to the tarantula in both contexts before treatment and with enhanced distinctiveness of the contexts by using rooms in different locations, of different size, and containing different salient visual cues, and by using experimenters of different sexes. All participants received one session of graded exposure trials, with participant modeling and then were reassessed 1 week later in either the exposure context or in a novel context. Results confirmed that treatment was highly effective in decreasing fear. Consistent with context-specificity renewal effects, participants tested in a novel context at follow-up demonstrated significantly more self-reported return of fear than participants tested in the same context. The effects were not large, however, and were limited to self-report (vs. behavioral or physiological indices). Despite the additional efforts to enhance their distinctiveness, the overall similarity between the contexts (rooms within a psychology department) may have again mitigated context effects. It is also conceivable that the chosen contexts were not relevant to the target stimulus (i.e., spiders) and that contexts with greater relevance may yield more potent context effects on return of fear. In other words, inherent contextual differences might affect treatment outcome or even return of fear. Furthermore, the fact that participants in the Mineka et al. (1999) study completed questionnaires in the same instruction room during treatment and during follow-up retesting may have limited context effects. According to Smith's (1988) outshining hypothesis, the impact of memory-enhancing cues is weakened by the presence of other competing cues during testing. Conceivably, starting the follow-up session in the same instruction room with similar questionnaires could dominate the perception of "context" and outshine the other novel cues that subsequently followed for the groups tested in the novel context.

With these issues in mind, Mystkowski, Craske, and Echiverri (2002) compared an outside context with the standard laboratory context. Because spiders' natural habitat is outdoors rather than indoors, the relevance of the context to the feared stimulus (i.e., context belongingness) was investigated as a moderator of renewal. The contexts were additionally differentiated by the sex of the experimenter and salient visual cues (i.e., color of treatment materials and therapist lab coats). Participants who were highly fearful of

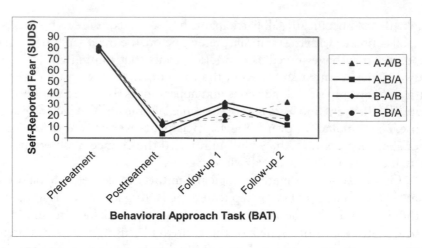

Figure 11.1. Mean self-reported fear for each group from the pretreatment to follow-up behavioral approach tasks. From "Treatment Context and Return of Fear in Spider Phobia," by J. L. Mystkowski, M. G. Craske, and A. M. Echiverri, 2002, *Behavior Therapy, 33*, pp. 399–416. Copyright 2002 by the Association for Advancement of Behavior Therapy. Reprinted with permission.

spiders were randomly assigned to graded exposure trials, with participant modeling, in either an inside (A) or outside (B) context. This study used a within-subjects paradigm, similar to designs used in the animal conditioning literature (e.g., Bouton & Brooks, 1993) to maximize power. Thus, 1 week later, participants were tested for return of fear in both the original treatment context and the different context in a counterbalanced order (AB or BA). Phobic fear was measured using subjective self-reports, behavioral avoidance, and heart rate, and self-report fear measures were administered in the experimental context throughout the study. Again, self-reported return of fear was greater when individuals confront a previously feared stimulus in a context different from the extinction context (see Figure 11.1). As predicted, the effect sizes and power observed in this study were much larger than in prior context studies, although the findings remained limited to self-reported fear obtained during behavioral approach tasks. Also, whereas the outside context did not lead to more self-reported return of fear at follow-up, it was associated with elevated heart rate. Taken together, the data lend mixed results as to the CS-context "belongingness" hypothesis and suggest that further research is needed to answer this question with regard to human fear renewal, perhaps using measures more sensitive than average heart rate.

Bouton and Swartzentruber (1991) suggested that mismatch of internal states during treatment and follow-up, manipulated using drug state, can lead to significant return of fear. Of course, this has direct relevance to the use of psychotropic medications in combination with exposure therapy for anxiety disorders and may explain the high rates of relapse when medications are withdrawn (e.g., Marks et al., 1993), particularly those medications that have a distinct effect on internal state (i.e., high-potency benzodiazepines).

We manipulated drug state as a context variable for human fears (Zoellner & Craske, 1998) by conducting exposure and retesting to spiders with and without alprazolam (i.e., alprazolam during exposure followed by retesting with vs. without alprazolam; and no alprazolam during exposure followed by retesting with and without alprazolam). No effect was found from shifting from a drug to a no-drug state or vice versa. Conceivably, the dosage levels of alprazolam (.25 mg) were too low to generate a sufficiently salient context.

More evidence for internal context specificity of extinction was demonstrated in a study that manipulated drug state through caffeine versus placebo ingestion for individuals fearful of spiders (Mystkowski, Mineka, Vernon, & Zinbarg, 2003). Participants received one session of exposure therapy under the influence of a randomly chosen drug condition (i.e., caffeine or placebo) and were reassessed 1 week later after ingesting a drink mixture that may or may not have been identical to the drink ingested during the previous treatment session. As predicted, participants experiencing incongruent drug states exhibited significantly greater self-reported return of fear, measured during a behavioral approach task, from posttreatment to follow-up than those participants experiencing congruent drug states. However, the effect sizes were smaller than those achieved using the inside–outside context shifts (Mystkowski et al., 2002).

In summary, a series of experimental studies have consistently demonstrated context-specificity effects of exposure therapy on circumscribed phobias. This represents an advance on prior investigations of return of fear that have yielded mostly contradictory results from mostly post hoc analyses. That the context effects are mostly limited to the self-report response domain may mean that self-report measurement is a more sensitive index of mild fear (return of fear is typically mild in severity) than are behavioral or physiological measures. The majority of effects are statistically but not clinically significant, although larger effects were obtained when more distinctly different contexts were used. Conceivably, even larger effects would be obtained if retesting occurred in the original fear acquisition context because in the animal literature the contextual control of return of fear is stronger when the animal is tested for renewal of fear in the context in which the fear was originally conditioned than when tested in a new context (Bouton & Brooks, 1993). Of course, it is not usually feasible to reconstruct the original sites of fear acquisition in human phobic samples.

EXPECTANCIES: EXPOSURE DURATION AND SPACING

Expectancies regarding the likelihood of aversive events are central to human fear conditioning. For example, contingency awareness (i.e., knowledge that a specific CS predicts a specific US), although of debatable necessity for conditioned responding (e.g., Lovibond & Shanks, 2002, vs. Öhman & Mineka, 2001) is a strong correlate of conditioned responding. Differential autonomic conditioning in particular is strongly associated with verbal measures of contingency knowledge (e.g., Purkis & Lipp, 2001). Expectancies also are important for extinction; extinction is posited to follow from a mismatch between the expectancy of an aversive event and the absence of its occurrence (Rescorla & Wagner, 1972) or from the perception of a negative change in the rate at which aversive events are associated with the CS (Gallistel & Gibbon, 2000). The duration for which exposure to the CS continues, therefore, may be critical in the process of extinction. Research with mice indicates that extinction is more effective when individual CS presentations are massed and blocks of massed CSs are spaced apart (Cain et al., 2003). These data have been interpreted to suggest that durations of a continuous CS presentation during extinction that exceed the length of the CS during acquisition induces extinction learning most effectively, but once induced, extinction learning is best consolidated with spaced training. (Notably, other research fails to support the role of spacing of extinction trials for extinction learning; see chap. 9, this volume.)

In accord with Cain and colleagues (2003), several studies of human phobic samples indicate that a single massed exposure is more effective than a series of short exposures of the same total duration, such as one 60-minute-duration exposure versus three 20-minute-duration exposures (e.g., Marshall, 1985). Conceivably, the lengthier (massed) exposure is more effective by virtue of providing sufficient time to learn that aversive outcomes do not occur (i.e., to disconfirm negative outcome expectancies). To date, no study has directly evaluated outcome expectancies or manipulated exposure duration in relation to outcome expectancies.

Related, however, is the body of work on the role of distraction during exposure, because distraction in essence represents disrupted (i.e., unmassed) exposure. Results regarding the detrimental effects of distraction during exposure therapy have been contradictory (e.g., Kamphuis & Telch, 2000, vs. Rodriguez & Craske, 1995; Oliver & Page, 2003; Rose & McGlynn, 1997). The equivocal nature of the findings may derive from lack of an operational definition of distraction, from confounds with the affective quality of the distracter, and from the unknown amount of distraction that actually takes place. Moreover, there is the possibility that external inhibition in the form of distraction influences performance but does not influence learning (Lovibond et al., 2000). However, if distraction was idiosyncratically designed in such a way that disconfirmation of expectancies for aversive outcomes was impeded (i.e., recognition of the absence of the US after the expected duration of exposure to the CS was impeded), then detrimental effects of distraction may be observed more reliably. Future research could evaluate this question by comparing the effect of distractions before versus after the point at which the aversive event is fully expected to occur.

Schedules of spacing *between* exposure days (as opposed to schedules within a single-exposure session) pertain to the issue of consolidation of learning. As noted, results with nonprimates indicate superior extinction with *spaced* blocks of massed exposure (Cain et al., 2003). Unfortunately, research in human samples has failed to address simultaneously massing within and spacing between exposure trials. That is, studies of spacing between exposure days have been conducted without assuring necessarily that exposure is sufficiently massed within each exposure day, and hence the results have been mixed. Foa, Jameson, Turner, and Payne (1980) found greater decrements in anxiety and avoidance behavior in those receiving massed rather than spaced exposure sessions for agoraphobia, whereas Ramsay, Barends, Breuker, and Kruseman (1966) found spaced schedules to be superior to massed schedules for desensitization to specific phobias. We observed less return of fear following an expanding spaced schedule of progressively longer intervals between exposure trials compared with consecutive days of exposure (Rowe & Craske, 1998a; Tsao & Craske, 2000). Many other studies show no differences between massed and spaced exposure-day schedules (e.g., Chambless, 1990). Some of the contradiction arises from inconsistent operationalization of massed and spaced scheduling across studies. Instead of drawing on principles of extinction theory to develop the most effective schedules of exposure, studies have compared arbitrarily chosen fixed durations and schedules of exposure, and sometimes what is labeled as massed in one study is labeled as spaced in another. If the research by Cain and colleagues (2003) is replicated and transfers to human samples, the most effective schedule would involve within-session durations of exposure that effectively violate aversive outcome expectancies, followed by schedules of exposure days that effectively consolidate the new learning regarding aversive outcomes. A major gap in the translation from basic science to clinical practice is research directly comparing exposure trials designed to disconfirm a priori expectancies and consolidate such learning.

EXCITATION AND EXPOSURE

Clinically, there is wide subscription to the theory that corrective learning is maximal when physiological arousal is initially activated and then subsides within and between exposure sessions (i.e., emotional processing theory; Foa & McNally, 1996). Empirical and theoretical developments suggest, however, that reduction of excitation is unimportant to outcome, and furthermore, sustained excitation during extinction training may even yield more effective results on retesting. Specifically, Cain, Blouin, and Barad (2004) have found that anxiogenic drugs such as yohimbine facilitate extinction in mice and in general suggested that drugs or conditions that enhance adrenergic transmission overcome a natural inhibitory constraint on extinction.

Evidence from the clinical literature is somewhat consistent with this point of view. First, there is some, albeit limited, data to indicate that exposure proceeds most effectively for participants in whom physiological reactivity is elevated initially (e.g., Kozak, Foa, & Steketee, 1988). Second, there is no consistent evidence to show that reduction in arousal (typically measured by heart rate) is important for the success of exposure therapy. Specifically, within-session reduction of heart rate did not correlate with treatment outcome for obsessive–compulsive disorder (Kozak et al., 1988). Nor did indices of within-session habituation, toward the beginning, middle, or end of an 8-week treatment program for panic disorder with agoraphobia, relate to outcome in another study (Riley et al., 1995), although exposure in this study was confounded by the addition of mild to moderate doses of alprazolam. Nor is there strong evidence that between-session reduction in arousal is important for treatment outcome. For example, Kozak and colleagues (1988) observed overall improvement in obsessive–compulsive symptoms despite absence of between-session reduction in heart rate. We found *less* return of fear in individuals fearful of spiders and of public speaking who underwent exposure conditions that sustained or elevated heart rate across exposure sessions compared with conditions in which heart rate declined across sessions (Rowe & Craske, 1998b; Tsao & Craske, 2000). In a study of patients with acrophobia, exposure conditions under which heart rate remained elevated across sessions was as effective as conditions under which heart rate declined (see Figure 11.2; A. J. Lang & Craske, 2000). Although these profiles were observed post hoc, they nonetheless raise the possibility that sustained heart rate elevation—representative of sustained excitation—is at least as effective if not more effective than diminution of excitation throughout exposure.

Sustained excitation may also explain the results obtained from random and variable exposures. In random practice, practice of a particular task is randomized with practice of another task, whereas in blocked practice, sequential performance of all trials for one task is conducted before proceeding to all trials for the next task. Most fear treatments use blocked practice, or repeated exposure to the same situation until fear declines, before moving to the next exposure task. Like random practice, variable practice enhances retention of nonemotional learning in the long term (e.g., Magill & Hall, 1990). These long-term benefits have been attributed to pairing the information to be learned with more retrieval cues thus enhancing retrievability, as well as by generation and application of a rule that captures the invariance among tasks (i.e., despite similarities, the basic principles are the same across tasks and can be applied regardless of situational dissimilarities; Schmidt & Bjork, 1992). Variation and randomness may additionally enhance learning, however, because they sustain higher levels of excitation throughout training than does blocked and constant training. We studied effects of random and variable, compared with blocked and constant, exposure for height phobias (A. J. Lang & Craske, 2000). In the random and variable exposure condi-

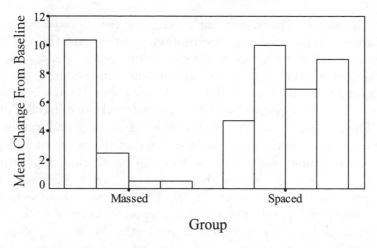

Figure 11.2. Average heart rate (beats per minute) during each treatment block. Bars represent blocks 1 through 4. From "Manipulations of Exposure-Based Therapy to Reduce Return of Fear: A Replication," by A. J. Lang and M. G. Craske, 2000, *Behaviour Research and Therapy, 38*, pp. 1–12. Copyright 2000 by Elsevier. Reprinted with permission.

tion, participants practiced exposure to heights in random order, such as 8th-floor, 2nd-floor, 10th-floor, and 3rd-floor balconies, and variable practice in more than one situation (e.g., inside vs. outside stairwell) and approached the precipice in different ways (e.g., looking out vs. down, leaning forward vs. backward against the balcony). This was compared with blocked exposure to the same balconies repeatedly before moving to the next floor, and the same manner of approaching the height during each exposure trial. As predicted, random and variable practice resulted in less anxiety at retesting 1 month later despite higher peak levels of anxiety throughout exposure.

The value of continued physiological reactivity and excitation may be caused by associative mechanisms, wherein greater associative learning derives from the absence of the aversive stimulus in the presence of multiple stimuli compared with single conditioned excitatory stimuli, for which support has been found in nonprimate studies (e.g., Rescorla, 2000). Thus, sustained physiological excitation may serve as an additional CS+ during extinction training, at least for individuals who are fearful of physiological responses. Laboratory studies in human samples, however, have not found extinction to be enhanced by additional conditioned exciters (Lovibond & Shanks, 2002; Vervliet et al., 2005). Alternatively, as suggested by Cain and colleagues (2004), excitation may represent enhanced adrenergic transmission that facilitates extinction by overcoming natural inhibitory mechanisms. Direct investigations of single versus multiple CSs, and incorporation of yohimbine during exposure therapy in human phobic samples are currently ongoing.

Contrasting with excitatory stimuli are conditioned inhibitors, or predictors of the absence of the unconditional stimulus, also known as safety signals. Common safety signals for patients with anxiety disorder are the presence of another person, therapists, medications, food, or drink (Barlow, 1988). Although they alleviate distress in the short term, safety signals are assumed to sustain anxiety in the long term, because when an excitatory stimulus is accompanied by an inhibitory CS, the excitatory stimulus may continue to elicit a conditioned response when subsequently tested alone (Siddle & Bond, 1988). These effects have been explained by associative and attributional mechanisms. The associative model assumes that the negative associative strength of the inhibitory stimulus cancels out the positive associative strength of the excitatory stimulus, so that there is no change from what is predicted by all cues (zero; Lovibond et al., 2000). The attributional model implies that if subjects attribute the absence of an expected outcome to the inhibitory stimulus, then there is no reason to change the causal status of the excitatory stimulus. Whether for associative or attributional reasons, safety signals have been presumed to contribute to the maintenance of phobias (see chap. 6, this volume).

Furthermore, inclusion of conditioned inhibitors during extinction training may interfere with extinction learning. Surprisingly, the animal literature on safety signals during extinction is mixed (Lovibond et al., 2000), and the only human laboratory study yielded negative results. That is, in a laboratory conditioning paradigm, Lovibond and colleagues (2000) demonstrated that extinction was blocked (using measures of expectancy and skin conductance) by an inhibitory stimulus; however, a conditioned excitor performed in the same way. It is interesting that the results were posited to be caused by context specificity, given that retesting of the excitatory stimulus alone served as a sufficiently different context from what occurred during the extinction trials when the excitatory stimulus was accompanied by either an excitatory stimulus or an inhibitory stimulus.

The investigation of safety signals during exposure therapy for phobias is limited to studies that either have failed to establish safety signals experimentally as conditioned inhibitors or have confounded safety signals with the primary conditional or phobic stimulus. Sloan and Telch (2002) reported that participants with claustrophobia who received an exposure treatment in which they were encouraged to use safety signals reported more fear at posttest and follow-up than those encouraged to focus on their fear during exposure. In a subsequent study, Powers, Smits, and Telch (2004) found that the perception of safety (i.e., availability of safety behaviors regardless of whether they were used) rather than use of safety was detrimental to treatment outcome because level of fear reduction was unaffected by actual use of safety behaviors. In both studies, however, the effects of safety-signal encouragement may have been attributable to distraction, and purported safety signals were not established experimentally as safety signals. Moreover, the safety signals (i.e., opening a window, unlocking a door lock) constituted behaviors that in essence degraded the CS (i.e., enclosed situations for participants with claustrophobia). Hence, they more closely represent avoidance responses rather than safety signals.

Avoidance responses may share some functional properties with Pavlovian safety signals, however. Consistent with this idea, Salkovskis and his colleagues (e.g., Salkovskis, 1991) have provided evidence that "within-situation safety behaviors"—equivalent to avoidance responses—interfere with the benefits of exposure therapy. Specifically, they showed that teaching anxious clients to refrain from these behaviors leads to greater fear reduction after an exposure session. It is clear that much more direct investigation is needed on the effects of safety signals and avoidance responses during exposure therapy, especially given the direct implications for clinical practice.

Such research may be directed at the role of medications as safety signals because their availability reassures that the dangers of extreme fear are controllable. Attribution of safety to medications impedes correction of misperceived danger (e.g., "It is safe for me to drive on the freeway even when unmedicated"), and attribution of therapeutic gains to a medication (alprazolam) in patients with panic disorder and agoraphobia predicted subsequent withdrawal symptoms and relapse (Basoglu, Marks, Kilic, Brewin, & Swinson, 1994). Thus, the greater relapse following exposure combined with anxiolytics (especially high-potency, short-acting drugs) compared with exposure alone (e.g., Marks et al., 1993) may be attributable not only to drug context shifts, described earlier, but also to medications functioning as safety signals. An interesting caveat arises with respect to safety signals in that they tend to lose their inhibitory properties with the passage of time: Conditional excitation is maintained for a considerably longer period of time than is conditional inhibition (e.g., Hendersen, 1985). Thus, occasions when anxiolytics "inexplicably" lose their effectiveness over time may be in part because of gradual depletion of their power to signal safety. Again, experimental investigation on the role of safety signals during exposure therapy is sorely needed.

CLINICAL APPLICATION

In this section, the clinical applications of basic research in extinction learning (context specificity, schedules of extinction, and level of excitation during extinction) are reviewed. Foremost, given that extinction is an active learning process, substances that facilitate N-methyl-D-aspartate receptor (NMDAr) glutamate receptors may facilitate the consolidation of extinction. As already mentioned, preliminary evidence, described in chapter 8 of this volume, supports this possibility. Replication of the effects of NMDAr glutamate in clinically disordered anxious populations would lay the groundwork for new, integrative treatments.

Context renewal effects imply that return of fear would be militated by conducting exposure in the same context in which fear was originally acquired or any context in which the CS is likely to be encountered in the future. Thus, clinically it may be wise to suggest to clients to return to their original fear acquisition context. Unfortunately, extinction in such contexts often is not feasible, given that many are unable to recall their fear onset and given the unavailability of original contexts. Consider, for example, the person whose initial panic attack occurred within the context of grieving the loss of a parent or of a major surgery. An alternative is to conduct extinction in as many contexts as possible to offset renewal caused by novel contexts, as supported by the research of Vansteenwegen and colleagues (in this volume). Notably, multiple contexts during extinction did not attenuate renewal in nonprimate samples (see chap. 9, this volume). The reasons for the discrepancy between nonprimate and human samples in this regard are not clear.

Because it is not always feasible to conduct exposure in original fear acquisition contexts or multiple contexts, we (Mystkowski et al., in press) sought to investigate whether a contextually based return of fear could be counteracted through mental rehearsal of extinction contexts (e.g., the therapist, treatment information, and the physical surroundings where treatment took place). Some support derives from nonemotional learning. Specifically, if participants are instructed to recall the original learning environment just before free recall of a list of words in an unfamiliar environment, a release from contextual dependence is observed, and performance is identical to that of participants tested in the original learning environment (Smith, 1979).

Thus, we evaluated the role of mental rehearsal of context on return of fear (Mystkowski et al., in press). Participants with spider phobias were treated and followed up in the same context (i.e., matched context groups) or treated and followed up in different contexts (i.e., mismatched context groups). Half of the participants in each group were instructed to rehearse mentally the treatment context and the material learned in that context before entering the test context at follow-up; the other half was asked to recall a neutral scenario. Therefore, there were two mental rehearsal conditions: treatment-related instructions (MR+) and treatment-unrelated instructions (MR–). Fear measurements included subjective, behavioral, and physiological measures taken during a behavioral approach task before and after treatment and at follow-up. Self-report data replicated previous research on contextually driven return of fear, with strong effect sizes between groups and a high degree of statistical power. Furthermore, participants who mentally rehearsed the treatment context, before encountering the phobic stimulus in a new context at follow-up, had less return of fear than those who did not (see Figure 11.3).

In addition to multiple contexts and mental rehearsal of treatment contexts, context-based return of fear may be attenuated by exposure therapy with altered presentations of a CS. For every CS (e.g., spider), there is a set of important characteristics that define that stimulus in an individual's mind (e.g., hairy legs, tiny eyes, rate of movement). Therefore, if exposure therapy was conducted with a CS that did not feature enough or all of the pertinent features stored in fear memory structures or if the exposure CS was not proto-

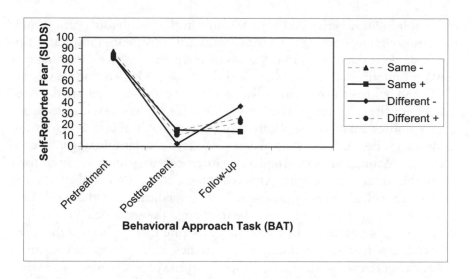

Figure 11.3. Mean self-reported fear for each group from the pretreatment to follow-up BATs. Groups "Same" had matched treatment and follow-up contexts, whereas "Different" had mismatched treatment and follow-up contexts. A plus sign (+) after the group name indicates treatment context mental rehearsal instructions, compared with a minus sign (–) for nontreatment context mental rehearsal instructions. From "Treatment Context and Return of Fear in Spider Phobia," by J. L. Mystkowski, J. S. Labus, A. M. Echiverri, and M. G. Craske, in press, *Behavior Therapy.* Copyright 2006 by the Association for Advancement of Behavior Therapy. Reprinted with permission.

typical of the feared CS, fear extinction may not generalize to other CSs, resulting in a more probable return of fear when changes in context occur. Thus, prototypical CSs are important to include in exposure.

Bouton and colleagues argued that context specificity of a CS exists not just for material learned during extinction but for the second meaning given to a CS, be it inhibitory or excitatory (Nelson & Bouton, 2002). Nelson (2002) found that initial training to develop inhibition to a neutral CS (i.e., conditioned inhibition) followed by excitatory conditioning of that CS led to transfer of inhibition across varying test contexts. If Nelson's (2002) findings in rats carry over to the treatment of human fears and anxiety, they would highlight the value of preventative exposure-type interventions for individuals at risk for developing anxious psychopathology (e.g., conducting exposures to CSs that are likely to be eventually associated with aversive USs, such as exposure to bodily sensations through vigorous exercise for individuals vulnerable to unexpected panic attacks). The preventative intervention, moreover, could include such skills as mental rehearsal of the prevention context, which could further minimize the impact of future anxious learning to a fewer number of contexts while maximizing the generalization of previous nonanxious learning to a larger number of contexts. In accord with Nelson (2002), this process would depend critically on the temporal order of inhibitory versus excitatory learning in that inhibitory learning must precede excitatory learning to obviate contextual constraints. Prospective evidence supports the merits of individuals who are anxiety prone learning preventative information about to-be-feared objects (e.g., Gardenswartz & Craske, 2001) and bolsters the movement within clinical psychology toward developing empirically validated prevention programs for anxious psychopathology.

Another important implication of context renewal effects pertains to medications because drug state may serve as a particular interoceptive context, and information learned under one interoceptive state may not transfer to another interoceptive state. As noted earlier, context renewal effects may contribute to high rates of relapse following medication withdrawal. One way to overcome these effects may be to change the sequencing of medication and exposure therapy by continuing exposure therapy beyond the point of withdrawal from medications. In most studies, medications are continued much longer than exposure therapy. Opportunities to practice exposure without being in a medicated state would overcome state dependency, however; this would also minimize the safety-signal status of medications. Medication tapering while exposure therapy is ongoing would probably require biweekly or monthly behavioral booster sessions after completion of acute exposure therapy.

With reference to the duration and spacing of exposures, we have suggested that exposure may be most effective when exposure trials are continued for the length of time necessary to violate aversive outcome expectancies. Experimental investigation of this proposal is needed. If confirmed, then rather than defining exposure trials in a standardized manner (e.g., 1 hour) or in terms of level of fear reduction (e.g., continue until fear reduces to 50%), it would be most beneficial to design exposures to be of the duration needed to convince patients that the aversive outcome did not and would not occur. We suggest that expectancies be elicited using interviews to ascertain the (a) nature of the expected aversive event in the phobic situation (e.g., suffocate, fall, faint) and (b) length of time in the feared situation at which expectancy for the aversive event is rated as extremely likely to occur (e.g., "I believe that the chances of fainting are extremely likely if I remain in the department store for 60 minutes") or the number of exposures to the feared situation by which expectancy for aversive event is rated as extremely likely to occur (e.g., "I believe that the chances of fainting are extremely likely if I go to the department store more than three times."). Exposures are then to be conducted for at least the length of time or number of times at which the aversive event is judged extremely likely to occur. Expectancies and durations are to be reestablished at the start of each exposure day. This type of exposure would function as massed exposure, to be consolidated by spaced, or expanding spaced, schedules between exposure days to consolidate extinction learning. Of course, such scheduling would be less applicable to fears involving undefined temporal events (e.g., the person with obsessive–compulsive disorder who fears punishment at some time in the future for his or her intrusive thoughts). Notably, our discussion has focused exclusively on expectancies for aversive outcomes; we have not addressed judgments of valence, which others have shown may persist even in the face of successful diminution of outcome expectancies and may contribute to return of fear (see chap. 10, this volume).

With regard to excitators and inhibitors during exposure, it is time to explore behavioral and pharmacological means of inducing more arousal or excitation during exposure (whether through multiple CS+s, randomness of exposures, or drug states) and to minimize conditioned inhibitors during exposure. More basic translational research is needed before drawing direct clinical applications.

CONCLUSIONS

In closing, the purpose of this chapter was to provide a bridge between basic extinction research and the clinical application of exposure therapy and to suggest avenues of research. To this end, we reviewed the role of excitation versus inhibition, violation of outcome expectancies, and context specificity with regard to exposure therapy. The "nonpermanence" of fear extinction was related to changes in context from successful exposure therapy to subsequent reexposure to a previously feared stimulus at a later point in time. Also, disconfirmation of the expectancy of an aversive outcome was presented as a possible key ingredient in the effective and efficient induction of extinction, a mechanism that awaits direct investigation in human samples. Finally, contrary to previously held beliefs about the importance of habituating physiological arousal for effective exposure therapy outcomes, maximizing excitation during exposure appears to offer much promise for clinically significant declines in anxious symptomatology.

In line with basic science in fear extinction, we have emphasized that performance during exposure therapy does not necessarily reflect learning at the process level. We suggest that it is time to shift away from an emphasis on fear reduction during exposure therapy as an index of learning at the process level and toward a model of exposure therapy that emphasizes the development of competing nonthreatening outcome expectancies, strengthening accessibility of nonthreatening outcome expectancies across stimuli and contexts, and weakening of avoidance and strengthening tolerance of aversive internal states and fear.

IV

FINAL THOUGHTS

FEAR AND LEARNING: DEBATES, FUTURE RESEARCH, AND CLINICAL IMPLICATIONS

DIRK HERMANS, DEBORA VANSTEENWEGEN,
AND MICHELLE G. CRASKE

This volume of chapters highlights empirical and theoretical developments in fear learning and their relevance to anxiety disorders. Those areas of theory and research that we believe will lead to advances in clinical practice were the basis for the selection of chapters for this book. The chapters also highlight the quickly progressing and already impressive cross-fertilization between neurobiology and learning theory.

ACQUISITION OF FEAR

Although differing in approach and emphasis, the chapters share a broad conceptualization of conditioning and learning. The association of an originally neutral conditioned stimulus (CS) with a traumatic or aversive experience (unconditioned stimulus [US]) is viewed as the basic mechanism underlying fear acquisition. As suggested by Eelen and Vervliet (chap. 1, this volume), the associative learning account is difficult to falsify. It is the theories that are derived from this functional perspective of behavior that can be tested and falsified. The broader perspective of human and nonhuman animals as learning organisms remains an axiom, a starting point for research and clinical practice.

One of the most important conditions for learning, as described in the well-known Rescorla–Wagner model, is that the CS is a valid predictor of the US. A propositional interpretation of this fundamental premise of learning is presented by both Davey and Lovibond in two chapters of this volume. Others, however, contest that although propositional features of learning (e.g., expectancies of negative consequences) play an important role in fear-related disorders, they are insufficient to explain the irrationality typical of many fears and the absence of change in behavior following change in knowledge or expectancies.

Dual-process accounts integrate propositional with lower, associative levels of fear learning. One example of a dual-process account is found in the context of evaluative conditioning research (for a review, see De Houwer et al., 2001) in which learning about expectancies is distinguished from referential learning. In referential learning, simple CS–US co-occurrences are registered on the basis of contiguity rather than contingency, such that likes and dislikes can be learned without learned expectancies. Evaluative conditioning has been found to be less sensitive to extinction than is expectancy-based learning (Baeyens, Eelen, & Crombez, 1995), and residual dislikes that remain after extinction of expectancies may play a role in return of fear (Hermans, Dirikx, Vansteenwegen, Baeyens, & Eelen, 2005). Hence, evaluative conditioning is potentially important for clinical practice. Systematic study of the development of likes and dislikes is warranted within typical fear-conditioning paradigms (e.g., Dirikx, Hermans, Vansteenwegen, Baeyens, & Eelen, 2004).

Another dual-process account is the evolved fear module theory of Öhman and Mineka (2001). Mineka and Sutton (chap. 4, this volume) argue that whereas all learning situations evoke propositional learning (which Öhman & Mineka, 2003, associated with hippocampal neurocircuitry), learning situations with fear-relevant stimuli, as first defined by Seligman, also evoke an automatic form of learning that is nonpropositional (which Öhman & Mineka, 2003, associated with amygdala neurocircuitry). The latter form of learning involves the fear module.

Comparable to dual processes in fear learning, social cognition researchers have studied dual processes in the (re)activation of knowledge from associative memory (e.g., Chaiken & Trope, 1999). For instance, it has been proposed that associations involved in attitudes can affect behavior through a low-level, automatic, and associative route or in a more propositional, deliberate fashion. Rather than trying to determine which model is more "correct," current research focuses on the situations that favor one mode of processing over the other (Fazio & Towles-Schwen, 1999). We believe that this perspective might be of value for the levels of learning discussion within fear conditioning. For example, milder USs are conceivably linked more directly with propositional processes in comparison to more intense USs. Thus, the question is not whether we are governed by low-level unconscious associations or by higher cognitions, expectancies, and beliefs, but rather under which circumstances they each play a role in the acquisition and extinction of fear. In addition, an important direction for future research is the degree to which individual differences in vulnerability to excessive fear and anxiety stem from low-level associations or from dysfunctional propositional knowledge (as described by Forsyth, chap. 7, this volume).

In terms of clinical application, the possibility of nonpropositional fear learning means that attempts to recall the onset of phobias may be sometimes misguided. Continued expression of fear without full conscious recognition of the phobic stimulus may explain unexpected fearful responding, and the apparent irrationality of phobic responding. Furthermore, the levels-of-learning approach raises the possibility that prevention efforts should be focused not only on information about the meaning of aversive stimuli (see chap. 5, this volume), but also on experiences that lessen the associative strength of pairing with such stimuli (i.e., latent inhibition).

Although the modulatory role of context is discussed in depth in several chapters in this volume, the idea that fear might be directly conditioned to the context has received less attention. Because fear of the context was found to be elicited by unpredictable US presentations (Grillon & Davis, 1997), Grillon (2002) proposed that fear could be distinguished from anxiety by conceptualizing fear as cue-specific (as in phobias) and anxiety as a future-oriented fear of context that is elicited by unpredictable situations. In other words, he conceptualized contextual fear as an analog for "anxiety" (e.g., generalized anxiety disorder). A possible consequence of this theory is that conditioning to a specific stimulus might promote predictability and restrict the range of stimuli that elicit fear, thus decreasing the amount of contextual fear as conditioning to the specific stimulus is strengthened. An important direction for future research will be to study cue-specific fear, contextual fear, and their interactions within the same conditioning paradigm. Such research would broaden the applicability of conditioning paradigms to more generalized anxiety problems as well as help to elucidate similarities and differences between phobic and nonphobic anxiety.

Reliance on self-report tools for measuring fear learning, most likely because of the ease with which paper-and-pencil tests can be implemented, is a limitation of current research. Fear learning involves physiological (i.e., skin conductance, startle eyeblink) and behavioral responses that should be measured in addition to self-report (see Lipp, chap. 2, this volume). A recent addition to behavioral measures of fear conditioning are reaction time procedures, some of which focus on evaluative changes that occur as a result of conditioning (e.g., affective priming procedure; Hermans, Baeyens, & Eelen,

2003), whereas others assess the salience that the CS acquires (or loses) as a result of conditioning. An example of the latter is the secondary probe reaction-time task (Dawson et al., 1982) that has been successfully used as a measure of allocation of processing capacities to the CS+ and CS– in studies of Pavlovian conditioning (e.g., Hermans et al., 2005). Other reaction-time procedures include the visual dot probe reaction-time task (e.g., Beaver, Mogg, & Bradley, 2005), the exogenous cuing paradigm (Koster et al., 2004), and the visual search task (Öhman et al., 2001).

Many of these behavioral paradigms were developed outside the domain of conditioning research by researchers in the field of social cognition and cognition–emotion interactions (for reviews, see Fazio & Olson, 2003). Learning theory will most likely benefit from the expertise that has accumulated with respect to these research methods (see Hermans et al., 2003).

EXTINCTION OF FEAR

Recent theoretical developments in the domain of extinction have instigated a line of research with important clinical implications.

Extinction and Erasure of Fear Memories

It is now widely accepted that extinction training serves to generate an alternative set of memory associations that compete with but do not erase original fear memory associations (Bouton, 1993), although not all concur with the emphasis on context effects (Lovibond et al., 1984; Rescorla & Cunningham, 1978). According to Bouton and colleagues, original fear memories are retrievable, as is evident in studies of spontaneous recovery, renewal, and reinstatement (see chap. 9, this volume). In a series of elegant studies reported by Rescorla (1996), devaluation procedures applied after extinction revealed the continued presence of CS–US associations. These data not only support the idea that extinction does not erase original CS–US associations but also suggest that extinction training does not modify these associations. This is an important qualification of the "extinction is not unlearning" idea (see also Delamater, 1996).

The extensive work of Bouton and colleagues has demonstrated the context specificity of extinction learning. Although the findings tend to be less robust in human samples than in nonprimates, the findings with analog and clinical human samples described by Vansteenwegen, Dirikx, Hermans, Vervliet, and Eelen (chap. 10, this volume) and by Craske and Mystkowski (chap. 11, this volume) similarly demonstrate a context specificity of extinction such that retesting of the CS in a context different from the extinction context is associated with more return of fear than is testing in a context that is the same as the extinction context. The clinical implications of this model of extinction are far reaching (see next section).

Two mechanisms may explain why extinction is more context-specific than acquisition: First, inhibitory learning is more context-dependent than excitatory conditioning (Riccio, Richardson, & Ebner, 1999) and, second, learned information is more context-dependent than first learned information (Bouton, Nelson, & Rosas, 1999). Demonstrations of context dependency in excitatory conditioning preparations and in situations in which no additional information is provided (Hall & Honey, 1990) discount the totality of these explanations. Nonetheless, if second learning is crucial, then an important goal for future research will be to elucidate whether context effects are as important for other types of behavior modification (e.g., counterconditioning) as they appear to be for extinction and exposure. Moreover, the second learning argument highlights the importance of prevention because first attitudes will be less vulnerable to context shifts than all modified attitudes that follow (Bouton, 2000).

Some evidence in the conditioning literature suggests that extinction might change the associative strength of the CS (e.g., Thomas & Ayres, 2004), and Barad (chap. 8, this volume) proposes that extinction may involve erasure of the synaptic connections that underlie conditional fear itself; that is, memory of fear conditioning may be erased from the amygdala, albeit conserved in another area such as the prefrontal cortex. At this point, it is unclear how to reconcile the possibility of a synaptic erasure with evidence for context specificity of extinction described here. Also, as stated by Barad, much finer grained physiological examinations of changes in synaptic strength in the amygdala during fear acquisition and extinction are needed. Conceivably, both erasure and context-specific inhibition occur, and future research will elucidate the various conditions under which each predominates.

The Difference Between Extinction Performance and Extinction Learning

Given their data to show that strength of responding during extinction training did not relate to extinction learning (assessed by degree of spontaneous recovery 72 hours later), Bouton and colleagues (chap. 9, this volume) propose that extinction training performance does not reflect extinction learning. This is critically relevant to the process of exposure therapy, because it has long been assumed that reduction in level of subjective and physiological responding during repeated exposures to the phobic stimulus is reflective of corrective learning and predictive of long-term treatment success. This premise began with the work of Wolpe (1958) on systematic desensitization and continues with current models of emotional processing theory (Foa & McNally, 1996). Much of clinical practice is guided by this principle, which has remained unchallenged largely because of the failure to follow exposure therapy trials with later retesting of reactivity to the phobic stimulus, because it is only through retesting that extinction learning (as opposed to extinction performance) can be evaluated. If these findings are replicated in clinical samples, clinicians should be encouraged to focus their attention away from fear reduction during exposure therapy and to retest fear to the phobic stimulus at a later point in time, after a series of exposure trials, to establish with more certainty the learning that has taken place.

It is also possible that rather than there being no relation between extinction training performance and extinction learning, as suggested by Bouton, there may be an inverse relationship in that sustained excitation during extinction training may facilitate extinction learning. That is, in accord with other evidence for the centrality of the amygdala to the expression of fear extinction, nonprimate work by Barad (chap. 8, this volume) suggests that excitation, in the form of agonists of beta-adrenergic transmission (i.e., yohimbine), facilitates extinction learning. Post hoc findings from clinical samples (chap. 11, this volume) support the role of sustained excitation, measured by heart rate responding throughout exposure to phobia stimuli. If supported with experimental designs, these findings suggest that exposure therapy would proceed more effectively by sustaining levels of excitation, through drugs such as yohimbine, unpredictable schedules of exposure, or multiple stimuli. It is clear that there is a need for direct research in both animal and human samples on the role of excitation during exposure that would be enormously helpful to the clinician.

Structure of Extinction Training

The way in which extinction training is structured dramatically affects the effectiveness of extinction, both within session and in the long term. Several methods for minimizing context specificity of extinction, such as extinction in multiple contexts and retrieval cues, are suggested in the animal literature (see chap. 10, this volume). Furthermore, exposure to the US during extinction trials also weakens reinstatement effects (e.g., Bouton, 1988), as long as the US is presented in the extinction context.

Spacing of extinction and exposure trials is another structural variable, but one for which the evidence is equivocal. Barad (chap. 8, this volume) presents evidence indicating that massing of extinction trials facilitates extinction learning. He reports that massed extinction trials with very short intertrial intervals function as one continuous trial that is lengthier than the duration of the CS during acquisition training. By virtue of these temporal relations, Barad suggests that subjects optimally learn that the US is no longer associated with the CS. Hence, Craske and Mystkowski (chap. 11, this volume) suggest that instead of designing exposure to continue for predetermined lengths of time, or until fear subsides, a more effective strategy may be to design exposure trials specifically to extend beyond the point at which the aversive outcome is considered most certain to happen. This theory of outcome expectancy violation awaits systematic evaluation in human samples, especially given Bouton and colleagues' (chap. 9, this volume) report that spacing of extinction trials had no effect on extinction learning as measured on retesting 72 hours later in nonprimates.

Finally, developments in the neurobiology of extinction are likely to lead to psychopharmacological products that specifically enhance exposure treatment (see chaps. 3, 8, this volume).

Context and Stimulus Valence in Extinction Training

Even though effect sizes for context specificity in human samples are relatively small, the model of context specificity of extinction suggests ways for offsetting renewal and reinstatement of fear. This may be important, especially if renewal and reinstatement set the scene for future relapse. Vansteenwegen and colleagues (chap. 10, this volume) present evidence to show that inclusion of multiple contexts throughout exposure in students with spider anxiety offsets renewal when a spider is presented in a new context. Bouton and colleagues (chap. 9, this volume), however, were not able to replicate the attenuating effects of multiple contexts in nonprimate samples. Thus, they concluded that renewal and reinstatement may be best minimized by creating bridging mechanisms between exposure and retest. An example of this is the mental rehearsal described by Craske and Mystkowksi (chap. 11, this volume) in which clinicians encourage clients to remind themselves of "where they were and what they did during exposure therapy" as they encounter their phobia stimulus in varied daily life contexts. The discord between the human and nonprimate findings regarding the role of multiple contexts throughout extinction training awaits further investigation; at present, it would seem beneficial for clinicians both to conduct exposure in multiple contexts and to encourage clients to reinstate mentally the exposure therapy in their daily lives.

Finally, there is evidence to indicate that despite downward shifts in aversive expectancies, the CS may remain negatively valenced at the end of extinction training. The possibility that this negative valence contributes to return of fear raises other questions for the clinician regarding prevention of return of fear (e.g., Hermans et al., 2005). Of course, such attempts would be based on the assumption that return of fear should be prevented; it might also be the case that episodes of return of fear might provide the opportunity for relearning in a way that enhances extinction learning. This, too, would be an avenue for fruitful exploration of basic and applied science.

CONCLUSION

We have summarized some of the issues, debates, areas for future research, and clinical implications of fear learning. We hope this collection of works both updates the clinical field and stimulates basic scientists to address the questions of most importance to clinical practice.

REFERENCES

Abramson, L. Y., Seligman, M. E. P., & Teasdale, J. D. (1978). Learned helplessness in humans: Critique and reformulation. *Journal of Abnormal Psychology, 87*, 49–74.

Adler, C. M., Craske, M. G., Kirshenbaum, S., & Barlow, D. H. (1989). Fear of panic: An investigation of its role in panic occurrence, phobic avoidance, and treatment outcome. *Behaviour Research and Therapy, 27*, 391–396.

Agras, W., & Jacob, R. (1981). Phobia: Nature and measurements. In M. Mavissakalian & D. H. Barlow (Eds.), *Phobia: Psychological and pharmacological treatment* (pp. 35–62). New York: Guilford Press.

Ainsworth, M. D., Blehar, M., Waters, E., & Wall, S. (1978). *Patterns of attachment.* Hillsdale, NJ: Erlbaum.

Alger, B. E., & Teyler, T. J. (1976). Long-term and short-term plasticity in the CA1, CA3 and dentate region of the rat hippocampal slice. *Brain Research, 110*, 463–480.

Allen, N. B., Wong, S., Kim, Y., & Trinder, J. (1996). Startle reflex and heart rate responses during appetitive and aversive anticipation [abstract]. *Psychophysiology, 33*, S18.

Amaral, D. G., & Witter, M. P. (1995). The hippocampal formation. In G. Paxinos (Ed.), *The rat nervous system* (pp. 443–493). San Diego, CA: Academic Press.

American Psychiatric Association. (1994). *Diagnostic and statistical manual of mental disorders* (4th ed.). Washington, DC: Author.

Anagnostaras, S. G., Gale, G. D., & Fanselow, M. S. (2001). Hippocampus and contextual fear conditioning: Recent controversies and advances. *Hippocampus, 11*, 8–17.

Anagnostaras, S. G., Maren, S., & Fanselow, M. S. (1999). Temporally graded retrograde amnesia of contextual fear after hippocampal damage in rats: Within-subjects examination. *Journal of Neuroscience, 19*, 1106–1114.

Annau, Z., & Kamin, L. J. (1961). The conditioned emotional response as a function of intensity of the US. *Journal of Comparative and Physiological Psychology, 54*, 428–432.

Arntz, A., Hildebrand, M., & van den Hout, M. (1994). Overprediction of anxiety and disconfirmatory processes in anxiety disorders. *Behaviour Research and Therapy, 32*, 709–722.

Arntz, A., Lavy, E., Van den Berg, G., & van Rijsoort, S. (1993). Negative beliefs of spider phobics: A psychometric evaluation of the Spider Phobia Beliefs Questionnaire. In Phobia: Etiological, cognitive, and physiological aspects [Special issue]. *Advances in Behaviour Research and Therapy, 15*, 257–277.

Arntz, A., Rauner, M., & van den Hout, M. (1995). "If I feel anxious, there must be danger": Ex-consequentia reasoning in inferring danger in anxiety disorders. *Behaviour Research and Therapy, 33*, 917–925.

Augustson, E. M., & Dougher, M. J. (1997). The transfer of avoidance evoking functions through stimulus equivalence classes. *Journal of Behavior Therapy and Experimental Psychiatry, 28*, 181–191.

Baas, J. M., Nugent, M., Lissek, S., Pine, D. S., & Grillon, C. (2004). Fear conditioning in virtual reality contexts: A new tool for the study of anxiety. *Biological Psychiatry, 55*, 1056–1060.

Baeyens, F., & De Houwer, J. (1995). Evaluative conditioning is a qualitatively distinct form of classical conditioning: A reply to Davey (1994). *Behaviour Research and Therapy, 33*, 825–831.

Baeyens, F., Eelen, P., & Crombez, G. (1995). Pavlovian associations are forever: On classical conditioning and extinction. *Journal of Psychophysiology, 9*, 127–141.

Bailey, D. J., Kim, J. J., Sun, W., Thompson, R. F., & Helmstetter, F. J. (1999). Acquisition of fear conditioning in rats requires the synthesis of mRNA in the amygdala. *Behavioral Neuroscience, 113*, 276–282.

Baker, A. G., Mercier, P., Gabel, J., & Baker, P. A. (1981). Contextual conditioning and the US preexposure effect in conditioned fear. *Journal of Experimental Psychology: Animal Behavior Processes, 7*, 109–128.

Baker, A. G., Steinwald, H., & Bouton, M. E. (1991). Contextual conditioning and reinstatement of extinguished instrumental responding. *Quarterly Journal of Experimental Psychology, 4B*, 199–218.

Baker, J. D., & Azorlosa, J. L. (1996). The NMDA antagonist MK-801 blocks the extinction of Pavlovian fear conditioning. *Behavioral Neuroscience, 110*, 618–620.

Ball, W., & Tronick, E. (1971, February 26). Infant responses to impending collision: Optical and real. *Science, 171*, 818–820.

Barela, P. B. (1999). Theoretical mechanisms underlying the trial-spacing effect in Pavlovian fear conditioning. *Journal of Experimental Psychology: Animal Behavior Processes, 25*, 177–193.

Barlow, D. H. (1988). *Anxiety and its disorders: The nature and treatment of anxiety and panic.* New York: Guilford Press.

Barlow, D. H. (2002). *Anxiety and its disorders: The nature and treatment of anxiety and panic* (2nd ed.). New York: Guilford Press.

Barlow, D. H., Allen, L. B., & Choate, M. L. (2004). Toward a unified treatment for emotional disorders. *Behavior Therapy, 35*, 205–230.

Barondes, S. H. (1970). Cerebral protein synthesis inhibitors block long-term memory. *International Review of Neurobiology, 12*, 177–205.

Barrientos, R. M., O'Reilly, R. C., & Rudy, J. W. (2002). Memory for context is impaired by injecting anisomycin into dorsal hippocampus following context exploration. *Behavioral Brain Research, 134*, 299–306.

Basoglu, M., Marks, I. M., Kilic, C., Brewin, C. R., & Swinson, R. P. (1994). Alprazolam and exposure for panic disorder with agoraphobia: Attribution of improvement to medication predicts subsequent relapse. *British Journal of Psychiatry, 164*, 652–659.

Bast, T., Zhang, W. N., & Feldon, J. (2001). The ventral hippocampus and fear conditioning in rats. Different anterograde amnesias of fear after tetrodotoxin inactivation and infusion of the GABA(A) agonist muscimol. *Experimental Brain Research, 139,* 39–52.

Bast, T., Zhang, W. N., & Feldon, J. (2003). Dorsal hippocampus and classical fear conditioning to tone and context in rats: Effects of local NMDA-receptor blockade and stimulation. *Hippocampus, 13,* 657–675.

Bauer, E. P., Schafe, G. E., & LeDoux, J. E. (2002). NMDA receptors and L-type voltage-gated calcium channels contribute to long-term potentiation and different components of fear memory formation in the lateral amygdala. *Journal of Neuroscience, 22,* 5239–5249.

Baum, M. (1970). Extinction of avoidance response through response prevention (flooding). *Psychological Bulletin, 74,* 276–284.

Baum, M. (1988). Spontaneous recovery from the effects of flooding (exposure) in animals. *Behaviour Research and Therapy, 26,* 185–186.

Beaver, J. D., Mogg, K., & Bradley, B. P. (2005). Emotional conditioning to masked stimuli and modulation of visuospatial attention. *Emotion, 5,* 67–79.

Bechara, A., Tranel, D., Damasio, H., Adolphs, R., Rockland, C., & Damasio, A. R. (1995, August 25). Double dissociation of conditioning and declarative knowledge relative to the amygdala and hippocampus in humans. *Science, 269,* 1115–1118.

Bechterev, V. M. (1913). *La psychologie objective.* Paris: Alcan.

Beck, A. T. (1972). *Depression: Causes and treatment.* Philadelphia: University of Pennsylvania Press.

Beck, A. T. (1987). Cognitive models of depression. *Journal of Cognitive Psychotherapy: An International Quarterly, 1,* 5–37.

Beck, A. T., & Clark, D. A. (1997). An information processing model of anxiety: Automatic and strategic processes. *Behaviour Research and Therapy, 35,* 49–58.

Beck, A. T., & Emery, G. (1985). *Anxiety disorders and phobias: A cognitive perspective.* New York: Basic Books.

Beck, A. T., Emery, G., & Greenberg, R. L. (1985). *Anxiety disorders and phobias: A cognitive perspective.* New York: Basic Books.

Bergin, A. E. (1971). The evaluation of therapeutic outcomes. In A. E. Bergin & S. Garfield (Eds.), *Handbook of psychotherapy and behavior change: An empirical analysis* (pp. 217–270). New York: Wiley.

Biederman, J., Rosenbaum, J., Hirshfeld, D., Faraone, S., Bolduc, E., Gersten, M., et al. (1990). Psychiatric correlates of behavioral inhibition in young children of parents with and without psychiatric disorders. *Archives of General Psychiatry, 47,* 21–26.

Biferno, M. A., & Dawson, M. E. (1977). The onset of contingency awareness and electrodermal classical conditioning: An analysis of temporal relationships during acquisition and extinction. *Psychophysiology, 14,* 164–171.

Birbaumer, N., Grodd, W., Diedrich, O., Klose, U., Erb, M., Lotze, M., et al. (1998). fMRI reveals amygdala activation to human faces in social phobics. *NeuroReport, 9,* 1223–1226.

Bjork, R. A., & Bjork, E. L. (1992). A new theory of disuse and an old theory of stimulus fluctuation. In A. Healy, S. Kosslyn, & R. Shiffrin (Eds.), *From learning processes to cognitive processes: Essays in honor of William K. Estes* (Vol. 2, pp. 35–67). Hillsdale, NJ: Erlbaum.

Blackledge, J. T., & Hayes, S. C. (2001). Emotion regulation in acceptance and commitment therapy. *JCLP/In session: Psychotherapy in Practice, 57,* 243–255.

Blair, H. T., Schafe, G. E., Bauer, E. P., Rodrigues, S. M., & LeDoux, J. E. (2001). Synaptic plasticity in the lateral amygdala: A cellular hypothesis of fear conditioning. *Learning & Memory, 8,* 229–242.

Blair, K. A., Denham, S. A., Kochanoff, A., & Whipple, B. (2004). Playing it cool: Temperament, emotion regulation, and social behavior in preschoolers. *Journal of School Psychology, 42,* 419–443.

Blanchard, D. C., & Blanchard, R. J. (1972). Innate and conditioned reactions to threat in rats with amygdaloid lesions. *Journal of Comparative and Physiological Psychology, 81,* 281–290.

Blanchard, D. C., Blanchard, R. J., Tom, P., & Rodgers, R. J. (1990). Diazepam changes risk assessment in an anxiety/defense test battery. *Psychopharmacology, 101,* 511–518.

Blanchard, D. C., Griebel, G., & Blanchard, R. J. (2001). Mouse defensive behaviors: Pharmacological and behavioral assays for anxiety and panic. *Neuroscience and Biobehavioral Reviews, 25,* 205–218.

Blanchard, R. J., & Blanchard, D. C. (1969). Passive and active reactions to fear-eliciting stimuli. *Journal of Comparative and Physiological Psychology, 68,* 129–135.

Blanchard, R. J., Mast, M., & Blanchard, D. C. (1975). Stimulus control of defensive reactions in the albino rat. *Journal of Comparative and Physiological Psychology, 88,* 81–88.

Bliss, T. V. P., & Gardner-Medwin, A. R. (1973). Long-lasting potentiation of synaptic transmission in the dentate area of the unanaesthetized rabbit following stimulation of the perforant path. *Journal of Physiology, 232,* 357–374.

Bliss, T. V. P., & Lomo, T. (1973). Long-lasting potentiation of synaptic transmission in the dentate area of the anaesthetized rabbit following stimulation of the perforant path. *Journal of Physiology, 232,* 331–356.

Block, A. T., Ghoneim, M. M., Fowles, D. C., Kumar, V., & Pathak, D. (1987). Effects of a subanesthetic concentration of nitrous oxide on establishment, elicitation, and semantic and phonemic generalization of classically conditioned skin conductance responses. *Pharmacology, Biochemistry and Behavior, 28*(1), 7–14.

Blumenthal, T. D., Cuthbert, B. N., Filion, D. L., Hackley, S., Lipp, O. V., & van Boxtel, A. (2005). Committee report: Guidelines for human startle eyeblink electromyographic studies. *Psychophysiology, 42,* 1–15.

Bohlin, G., & Kjellberg, A. (1979). Orienting activity in two stimulus paradigms as reflected in heart rate. In H. D. Kimmel, E. H. van Olst, & J. F. Orlebehe (Eds.), *The orienting reflex in humans* (pp. 169–197). Hillsdale, NJ: Erlbaum.

Bolles, R. C. (1970). Species-specific defense reactions and avoidance learning. *Psychological Review, 77,* 32–48.

Bolles, R. C., & Fanselow, M. S. (1980). A perceptual-defensive-recuperative model of fear and pain. *Behavioral and Brain Sciences, 3*, 291–301.

Bonanno, G. A., Papa, A., LaLande, K., Westphal, M., & Coifman, K. (2004). The importance of being flexible: The ability to both enhance and suppress emotional expression predicts long-term adjustment. *Psychological Science, 15*, 482–487.

Booth, R., & Rachman, S. J. (1992). The reduction of claustrophobia: I. *Behaviour Research and Therapy, 30*, 207–221.

Borowski, T. B., & Kokkinidis, L. (1998). The effects of cocaine, amphetamine, and the dopamine D1 receptor agonist SKF 38393 on fear extinction as measured with potentiated startle: Implications for psychomotor stimulant psychosis. *Behavioral Neuroscience, 112*, 952–965.

Bourtchuladze, R., Frenguelli, B., Blendy, J., Cioffi, C., Schutz, G., & Silva, A. J. (1994). Deficient long-term memory in mice with a targeted mutation of the camp-responsive element-binding protein. *Cell, 79*, 59–68.

Bouton, M. E. (1984). Differential control by context in the inflation and reinstatement paradigms. *Journal of Experimental Psychology: Animal Behavior Processes, 10*, 56–74.

Bouton, M. E. (1988). Context and ambiguity in the extinction of emotional learning: Implications for exposure therapy. *Behaviour Research and Therapy, 26*, 137–149.

Bouton, M. E. (1991a). Context and retrieval in extinction and in other examples of interference in simple associative learning. In L. Dachowski & C. F. Flaherty (Eds.), *Current topics in animal learning: Brain, emotion, and cognition* (pp. 25–53). Hillsdale, NJ: Erlbaum.

Bouton, M. E. (1991b). A contextual analysis of fear extinction. In P. R. Martin (Ed.), *Handbook of behavior therapy and psychological science: An integrative approach* (pp. 435–453). Elmsford, NY: Pergamon Press.

Bouton, M. E. (1993). Context, time and memory retrieval in the interference paradigms of Pavlovian learning. *Psychological Bulletin, 114*, 90–99.

Bouton, M. E. (1994). Context, ambiguity, and classical conditioning. *Current Directions in Psychological Science, 3*, 49–53.

Bouton, M. E. (2000). A learning theory perspective on lapse, relapse, and the maintenance of behavior change. *Health Psychology, 19*(Suppl. 1), 57–63.

Bouton, M. E. (2002). Context, ambiguity, and unlearning: Sources of relapse after behavioral extinction. *Biological Psychiatry, 52*, 976–986.

Bouton, M. E. (2004). Context and behavioral process in extinction. *Learning & Memory, 11*, 485–494.

Bouton, M. E., & Bolles, R. C. (1979). Role of conditioned contextual stimuli in reinstatement of extinguished fear. *Journal of Experimental Psychology: Animal Behavior Processes, 5*, 368–378.

Bouton, M. E., & Bolles, R. C. (1980). Conditioned fear assessed by freezing and by the suppression of three different baselines. *Animal Learning & Behavior*, 8, 429–434.

Bouton, M. E., & Brooks, D. C. (1993). Time and context effects on performance in a Pavlovian discrimination reversal. *Journal of Experimental Psychology: Animal Behavior Processes*, 19, 165–179.

Bouton, M. E., García-Gutiérrez, A., Zilski, J., & Moody, E. W. (in press). Extinction in multiple contexts does not necessarily make extinction less vulnerable to relapse. *Behaviour Research and Therapy*.

Bouton, M. E., Kenney, F. A., & Rosengard, C. (1990). State-dependent fear extinction with 2 benzodiazepine tranquilizers. *Behavioural Neuroscience*, 104, 44–55.

Bouton, M. E., & King, D. A. (1983). Contextual control of the extinction of conditioned fear: Tests for the associative value of the context. *Journal of Experimental Psychology: Animal Behavior Processes*, 9, 248–265.

Bouton, M. E., & King, D. A. (1986). Effect of context on performance to conditioned stimuli with mixed histories of reinforcement and nonreinforcement. *Journal of Experimental Psychology: Animal Behavior Processes*, 12, 4–15.

Bouton, M. E., Mineka, S., & Barlow, D. H. (2001). A modern learning theory perspective on the etiology of panic disorder. *Psychological Review*, 108, 4–32.

Bouton, M. E., & Nelson, J. B. (1998). The role of context in classical conditioning: Some implications for cognitive behavior therapy. In W. T. O'Donohue (Ed.), *Learning theory and behavior therapy* (pp. 59–83). Needham Heights, MA: Allyn & Bacon.

Bouton, M. E., Nelson, J. B., & Rosas, J. M. (1999). Stimulus generalization, context change, and forgetting. *Psychological Bulletin*, 125, 171–186.

Bouton, M. E., & Peck, C. A. (1992). Spontaneous recovery in cross-motivational transfer (counterconditioning). *Animal Learning & Behavior*, 20, 313–321.

Bouton, M. E., & Ricker, S. T. (1994). Renewal of extinguished responding in a 2nd context. *Animal Learning & Behavior*, 22, 317–324.

Bouton, M. E., & Sunsay, C. (2003). Importance of trials versus accumulating time across trials in partially reinforced appetitive conditioning. *Journal of Experimental Psychology: Animal Behavior Processes*, 29, 62–77.

Bouton, M. E., & Swartzentruber, D. (1989). Slow reacquisition following extinction: Context, encoding, and retrieval mechanisms. *Journal of Experimental Psychology: Animal Behavior Processes*, 15, 43–53.

Bouton, M. E., & Swartzentruber, D. (1991). Sources of relapse after extinction in Pavlovian and instrumental learning. *Clinical Psychology Review*, 11, 123–140.

Bouton, M. E., Woods, A. M., & Pineño, O. (2004). Occasional reinforced trials during extinction can slow the rate of rapid reacquisition. *Learning and Motivation*, 35, 371–390.

Bower, G. H. (1981). Mood and memory. *American Psychologist*, 36, 129–148.

Bowery, N. G. (1987). Glycine-binding sites and NMDA receptors in brain. *Nature*, 326, 338.

Bradburn, N. M., Rips, L. J., & Shevell, S. K. (1987, April 10). Answering autobiographical questions: The impact of memory and inference on surveys. *Science*, *236*, 157–161.

Bradley, B. P., Mogg, K., Falla, S. J., & Hamilton, L. R. (1998). Attentional bias for threatening facial expressions in anxiety: Manipulation of stimulus duration. *Cognition & Emotion*, *12*, 737–753.

Bradley, B. P., Mogg, K., Millar, N., Bonham-Carter, C., Fergusson, E., Jenkins, J., & Parr, M. (1997). Attentional biases for emotional faces. *Cognition & Emotion*, *11*, 25–42.

Bradley, B. P., Mogg, K., White, J., Groom, C., & de Bono, J. (1999). Attentional bias for emotional faces in generalized anxiety disorder. *British Journal of Clinical Psychology*, *38*, 267–278.

Bradley, M. M. (2000). Emotion and motivation. In J. T. Cacioppo, L. G. Tassinary, & G. G. Berntson (Eds.), *Handbook of psychophysiology* (pp. 602–642). New York: Cambridge University Press.

Brandon, T. H., Collins, B. N., Juliano, L. M., & Lazev, A. B. (2000). Preventing relapse among former smokers: A comparison of minimal interventions through telephone and mail. *Journal of Consulting and Clinical Psychology*, *68*, 103–113.

Brewer, W. F. (1974). There is no convincing evidence for operant or classical conditioning in adult humans. In W. B. Weimer & D. S. Palermo (Eds.), *Cognition and the symbolic processes* (pp. 1–42). Hillsdale, NJ: Erlbaum.

Brewin, C. R., Andrews, B., & Gotlib, I. H. (1993). Psychopathology and early experience: A reappraisal of retrospective reports. *Psychological Bulletin*, *113*, 82–98.

Brewin, C. R., Dalgleish, T., & Joseph, S. (1996). A dual representation theory of post traumatic stress disorder. *Psychological Review*, *103*, 670–686.

Brewin, C. R., & Holmes, E. A. (2003). Psychological theories of posttraumatic stress disorder. *Clinical Psychology Review*, *23*, 339–376.

Breznitz, S. (1983). *The denial of stress*. New York: International Universities Press.

Brooks, D. C. (2000). Recent and remote extinction cues reduce spontaneous recovery. *Quarterly Journal of Experimental Psychology*, *53B*, 25–58.

Brooks, D. C., & Bouton, M. E. (1993). A retrieval cue for extinction attenuates spontaneous recovery. *Journal of Experimental Psychology: Animal Behavior Processes*, *19*, 77–89.

Brooks, D. C., & Bouton, M. E. (1994). A retrieval cue for extinction attenuates response recovery (renewal) caused by a return to the conditioning context. *Journal of Experimental Psychology: Animal Behavior Processes*, *20*, 366–379.

Brooks, D. C., Hale, B., Nelson, J. B., & Bouton, M. E. (1995). Reinstatement after counterconditioning. *Animal Learning & Behavior*, *23*, 383–390.

Brooks, D. C., Palmatier, M. I., Garcia, L. O., & Johnson, J. L. (1999). An extinction cue reduces spontaneous recovery of a conditioned taste aversion. *Animal Learning & Behavior*, *27*, 77–88.

Brooks, D. C., Vaughn, J. M., Freeman, A. J., & Woods, A. M. (2004). An extinction cue reduces spontaneous recovery of ethanol tolerance in rats. *Psychopharmacology*, *176*, 256–265.

Brown, G. W., & Harris, T. (1982). Fall-off in the reporting of life events. *Social Psychiatry, 17,* 23–28.

Brown, J. S., Kalish, H. I., & Farber, I. E. (1951). Conditioned fear as revealed by magnitude of startle response to an auditory stimulus. *Journal of Experimental Psychology, 41,* 317–327.

Brown, T. A., Chorpita, B. F., & Barlow, D. H. (1998). Structural relationships among dimensions of the DSM–IV anxiety and mood disorders and dimensions of negative affect, positive affect, and autonomic arousal. *Journal of Abnormal Psychology, 107,* 179–192.

Brownley, K. A., Hurwitz, B. E., & Schneiderman, N. (2000). Cardiovascular psychophysiology. In J. T. Cacioppo, L. G. Tassinary, & G. G. Berentson (Eds.), *Handbook of psychophysiology* (pp. 224–264). New York: Cambridge University Press.

Brunzell, D. H., & Kim, J. J. (2001). Fear conditioning to tone, but not to context, is attenuated by lesions of the insular cortex and posterior extension of the intralaminar complex in rats. *Behavioral Neuroscience, 115,* 365–375.

Bryant, R. A., & Harvey, A. G. (1997). Attentional bias in posttraumatic stress disorder. *Journal of Traumatic Stress, 10,* 635–644.

Büchel, C., & Dolan, R. J. (2000). Classical fear conditioning in functional neuroimaging. *Current Opinion in Neurobiology, 10,* 219–223.

Büchel, C., Morris, J., Dolan, R. J., & Friston, K. J. (1998). Brain systems mediating aversive conditioning: An event-related fMRI study. *Neuron, 20,* 947–957.

Burwell, R. D., Saddoris, M. P., Bucci, D. J., & Wiig, K. A. (2004). Corticohippocampal contributions to spatial and contextual learning. *Journal of Neuroscience, 24,* 3826–3836.

Butler, E. A., & Gross, J. J. (2004). Hiding feelings in social contexts: Out of sight is not out of mind. In P. Philippot & R. S. Feldman (Eds.), *The regulation of emotion* (pp. 101–126). Mahwah, NJ: Erlbaum.

Cain, C. K., Blouin, A. M., & Barad, M. (2002). L-type voltage-gated calcium channels are required for extinction, but not for acquisition or expression, of conditional fear in mice. *Journal of Neuroscience, 22,* 9113–9121.

Cain, C. K., Blouin, A. M., & Barad, M. (2003). Temporally massed CS presentations generate more fear extinction than spaced presentations. *Journal of Experimental Psychology: Animal Behavior Processes, 29,* 323–333.

Cain, C. K., Blouin, A. M., & Barad, M. (2004). Adrenergic transmission facilitates extinction of conditional fear in mice. *Learning & Memory, 11,* 179–187.

Cain, C. K., Jami, S., Ponnusamy, R., & Barad, M. (2005). *Local infusion into basolateral amygdala of an antagonist or an agonist of L-type voltage gated calcium channels blocks or facilitates conditioned fear extinction.* Manuscript in preparation.

Cain, M. E., Kapp, B. S., & Puryear, C. B. (2002). The contribution of the amygdala to conditioned thalamic arousal. *Journal of Neuroscience, 22,* 11026–11034.

Campbell, D. H., Sanderson, R. E., & Laverty, S. G. (1964). Characteristics of a conditioned response in human subjects during extinction trials following a single traumatic conditioning trial. *Journal of Abnormal and Social Psychology, 68,* 627–639.

Campeau, S., & Davis, M. (1995). Involvement of the central nucleus and basolateral complex of the amygdala in fear conditioning measured with fear-potentiated startle in rats trained concurrently with auditory and visual conditioned stimuli. *Journal of Neuroscience, 15,* 2301–2311.

Capaldi, E. J. (1994). The sequential view: From rapidly fading stimulus traces to the organization of memory and the abstract concept of number. *Psychonomic Bulletin & Review, 1,* 156–181.

Carew, T. J., & Kandel, E. R. (1973, December 14). Acquisition and retention of long-term habituation in Aplysia: Correlation of behavioral and cellular processes. *Science, 182,* 1158–1160.

Cavanagh, K., & Davey, G. C. L. (2000). UCS expectancy biases in spider phobics: Underestimation of aversive consequences following fear irrelevant stimuli. *Behaviour Research and Therapy, 38,* 641–651.

Cavanagh, K., & Davey, G. C. L. (2001). The use of stimulus dimensions in judgment making in spider fearful and nonfearful individuals. *Behaviour Research and Therapy, 39,* 1199–1211.

Cavanagh, K., & Davey, G. C. L. (2004). Access to information about harm and safety in spider fearful and non-fearful individuals: When they were good they were very very good but when they were bad they were horrid. *Journal of Behavior Therapy and Experimental Psychiatry, 34,* 269–281.

Center for the Study of Emotion and Attention [CSEA-NIHM]. (1999). *The international affective picture system: Digitized photographs.* Gainesville, FL: Center for Research in Psychophysiology, University of Florida.

Chaiken, S., & Trope, Y. (1999). *Dual-process theories in social psychology.* New York: Guilford Press.

Chambless, D. L. (1990). Spacing of exposure sessions in treatment of agoraphobia and simple phobia. *Behavior Therapy, 21,* 217–229.

Chambless, D. L., Sanderson, W. C., Shoham, V., Bennett Johnson, S., Pope, K. S., Crits-Christoph, P., et al. (1996). An update on empirically validated therapies. *Clinical Psychologist, 49,* 5–18.

Chapman, P. F., Kairiss, E. W., Keenan, C. L., & Brown, T. H. (1990). Long-term synaptic potentiation in the amygdala. *Synapse, 6,* 271–278.

Charney, D. S., Woods, S. W., Krystal, J. H., Nagy, L. M., & Heninger, G. R. (1992). Noradrenergic neuronal dysregulation in panic disorder: The effects of intravenous yohimbine and clonidine in panic disorder patients. *Acta Psychiatrica Scandinavica, 8,* 273–282.

Chelonis, J. J., Calton, J. L., Hart, J. A., & Schachtman, T. R. (1999). Attenuation of the renewal effect by extinction in multiple contexts. *Learning and Motivation, 30,* 1–14.

Chhatwal, J. P., Davis, M., Maguschak, K. A., & Ressler, K. J. (2005). Enhancing cannabinoid neurotransmission augments the extinction of conditioned fear. *Neuropsychopharmacology, 30,* 516–524.

Chhatwal, J. P., Myers, K. M., Ressler, K. J., & Davis, M. (2005). Regulation of gephyrin and GABAA receptor binding within the amygdala after fear acquisition and extinction. *Journal of Neuroscience, 25*, 502–506.

Chorpita, B. F. (2001). Control and the development of negative emotions. In M. W. Vasey & M. R. Dadds (Eds.), *The developmental psychopathology of anxiety* (pp. 112–142). New York: Oxford University Press.

Church, R. M., & Deluty, M. Z. (1977). Bisection of temporal intervals. *Journal of Experimental Psychology: Animal Behavior Processes, 3*, 216–228.

Clark, D. M. (1986). A cognitive approach to panic disorder. *Behaviour Research and Therapy, 24*, 461–470.

Clugnet, M. C., & LeDoux, J. E. (1990). Synaptic plasticity in fear conditioning circuits: Induction of LTP in the lateral nucleus of the amygdala by stimulation of the medial geniculate body. *Journal of Neuroscience, 10*, 2818–2824.

Coles, M. E., & Heimberg, R. G. (2002). Memory biases in the anxiety disorders: Current status. *Clinical Psychology Review, 22*, 587–627.

Collingridge, G. L., Kehl, S. J., & McLennan, H. (1983). Excitatory amino acids in synaptic transmission in the Schaffer-commissural pathway of the rat hippocampus. *Journal of Physiology, 334*, 33–46.

Collins, B. N., & Brandon, T. H. (2002). Effects of extinction context and retrieval cues on alcohol cue reactivity among nonalcoholic drinkers. *Journal of Consulting and Clinical Psychology, 70*, 390–397

Collins, D. J., & Shanks, D. R. (2002). Momentary and integrative response strategies in causal judgment. *Memory & Cognition, 30*, 1138–1147.

Colwill, R. M., & Rescorla, R. A. (1990). Effect of reinforcer devaluation on discriminative control of instrumental behavior. *Journal of Experimental Psychology: Animal Behavior Processes, 16*, 40–47.

Cook, E. W., III., Hodes, R. L., & Lang, P. J. (1986). Preparedness and phobia: Effects of stimulus content on human visceral conditioning. *Journal of Abnormal Psychology, 95*, 195–207.

Cook, M., & Mineka, S. (1989). Observational conditioning of fear to fear-relevant versus fear-irrelevant stimuli in rhesus monkeys. *Journal of Abnormal Psychology, 98*, 448–459.

Cook, M., & Mineka, S. (1990). Selective associations in the observational conditioning of fear in monkeys. *Journal of Experimental Psychology: Animal Behavior Processes, 16*, 372–389.

Cook, M., Mineka, S., Wolkenstein, B., & Laitsch, K. (1985). Observational conditioning of snake fear in unrelated rhesus monkeys. *Journal of Abnormal Psychology, 94*, 591–610.

Corcoran, K. A., & Maren, S. (2001). Hippocampal inactivation disrupts contextual retrieval of fear memory after extinction. *Journal of Neuroscience, 21*, 1720–1726.

Cracknell, S., & Davey, G. C. L. (1988). The effects of perceived unconditioned response strength on conditioned responding in humans. *Medical Science Research, 16*, 169–170.

Craske, M. G. (1999). *Anxiety disorders: Psychological approaches to theory and treatment*. Boulder, CO: Westview Press.

Craske, M. G. (2003). *The origins of phobias and anxiety disorders: Why more women than men*. Oxford, England: Elsevier.

Craske, M. G., DeCola, J. P., Sachs, A. D., & Pontillo, D. C. (2003). Panic control treatment for agoraphobia. *Journal of Anxiety Disorders, 17,* 321–333.

Craske, M. G., Miller, P. P., Rotunda, R., & Barlow, D. H. (1990). A descriptive report of features of initial unexpected panic attacks in minimal and extensive avoiders. *Behaviour Research and Therapy, 28,* 395–400.

Craske, M. G., & Rachman, S. J. (1987). Return of fear: Perceived skill and heart rate responsivity. *British Journal of Clinical Psychology, 26,* 187–199.

Craske, M. G., Rowe, M., Lewin, M., & Noriega-Dimitri, R. (1997). Interoceptive exposure versus breathing retraining within cognitive-behavioural therapy for panic disorder with agoraphobia. *British Journal of Clinical Psychology, 36,* 85–99.

Craske, M. G., Sanderson, W. C., & Barlow, D. H. (1987). How do desynchronous response systems relate to the treatment of agoraphobia: A follow-up evaluation. *Behaviour Research and Therapy, 25,* 117–122.

Craske, M. G., Street, L., & Barlow, D. H. (1989). Instructions to focus upon or distract from internal cues during exposure treatment of agoraphobic avoidance. *Behaviour Research and Therapy, 27,* 663–672.

Cruikshank, S. J., Edeline, J. M., & Weinberger, N. M. (1992). Stimulation at a site of auditory-somatosensory convergence in the medial geniculate nucleus is an effective unconditioned stimulus for fear conditioning. *Behavioral Neuroscience, 106,* 471–483.

Cunningham, C. L. (1979). Alcohol as a cue for extinction: State dependency produced by conditioned inhibition. *Animal Learning & Behavior, 7,* 45–52.

Cuthbert, B. N., Bradley, M. M., & Lang, P. J. (1996). Probing picture perception: Activation and emotion. *Psychophysiology, 33,* 103–112.

Dadds, M. R., Davey, G. C., & Field, A. P. (2001). Developmental aspects of conditioning processes in anxiety disorders. In M. W. Vasey & M. R. Dadds (Eds.), *The developmental psychopathology of anxiety* (pp. 205–230). New York: Oxford University Press.

Davey, G. C. L. (1987). An integration of human and animal models of Pavlovian conditioning: Associations, cognitions and attributions. In G. C. L. Davey (Ed.), *Cognitive processes and Pavlovian conditioning in humans* (pp. 83–114). Oxford, England: Wiley.

Davey, G. C. L. (1988). Pavlovian conditioning in humans: UCS revaluation and the self-observation of responding. *Medical Science Research, 16,* 957–961.

Davey, G. C. L. (1989). UCS revaluation and conditioning models of acquired fears. *Behaviour Research and Therapy, 27,* 521–528.

Davey, G. C. L. (1992a). Classical conditioning and the acquisition of human fears and phobias: A review and synthesis of the literature. *Advances in Behaviour Research and Therapy, 14,* 29–66.

Davey, G. C. L. (1992b). An expectancy model of laboratory preparedness effects. *Journal of Experimental Psychology: General, 121*, 24–40.

Davey, G. C. L. (1993). A comparison of three cognitive appraisal strategies: The role of threat devaluation in problem-focused coping. *Personality and Individual Differences, 14*, 535–546.

Davey, G. C. L. (1994a). An expectancy model of laboratory preparedness effects. *Journal of Experimental Psychology: General, 121*, 24–40.

Davey, G. C. L. (1994b). The "disgusting" spider: The role of disease and illness in the perpetuation of fear of spiders. *Society & Animals, 2*, 17–25.

Davey, G. C. L. (1995). Preparedness and phobias: Specific evolved associations or a generalized expectancy bias. *Behavioral and Brain Sciences, 18*, 289–325.

Davey, G. C. L. (1997). A conditioning model of phobias. In G. C. L. Davey (Ed.), *Phobias: A handbook of theory, research and assessment* (pp. 301–322). Oxford, England: Wiley.

Davey, G. C. L., Burgess, I., & Rashes, R. (1995). Coping strategies and phobias: The relationship between, fears, phobias and methods of coping with stressors. *British Journal of Clinical Psychology, 34*, 423–434.

Davey, G. C. L., & Craigie, P. (1997). Manipulation of dangerousness judgments to fear-relevant stimuli: Effects on a priori UCS expectancy and a posteriori covariation assessment. *Behaviour Research and Therapy, 35*, 607–617.

Davey, G. C. L., de Jong, P. J., & Tallis, F. (1993). UCS inflation in the aetiology of a variety of anxiety disorders: Some case histories. *Behaviour Research and Therapy, 31*, 495–498.

Davey, G. C. L., & Dixon, A. (1996). The expectancy bias model of selective associations: The relationship of judgments of CS dangerousness, CS-UCS similarity and prior fear to a priori and a posteriori co-variation assessments. *Behaviour Research and Therapy, 34*, 235–252.

Davey, G. C. L., Hampton, J., Farrell, J., & Davidson, S. (1992). Some characteristics of worrying: Evidence for worrying and anxiety as separate constructs. *Personality and Individual Differences, 13*, 133–147.

Davey, G. C. L., & Levy, S. (1998). Catastrophic worrying: Personal inadequacy and a perseverative iterative style as features of the catastrophising process. *Journal of Abnormal Psychology, 107*, 576–586.

Davey, G. C. L., & Matchett, G. (1994). UCS rehearsal and the enhancement and retention of differential "fear" conditioning: Effects of trait and state anxiety. *Journal of Abnormal Psychology, 104*, 708–718.

Davey, G. C. L., & Matchett, G. (1996). The effects of response feedback on conditioned responding during extinction: Implications for the role of interoception in anxiety-based disorders. *Journal of Psychophysiology, 10*, 291–302.

Davey, G. C. L., & McDonald, A. S. (2000). Cognitive neutralising strategies and their use across differing stressor types. *Anxiety, Stress & Coping, 13*, 115–141.

Davey, G. C. L., & McKenna, I. (1983). The effects of postconditioning revaluation of CS1 and UCS following Pavlovian second-order electrodermal conditioning in humans. *Quarterly Journal of Experimental Psychology, 35B*, 125–133.

Davis, H. P., & Squire, L. R. (1984). Protein synthesis and memory: A review. *Psychological Bulletin, 96,* 518–559.

Davis, M. (1986). Pharmacological and anatomical analysis of fear conditioning using the fear-potentiated startle paradigm. *Behavioral Neuroscience, 100,* 814–824.

Davis, M. (1992a). The role of the amygdala in fear and anxiety. *Annual Review of Neuroscience, 15,* 353–375.

Davis, M. (1992b). The role of the amygdala in fear-potentiated startle: Implications for animal models of anxiety. *Trends in Pharmacological Science, 13,* 35–41.

Dawson, M. E. (1973). Can classical conditioning occur without contingency learning? A review and evaluation of the evidence. *Psychophysiology, 10,* 82–86.

Dawson, M. E., Catania, J. J., Schell, A. M., & Grings, W. W. (1979). Autonomic classical conditioning as a function of awareness of stimulus contingencies. *Biological Psychology, 9,* 23–40.

Dawson, M. E., & Furedy, J. J. (1976). The role of awareness in human differential autonomic classical conditioning: The necessary-gate hypothesis. *Psychophysiology, 13,* 50–53.

Dawson, M. E., & Reardon, P. (1973). Construct validity of recall and recognition post conditioning measures of awareness. *Journal of Experimental Psychology, 98,* 308–315.

Dawson, M. E., & Schell, A. M. (1985). Information processing and human autonomic classical conditioning. In P. K. Ackles, J. R. Jennings, & M. Coles (Eds.), *Advances in psychophysiology* (Vol. I, pp. 89–165). Greenwich, CT: JAI Press.

Dawson, M. E., & Schell, A. M. (1987). The role of "controlled" and "automatic" cognitive processes in human autonomic classical conditioning. In G. C. L. Davey (Ed.), *Cognitive processes and Pavlovian conditioning in humans* (pp. 27–55). New York: Wiley.

Dawson, M. E., Schell, A. M., Beers, J. R., & Kelly, A. (1982). Allocation of cognitive processing capacity during human autonomic classical conditioning. *Journal of Experimental Psychology, 111,* 273–294.

Dawson, M. E., Schell, A. M., & Böhmelt, A. H. (1999). *Startle modification: Implications for neuroscience, cognitive science, and clinical science.* New York: Cambridge University Press.

Dawson, M. E., Schell, A. M., & Filion, D. L. (2000). The electrodermal system. In J. T. Cacioppo, L. G. Tassinary, & G. G. Berentson (Eds.), *Handbook of psychophysiology* (pp. 200–223). New York: Cambridge University Press.

Dawson, M. E., Schell, A. M., & Tweddle-Banis, H. (1986). Greater resistance to extinction of electrodermal responses conditioned to potentially phobic CSs: A noncognitive process? *Psychophysiology, 23,* 552–561.

De Houwer, J., Baeyens, F., & Field, A. P. (2005). Associative learning of likes and dislikes: Some current controversies and possible ways forward. *Cognition & Emotion, 19,* 161–174.

De Houwer, J., Crombez, G., & Baeyens, F. (2005). Avoidance behaviour can function as a negative occasion setter. *Journal of Experimental Psychology: Animal Behavior Processes, 31,* 101–106.

De Houwer, J., Thomas, S., & Baeyens, F. (2001). Associative learning of likes and dislikes: A review of 25 years of research on human evaluative conditioning. *Psychological Bulletin, 127,* 853–869.

de Jong, P. J., Haenen, M. A., Schmidt, A., & Mayer, B. (1998). Hypochondriasis: The role of fear-confirming reasoning. *Behaviour Research and Therapy, 36,* 65–74.

de Jong, P. J., Merckelbach, H., Arntz, A., & Nijman, H. (1992). Co-variation detection in treated and untreated spider phobics. *Journal of Abnormal Psychology, 101,* 724–727.

de Jong, P. J., Weertman, A., Horselenberg, R., & van den Hout, M. A. (1997). Deductive reasoning and pathological anxiety: Evidence for a relatively strong "belief bias" in phobic subjects. *Cognitive Therapy and Research, 21,* 647–662.

Delamater, A. R. (1996). Effects of several extinction treatments upon the integrity of Pavlovian stimulus-outcome associations. *Animal Learning & Behavior, 24,* 437–449.

Delamater, A. R. (1997). Selective reinstatement of stimulus-outcome associations. *Animal Learning & Behaviour, 15,* 400–412.

Delamater, A. R. (2004). Experimental extinction in Pavlovian conditioning: Behavioural and neuroscience perspectives. *Quarterly Journal of Experimental Psychology, 57B,* 97–132.

Denniston, J. C., Chang, R. C., & Miller, R. R. (2003). Massive extinction treatment attenuates the renewal effect. *Learning and Motivation, 34,* 68–86.

Denollet, J., Sys, S. U., Stoobant, N., Rombouts, H., Gillebert, T. C., & Brutsaert, D. L. (1996). Personality as an independent predictor of long-term mortality in patients with coronary heart disease. *The Lancet, 347,* 417–421.

DeOca, B. M., DeCola, J. P., Maren, S., & Fanselow, M. S. (1998). Distinct regions of the periaqueductal gray are involved in the acquisition and expression of defensive responses. *Journal of Neuroscience, 18,* 3426–3432.

De Silva, P., Rachman, S. J., & Seligman, M. E. P. (1977). Prepared phobias and obsessions: Therapeutic outcome. *Behaviour Research and Therapy, 15,* 65–77.

Diamond, D., Matchett, G., & Davey, G. C. L. (1995). The effect of prior fear levels on UCS-expectancy ratings to a fear-relevant stimulus. *Quarterly Journal of Experimental Psychology, 48A,* 237–247.

Dickinson, A. (2001). Causal learning: An associative analysis. *Quarterly Journal of Experimental Psychology, 54B,* 3–25.

Dimberg, U. (1987). Facial reactions, autonomic activity, and experienced emotion: A three-component model of emotional conditioning. *Biological Psychology, 24,* 105–122.

Dirikx, T., Hermans, D., Vansteenwegen, D., Baeyens, F., & Eelen, P. (in press). Reinstatement of conditioned responses in human differential fear conditioning. *Journal of Behavior Therapy and Experimental Psychiatry.*

Dirikx, T., Hermans, D., Vansteenwegen, D., Baeyens, F., & Eelen, P. (2004). Reinstatement of extinguished conditioned responses and negative stimulus valence as a pathway to return of fear in humans. *Learning & Memory, 11*, 549–554.

Dollard, J., & Miller, N. E. (1950). *Personality and psychotherapy: An analysis in terms of learning, thinking, and culture.* New York NY: McGraw-Hill.

Domjan, M. (2005). Pavlovian conditioning. *Annual Review of Psychology, 56*, 179–206.

Dunlap, K. (1932). *Habits, their making and unmaking.* New York: Liveright.

Ebbinghaus, H. (1885/1913). *Memory: A contribution to experimental psychology* (H. A. Ruger & C. E. Bussenius, Trans.). New York: Teachers College, Columbia University.

Edmunds, M. (1974). *Defence in animals.* Burnt Mill, England: Longman.

Eelen, P., Hermans, D., & Baeyens, F. (2001). Learning perspectives on anxiety disorders. In E. J. L. Griez, C. Faravelli, D. Nutt, & J. Zohar (Eds.), *Anxiety disorders: An introduction to clinical management and research* (pp. 249–264). New York: Wiley.

Eifert, G. H., & Forsyth, J. P. (2005). *Acceptance and commitment therapy for anxiety disorders: A practitioner's treatment guide to using mindfulness, acceptance, and value-based behavior change strategies.* Oakland, CA: New Harbinger.

Eifert, G. H., & Heffner, M. (2003). The effects of acceptance versus control contexts on avoidance of panic-related symptoms. *Journal of Behavior Therapy and Experimental Psychiatry, 34*, 293–312.

El-Ghundi, M., O'Dowd, B. F., & George, S. R. (2001). Prolonged fear responses in mice lacking dopamine D1 receptor. *Brain Research, 892*, 86–93.

Ellis, A. (1962). *Reason and emotion in psychotherapy.* New York: Lyle Stuart.

Estes, W. K. (1955a). Statistical theory of distributional phenomena in learning. *Psychological Review, 62*, 369–377.

Estes, W. K. (1955b). Statistical theory of spontaneous recovery and regression. *Psychological Review, 62*, 145–154.

Estes, A. (1959). The statistical approach to learning theory. In S. Koch (Ed.), *Psychology: A study of a science* (Vol. 2, pp. 380–491). New York: McGraw-Hill.

Estes, W. K., & Skinner, B. F. (1941). Some quantitative properties of anxiety. *Journal of Experimental Psychology, 29*, 390–400.

Eysenck, H. J. (1952). The effects of psychotherapy: An evaluation. *Journal of Consulting Psychology, 16*, 319–324.

Eysenck, H. J. (1960). The effects of psychotherapy. In H. J. Eysenck (Ed.), *Handbook of abnormal psychology: An experiential approach* (pp. 675–725). London: Pitman Medical.

Eysenck, H. J. (1963). Editorial. *Behaviour Research and Therapy, 1*, 1–2.

Eysenck, H. J. (1967). *The biological basis of personality.* Springfield, IL: Charles C Thomas.

Eysenck, H. J. (1968). A theory of the incubation of anxiety/fear responses. *Behaviour Research and Therapy, 6*, 309–321.

Eysenck, H. J. (1976). The learning theory model of neurosis—A new approach. *Behaviour Research and Therapy, 14*, 251–267.

Eysenck, H. J. (1979). The conditioning model of neurosis. *Behavioral and Brain Sciences, 2*, 155–199.

Eysenck, H. J. (1980). Autobiography. In G. Lindzey (Ed.), *A history of psychology in autobiography* (Vol. VII, pp. 153–187). San Francisco: W. H. Freeman.

Eysenck, M. W. (1997). *Anxiety and cognition: A unified theory.* Hove, England: Erlbaum.

Falls, W. A., Miserendino, M. J., & Davis, M. (1992). Extinction of fear-potentiated startle: Blockade by infusion of an NMDA antagonist into the amygdala. *Journal of Neuroscience, 12*, 854–863.

Fanselow, M. S. (1980). Conditional and unconditional components of post-shock freezing. *Pavlovian Journal of Biological Sciences, 15*, 177–182.

Fanselow, M. S. (1982). The post-shock activity burst. *Animal Learning & Behavior, 10*, 448–454.

Fanselow, M. S. (1986). Associative vs. topographical accounts of the immediate shock freezing deficit in rats: Implications for the response selection rules governing species specific defensive reactions. *Learning and Motivation, 17*, 16–39.

Fanselow, M. S. (1990). Factors governing one-trial contextual conditioning. *Animal Learning & Behavior, 18*, 264–270.

Fanselow, M. S. (1993). Associations and memories: The role of NMDA receptors and long-term potentiation. *Current Directions in Psychological Science, 2*, 152–156.

Fanselow, M. S. (1994). Neural organization of the defensive behavior system responsible for fear. *Psychonomic Bulletin & Review, 14*, 429–438.

Fanselow, M. S. (1998). Pavlovian conditioning, negative feedback, and blocking: Mechanisms that regulate association formation. *Neuron, 20*, 625–627.

Fanselow, M. S., & Baackes, M. P. (1982). Conditioned fear-induced opiate analgesia on the formalin test: Evidence for two aversive motivational systems. *Learning & Motivation, 13*, 200–221.

Fanselow, M. S., & Bolles, R. C. (1979). Triggering of the endorphin analgesic reaction by a cue previously associated with shock: Reversal by naloxone. *Bulletin of the Psychonomic Society, 14*, 88–90.

Fanselow, M. S., DeCola, J. P., & Young, S. L. (1993). Mechanisms responsible for reduced contextual conditioning with massed unsignaled unconditional stimuli. *Journal of Experimental Psychology: Animal Behavior Processes, 19*, 121–137.

Fanselow, M. S., & Kim, J. J. (1994). Acquisition of contextual Pavlovian fear conditioning is blocked by application of an NMDA receptor antagonist D,L-2-amino-5-phosphonovaleric acid to the basolateral amygdala. *Behavioral Neuroscience, 108*, 210–212.

Fanselow, M. S., & LeDoux, J. E. (1999). Why we think plasticity underlying Pavlovian fear conditioning occurs in the basolateral amygdala. *Neuron, 23,* 229–232.

Fanselow, M. S., & Lester, L. S. (1988). A functional behavioristic approach to aversively motivated behavior: Predatory imminence as a determinant of the topography of defensive behavior. In R. Bolles & M. Beecher (Eds.), *Evolution and learning* (pp. 185–211). Hillsdale, NJ: Erlbaum.

Fanselow, M. S., Lester, L. S., & Helmstetter, F. J. (1988). Changes in feeding and foraging patterns as an antipredator defensive strategy: A laboratory simulation using aversive stimulation in a closed economy. *Journal of the Experimental Analysis of Behavior, 50,* 361–374.

Fanselow, M. S., & Poulos, A. M. (2005). The neuroscience of mammalian associative learning. *Annual Review of Psychology, 56,* 207–234.

Fanselow, M. S., & Tighe, T. J. (1988). Contextual conditioning with massed versus distributed unconditional stimuli in the absence of explicit conditional stimuli. *Journal of Experimental Psychology. Animal Behavior Processes, 14,* 187–199.

Farchione, T. J. (2002). Effects of overlearning on return of fear. *Dissertation Abstracts International: Section B: The Sciences & Engineering, 62,* 5371.

Fazio, R. H., & Olson, M. A. (2003). Implicit measures in social cognition research: Their meaning and use. *Annual Review of Psychology, 54,* 297–327.

Fazio, R. H., & Towles-Schwen, T. (1999). The MODE model of attitude-behavior processes. In S. Chaiken & Y. Trope (Eds.), *Dual-process theories in social psychology* (pp. 97– 116). New York: Guilford Press.

Feldner, M. T., Zvolensky, M. J., Eifert, G. H., & Spira, A. P. (2003). Emotional avoidance: An experimental test of individual differences and response suppression during biological challenge. *Behaviour Research and Therapy, 41,* 403–411.

Feldner, M. T., Zvolensky, M. J., & Leen-Feldner, E. W. (2004). A critical review of the empirical literature on coping and panic disorder. *Clinical Psychology Review, 24,* 123–148.

Fendt, M., & Fanselow, M. S. (1999). The neuroanatomical and neurochemical basis of conditioned fear. *Neuroscience and Biobehavioral Reviews, 23,* 743–760.

Fernandez Espejo, E. (2003). Prefrontocortical dopamine loss in rats delays long-term extinction of contextual conditioned fear, and reduces social interaction without affecting short-term social interaction memory. *Neuropsychopharmacology, 28,* 490–498.

Field, A. P., Argyris, N. G., & Knowles, K. A. (2001). Who's afraid of the big bad wolf: A prospective paradigm to test Rachman's indirect pathways in children. *Behaviour Research and Therapy, 39,* 1259–1276.

Field, A. P., & Lawson, J. (2003). Fear information and the development of fears during childhood: effects on implicit fear responses and behavioural avoidance. *Behaviour Research and Therapy, 41,* 1277–1293.

Fischer, A., Sananbenesi, F., Schrick, C., Spiess, J., & Radulovic, J. (2004). Distinct roles of hippocampal de novo protein synthesis and actin rearrangement in extinction of contextual fear. *Journal of Neuroscience, 24,* 1962–1966.

Flint, J. (2004). The genetic basis of neuroticism. *Neuroscience and Biobehavioral Reviews, 28,* 307–316.

Foa, E. B. (1997). Trauma and women: Course, predictors, and treatment. *Journal of Clinical Psychology, 58*(Suppl. 9), 25–28.

Foa, E. B., Jameson, J. S., Turner, R. M., & Payne, L. L. (1980). Massed versus spaced exposure sessions in the treatment of agoraphobia. *Behaviour Research and Therapy, 18,* 333–338.

Foa, E. B., & Kozak, M. J. (1986). Emotional processing of fear: Exposure to corrective information. *Psychological Bulletin, 99,* 20–35.

Foa, E. B., & McNally, R. J. (1996). Mechanisms of change in exposure therapy. In M. Rapee (Ed.), *Current controversies in the anxiety disorders* (pp. 329–343). New York: Guilford Press.

Foa, E. B., McNally, R. J., Steketee, G. S., & McCarthy, P. R. (1991). A test of preparedness theory in anxiety-disordered patients using an avoidance paradigm. *Journal of Psychophysiology, 5,* 159–163.

Foa, E. B., Steketee, R. S., & Rothbaum, B. O. (1989). Behavioral–cognitive conceptualizations of posttraumatic stress disorder. *Behavior Therapy, 20,* 155–176.

Forsyth, J. P., & Eifert, G. H. (1996a). Systemic alarms in fear conditioning I: A reappraisal of what is being conditioned. *Behavior Therapy, 27,* 441–462.

Forsyth, J. P., & Eifert, G. H. (1996b). The language of feeling and the feeling of anxiety: Contributions of the behaviorisms toward understanding the function-altering effects of language. *Psychological Record, 46,* 607–649.

Forsyth, J. P., & Eifert, G. H. (1998). Response intensity in content-specific fear conditioning comparing 20% versus 13% CO_2-enriched air as unconditioned stimuli. *Journal of Abnormal Psychology, 107,* 291–304.

Fowles, D. C., Christie, M. J., Edelberg, R., Grings, W. W., Lykken, D. T., & Venables, P. H. (1981). Publication recommendations for electrodermal measurements. *Psychophysiology, 18,* 232–239.

Fox, E. (2004). Maintenance or capture of attention in anxiety-related biases? In J. Yiend (Ed.), *Cognition, emotion, and psychopathology* (pp. 86–105). New York: Cambridge University Press.

Fox, E., Russo, R., Bowles, R., & Dutton, K. (2001). Do threatening stimuli draw or hold attention in subclinical anxiety? *Journal of Experimental Psychology: General, 130,* 681–700.

Fox, N. A., Henderson, H. A., Marshall, P. J., Nichols, K. E., & Ghera, M. M. (2005). Behavioral inhibition: Linking biology and behavior within a developmental framework. *Annual Review of Psychology, 56,* 235–262.

Freudenthal, R., Locatelli, F., Hermitte, G., Maldonado, H., Lafourcade, C., Delorenzi, A., et al. (1998). Kappa-B like DNA-binding activity is enhanced after spaced training that induces long-term memory in the crab Chasmagnathus. *Neuroscience Letters, 242,* 143–146.

Frey, P. W., & Butler, C. S. (1977). Extinction after aversive conditioning: An associative or nonassociative process? *Learning and Motivation, 8,* 1–17.

Frohardt, R. J., Guarraci, F. A., & Bouton, M. E. (2000). The effects of neurotoxic hippocampal lesions on two effects of context after fear extinction. *Behavioural Neuroscience, 114,* 227–240.

Gale, G. D., Anagnostaras, S. G., & Fanselow, M. S. (2001). Cholinergic modulation of Pavlovian fear conditioning: Effects of intrahippocampal scopolamine infusion. *Hippocampus, 11,* 371–376.

Gale, G. D., Anagnostaras, S. G., Godsil, B. P., Mitchell, S., Nozawa, T., Sage, J. R., et al. (2004). Role of the basolateral amygdala in the storage of fear memories across the adult lifetime of rats. *Journal of Neuroscience, 24,* 3810–3815.

Gallistel, C. R., & Gibbon, J. (2000). Time, rate, and conditioning. *Psychological Review, 107,* 289–344.

Gantt, W. H. (1944). *Experimental basis for neurotic behavior: Origin and development of artificially produced disturbances of behavior in dogs.* New York: Paul B. Hoeber.

García-Gutiérrez, A., & Rosas, J. M. (2003a). Empirical and theoretical implications of additivity between reinstatement and renewal after interference in causal learning. *Behavioral Processes, 63,* 21–31.

García-Gutiérrez, A., & Rosas, J. M. (2003b). Context change as the mechanism of reinstatement in causal learning. *Journal of Experimental Psychology: Animal Behavior Processes, 29,* 292–310.

Gardenswartz, C. A., & Craske, M. G. (2001). Prevention of panic disorder. *Behavior Therapy, 32,* 725–738.

Garnefski, N., & Spinhoven, K. P. (2001). Negative life events, cognitive emotion regulation, and emotional problems. *Personality and Individual Differences, 30,* 1311–1327.

Garnefski, N., van den Kommer, T., Kraaij, V., Terrds, J., Legerstee, J., & Onstein, E. (2002). The relationship between cognitive emotion regulation strategies and emotional problems: Comparison between a clinical and non-clinical sample. *European Journal of Personality, 16,* 403–420.

Gerren, R. A., & Weinberger, N. M. (1983). Long-term potentiation in the magnocellular medial geniculate nucleus of the anesthetized cat. *Brain Research, 265,* 138–142.

Gerull, F., & Rapee, R. (2002). Mother knows best: Effects of maternal modeling on the acquisition of fear and avoidance behaviour in toddlers. *Behaviour Research and Therapy, 40,* 279–287.

Gewirtz, J. C., Falls, W. A., & Davis, M. (1997). Normal conditioned inhibition and extinction of freezing and fear-potentiated startle following electrolytic lesions of medical prefrontal cortex in rats. *Behavioural Neuroscience, 111,* 712–726.

Gibbon, J. (1977). Trial and intertrial durations in autoshaping. *Journal of Experimental Psychology: Animal Behavior Processes, 3,* 264–284.

Gibson, E. J., & Walk, R. D. (1960). The "visual cliff." *Scientific American, 202,* 64–71.

Globisch, J., Hamm, A. O., Esteves, F., & Öhman, A. (1999). Fear appears fast: Temporal course of startle reflex potentiation in animal fearful subjects. *Psychophysiology, 36,* 66–75.

Godsil, B. P., Quinn, J. J., & Fanselow, M. S. (2000). Body temperature as a conditional response measure for Pavlovian fear conditioning. *Learning & Memory, 7,* 353–356.

Godsil, B. P., Tinsley, M. R., & Fanselow, M. S. (2003). Motivation. In A. F. Healy & R. W. Proctor (Eds.), *Handbook of psychology: Experimental psychology* (Vol. 4, pp. 33–60). New York: Wiley.

Goosens, K. A., Holt, W., & Maren, S. (2000). A role for amygdaloid PKA and PKC in the acquisition of long-term conditional fear memories in rats. *Behavioral Brain Research, 114,* 145–152.

Goosens, K. A., & Maren, S. (2001). Contextual and auditory fear conditioning are mediated by the lateral, basal, and central amygdaloid nuclei in rats. *Learning & Memory, 8,* 148–155.

Goosens, K. A., & Maren, S. (2003). Pretraining NMDA receptor blockade in the basolateral complex, but not the central nucleus, of the amygdala prevents savings of conditional fear. *Behavioral Neuroscience, 117,* 738–750.

Graham, J., & Gaffan, E. A. (1997). Fear of water in children and adults: Etiology and familial effects. *Behaviour Research and Therapy, 35,* 91–108.

Gray, J. A. (1975). *Elements of a two-process theory of learning.* London: Academic Press.

Gray, J. A. (1987). *The psychology of fear and stress.* New York: Cambridge University Press.

Gray, J. A. (1990). Brain systems that mediate both emotion and cognition. *Cognition & Emotion, 4,* 269–288.

Grey, S., Rachman, S., & Sartory, G. (1981). Return of fear: The role of inhibition. *Behaviour Research and Therapy, 19,* 135–143.

Green, G., & Osborne, J. (1985). Does vicarious instigation provide support for observational learning theories? A critical review. *Psychological Bulletin, 38,* 3–17.

Grillon, C. (2002). Startle reactivity and anxiety disorders: Aversive conditioning, context, and neurobiology. *Biological Psychiatry, 52,* 958–975.

Grillon, C., & Ameli, R. (1998). Effects of threat and safety signals on startle during anticipation of aversive shocks, sounds, and airblasts. *Journal of Psychophysiology, 12,* 329–337.

Grillon, C., Ameli, R., Woods, S. W., Merikangas, K., & Davis, M. (1991). Fear-potentiated startle in humans: Effects of anticipatory anxiety on the acoustic blink reflex. *Psychophysiology, 28,* 588–595.

Grillon, C., & Davis, M. (1997). Effects of stress and shock anticipation on prepulse inhibition of the startle reflex. *Psychophysiology, 34,* 511–517.

Grillon, C., & Morgan, C. A., III (1999). Fear-potentiated startle conditioning to explicit and contextual cues in gulf war veterans with posttraumatic stress disorder. *Journal of Abnormal Psychology, 108,* 134–142.

Gross, J. J. (1998). Antecedent- and response-focused emotion regulation: Divergent consequences for experience, expression, and physiology. *Journal of Personality and Social Psychology, 74,* 224–237.

Gross, J. J. (2002). Emotion regulation: Affective, cognitive, and social consequences. *Psychophysiology, 39,* 281–291.

Gross, J. J., & John, O. P. (2003). Individual differences in two emotion regulation processes: Implications for affect, relationships, and well-being. *Journal of Personality and Social Psychology, 85,* 348–362.

Gross, J. J., & Levenson, R. W. (1997). Hiding feelings: The acute effects of inhibiting negative and positive emotion. *Journal of Abnormal Psychology, 106,* 95–103.

Gross, J. J., & Muñoz, R. F. (1995). Emotion regulation and mental health. *Clinical Psychology: Science and Practice, 2,* 151–164.

Gross, J. J., Sutton, S. K., & Ketelaar, T. V. (1998). Relations between affect and personality: Support for the affect-level and affective-reactivity views. *Personality and Social Psychology Bulletin, 24,* 279–288.

Groves, P. M., & Thompson, R. F. (1970). Habituation: A dual-process theory. *Psychological Review, 77,* 419–450.

Gunther, L. M., Denniston, J. C., & Miller, R. R. (1998). Conducting exposure treatment in multiple contexts can prevent relapse. *Behaviour Research and Therapy, 36,* 75–91.

Guthrie, E. R. (1935). *The psychology of learning.* New York: Harper.

Halberstadt, J. B., & Niedenthal, P. M. (1997). Emotional state and the use of stimulus dimensions in judgement. *Journal of Personality and Social Psychology, 72,* 1017–1033.

Hall, G., & Honey, R. C. (1990). Context-specific conditioning in the conditioned-emotional-response procedure. *Journal of Experimental Psychology: Animal Behavior Processes, 16,* 271–278.

Hamm, A. O., & Vaitl, D. (1996). Affective learning: Awareness and aversion. *Psychophysiology, 33,* 698–710.

Hamm, A. O., Vaitl, D., & Lang, P. J. (1989). Fear conditioning, meaning, and belongingness: A selective association analysis. *Journal of Abnormal Psychology, 98,* 395–406.

Hardwick, S., & Lipp, O. V. (2000). Modulation of affective learning: An occasion for evaluative conditioning. *Learning and Motivation, 31,* 251–271.

Harris, E. W., Ganong, A. H., & Cotman, C. W. (1984). Long-term potentiation in the hippocampus involves activation of N-methyl-D-aspartate receptors. *Brain Research, 323,* 132–137.

Harris, J. A., & Westbrook, R. F. (1998). Evidence that GABA transmission mediates context-specific extinction of learned fear. *Psychopharmacology, 140,* 105–115.

Harris, J. A., & Westbrook, R. F. (1999). The benzodiazepine midazolam does not impair Pavlovian fear conditioning but regulates when and where fear is expressed. *Journal of Experimental Psychology: Animal Behavior Processes, 25*, 236–246.

Hawton, K., Salkovskis, P. M., Kirk, J., & Clark, D. M. (1989). *Cognitive behaviour therapy for psychiatric problems: A practical guide*. London: Oxford University Press.

Hayes, S. C. (1976). The role of approach contingencies in phobic behavior. *Behavior Therapy, 7*, 28–36.

Hayes, S. C. (2004a). Acceptance and commitment therapy, relational frame theory, and the third wave of behavioral and cognitive therapies. *Behavior Therapy, 35*, 639–666.

Hayes, S. C. (Ed.). (2004b). *Rule-governed behavior: Cognition, contingencies, and instructional control*. Reno, NV: Context Press.

Hayes, S. C., Barnes-Holmes, D., & Roche, B. (2001). *Relational frame theory: A post-Skinnerian account of human language and cognition*. New York: Kluwer Academic.

Hayes, S. C., Brownstein, A. J., Zettle, R. D., Rosenfarb, I., & Korn, Z. (1986). Rule-governed behavior and sensitivity to changing consequences of responding. *Journal of the Experimental Analysis of Behavior, 45*, 237–256.

Hayes, S. C., Lattal, K. A., & Myerson, W. A. (1979). Strength of experimentally induced phobic behavior in rats: Avoidance versus dual-component formulations. *Psychological Reports, 44*, 891–894.

Hayes, S. C., Strosahl, K. D., & Wilson, K. G. (1999). *Acceptance and commitment therapy: An experiential approach to behavior change*. New York: Guilford Press.

Hayes, S. C., Strosahl, K. D., Wilson, K. G., Bissett, R. T., Pistorello, J., Toarmino, D., et al. (2004). Measuring experiential avoidance: A preliminary test of a working model. *The Psychological Record, 54*, 553–578.

Hayes, S. C., Wilson, K. G., Gifford, E. V., Follette, V. M., & Strosahl, K. (1996). Experiential avoidance and behavioral disorders: A functional dimensional approach to diagnosis and treatment. *Journal of Consulting and Clinical Psychology, 64*, 1152–1168.

Hayes, W. N., & Saiff, E. I. (1967). Visual alarm reactions in turtles. *Animal Behaviour, 15*, 102–106.

Hayward, C., Killen, J. D., Kraemer, H. C., & Taylor, C. B. (2000). Predictors of panic attacks in adolescents. *Journal of American Academy of Child Adolescent Psychiatry, 39*, 207–214.

Helmstetter, F. J., & Bellgowan, P. S. (1994). Effects of muscimol applied to the basolateral amygdala on acquisition and expression of contextual fear conditioning in rats. *Behavioral Neuroscience, 108*, 1005–1009.

Helmstetter, F. J., & Tershner, S. A. (1994). Lesions of the periaqueductal gray and rostral ventromedial medulla disrupt antinociceptive but not cardiovascular aversive conditional responses. *Journal of Neuroscience, 14*, 7099–7108.

Hendersen, R. W. (1978). Forgetting of conditioned fear inhibition. *Learning and Motivation, 9*, 16–30.

Hendersen, R. W. (1985). Fearful memories: The motivational significance of forgetting. In F. R. Brush & J. B. Overmier (Eds.), *Affect, conditioning, and cognition: Essays on the determinants of behavior* (pp. 43–54). Hillsdale, NJ: Erlbaum.

Henry, B., Moffitt, T. E., Caspi, A., Langley, J., & Silva, P. A. (1994). On the "Remembrance of Things Past": A longitudinal evaluation of the retrospective method. *Psychological Assessment, 6,* 92–101.

Hermans, D., Baeyens, F., & Eelen, P. (2003). On the acquisition and activation of evaluative information in memory: The study of evaluative learning and affective priming combined. In J. Musch & K. C. Klauer (Eds.), *The psychology of evaluation: Affective processes in cognition and emotion* (pp. 139–168). Mahwah, NJ: Erlbaum.

Hermans, D., Crombez, G., Vansteenwegen, D., Baeyens, F., & Eelen, P. (2002). Expectancy-learning and evaluative learning in human classical conditioning: differential extinction effects. In S. P. Shohov (Ed.), *Advances in psychology research* (pp. 17–42). Hauppauge, NY: Nova Science.

Hermans, D., Dirikx, T., Vansteenwegen, D., Baeyens, F., & Eelen, P. (2005). Reinstatement of fear responses in human aversive conditioning. *Behaviour Research and Therapy, 43,* 533–551.

Hermans, D., Dirikx, T., Vansteenwegen, D., Baeyens, F., Van den Bergh, O., & Eelen, P. (2005). Reinstatement of fear responses in human aversive conditioning. *Behaviour Research and Therapy, 43,* 533–551.

Hermans, D., Spruyt, A., & Eelen, P. (2003). Automatic affective priming of recently acquired stimulus valence: Priming at SOA 300 but not at SOA 1000. *Cognition & Emotion, 17,* 83–99.

Hermans, D., Vansteenwegen, D., Crombez, G., Baeyens, F., & Eelen, P. (2002). Expectancy-learning and evaluative learning in human classical conditioning: Affective priming as an indirect and unobtrusive measure of conditioned stimulus valence. *Behaviour Research and Therapy, 40,* 217–234.

Herrnstein, R. J. (1969). Method and theory in the study of avoidance. *Psychological Review, 76,* 49–69.

Herry, C., & Garcia, R. (2002). Prefrontal cortex long-term potentiation, but not long-term depression, is associated with the maintenance of extinction of learned fear in mice. *Journal of Neuroscience, 22,* 577–583.

Hertel, P. T., Mathews, A., Peterson, S., & Kintner, K. (2003). Transfer of training emotionally biased interpretations. *Applied Cognitive Psychology, 17,* 775–784.

Hiss, H., Foa, E. B., & Kozak, M. J. (1994). Relapse prevention program for treatment of obsessive-compulsive disorder. *Journal of Consulting and Clinical Psychology, 162,* 801–808.

Hitchcock, J. M., & Davis, M. (1991). Efferent pathway of the amygdala involved in conditioned fear as measured with the fear-potentiated startle paradigm. *Behavioral Neuroscience, 105,* 826–842.

Honey, R. C., & Hall, G. (1989). Acquired equivalence and distinctiveness of cues. *Journal of Experimental Psychology: Animal Behavior Processes, 15,* 338–346.

Honeybourne, C., Matchett, G., & Davey, G. C. L. (1993). An expectancy model of preparedness effects: A UCS-expectancy bias in phylogenetic and ontogenetic fear-relevant stimuli. *Behavior Therapy, 24,* 253–264.

Huerta, P. T., Sun, L. D., Wilson, M. A., & Tonegawa, S. (2000). Formation of temporal memory requires NMDA receptors within CA1pyramidal neurons. *Neuron, 25,* 473–480.

Huff, N. C., & Rudy, J. W. (2004). The amygdala modulates hippocampus-dependent context memory formation and stores cue-shock associations. *Behavioral Neuroscience, 118,* 53– 62.

Hull, C. L. (1935). The conflicting psychologies of learning—A way out. *Psychological Review, 42,* 491–516.

Hull, C. L. (1952). *Behavior System.* New Haven, NJ: Yale University Press.

Humphreys, L. (1940). Distributed practice in the development of the conditioned eyelid reaction. *Journal of General Psychology, 22,* 379–385.

Hyman, I. E., Jr., & Loftus, E. F. (1998). Errors in autobiographical memory. *Clinical Psychology Review, 18,* 935–947.

Insausti, R., Herrero, M. T., & Witter, M. P. (1997). Entorhinal cortex of the rat. Cytoarchitectonic subdivisions and the origin and distribution of cortical efferents. *Hippocampus, 7,* 146–183.

Iwata, J., & LeDoux, J. E. (1988). Dissociation of associative and nonassociative concomitants of classical fear conditioning in the freely behaving rat. *Behavioral Neuroscience, 102,* 66–76.

Jacobs, W. J., & Nadel, L. (1985). Stress-induced recovery of fears and phobias. *Psychological Review, 92,* 512–531.

Jacobson, E. (1938). *Progressive relaxation.* Chicago: University of Chicago Press.

Jami, S., & Barad, M. S. (2005). *Systemic injection or local basolateral amygdala infusion of GABA$_A$ receptor antagonists reversibly block the expression of conditioned fear extinction.* Manuscript in preparation.

Jasmin, L., Burkey, A. R., Granato, A., & Ohara, P. T. (2004). Rostral agranular insular cortex and pain areas of the central nervous system: A tract-tracing study in the rat. *Journal of Comparative Neurology, 468,* 425–440.

Jenkins, H. M., Barnes, R. A., & Barrera, J. (1981). Why autoshaping depends on trial spacing. In C. Locurto, H. S. Terrace, & J. Gibbon (Eds.), *Autoshaping and conditioning theory* (pp. 255–284). New York: Academic Press.

Jennings, J. R., Berg, W. K., Hutchenson, J. S., Obrist, P., Porges, S. W., & Turpin, G. (1981). Publication guidelines for heart rate studies in man. *Psychophysiology, 18,* 226–231.

John, O. P., & Gross, J. J. (2004). Healthy and unhealthy emotion regulation: Personality processes, individual differences, and life span development. *Journal of Personality, 72,* 1301–1333.

Jones, M. C. (1924a). The elimination of children's fears. *Journal of Experimental Psychology, 7,* 382–390.

Jones, M. C. (1924b). A laboratory study of fear: The case of Peter. *Pedagogical Seminary and Journal of Genetic Psychology, 31,* 308–315.

Jones, T., & Davey, G. C. L. (1990). The effects of cued UCS rehearsal on the retention of differential "fear" conditioning: An experimental analogue of the "worry" process. *Behaviour Research and Therapy, 28,* 159–164.

Josselyn, S. A., Shi, C., Carlezon, W. A., Neve, R. L., Nestler, E. J., & Davis, M. (2001). Long-term memory is facilitated by camp response element-binding protein overexpression in the amygdala. *Journal of Neuroscience, 21,* 2404–2412.

Kagan, J. (1989). Temperamental contributions to social behavior. *American Psychologist, 44,* 668–674.

Kagan, J., & Snidman, N. (1999). Early childhood predictors of adult anxiety disorders. *Biological Psychiatry, 46,* 1536–1541.

Kalin, N. H., Shelton, S. E., & Davidson, R. J. (2004). The role of the central nucleus of the amygdala in mediating fear and anxiety in the primate. *Journal of Neuroscience, 24,* 5506–5515.

Kamin, L. J. (1969). Predictability, surprise, attention and conditioning. In B. A. Campbell & R. M. Church (Eds.), *Punishment and aversive behavior* (pp. 279–296). New York: Appleton-Century-Crofts.

Kamphuis, J. H., & Telch, M. J. (2000). Effects of distraction and guided threat reappraisal on fear reduction during exposure-based treatments for specific fears. *Behaviour Research and Therapy, 38,* 1163–1181.

Karekla, M., Forsyth, J. P., & Kelly, M. M. (2004). Emotional avoidance and panicogenic responding to a biological challenge procedure. *Behavior Therapy, 35,* 725–746.

Kashdan, T. B., Barrios, V., Forsyth, J. P., & Steger, M. F. (in press). Experiential avoidance as a generalized psychological vulnerability: Comparisons with coping and emotion regulation strategies. *Behaviour Research and Therapy.*

Kazdin, A. E., & Wilcoxon, I. A. (1976). Systematic desensitization and nonspecific treatment effects: A methodological evaluation. *Psychological Bulletin, 83,* 729–758.

Kehoe, E. J. (1988). A layered network model of associative learning: Learning to learn and configuration. *Psychological Review, 95,* 411–433.

Kehoe, E. J., & Macrae, M. (1997). Savings in animal learning: Implications for relapse and maintenance after therapy. *Behavior Therapy, 28,* 141–155.

Keller, M. B., Yonkers, K. A., Warshaw, M. G., Pratt, L. A., Gollan, J. K., Massion, A. O., et al. (1994). Remission and relapse in subjects with panic disorder and panic with agoraphobia. *Journal of Nervous and Mental Disease, 182,* 290–296.

Kelso, S. R., & Brown, T. H. (1986, April 4). Differential conditioning of associative synaptic enhancement in hippocampal brain slices. *Science, 232,* 85–87.

Kendler, K. S., Heath, A. C., Martin, N. G., & Eaves, L. J. (1987). Symptoms of anxiety and symptoms of depression: Same genes, different environments? *Archives of General Psychiatry, 44,* 451–457.

Kendler, K. S., Myers, J., & Prescott, C. A. (2002). The etiology of phobias: An evaluation of the stress-diathesis model. *Archives of General Psychiatry, 59,* 242–248.

Kent, G. (1997). Dental phobias. In G. C. Davey (Ed.), *Phobias: A handbook of theory, research and treatment* (pp. 107–127). Chichester, England: Wiley.

Kessler, R., McGonagle, K., Zhao, S., Nelson, C., Hughes, M., Eshelman, S., et al. (1994). Lifetime and 12-month prevalence of DSM–III–R psychiatric disorders in the United States: Results from the National Comorbidity Survey. *Archives of General Psychiatry, 51,* 8–19.

Kheriaty, E., Kleinknecht, R. A., & Hyman, I. E., Jr. (1999). Recall and validation of phobia origins as a function of a structured interview versus the Phobic Origins Questionnaire. *Behavior Modification, 23,* 61–78.

Kida, S., Josselyn, S. A., de Ortiz, S. P., Kogan, J. H., Chevere, I., Masushige, S., & Silva, A. J. (2002). CREB required for the stability of new and reactivated fear memories. *Nature Neuroscience, 5,* 348–355.

Killcross, S., Robbins, T. W., & Everitt, B. J. (1997). Different types of fear-conditioned behaviour mediated by separate nuclei within amygdala. *Nature, 388,* 377–380.

Kim, J. J., Clark, R. E., & Thompson, R. F. (1995). Hippocampectomy impairs the memory of recently, but not remotely, acquired trace eyeblink conditioned responses. *Behavioral Neuroscience, 109,* 195–203.

Kim, J. J., DeCola, J. P., Landeira-Fernandez, J., & Fanselow, M. S. (1991). N-methyl-d-aspartate receptor antagonist APV blocks acquisition but not expression of fear conditioning. *Behavioral Neuroscience, 105,* 126–133.

Kim, J. J., & Fanselow, M. S. (1992, May 1). Modality specific retrograde amnesia of fear following hippocampal lesions. *Science, 256,* 675–677.

Kimmel, H. D., King, J., Huddy, J. J., & Gardner, K. A. (1980). A mutual inductance shocker. *Behavior Research Methods, Instruments and Computers, 12,* 605–606.

Kirsch, I., Tennen, H., Wickless, C., Saccone, A. J., & Cody, S. (1983). The role of expectancy on the reduction of fear. *Behavior Therapy, 14,* 520–533.

Klauer, K. C., & Musch, J. (2003). Affective priming: Findings and theories. In J. Musch & K. C. Klauer (Eds.), *The psychology of evaluation: Affective processes in cognition and emotion* (pp. 7–49). Mahwah, NJ: Erlbaum.

Kleinknecht, R. A. (2002). Comments on: Non-associative fear acquisition: A review of the evidence from retrospective and longitudinal research. *Behaviour Research and Therapy, 40,* 159–163.

Knight, D. C., Smith, C. N., Stein, E. A., & Helmstetter, F. J. (1999). Functional MRI of human Pavlovian fear conditioning: Patterns of activation as a function of learning. *NeuroReport, 10,* 3665–3670.

Kogan, J. H., Frankland, P. W., Blendy, J. A., Coblentz, J., Marowitz, Z., Schutz, G., et al. (1997). Spaced training induces normal long-term memory in CREB mutant mice. *Current Biology 7,* 1–11.

Konorski, J. (1967). *Integrative activity of the brain.* Chicago: University of Chicago Press.

Koster, E. H. W., Crombez, G., Van Damme, S., Verschuere, B., & De Houwer, J. (2004). Does imminent threat capture and hold attention? *Emotion, 4,* 312–317.

Kozak, M. J., Foa, E. B., & Steketee, G. (1988). Process and outcome of exposure treatment with obsessive-compulsives: Psychophysiological indicators of emotional processing. *Behavior Therapy, 19*, 157–169.

LaBar, K. S., LeDoux, J. E., Spencer, D. D., & Phelps, E. A. (1995). Impaired fear conditioning following unilateral temporal lobectomy in humans. *Journal of Neuroscience, 15*, 6846–6855.

Lachnit, H. (1986). Transswitching and contextual conditioning: Relevant aspects of time. *Pavlovian Journal of Biological Science, 21*, 160–172.

Lake, R. I. E., Eaves, L. J., Maes, H. H. M., Heath, A. C., & Martin, N. G. (2000). Further evidence against the environmental transmission of individual differences in neuroticism from a collaborative study of 45,850 twins and relatives of two continents. *Behavior Genetics, 30*, 223–233.

Landau, R. J. (1980). The role of semantic schemata in phobic word interpretation. *Cognitive Therapy and Research, 4*, 427–434.

Lang, A. J., & Craske, M. G. (2000). Manipulations of exposure-based therapy to reduce return of fear: A replication. *Behaviour Research and Therapy, 38*, 1–12.

Lang, A. J., Craske, M. G., & Bjork, R. A. (1999). Implications of a new theory of disuse for the treatment of emotional disorders. *Clinical Psychology: Science & Practice, 6*, 80–94.

Lang, P. J. (1971). The application of psychophysiological methods to the study of psychotherapy and behavior change. In A. E. Bergin & S. L. Garfield (Eds.), *Handbook of psychotherapy and behavior change: An empirical analysis* (pp. 75–125). New York: Wiley.

Lang, P. J. (1985). The cognitive psychophysiology of emotion: Fear and anxiety. In A. H. Tuma & J. D. Maser (Eds.), *Anxiety and the anxiety disorders* (pp. 131–170). Hillsdale, NJ: Erlbaum.

Lang, P. J., Bradley, M. M., & Cuthbert, B. N. (1990). Emotion, attention and the startle reflex. *Psychological Review, 97*, 377–395.

Lang, P. J., Bradley, M. M., & Cuthbert, B. N. (1997). Motivated attention: Affect, activation and action. In P. J. Lang, R. F. Simons, & M. T. Balaban (Eds.), *Attention and orienting: Sensory and motivational processes* (pp. 97–396). New York: Erlbaum.

Lang, P. J., Davis, M., & Öhman, A. (2000). Fear and anxiety: Animal models and human cognitive psychophysiology. *Journal of Affective Disorders, 61*, 137–159.

Lang, P. J., Greenwald, M. K., Bradley, M. M., & Hamm, A. O. (1993). Looking at pictures: Affective, facial, visceral, and behavioral reactions. *Psychophysiology, 30*, 261–273.

Lanuza, E., Nader, K., & LeDoux, J. E. (2004). Unconditioned stimulus pathways to the amygdala: Effects of posterior thalamic and cortical lesions on fear conditioning. *Neuroscience, 125*, 305–315.

Larsen, R. J., & Ketelaar, T. (1989). Extraversion, neuroticism, and susceptibility to positive and negative mood induction procedures. *Personality and Individual Differences, 10*, 1221–1228.

Lazarus, R. S., & Alfert, E. (1964). Short-circuiting of threat by experimentally altering cognitive appraisal. *Journal of Abnormal and Social Psychology, 69*, 195–205.

Lazarus, R. S., & Folkman, S. (1984). *Stress, appraisal and coping.* New York: Springer Publishing Company.

Lebron, K., Milad, M. R., & Quirk, G. J. (2004). Delayed recall of fear extinction in rats with lesions of ventral medial prefrontal cortex. *Learning & Memory, 11*, 544–548.

Ledgerwood, L., Richardson, R., & Cranney, J. (2003). Effects of D-cycloserine on extinction of conditioned freezing. *Behavioral Neuroscience, 117*, 341–349.

Ledgerwood, L., Richardson, R., & Cranney, J. (2004). D-cycloserine and the facilitation of extinction of conditioned fear: consequences for reinstatement. *Behavioral Neuroscience, 118*, 505–513.

LeDoux, J. E. (1993). Emotional memory: In search of systems and synapses. *Annals of the New York Academy of Sciences, 702*, 149–157.

LeDoux, J. E. (2000). Emotion circuits in the brain. *Annual Review of Neuroscience, 23*, 155–184.

LeDoux, J. E., Iwata, J., Cicchetti, P., & Reis, D. J. (1988). Different projections of the central amygdaloid nucleus mediate autonomic and behavioral correlates of conditioned fear. *Journal of Neuroscience, 8*, 2517–2529.

LeDoux, J. E., Ruggiero, D. A., Forest, R., Stornetta, R., & Reis, D. J. (1987). Topographic organization of convergent projections to the thalamus from the inferior colliculus and spinal cord in the rat. *Journal of Comparative Neurology, 264*, 123–146.

Lee, K. S. (1982). Sustained enhancement of evoked potentials following brief, high frequency stimulation of the cerebral cortex in vitro. *Brain Research, 239*, 617–623.

Lee, Y., & Davis, M. (1997). Role of the hippocampus, the bed nucleus of the stria terminalis, and the amygdala in the excitatory effect of corticotropin-releasing hormone on the acoustic startle reflex. *Journal of Neuroscience, 17*, 6434–6446.

Lee, Y., Walker, D. L., & Davis, M. (1996). Lack of a temporal gradient of retrograde amnesia following NMDA-induced lesions of the basolateral amygdala assessed with the fear-potentiated startle paradigm. *Behavioral Neuroscience, 110*, 836–839.

Leen-Feldner, E. W., Zvolensky, M. J., Feldner, M. T., & Lejuez, C. W. (2004). Behavioral inhibition: Relation to negative emotion regulation and reactivity. *Personality and Individual Differences, 36*, 1235–1247.

Levey, A., & Martin, I. (1981). Personality and conditioning. In H. Eysenck (Ed.), *A model for personality* (pp. 123–168). Berlin, Germany: Springer-Verlag.

Levis, D. J. (1985). Implosive theory: A comprehensive extension of conditioning theory of fear/anxiety to psychopathology. In S. Reiss & R. R. Bootzin (Eds.), *Theoretical issues in behavior therapy* (pp. 49–82). New York: Academic Press.

Levis, D. J., & Levin, H. S. (1972). Escape maintenance under serial and simultaneous compound presentation of separately established conditioned stimuli. *Journal of Experimental Psychology, 95,* 451–452.

Levitt, J. T., Brown, T. A., Orsillo, S. M., & Barlow, D. H. (2004). The effects of acceptance versus suppression of emotion on subjective and psychophysiological response to carbon dioxide challenge in patients with panic disorder. *Behavior Therapy, 35,* 747–766.

Levy, W. B., & Steward, O. (1979). Synapses as associative memory elements in the hippocampal formation. *Brain Research, 175,* 233–245.

Lewis, J. W., Sherman, J. E., & Liebeskind, J. C. (1981). Opioid and non-opioid stress analgesia: Assessment of tolerance and cross-tolerance with morphine. *Journal of Neuroscience, 1,* 358–363.

Liddell, H. S. (1949). *Emotional hazards in animals and man.* Springfield, IL: Charles C Thomas.

Likierman, H., & Rachman, S. J. (1980). Spontaneous decay of compulsive urges: Cumulative effects. *Behaviour Research and Therapy, 18,* 387–394.

Lin, C.-H., Lee, C.-C., & Gean, P.-W. (2003). Involvement of a calcineurin cascade in amygdala depotentiation and quenching of fear memory. *Molecular Pharmacology, 63,* 44–52.

Lin, C.-H., Yeh, S.-H., Leu, T.-H., Chang, W.-C., Wang, S.-T., & Gean, P.-W. (2003). Identification of calcineurin as a key signal in the extinction of fear memory. *Journal of Neuroscience, 23,* 1574–1579.

Lin, C.-H., Yeh, S.-H., Lu, H.-Y., & Gean, P.-W. (2003). The similarities and diversities of signal pathways leading to consolidation of conditioning and consolidation of extinction of fear memory. *Journal of Neuroscience, 23,* 8310–8317.

Lindquist, D. H., & Brown, T. H. (2004). Amygdalar NMDA receptors control the expression of associative reflex facilitation and three other conditional responses. *Behavioral Neuroscience, 118,* 36–52.

Linke, R., Braune, G., & Schwegler, H. (2000). Differential projection of the posterior paralaminar thalamic nuclei to the amygdaloid complex in the rat. *Experimental Brain Research, 134,* 520–532.

Lipp, O. V., Cox, D., & Siddle, D. A. T. (2001). Blink startle modulation during anticipation of pleasant and unpleasant stimuli. *Journal of Psychophysiology, 15,* 155–162.

Lipp, O. V., Oughton, N., & LeLievre, J. (2003). Evaluative learning in human Pavlovian conditioning: Extinct, but still there? *Learning and Motivation, 34,* 219–239.

Lipp, O. V., & Purkis, H. M. (2005). No support for dual process accounts of human affective learning in simple Pavlovian conditioning. *Cognition & Emotion, 19,* 269–282.

Lipp, O. V., Sheridan, J., & Siddle, D. A. T. (1994). Human blink startle during aversive and nonaversive Pavlovian conditioning. *Journal of Experimental Psychology: Animal Behavior Processes, 20,* 380–389.

Lipp, O. V., Siddle, D. A. T., & Dall, P. J. (1998). Effects of stimulus modality and task condition on blink startle modification and on electrodermal responses. *Psychophysiology, 35*, 452–461.

Lipp, O. V., Siddle, D. A. T., & Dall, P. J. (2003). The effects of unconditional stimulus valence and conditioning paradigm on verbal, skeleto-motor, and autonomic indices of human Pavlovian conditioning. *Learning and Motivation, 34*, 32–51.

Lipp, O. V., & Vaitl, D. (1990). Reaction time task as unconditional stimulus: Comparing aversive and non-aversive unconditional stimuli. *Pavlovian Journal of Biological Science, 25*, 77–83.

Lissek, S., Baas, J., Pine, D. S., Orme, K., Dvir, S., Nugent, M., et al. (2005). Airpuff startle probes: An efficacious and less aversive alternative to white-noise? *Biological Psychology, 68*, 283–299.

Locke, J. (1894). *An essay concerning human understanding.* London: Routledge. (Original work published 1690)

Lovibond, P. F. (1993). Conditioning and cognitive–behaviour therapy. *Behaviour Change, 10*, 119–130.

Lovibond, P. F. (2003). Causal beliefs and conditioned responses: Retrospective revaluation induced by experience and by instruction. *Journal of Experimental Psychology: Learning, Memory, and Cognition, 29*, 97–106.

Lovibond, P. F., Davis, N. R., & O'Flaherty, A. S. (2000). Protection from extinction in human fear conditioning. *Behaviour Research and Therapy, 38*, 967–983.

Lovibond, P. F., Mitchell, C. J., Minard, E., & Brady, A. (2005). *Safety behaviours preserve threat beliefs: Protection from extinction by an avoidance response in a laboratory model of fear.* Manuscript submitted for publication.

Lovibond, P. F., Preston, G. C., & Mackintosh, N. J. (1984). Context specificity of conditioning extinction, and latent inhibition. *Journal of Experimental Psychology: Animal Behavior Processes, 10*, 360–375.

Lovibond, P. F., Saunders, J. C., Brady, A., & Mitchell, C. J. (in press). Evidence for expectancy as a mediator of avoidance and anxiety in a laboratory model of human avoidance learning. *Quarterly Journal of Experimental Psychology.*

Lovibond, P. F., & Shanks, D. R. (2002). The role of awareness in Pavlovian conditioning: Empirical evidence and theoretical implications. *Journal of Experimental Psychology: Animal Behavior Processes, 28*, 3–26.

Lu, K. T., Walker, D. L., & Davis, M. (2001). Mitogen-activated protein kinase cascade in the basolateral nucleus of amygdala is involved in extinction of fear-potentiated startle. *Journal of Neuroscience, 21*, RC162.

Lubow, R. E. (1998). Latent inhibition and behavior pathology: Prophylactic and other possible effects of stimulus preexposure. In W. O'Donohue (Ed.), *Learning and behavior therapy* (pp. 107–121). Needham Heights, MA: Allyn & Bacon.

Lucock, M. P., & Salkovskis, P. M. (1988). Cognitive factors in social anxiety and its treatment. *Behaviour Research and Therapy, 26*, 297–302.

Lynch, G., Larson, J., Kelso, S., Barrionuevo, G., & Schottler, F. (1983). Intracellular injections of EGTA block induction of hippocampal long-term potentiation. *Nature, 305,* 719–721.

MacLeod, C., & Cohen, I. L. (1993). Anxiety and the interpretation of ambiguity—a text comprehension study. *Journal of Abnormal Psychology, 102,* 238–247.

MacLeod, C., Mathews, A., & Tata, P. (1986). Attentional bias in emotional disorders. *Journal of Abnormal Psychology, 95,* 15–20.

Magill, R. A., & Hall, K. G. (1990). A review of the contextual interference effect in motor skill acquisition. *Human Movement Science, 9,* 241–289.

Majak, K., & Pitkanen, A. (2003). Projections from the periamygdaloid cortex to the amygdaloid complex, the hippocampal formation, and the parahippocampal region: A PHA-L study in the rat. *Hippocampus, 13,* 922–942.

Malenka, R. C. (1991). The role of postsynaptic calcium in the induction of long-term potentiation. *Molecular Neurobiology, 5,* 289–295.

Malenka, R. C., & Bear, M. F. (2004). LTP and LTD: An embarrassment of riches. *Neuron, 44,* 5–21.

Malenka, R. C., Kauer, J. A., Zucker, R. S., & Nicoll, R. A. (1988, October 7). Postsynaptic calcium is sufficient for potentiation of hippocampal synaptic transmission. *Science, 242,* 81–84.

Malloy, P. F., & Levis, D. J. (1988). A laboratory demonstration of persistent human avoidance. *Behavior Therapy, 19,* 229–241.

Manns, J. R., Clark, R. E., & Squire, L. R. (2002). Standard delay eyeblink conditioning is independent of awareness. *Journal of Experimental Psychology: Animal Behavior Processes, 28,* 32–37.

Marcks, B. A., & Woods, D. W. (2005). A comparison of thought suppression to an acceptance-based technique in the management of personal intrusive thoughts: A controlled evaluation. *Behaviour Research and Therapy, 43,* 433–445.

Maren, S. (1998). Overtraining does not mitigate contextual fear conditioning deficits produced by neurotoxic lesions of the basolateral amygdala. *Journal of Neuroscience, 18,* 3088–3097.

Maren, S. (1999). Neurotoxic basolateral amygdala lesions impair learning and memory but not the performance of conditional fear in rats. *Journal of Neuroscience, 19,* 8696–8703.

Maren, S. (2003). The amygdala, synaptic plasticity, and fear memory. *Annual New York Academy of Sciences, 985,* 106–113.

Maren, S., Aharonov, G., & Fanselow, M. S. (1996). Retrograde abolition of conditional fear after excitotoxic lesions in the basolateral amygdala of rats: Absence of a temporal gradient. *Behavioral Neuroscience, 110,* 718–726.

Maren, S., Aharonov, G., & Fanselow, M. S. (1997). Neurotoxic lesions of the dorsal hippocampus and Pavlovian fear conditioning in rats. *Behavioral Brain Research, 88,* 261–274.

Maren, S., & Fanselow, M. S. (1995). Synaptic plasticity in the basolateral amygdala induced by hippocampal formation stimulation in vivo. *Journal of Neuroscience*, *15*, 7548–7564.

Maren, S., Ferrario, C. R., Corcoran, K. A., Desmond, T. J., & Frey, K. A. (2003). Protein synthesis in the amygdala, but not the auditory thalamus, is required for consolidation of Pavlovian fear conditioning in rats. *European Journal of Neuroscience*, *18*, 3080–3088.

Marescau, V., Vansteenwegen, D., Vervliet, B., & Eelen, P. (2006). *The attenuation of renewal by an extinction retrieval cue in human contingency learning*. Manuscript in preparation.

Marks, I. M. (1987). *Fears, phobias and rituals: Panic, anxiety and their disorders*. New York, NY: Academic Press.

Marks, I. M., Lovell, K., Noshirvani, H., Livanou, M., & Thrasher, S. (1998). Treatment of posttraumatic stress disorder by exposure and/or cognitive restructuring: A controlled study. *Archives of General Psychiatry*, *55*, 317–325.

Marks, I. M., Swinson, R. P., Basoglu, M., Kuch, K., Noshirvani, H., O'Sullivan, G., et al. (1993). Alprazolam and exposure alone and combined in panic disorder with agoraphobia: A controlled study in London and Toronto. *British Journal of Psychiatry*, *162*, 776–787.

Marshall, W. L. (1985). The effects of variable exposure in flooding therapy. *Behavior Therapy*, *16*, 117–135.

Marsicano, G., Wotjak, C. T., Azad, S. C., Bisogno, T., Rammes, G., Cascio, M. G., et al. (2002). The endogenous cannabinoid system controls extinction of aversive memories. *Nature*, *418*, 530–534.

Martin, I., & Levey, A. B. (1978). Evaluative conditioning. *Advances in Behaviour Research and Therapy*, *1*, 57–102.

Martin, I., & Levey, A. B. (1989). Propositional knowledge and mere responding. *Biological Psychology*, *28*, 149–155.

Marx, B. P., & Sloan, D. M. (2002). The role of emotion in the psychological functioning of adult survivors of childhood sexual abuse. *Behavior Therapy*, *33*, 563–577.

Mason, S. T. (1983). The neurochemistry and pharmacology of extinction behavior. *Neuroscience and Biobehavioural Review*, *7*, 325–347.

Masserman, J. H. (1943). *Behavior and neurosis: An experimental psycho-analytic approach to psychobiologic principles*. Chicago: University of Chicago Press.

Massicotte, G., & Baudry, M. (2004). Brain plasticity and remodeling of AMPA receptor properties by calcium-dependent enzymes. *Genetic Engineering*, *26*, 239–254.

Mathews, A. (1990). Why worry—the cognitive function of anxiety. *Behaviour Research and Therapy*, *28*, 455–468.

Mathews, A., & Mackintosh, B. (1998). A cognitive model of selective processing in anxiety. *Cognitive Therapy and Research*, *22*, 539–560.

Mathews, A., & Mackintosh, B. (2000). Induced emotional interpretation bias and anxiety. *Journal of Abnormal Psychology*, *109*, 602–615.

Mathews, A., & Macleod, C. (1985). Selective processing of threat cues in anxiety states. *Behaviour Research and Therapy, 23,* 563–569.

Mathews, A., & MacLeod, C. (1994). Cognitive approaches to emotion and emotional disorders. *Annual Review of Psychology, 45,* 25–50.

Mathews, A., & MacLeod, C. (2002). Induced processing biases have causal effects on anxiety. *Cognition & Emotion, 16,* 331–354.

Mathews, A., Richards, A., & Eysenck, M. (1989). Interpretation of homophones related to threat in anxiety-states. *Journal of Abnormal Psychology, 98,* 31–34.

McEchron, M. D., Bouwmeester, H., Tseng, W., Weiss, C., & Disterhoft, J. F. (1998). Hippocampectomy disrupts auditory trace fear conditioning and contextual fear conditioning in the rat. *Hippocampus, 8,* 638–646.

McEchron, M. D., Tseng, W., & Disterhoft, J. F. (2000). Neurotoxic lesions of the dorsal hippocampus disrupt auditory-cued trace heart rate (fear) conditioning in rabbits. *Hippocampus, 10,* 739–751.

McGaugh, J. L. (2000, January 14). Memory: A century of consolidation. *Science, 287,* 248–251.

McGaugh, J. L., Castellano, C., & Brioni, J. (1990). Picrotoxin enhances latent extinction of conditioned fear. *Behavioral Neuroscience, 104,* 264–267.

McGee, R., Feehan, M., Williams, S., Partridge, F., Silva, P. A., & Kelly, J. (1990). DSM–III disorders in a large sample of adolescents, *Journal of the American Academy of Child & Adolescent Psychiatry, 29,* 611–619.

McGregor, I. S., Schrama, L., Ambermoon, P., & Dielenberg, R. A. (2002). Not all "predator odours" are equal: Cat odour but not 2,4,5 trimethylthiazoline (TMT; fox odour) elicits specific defensive behaviours in rats. *Behavioral Brain Research, 129,* 1–16.

McLaren, S., & Crowe, S. F. (2003). The contribution of perceived control of stressful life events and thought suppression to the symptoms of obsessive-compulsive disorder in both non-clinical and clinical samples. *Journal of Anxiety Disorders, 17,* 389–403.

McNally, R. J. (1987). Preparedness and phobias: A review. *Psychological Bulletin, 101,* 283–303.

McNally, R. J., & Heatherton, T. F. (1993). Are co-variation biases attributable to a priori expectancy biases? *Behaviour Research and Therapy, 31,* 653–658.

McNally, R. J., & Steketee, G. S. (1985). The etiology and maintenance of severe animal phobias. *Behaviour Research and Therapy, 23,* 430–435.

Menzies, R. G., & Clarke, J. C. (1995a). The etiology of phobias: A nonassociative account. *Clinical Psychology Review, 15,* 23–48.

Menzies, R. G., & Clarke, J. C. (1995b). Danger expectancies and insight in acrophobia. *Behaviour Research and Therapy, 33,* 215–221.

Menzies, R. G., & Harris, L. M. (2001). Nonassociative factors in the development of phobias. In M. E. Vasey & M. R. Dadds (Eds.), *The developmental psychopathology of anxiety* (pp. 183–204). Oxford, England: Oxford University Press.

Menzies, R. G., & Parker, L. (2001). The origins of height fear: An evaluation of neoconditioning explanations. *Behaviour Research and Therapy, 39,* 185–199.

Merckelbach, H., Muris, P., & van Schouten, E. (1996). Pathways to fear in spider phobic children. *Behaviour Research and Therapy, 34*, 935–938.

Milad, M. R., & Quirk, G. J. (2002). Neurons in medial prefrontal cortex signal memory for fear extinction. *Nature, 420*, 70–74.

Miller, R. R., & Matzel, L. D. (1988). The comparator hypothesis: A response rule for the expression of associations. In G. H. Bower (Ed.), *The psychology of learning and motivation: Advances in research and theory* (Vol. 22, pp. 51–92). San Diego, CA: Academic Press.

Mineka, S. (1979). The role of fear in theories of avoidance learning, flooding, and extinction. *Psychological Bulletin, 86*, 985–1010.

Mineka, S. (1985). Animal models of anxiety-based disorders: Their usefulness and limitations. In J. Maser & A. Tuma (Eds.), *Anxiety and the anxiety disorders* (pp. 199–244). Hillsdale, NJ: Erlbaum.

Mineka, S., & Cook, M. (1986). Immunization against the observational conditioning of snake fear in rhesus monkeys. *Journal of Abnormal Psychology, 95*, 307–318.

Mineka, S., & Cook, M. (1993). Mechanisms underlying observational conditioning of fear in monkeys. *Journal of Experimental Psychology: General, 122*, 23–38.

Mineka, S., Cook, M., & Miller, S. (1984). Fear conditioned with escapable and inescapable shock: The effects of a feedback stimulus. *Journal of Experimental Psychology: Animal Behavior Processes, 10*, 307–323.

Mineka, S., Davidson, M., Cook, M., & Keir, R. (1984). Observational conditioning of snake fear in rhesus monkeys. *Journal of Abnormal Psychology, 93*, 355–372.

Mineka, S., & Gino, A. (1980). Dissociation between conditioned emotional response and extended avoidance performance. *Learning and Motivation, 11*, 476–502.

Mineka, S., Gunnar, M., & Champoux, M. (1986). Control and early socioemotional development: Infant rhesus monkeys reared in controllable versus uncontrollable environments. *Child Development, 57*, 1241–1256.

Mineka, S., & Kihlstrom, J. (1978). Unpredictable and uncontrollable aversive events. *Journal of Abnormal Psychology, 87*, 256–271.

Mineka, S., Mystkowski, J., Hladek, D., & Rodriguez, B. (1999). The effects of changing contexts on return of fear following exposure treatment for spider fear. *Journal of Consulting and Clinical Psychology, 67*, 599–604.

Mineka, S., & Öhman, A. (2002a). Born to fear: Non-associative versus associative factors in the etiology of phobias. *Behaviour Research and Therapy, 40*, 173–184.

Mineka, S., & Öhman, A. (2002b). Phobias and preparedness: The selective, automatic and encapsulated nature of fear. *Biological Psychiatry, 52*, 927–937.

Mineka, S., & Zinbarg, R. (1996). Conditioning and ethological models of anxiety disorders. *Nebraska Symposium on Motivation, 43*, 135–210.

Miserendino, M. J., Sananes, C. B., Melia, K. R., & Davis, M. (1990). Blocking of acquisition but not expression of conditioned fear-potentiated startle by NMDA antagonists in the amygdala. *Nature, 345*, 716–718.

Mitchell, C. J., & Lovibond, P. F. (2002). Backward and forward blocking in human electrodermal conditioning: Blocking requires an assumption of outcome additivity. *Quarterly Journal of Experimental Psychology, 55B,* 311–329.

Mogg, K., & Bradley, B. P. (1998). A cognitive-motivational analysis of anxiety. *Behaviour Research and Therapy, 35,* 297–303.

Mogg, K., & Bradley, B. P. (1999). Selective attention and anxiety: A cognitive-motivational perspective. In T. Dalgleish & M. J. Power (Eds.), *Handbook of cognition and emotion* (pp. 145–170). Chichester, England: Wiley.

Mogg, K., Bradley, B. P., & Halliwell, N. (1994). Attentional bias to threat: Roles of trait anxiety, stressful events, and awareness. *Quarterly Journal of Experimental Psychology, 47A,* 841–864.

Mogg, K., Bradley, B. P., Williams, R., & Mathews, A. (1993). Subliminal processing of emotional information in anxiety and depression. *Journal of Abnormal Psychology, 109,* 695–704.

Mogg, K., Mathews, A., & Weinman, J. (1989). Selective processing of threat cues in anxiety states: A replication. *Behaviour Research and Therapy, 27,* 317–323.

Moody, E. W., Sunsay, C., & Bouton, M. E. (in press). Priming and trial-spacing in extinction: Effects on extinction performance, spontaneous recovery, and reinstatement in appetitive conditioning. *Quarterly Journal of Experimental Psychology.*

Monroe, S. M. (1982). Assessment of life events: Retrospective vs. concurrent strategies. *Archives of General Psychiatry, 39,* 606–610.

Morgan, M. A., Romanski, L. M., & LeDoux, J. E. (1993). Extinction of emotional learning: contribution of medial prefrontal cortex. *Neuroscience Letters, 163,* 109–113.

Morris, R. G. M. (1975). Preconditioning of reinforcing properties of an exteroceptive feedback stimulus. *Learning and Motivation, 6,* 289–298.

Morris, R. G. M., Anderson, E., Lynch, G. S., & Baudry, M. (1986). Selective impairment of learning and blockade of long-term potentiation by an N-methyl-D-aspartate receptor antagonist, APV. *Nature, 319,* 774–776.

Morris, R. W., Furlong, T. M., & Westbrook, R. F. (2005). Recent exposure to a dangerous context impairs extinction and reinstates lost fear reactions. *Journal of Experimental Psychology: Animal Behavior Processes, 31,* 40–55.

Morris, R. G., Moser, E. I., Riedel, G., Martin, S. J., Sandin, J., Day, M., et al. (2003). Elements of a neurobiological theory of the hippocampus: the role of activity-dependent synaptic plasticity in memory. *Philosophical Transactions of the Royal Society of London. Series B, Biological Sciences, 358,* 773–786.

Mowrer, O. H. (1947). On the dual nature of learning: A re-interpretation of "conditioning" and "problem-solving." *Harvard Educational Review, 17,* 102–148.

Mowrer, O. H. (1960). "Sin," the lesser of two evils. *American Psychologist, 15,* 301–304.

Mowrer, O. H. (1963). Freudianism, behaviour therapy and self-disclosure. *Behaviour Research and Therapy, 1,* 321–337.

Mowrer, O. H., & Mowrer, W. M. (1938). Enuresis: A method for its study and treatment. *American Journal of Orthopsychiatry, 8,* 436–459.

Mowrer, O. H., & Viek, P. (1948). An experimental analogue of fear from a sense of helplessness. *Journal of Abnormal and Social Psychology, 43,* 193–200.

Muller, D., Joly, M., & Lynch, G. (1988, December 23). Contributions of quisqualate and NMDA receptors to the induction and expression of LTP. *Science, 242,* 1694–1697.

Muller, J., Corodimas, K. P., Fridel, Z., & LeDoux, J. E. (1997). Functional inactivation of the lateral and basal nuclei of the amygdala by muscimol infusion prevents fear conditioning to an explicit conditioned stimulus and to contextual stimuli. *Behavioral Neuroscience, 111,* 683–691.

Muris, P., Bodden, D., Merckelbach, H., Ollendick, T., & King, N. (2003). Fear of the beast: A prospective study on the effects of negative information on childhood fear. *Behaviour Research and Therapy, 41,* 195–208.

Muris, P., & Merckelbach, H. (2001). The etiology of childhood specific phobia: A multifactorial model. In M. W. Vasey & M. R. Dadds (Eds.), *The developmental psychopathology of anxiety* (pp. 355–385). New York: Oxford University Press.

Muris, P., Merckelbach, H., & van Spauwen, I. (2003). The emotional reasoning heuristic in children. *Behaviour Research and Therapy, 41,* 261–272.

Myers, K. M., & Davis, M. (2002). Behavioral and neural analysis of extinction. *Neuron, 36,* 567–584.

Mystkowski, J. L., Craske, M. G., & Echiverri, A. M. (2002). Treatment context and return of fear in spider phobia. *Behavior Therapy, 33,* 399–416.

Mystkowski, J. L., Echiverri, A. M., Labus, J. S., & Craske, M. G. (in press). Mental reinstatement of context and return of fear in spider phobia. *Behavior Therapy.*

Mystkowski, J. L., Mineka, S., Vernon, L. L., & Zinbarg, R. E. (2003). Changes in caffeine state enhance return of fear in spider phobia. *Journal of Consulting and Clinical Psychology, 71,* 243–250.

Nader, K., & LeDoux, J. (1999). The dopaminergic modulation of fear: Quinpirole impairs the recall of emotional memories in rats. *Behavioral Neuroscience, 113,* 152–165.

Nader, K., Majidishad, P., Amorapanth, P., & LeDoux, J. E. (2001). Damage to the lateral and central, but not other, amygdaloid nuclei prevents the acquisition of auditory fear conditioning. *Learning & Memory, 8,* 156–163.

Nader, K., Schafe, G. E., & LeDoux, J. E. (2000). Fear memories require protein synthesis in the amygdala for reconsolidation after retrieval [see comments]. *Nature, 406,* 722–726.

Napier, R. M., Macrae, M., & Kehoe, E. J. (1992). Rapid reacquisition in conditioning of the rabbit's nictitating membrane response. *Journal of Experimental Psychology: Animal Behavior Processes, 18,* 182–192.

Nardone, G., & Watzlawick, P. (1993). Clinical practice, processes, and procedures. In G. Nardone & P. Watzlawick (Eds.), *The art of change* (pp. 45–72). San Francisco: Jossey-Bass.

Neisser, U. (2004). Memory development: New questions and old. *Developmental Review, 24,* 154–158.

Nelson, J. B. (2002). Context specificity of excitation and inhibition in ambiguous stimuli. *Learning and Motivation, 33,* 284–310.

Nelson, J. B., & Bouton, M. E. (2002). Extinction, inhibition, and emotional intelligence. In L. F. Barrett (Ed.), *The wisdom in feeling: Psychological processes in emotional intelligence. Emotions and social behavior* (pp. 60–85). New York: Guilford Press.

Neumann, D. L., Lipp, O. V., & Siddle, D. A. T. (1997). Conditioned inhibition of autonomic Pavlovian conditioning in humans. *Biological Psychology, 46,* 223–233.

Norton, G. R., Cox, B. J., & Malan, J. (1992). Nonclinical panickers: A critical review. *Clinical Psychology Review, 12,* 121–139.

Ochsner, K. N., Ray, R. D., Cooper, J. C., Robertson, E. R., Chopra, S., Gabrieli, J. D. E., & Gross, J. J. (2004). For better or for worse: Neural systems supporting cognitive down- and up-regulation of negative emotion. *Neuroimage, 23,* 483–499.

Öhman, A. (1986). Face the beast and fear the face: Animal and social fears as prototypes for evolutionary analyses of emotion. *Psychophysiology, 23,* 123–145.

Öhman, A. (1987). The psychophysiology of emotion: An evolutionary–cognitive perspective. *Advances in Psychophysiology, 2,* 79–127.

Öhman, A. (1997). Unconscious pre-attentive mechanisms in the activation of phobic fear. In G. C. L. Davey (Ed.), *Phobias: A handbook of theory, research and treatment* (pp. 349–374). Chichester, England: Wiley.

Öhman, A., Dimberg, U., & Öst, L. G. (1985). Animal and social phobias: Biological constraints on learned fear responses. In S. Reiss & R. R. Bootzin (Eds.), *Theoretical issues in behavior therapy* (pp. 123–178). Orlando, FL: Academic Press.

Öhman, A., Ellstrom, P. E., & Bjorkstrand, P. A. (1976). Electrodermal responses and subjective estimates of UCS probability in a longer interstimulus interval conditioning paradigm. *Psychophysiology, 13,* 121–127.

Öhman, A., Flykt, A., & Esteves, F. (2001). Emotion drives attention: Detecting the snake in the grass. *Journal of Experimental Psychology: General, 130,* 466–478.

Öhman, A., Hamm, A. O., & Hugdahl, K. (2000). Cognition and the autonomic nervous system: Orienting, anticipation, and conditioning. In J. T. Cacioppo, L. G. Tassinary, & G. G. Berntson (Eds.), *Handbook of psychophysiology* (pp. 533–575). New York: Cambridge University Press.

Öhman, A., & Mineka, S. (2001). Fears, phobias, and preparedness: Toward an evolved module of fear and fear learning. *Psychological Review, 108,* 483–522.

Öhman, A., & Mineka, S. (2003). The malicious serpent: Snakes as a prototypical stimulus for an evolved module of fear. *Current Directions in Psychological Science, 12,* 5–9.

Öhman, A., & Soares, J. (1993). On the automatic nature of phobic fear: Conditioned electrodermal responses to masked fear-relevant stimuli. *Journal of Abnormal Psychology, 102,* 121–132.

Öhman, A., & Soares, J. (1994). "Unconscious anxiety": Phobic responses to masked stimuli. *Journal of Abnormal Psychology, 103,* 231–240.

Öhman, A., & Soares, J. (1998). Emotional conditioning to masked stimuli: Expectancies for aversive outcomes following nonrecognized fear-relevant stimuli. *Journal of Experimental Psychology: General, 127,* 69–82.

O'Keefe, J., & Nadel, L. (1978). *The hippocampus as a cognitive map.* Oxford, England: Oxford University Press, Clarendon Press.

Olfson, M., Fireman, B., Weissman, M. M., Leon, A. C., Sheehan, D. V., Dathol, R. G., et al. (1997). Mental disorder and disability among patients in a primary group practice. *American Journal of Psychiatry, 154,* 1734–1740.

Oliver, N. S., & Page, A. C. (2003). Fear reduction during in vivo exposure to blood-injection stimuli: Distraction vs. attentional focus. *British Journal of Clinical Psychology, 24,* 13–25.

Ollendick, T. H., Yule, W., & Ollier, K. (1991). Fears in British children and their relationship to manifest anxiety and depression. *Journal of Child Psychiatry, 32,* 321–331.

Öst, L.-G. (1997). Rapid treatment of specific phobias. In G. C. L. Davey (Ed.), *Phobias: A handbook of theory, research and treatment* (pp. 227–246). Chichester, England: Wiley.

Öst, L.-G., & Hugdahl, K. (1981). Acquisition of phobias and anxiety response patterns in clinical patients. *Behaviour Research and Therapy, 19,* 439–447.

Ottersen, O. P. (1982). Connections of the amygdala of the rat. IV: Corticoamygdaloid and intraamygdaloid connections as studies with axonal transport of horseradish peroxidase. *Journal of Comparative Neurology, 205,* 30–48.

Overton, D. A., & Winter, J. C. (1974). Discriminable properties of drugs and state-dependent learning. Introduction. *Federation Proceedings, 33,* 1785–1786.

Oxford English Dictionary (2nd ed.). (1989). Oxford, England: Oxford University Press.

Pavlov, I. P. (1927). *Conditioned reflexes: An investigation of the physiological activity of the cerebral cortex* (G. V. Anrep, Ed. & Trans.). London: Oxford University Press.

Paxinos, G., & Watson, C. (1997). *The rat brain in stereotaxic coordinates.* New York: Academic Press.

Pearce, J. M., & Hall, G. (1980). A model for Pavlovian learning: Variations in the effectiveness of conditioned but not of unconditioned stimuli. *Psychological Review, 87,* 532–552.

Peck, C. A., & Bouton, M. E. (1990). Context and performance in aversive-to-appetitive transfer. *Learning and Motivation, 21,* 1–31.

Petrovich, G. D., & Swanson, L. W. (1997). Projections from the lateral part of the central amygdalar nucleus to the postulated fear conditioning circuit. *Brain Research, 763,* 247– 254.

Philips, H. C. (1985). Return of fear in the treatment of a fear of vomiting. *Behaviour Research and Therapy, 23,* 45–52.

Phillips, R. G., & LeDoux, J. E. (1992). Differential contribution of amygdala and hippocampus to cued and contextual fear conditioning. *Behavioral Neuroscience, 106,* 274–285.

Pillemer, D. B. (1998). What is remembered about early childhood events? *Clinical Psychology Review, 18*, 895–913.

Ponnusamy, R., & Barad, M. (2005). *Blockade of muscarinic receptors has no effect on conditioned fear extinction.* Manuscript in preparation.

Ponnusamy, R., Nissim, H. A., & Barad, M. (2005). Systemic blockade of D2-like dopamine receptors facilitates extinction of conditioned fear in mice. *Learning & Memory, 12*, 399–406.

Poulton, R., & Menzies, R. G. (2002a). Non-associative fear acquisition: A review of the evidence from retrospective and longitudinal research. *Behaviour Research and Therapy, 40*, 127–149.

Poulton, R., & Menzies, R. G. (2002b). Fears born and bred: Toward a more inclusive theory of fear acquisition. *Behaviour Research and Therapy, 40*, 197–208.

Poulton, R., Waldie, K. E., Craske, M. G., Menzies, R. G., & McGee, R. (2000). Dishabituation processes in height fear and dental fear: An indirect test of the nonassociative model of fear acquisition. *Behaviour Research and Therapy, 38*, 909–919.

Powers, M. B., Smits, J. A. J., & Telch, M. J. (2004). Disentangling the effects of safety-behavior utilization and safety-behavior availability during exposure-based treatment: A placebo-controlled trial. *Journal of Consulting and Clinical Psychology, 72*, 448–454.

Prado-Alcala, R. A., Haiek, M., Rivas, S., Roldan-Roldan, G., & Quirarte, G. L. (1994). Reversal of extinction by scopolamine. *Physiology & Behavior, 56*, 27–30.

Prokasy, W. F. (1977). First interval skin conductance responses: Conditioned or orienting responses? *Psychophysiology, 14*, 360–367.

Prokasy, W. F., & Kumpfer, K. L. (1973). Classical conditioning. In W. F. Prokasy & D. C. Raskin (Eds.), *Electrodermal activity in psychological research* (pp. 157–202). San Diego, CA: Academic Press.

Purdon, C. (1999). Thought suppression and psychopathology. *Behaviour Research and Therapy, 37*, 1029–1054.

Purkis, H. M. (2004). *Why do we fear what we fear: Evidence for a learning-based account of stimulus fear relevance.* Unpublished doctoral dissertation, University of Queensland, Australia.

Purkis, H. M., & Lipp, O. V. (2001). Does affective learning exist in the absence of contingency awareness? *Learning and Motivation, 32*, 84–99.

Putnam, L. E., Johnson, R., Jr., & Roth, W. T. (1992). Guidelines for reducing the risk of disease transmission in the psychophysiological laboratory. *Psychophysiology, 29*, 127–141.

Quilty, L. C., Van Ameringen, M., Mancini, C., Oakman, J., & Farvolden, P. (2003). Quality of life and the anxiety disorders. *Journal of Anxiety Disorders, 17*, 405–426.

Quinn, J. J., Loya, F., Ma, Q. D., & Fanselow, M. S. (2005). Dorsal hippocampus NMDA receptors differentially mediate trace and contextual fear conditioning. *Hippocampus, 15*, 665–674.

Quinn, J. J., Oommen, S. S., Morrison, G. E., & Fanselow, M. S. (2002). Post-training excitotoxic lesions of the dorsal hippocampus attenuate forward trace, backward trace, and delay fear conditioning in a temporally specific manner. *Hippocampus, 12*, 495–504.

Quirk, G. J., Repa, C., & LeDoux, J. E. (1995). Fear conditioning enhances short-latency auditory responses of lateral amygdala neurons: Parallel recordings in the freely behaving rat. *Neuron, 15*, 1029–1039.

Quirk, G. J., Russo, G. K., Barron, J. L., & Lebron, K. (2000). The role of ventromedial prefrontal cortex in the recovery of extinguished fear. *Journal of Neuroscience, 20*, 6225–6231.

Rachman, S. (1966). Studies in desensitization: III. Speed of generalization. *Behaviour Research and Therapy, 4*, 7–15.

Rachman, S. (1976). The passing of the two-stage theory of fear and avoidance: Fresh possibilities. *Behaviour Research and Therapy, 14*, 125–131.

Rachman, S. (1989). The return of fear: Review and prospect. *Clinical Psychology Review, 9*, 147–168.

Rachman, S. (1990). *Fear and courage* (2nd ed.). New York: Freeman.

Rachman, S. (1991). Neo-conditioning and the classical theory of fear acquisition. *Clinical Psychology Review, 11*, 155–173.

Rachman, S., Craske, M. G., Tallman, K., & Solyom, C. (1986). Does escape behavior strengthen agoraphobic avoidance? A replication. *Behavior Therapy, 17*, 366–384.

Rachman, S., & Lopatka, C. L. (1988). Return of fear: Underlearning and overlearning. *Behaviour Research and Therapy, 26*, 99–104.

Rachman, S., Robinson, S., & Lopatka, C. (1987). Is incomplete fear-reduction followed by a return of fear? *Behaviour Research and Therapy, 25*, 67–69.

Rachman, S., & Whittal, M. (1989a). The effect of an aversive event on the return of fear. *Behaviour Research and Therapy, 27*, 513–520.

Rachman, S., & Whittal, M. (1989b). Fast, slow and sudden reductions in fear. *Behaviour Research and Therapy, 27*, 613–620.

Ramsay, R. W., Barends, J., Breuker, J., & Kruseman, A. (1966). Massed versus spaced desensitization of fear. *Behaviour Research and Therapy, 4*, 205–207.

Rau, V., DeCola, J. P., & Fanselow, M. S. (2005). Stress-induced enhancement of fear learning: An animal model of posttraumatic stress disorder. *Neuroscience & Biobehavioral Reviews, 29*, 1207–1223.

Rauhut, A. S., Thomas, B. L., & Ayres, J. B. (2001). Treatments that weaken Pavlovian conditioned fear and thwart its renewal in rats: Implications for treating human phobias. *Journal of Experimental Psychology: Animal Behavior Processes, 27*, 99–114.

Razran, G. (1955). Conditioning and perception. *Psychological Review, 62*, 83–95.

Razran, G. (1961). The observable unconscious and the inferable conscious in current Soviet psychophysiology: Interoceptive conditioning, semantic conditioning, and the orienting reflex. *Psychological Review, 69*, 81–150.

Reiss, S. (1991). Expectancy model of fear, anxiety, and panic. *Clinical Psychology Review, 11*, 141–153.

Rescorla, R. A. (1967). Pavlovian conditioning and its proper control procedures. *Psychological Review, 74*, 71–80.

Rescorla, R. A. (1974). Effect of inflation of the unconditioned stimulus value following conditioning. *Journal of Comparative and Physiological Psychology, 86*, 101–106.

Rescorla, R. A. (1980). *Pavlovian second-order conditioning.* Hillsdale, NJ: Erlbaum.

Rescorla, R. A. (1985). Conditioned inhibition and facilitation. In R. R. Miller & N. E. Spear (Eds.), *Information processing in animals: Conditioned inhibition* (pp. 299–326). Hillsdale, NJ: Erlbaum.

Rescorla, R. A. (1996). Preservation of Pavlovian associations through extinction. *Quarterly Journal of Experimental Psychology, 49B*, 245–258.

Rescorla, R. A. (2000). Extinction can be enhanced by a concurrent excitor. *Journal of Experimental Psychology: Animal Behavior Processes, 26*, 251–260.

Rescorla, R. A. (2001). Experimental extinction. In R. R. Mowrer & S. B. Klein (Eds.), *Handbook of contemporary learning theories* (pp. 119–154). Mahwah, NJ: Erlbaum.

Rescorla, R. A. (2003). Protection from extinction. *Learning & Behavior, 31*, 124–132.

Rescorla, R. A. (2004). Spontaneous recovery. *Learning & Memory, 11*, 501–509.

Rescorla, R. A., & Cunningham, C. L. (1978). Recovery of the US representation over time during extinction. *Learning and Motivation, 9*, 373–391.

Rescorla, R. A., & Durlach, P. J. (1987). The role of context in intertrial interval effects in autoshaping. *Quarterly Journal of Experimental Psychology, 39B*, 35–48.

Rescorla, R. A., & Heth, C. D. (1975). Reinstatement of fear to an extinguished conditioned stimulus. *Journal of Experimental Psychology: Animal Behavior Processes, 104*, 88–96.

Rescorla, R. A., & LoLordo, V. M. (1965). Inhibition of avoidance behaviour. *Journal of Comparative and Physiological Psychology, 59*, 406–412.

Rescorla, R. A., & Wagner, A. R. (1972). A theory of Pavlovian conditioning: Variations in the effectiveness of reinforcement and nonreinforcement. In A. H. Black & W. F. Prokasy (Eds.), *Classical conditioning II: Current research and theory* (pp. 64–99). New York: Appleton-Century-Crofts.

Ressler, K. J., Rothbaum, B. O., Tannenbaum, L., Anderson, P., Graap, K., Zimand, E., et al. (2004). Cognitive enhancers as adjuncts to psychotherapy: Use of D-cycloserine in phobics to facilitate extinction of fear. *Archives of Psychiatry, 66*, 1136–1144.

Riccio, D. C., Richardson, R., & Ebner, D. L. (1999). The contextual change in paradox is still unresolved: Comment on Bouton, Nelson, and Rose (1999). *Psychological Bulletin, 125*, 187–189.

Richards, J. M., & Gross, J. J. (2000). Emotion regulation and memory: The cognitive costs of keeping one's cool. *Journal of Personality and Social Psychology, 79*, 410–424.

Richardson, R., Duffield, T., Bailey, G. K., & Westbrook, R. F. (1999). Reinstatement of fear to an extinguished conditioned context. *Animal Learning & Behavior, 27,* 399–415.

Ricker, S. T., & Bouton, M. E. (1996). Reacquisition following extinction in appetitive conditioning. *Animal Learning & Behavior, 24,* 423–436.

Riley, W. T., McCormick, M. G. F., Simon, E. M., Stack, K., Pushkin, Y., Overstreet, M. M., et al. (1995). Effects of alprazolam dose on the induction and habituation processes during behavioral panic induction treatment. *Journal of Anxiety Disorders, 9,* 217–227.

Rodriguez, B. I., & Craske, M. G. (1995). Does distraction interfere with fear reduction during exposure: A test with animal-fearful subjects. *Behavior Therapy, 26,* 337–350.

Rodriguez, B. I., Craske, M. G., Mineka, S., & Hladek, D. (1999). Context-specificity of relapse: Effects of therapist and environmental context on return of fear. *Behaviour Research and Therapy, 37,* 845–862.

Rogan, M. T., Staubli, U. V., & LeDoux, J. E. (1997). Fear conditioning induces associative long-term potentiation in the amygdala. *Nature, 390,* 604–607.

Rohrbaugh, M., & Riccio, D. C. (1970). Paradoxical enhancement of learned fear. *Journal of Abnormal Psychology, 75,* 210–216.

Romanski, L. M., Clugnet, M. C., Bordi, F., & LeDoux, J. E. (1993). Somatosensory and auditory convergence in the lateral nucleus of the amygdala. *Behavioral Neuroscience, 107,* 444–450.

Romanski, L. M., & LeDoux, J. E. (1992). Equipotentiality of thalamo-amygdala and thalamo-cortico-amygdala circuits in auditory fear conditioning. *Journal of Neuroscience, 12,* 4501–4509.

Rosas, J. M., Vila, N. J., Lugo, M., & Lopez, L. (2001). Combined effect of context change and retention interval on interface in causality judgments. *Journal of Experimental Psychology: Animal Behavior Processes, 27,* 153–164.

Rose, M. P., & McGlynn, D. (1997). Toward a standard experiment for studying post-treatment return of fear. *Journal of Anxiety Disorders, 11,* 263–277.

Rosen, J. B. (2004). The neurobiology of conditioned and unconditioned fear: A neurobehavioral system analysis of the amygdala. *Behavioral and Cognitive Neuroscience Reviews, 3,* 23–41.

Rosen, J. B., Fanselow, M. S., Young, S. L., Sitcoske, M., & Maren, S. (1998). Immediate-early gene expression in the amygdala following footshock stress and contextual fear conditioning. *Brain Research, 796,* 132–142.

Rosen, J. B., Hitchcock, J. M., Sananes, C. B., Miserendino, M. J., & Davis, M. (1991). A direct projection from the central nucleus of the amygdala to the acoustic startle pathway: Anterograde and retrograde tracing studies. *Behavioral Neuroscience, 105,* 817–825.

Rosen, J. B., & Schulkin, J. (1998). From normal fear to pathological anxiety. *Psychological Review, 105,* 325–350.

Rowe, M. K., & Craske, M. G. (1998a). Effects of an expanding-spaced vs. massed exposure schedule on fear reduction and return of fear. *Behaviour Research and Therapy, 36,* 701–717.

Rowe, M. K., & Craske, M. G. (1998b). Effects of varied-stimulus exposure training on fear reduction and return of fear. *Behaviour Research and Therapy, 36,* 719–734

Rubin, M. A., Berlese, D. B., Stiegemeier, J. A., Volkweis, M. A., Oliveira, D. M., dos Santos, et al. (2004). Intra-amygdala administration of polyamines modulate fear conditioning in rats. *Journal of Neuroscience, 24,* 2328–2334.

Rumpel, S., LeDoux, J., Zador, A., & Malinow, R. (2005, April 1). Postsynaptic receptor trafficking underlying a form of associative learning. *Science, 308,* 83–88.

Russell, C., & Davey, G. C. L. (1991). The effects of false response feedback on human "fear" conditioning. *Behaviour Research and Therapy, 29,* 191–196.

Rusting, C. L. (1998). Personality, mood, and cognitive processing of emotional information: Three conceptual frameworks. *Psychological Bulletin, 124,* 165–196.

Salkovskis, P. M. (1991). The importance of behaviour in the maintenance of anxiety and panic: A cognitive account. *Behavioural Psychotherapy, 19,* 6–19.

Salkovskis, P. M., Clark, D. M., & Gelder, M. (1996). Cognition-behaviour links in the persistence of panic. *Behaviour Research and Therapy, 34,* 453–458.

Salkovskis, P. M., & Mills, I. (1994). Induced mood, phobic responding and the return of fear. *Behaviour Research and Therapy, 32,* 439–445.

Salter, A. (1949). *Conditioned reflex therapy: The direct approach to the reconstruction of personality.* New York: Creative Age Press.

Santini, E., Ge, H., Ren, K., Pena de Ortiz, S., & Quirk, G. J. (2004). Consolidation of fear extinction requires protein synthesis in the medial prefrontal cortex. *Journal of Neuroscience, 24,* 5704–5710.

Santini, E., Muller, R. U., & Quirk, G. J. (2001). Consolidation of extinction learning involves transfer from NMDA-independent to NMDA-dependent memory. *Journal of Neuroscience, 21,* 9009–9017.

Sartory, G., Rachman, S., & Grey, S. J. (1982). Return of fear: The role of rehearsal. *Behaviour Research and Therapy, 20,* 123–133.

Scarr, S., & Salapatek, P. (1970). Patterns of fear development during infancy. *Merrill Palmer Quarterly, 16,* 53–90.

Scatton, B. (1993). The NMDA receptor complex. *Fundamental & Clinical Pharmacology, 7,* 389–400.

Schafe, G. E., & LeDoux, J. E. (2000). Memory consolidation of auditory Pavlovian fear conditioning requires protein synthesis and protein kinase A in the amygdala. *Journal of Neuroscience, 20,* RC96.

Schafe, G. E., Nadel, N. V., Sullivan, G. M., Harris, A., & LeDoux, J. E. (1999). Memory consolidation for contextual and auditory fear conditioning is dependent on protein synthesis, PKA, and MAP kinase. *Learning & Memory, 6,* 97–110.

Scharf, M. T., Woo, N. H., Lattal, K. M., Young, J. Z., Nguyen, P. V., & Abel, T. (2002). Protein synthesis is required for the enhancement of long-term potentiation and long-term memory by spaced training. *Journal of Neurophysiology, 87,* 2770–2777.

Scheier, M. F., & Carver, C. S. (1992). Effects of optimism on psychological and physical well-being: Theoretical overview and empirical update. *Cognitive Therapy and Research, 16,* 201–228.

Schell, A. M., Dawson, M. E., & Marinkovic, K. (1991). Effects of potentially phobic conditioned stimuli on retention, reconditioning, and extinction of the conditioned skin conductance response. *Psychophysiology, 28,* 140–153.

Schmid, A., Koch, M., & Schnitzler, H-U. (1995). Rapid communication: Conditioned pleasure attenuates the startle response in rats. *Neurobiology of Learning and Memory, 34,* 1–3.

Schmidt, N. B., Woolaway-Bickel, K., Trakowski, J., Santiago, H., Storey, J., Koselka, M., & Cook, J. (2000). Dismantling cognitive-behavioral treatment for panic disorder: Questioning the utility of breathing retraining. *Journal of Consulting and Clinical Psychology, 68,* 417–424.

Schmidt, R. A., & Bjork, R. A. (1992). New conceptualizations of practice: Common principles in three paradigms suggest new concepts for training. *Psychological Science, 3,* 207–217.

Schwartz, C., Snidman, N., & Kagan, J. (1999). Adolescent social anxiety as an outcome of inhibited temperament in childhood. *Journal of American Academy of Child and Adolescent Psychiatry, 38,* 1008–1015.

Scicli, A. P., Petrovich, G. D., Swanson, L. W., & Thompson, R. F. (2004). Contextual fear conditioning is associated with lateralized expression of the immediate early gene c-fos in the central and basolateral amygdalar nuclei. *Behavioral Neuroscience, 118,* 5–14.

Sechenov, I. (1965). Reflexes of the brain. In S. Belsky (Trans.), *Reflexes of the brain.* Cambride, MA: MIT Press. (Original work published in 1863)

Seligman, M. E. P. (1968). Chronic fear produced by unpredictable electric shock. *Journal of Comparative and Physiological Psychology, 66,* 402–411.

Seligman, M. E. P. (1971). Phobias and preparedness. *Behavior Therapy, 2,* 307–320.

Seligman, M. E. P., & Johnston, J. (1973). A cognitive theory of avoidance learning. In F. J. McGuigan & D. B. Lumsden (Eds.), *Contemporary approaches to conditioning and learning* (pp. 69–110). Washington, DC: Winston.

Shafran, R., Booth, R., & Rachman, S. (1993). The reduction of claustrophobia: II: Cognitive analyses. *Behaviour Research and Therapy, 31,* 75–85.

Shanks, D. R., & Lovibond, P. F. (2002). Autonomic and eyeblink conditioning are closely related to contingency awareness: Reply to Wiens and Öhman (2002) and Manns et al. (2002). *Journal of Experimental Psychology: Animal Behavior Processes, 28,* 38–42.

Shanks, D. R., & St. John, M. F. (1994). Characteristics of dissociable human learning systems. *Behavioral and Brain Sciences, 17,* 367–447.

Shi, C. J., & Cassell, M. D. (1998a). Cascade projections from somatosensory cortex to the rat basolateral amygdala via the parietal insular cortex. *Journal of Comparative Neurology, 399,* 469–491.

Shi, C. J., & Cassell, M. D. (1998b). Cortical, thalamic, and amygdaloid connections of the anterior and posterior insular cortices. *Journal of Comparative Neurology, 399,* 440–468.

Shi, C., & Davis, M. (1999). Pain pathways involved in fear conditioning measured with fear-potentiated startle: Lesion studies. *Journal of Neuroscience, 19,* 420–430.

Shimizu, E., Tang, Y., Rampon, C., & Tsien, J. Z. (2000, November 10). NMDA receptor-dependent synaptic reinforcement as a crucial process for memory consolidation. *Science, 290,* 1170–1174.

Siddle, D. A. T., & Bond, N. W. (1988). Avoidance learning, Pavlovian conditioning, and the development of phobias. *Biological Psychology, 27,* 167–183.

Silvestri, R., Rohrbaugh, M., & Riccio, D. C. (1970). Conditions influencing the retention of learned fear in young rats. *Developmental Psychology, 2,* 389–395.

Sloan, D. M. (2004). Emotion regulation in action: Emotional reactivity in experiential avoidance. *Behaviour Research and Therapy, 42,* 1257–1270.

Sloan, T., & Telch, M. J. (2002). The effects of safety-seeking behavior and guided threat reappraisal on fear reduction during exposure: An experimental investigation. *Behaviour Research and Therapy, 40,* 235–251.

Smeets, G., de Jong, P. J., & Mayer, B. (2000). If you suffer from a headache, then you have a brain tumour: Domain-specific reasoning "bias" and hypochondriasis. *Behaviour Research and Therapy, 38,* 763–776.

Smith, S. M. (1979). Remembering in and out of context. *Journal of Experimental Psychology: Human Learning and Memory, 5,* 460–471.

Smith, S. M. (1982). Enhancement of recall using multiple environmental contexts during learning. *Memory & Cognition, 10,* 405–412.

Smith, S. M. (1988). Environmental context-dependent memory. In G. M. Davies & D. M. Thomson (Eds.), *Memory in context: Context in memory* (pp. 13–34). NJ: Wiley.

Smith, S. M., & Vela, E. (2001). Environmental context-dependent memory: A review and meta-analysis. *Psychonomic Bulletin & Review, 8,* 203–220.

Soares, J., & Öhman, A. (1993). Preattentive processing, preparedness and phobias: Effects of instruction on conditioned electrodermal responses to masked and non-masked fear-relevant stimuli. *Behaviour Research and Therapy, 31,* 87–95.

Sokolowska, M., Siegel, S., & Kim, J. A. (2002). Intraadministration associations: Conditional hyperalgesia elicited by morphine onset cues. *Journal of Experimental Psychology. Animal Behavior Processes, 28,* 309–320.

Solomon, Z., Garb, R., Bleich, A., & Grupper, D. (1987). Reactivation of combat-related posttraumatic stress disorder. *American Journal of Psychiatry, 144,* 51–55.

Solomon, R. L., Kamin, L. J., & Wynne, L. C. (1953). Traumatic avoidance learning: the outcomes of several extinction procedures with dogs. *Journal of Abnormal and Social Psychology, 48*, 291–302.

Soltysik, S. S., Wolfe, G. E., Nicholas, T., Wilson, W. J., & Garcia-Sanchez, J. L. (1983). Blocking of inhibitory conditioning within a serial conditioned stimulus-conditioned inhibitor compound: Maintenance of acquired behavior without an unconditioned stimulus. *Learning and Motivation, 14*, 1–29.

Southwick, S. M., Krystal, J. H., Morgan, C. A., Johnson, D., Nagy, L. M., Nicolaou, A., et al. (1993). Abnormal noradrenergic function in posttraumatic stress disorder. *Archives of General Psychiatry, 50*, 266–274.

Spence, K. W., & Norris, E. B. (1950). Eyelid conditioning as a function of the intertrial interval. *Journal of Experimental Psychology, 40*, 716–720.

Spira, A. P., Zvolensky, M. J., Eifert, G. H., & Feldner, M. T. (2004). Avoidance-oriented coping as a predictor of anxiety-based physical stress: A test using biological challenge. *Journal of Anxiety Disorders, 18*, 309–323.

Spruyt, A., Hermans, D., De Houwer, J., & Eelen, P. (2004). Automatic non-associative semantic priming: Episodic affective priming of naming responses. *Acta Psychologica, 116*, 39–54.

Squire, L. R. (1994). Declarative and nondeclarative memory: Multiple brain systems supporting learning and memory. In D. L. Schacter & E. Tulving (Eds.), *Memory systems* (pp. 203–231). Cambridge, MA: MIT Press.

Stampfl, T. G., & Levis, D. J. (1967). The essentials of implosive therapy: A learning-theory-based psychodynamic behavioral therapy. *Journal of Abnormal Psychology, 72*, 496–503.

Stanton, P. K. (1996). LTD, LTP, and the sliding threshold for long-term synaptic plasticity. *Hippocampus, 6*, 35–42.

Starr, M. D., & Mineka, S. (1977). Determinants of fear over the course of avoidance learning. *Learning and Motivation, 8*, 332–350.

Stein, M. B., Walker, J. R., & Forde, D. R. (1996). Public-speaking fears in a community sample. Prevalence, impact on functioning, and diagnostic classification. *Archives of General Psychiatry, 53*, 169–174.

Stote, D. L., & Fanselow, M. S. (2004). NMDA receptor modulation of incidental learning in Pavlovian context conditioning. *Behavioral Neuroscience, 118*, 253–257.

Stroop, J. R. (1935). Studies of interference in serial verbal reactions. *Journal of Experimental Psychology, 18*, 643–661.

Sunsay, C., & Bouton, M. E. (2006). Analysis of a trial spacing effect with relatively long intertrial intervals. Manuscript submitted for publication.

Sunsay, C., Stetson, L., & Bouton, M. E. (2004). Memory priming and trial spacing effects in Pavlovian learning. *Learning & Behavior, 32*, 220–229.

Suomi, S. J. (1999). Attachment in rhesus monkeys. In J. Cassidy & P. R. Shaver (Eds.), *Handbook of attachment: Theory, research, and clinical application* (pp. 181–197). New York: Guilford Press.

Suzuki, A., Josselyn, S. A., Frankland, P. W., Masushige, S., Silva, A. J., & Kida, S. (2004). Memory reconsolidation and extinction have distinct temporal and biochemical signatures. *Journal of Neuroscience, 24,* 4787–4795.

Swanson, L. W. (2003). The amygdala and its place in the cerebral hemisphere. *Annals of the New York Academy of Sciences, 985,* 174–184.

Swendsen, J. D., Merikangas, K. R, Canino, G. J., Kessler, R. C., Rubio-Stipec, M., & Angst, J. (1998). The comorbidity of alcoholism with anxiety and depressive disorders in four geographic communities. *Comprehensive Psychiatry, 39,* 176–184.

Takehara, K., Kawahara, S., & Kirino, Y. (2003). Time-dependent reorganization of the brain components underlying memory retention in trace eyeblink conditioning. *Journal of Neuroscience, 23,* 9897–9905.

Takehara, K., Kawahara, S., Takatsuki, K., & Kirino, Y. (2002). Time-limited role of the hippocampus in the memory for trace eyeblink conditioning in mice. *Brain Research, 951,* 183–190.

Tamai, N., & Nakajima, S. (2000). Renewal of formerly conditioned fear in rats after extinction training. *International Journal of Comparative Psychology, 13,* 137–146.

Tang, Y. P., Shimizu, E., Dube, G. R., Rampon, C., Kerchner, G. A., Zhuo, M., et al. (1999). Genetic enhancement of learning and memory in mice. *Nature, 401,* 63–69.

Taylor, J. E., Deane, F. P., & Podd, J. V. (1999). Stability of driving fear acquisition pathways over one year. *Behaviour Research and Therapy, 37,* 927–939.

Taylor, S., & Rachman, S. J. (1994). Stimulus estimation and the overprediction of fear. *British Journal of Clinical Psychology, 33,* 173–181.

Teachman, B. A., & Woody, S. R. (2003). Automatic processing in spider phobia: Implicit fear associations over the course of treatment. *Journal of Abnormal Psychology, 112,* 100–109.

Telch, M. J., Valentiner, D., & Bolte, M. (1994). Proximity to safety and its effects on fear prediction bias. *Behaviour Research and Therapy, 32,* 747–751.

Tellegen, A. (1985). Structure of mood and personality and their relevance to assessing anxiety, with an emphasis on self-report. In A. H. Tuma & J. D. Maser (Eds.), *Anxiety and the anxiety disorders* (pp. 681–706). Hillsdale, NJ: Erlbaum.

Terrace, H. S., Gibbon, J., Farrell, L., & Baldock, M. D. (1975). Temporal factors influencing the acquisition and maintenance of an autoshaped keypeck. *Animal Learning & Behavior, 3,* 53–62.

Tesser, A. (1978). Self-generated attitude change. In L. Berkowitz (Ed.), *Advances in experimental social psychology* (Vol. 11, pp. 290–339). New York: Academic Press.

Thomas, B. L., & Ayres, J. J. B. (2004). Use of the ABA fear renewal paradigm to assess the effects of extinction with co-present fear inhibitors or excitors: Implications for theories of extinction and for treating human fears and phobias. *Learning and Motivation, 35,* 22–52.

Thomas, B. L., Larsen, N., & Ayres, J. J. B. (2003). Role of context similarity in ABA, ABC and AAB renewal paradigms: Implications for theories of renewal and for treating human phobias. *Learning and Motivation, 34,* 410–436.

Thorpe, S. J., & Salkovskis, P. M. (1995). Phobic beliefs: Do cognitive factors play a role in specific phobias? *Behaviour Research and Therapy, 33,* 805–816.

Thorpe, S. J., & Salkovskis, P. M. (1997). The effect of one-session treatment for spider phobia on attentional bias and beliefs. *British Journal of Clinical Psychology, 36,* 225–241.

Thorpe, S. J., & Salkovskis, P. M. (1998). Selective attention to real phobic and safety stimuli *Behaviour Research and Therapy, 36,* 471–481.

Tooby, J., & Cosmides, L. (1992). The psychological foundations of culture. In J. H. Barkow, L. Cosmides, & J. Tooby (Eds.), *The adapted mind: Evolutionary psychology and the generation of culture* (pp. 19–136). London: Oxford University Press.

Toren, P., Wolmer, L., Weizman, R., Magal-Vardi, O., & Laor, N. (2002). Retraumatization of Israeli civilians during a reactivation of the Gulf War threat. *Journal of Nervous and Mental Disease, 190,* 43–45.

Tsao, J. C. I., & Craske, M. G. (2000). Timing of treatment and return of fear: Effects of massed, uniform-, and expanding-spaced exposure schedules. *Behavior Therapy, 31,* 479–497.

Tully, T., Preat, T., Boynton, S. C., & Del Vecchio, M. (1994). Genetic dissection of consolidated memory in Drosophila. *Cell, 79,* 35–47.

Tursky, B., Watson, P. D., & O'Connell, D. N. (1965). A concentric shock electrode for pain stimulation. *Psychophysiology, 1,* 582–591.

Tversky, A., & Kahneman, D. (1973). Availability: A heuristic for judging frequency and probability. *Cognitive Psychology, 5,* 207–232.

Tyrer, P., Alexander, J., Remington, M., & Riley, P. (1987). Relationship between neurotic symptoms and neurotic diagnosis: A longitudinal study. *Journal of Affective Disorders, 13,* 13–21.

Unger, W., Evans, I. M., Rourke, P., & Levis, D. J. (2003). The S-S construct of expectancy versus the S-R construct of fear: Which motivates the acquisition of avoidance behavior? *Journal of General Psychology, 130,* 131–147.

Usher, J. A., & Neisser, U. (1993). Childhood amnesia and the beginnings of memory for four early life events. *Journal of Experimental Psychology: General, 122,* 155–165.

Valentiner, D. P., Telch, M. J., Petruzzi, D. C., & Bolte, M. C. (1996). Cognitive mechanisms in claustrophobia: An examination of Reiss and McNally's expectancy model and Bandura's self-efficacy theory. *Cognitive Therapy and Research, 20,* 593–612.

Valins, S. (1966). Cognitive effects of false heart-rate feedback. *Journal of Personality and Social Psychology, 4,* 400–408.

van Groen, T., & Wyss, J. M. (1990). Extrinsic projections from area CA1 of the rat hippocampus: Olfactory, cortical, subcortical, and bilateral hippocampal formation projections. *Journal of Comparative Neurology, 302,* 515–528.

van Hout, W. J. P. J., & Emmelkamp, P. M. G. (1994). Overprediction of fear in panic disorder patients with agoraphobia: Does the (mis)match model generalize to exposure in vivo therapy? *Behaviour Research and Therapy, 32,* 723–734.

Vansteenwegen, D., Crombez, G., Baeyens, F., & Eelen, P. (1998). Extinction in fear conditioning: Effects on startle modulation and evaluative self reports. *Psychophysiology, 35,* 729–736.

Vansteenwegen, D., Francken, G., Vervliet, B., Declerq, A., & Eelen, P. (2006). Resistance to extinction in evaluative conditioning. *Journal of Experimental Psychology: Animal Behavior Processes, 32,* 71–79.

Vansteenwegen, D., Hermans, D., Vervliet, B., Francken, G., Beckers, T., Baeyens, F., et al. (2005). Return of fear in a human differential conditioning paradigm caused by a return to the original acquisition context. *Behaviour Research and Therapy, 43,* 323–336.

Vansteenwegen, D., Vervliet, B., Hermans, D., Baeyens, F., & Van den Bergh, O. (2006). *The repeated confrontation with videotapes of spiders in multiple contexts attenuates renewal of fear in spider anxious students.* Manuscript submitted for publication.

Vansteenwegen, D., Vervliet, B., Hermans, D., Beckers, T., Baeyens, F., & Eelen, P. (in press). Stronger renewal in human fear conditioning when tested with an acquisition retrieval cue than with an extinction retrieval cue. *Behaviour Research and Therapy.*

Vasey, M., & Borkovec, T. D. (1992). A catastrophising assessment of worrisome thoughts. *Cognitive Therapy and Research, 16,* 505–520.

Veronen, L. J., & Kilpatrick, D. G. (1983). Stress management for rape victims. In D. Meichenbaum & M. E. Jaremko (Eds.), *Stress reduction and prevention* (pp. 341–374). New York: Plenum Press.

Vervliet, B. (2004). *Relapse into generalizations: An experimental analysis of the stimulus-specificity of extinction.* Unpublished master's thesis, Department of Psychology, University of Leuven, Belgium.

Vervliet, B., Vansteenwegen, D., Baeyens, F., Hermans, D., & Eelen, P. (2005). Return of fear in a human differential conditioning paradigm caused by a stimulus change after extinction. *Behaviour Research and Therapy, 43,* 357–371.

Vervliet, B., Vansteenwegen, D., & Eelen, P. (2004). Generalization of extinguished skin conductance responding in human fear conditioning. *Learning & Memory, 11,* 555–558.

Vervliet, B., Vansteenwegen, D., & Eelen, P. (in press). Generalization gradients for acquisition and extinction in human contingency learning. *Experimental Psychology.*

Vianna, M. R., Szapiro, G., McGaugh, J. L., Medina, J. H., & Izquierdo, I. (2001). Retrieval of memory for fear-motivated training initiates extinction requiring protein synthesis in the rat hippocampus. *Proceedings of the National Academy of Sciences of the United States of America, 98,* 12251–12254.

Vila, N. J., & Rosas, J. M. (2001). Reinstatement of acquisition performance by the presentation of the outcome after extinction in causality judgements. *Behavioral Processes, 56,* 147–154.

Wagner, A. R. (1969). Stimulus selection and a "modified continuity theory." In G. H. Bower & J. T. Spence (Eds.), *The psychology of learning and motivation* (Vol. 3, pp. 1–41). Oxford, England: Academic Press.

Wagner, A. R. (1981). SOP: A model of automatic memory processing in animal behavior. In N. E. Spear & R. R. Miller (Eds.), *Information processing in animals: Memory mechanisms* (pp. 5–47). Hillsdale, NJ: Erlbaum.

Wagner, A. R., & Brandon, S. E. (1989). Evolution of a structured connectionist model of Pavlovian conditioning (SOP). In S. B. Klein & R. R. Mowrer (Eds.), *Contemporary learning theories: Pavlovian conditioning and the status of traditional learning theory* (pp. 149–189). Hillsdale, NJ: Erlbaum.

Wagner, A. R., & Brandon, S. E. (2001). A componential theory of Pavlovian conditioning. In S. B. Klein & R. R. Mowrer (Eds.), *Handbook of contemporary learning theories* (pp. 23–64). Hillsdale, NJ: Erlbaum.

Wagner, A. R., & Rescorla, R. A. (1972). Inhibition in Pavlovian conditioning: Application of a theory. In R. A. Boakes & M. S. Halliday (Eds.), *Inhibition and learning* (pp. 301–336). London, England: Academic Press.

Walker, D. L., & Davis, M. (1997). Double dissociation between the involvement of the bed nucleus of the stria terminalis and the central nucleus of the amygdala in startle increases produced by conditioned versus unconditioned fear. *Journal of Neuroscience, 17*, 9375–9383.

Walker, D. L., Ressler, K. J., Lu, K. T., & Davis, M. (2002). Facilitation of conditioned fear extinction by systemic administration or intra-amygdala infusions of D-cycloserine as assessed with fear-potentiated startle in rats. *Journal of Neuroscience, 22*, 2343–2351.

Watson, J. B. (1913). Psychology as the behaviorist views it. *Psychological Review, 20*, 158–177.

Watson, J. B. (1924). *Behaviorism*. Chicago, IL: The People's Institute. (Rev. ed., 1966: Chicago: University of Chicago Press)

Watson, J. B., & Rayner, R. (1920). Conditioned emotional reactions. *Journal of Experimental Psychology, 3*, 1–14.

Watson, J. S. (1979). Perception of contingency as a determinant of social responsiveness. In E. Thomas (Ed.), *Origins of infant's social responsiveness* (pp. 33–64). New York: Erlbaum.

Watson, R. I. (1979). *Basic writings in the history of psychology*. New York: Oxford University Press.

Watts, F. N., McKenna, F. P., Sharrock, R., & Trezise, L. (1986). Color naming of phobia-related words. *British Journal of Psychology, 77*, 97–108.

Wegner, D. M. (1994). Ironic processes of mental control. *Psychological Review, 101*, 34–52.

Weisman, R. G., & Litner, J. S. (1972). The role of Pavlovian events in avoidance training. In R. A. Boakes & M. S. Halliday (Eds.), *Inhibition and learning* (pp. 253–270). New York: Academic Press.

Wells, A., Clark, D. M., Salkovskis, P., Ludgate, J., Hackmann, A., & Gelder, M. (1995). Social phobia: The role of in-situation safety behaviours in maintaining anxiety and negative beliefs. *Behavior Therapy, 26,* 153–161.

Westbrook, R. F., Smith, F. J., & Charnock, D. J. (1985). The extinction of an aversion: Role of the interval between non-reinforced presentations of the averted stimulus. *Quarterly Journal of Experimental Psychology, 37B,* 255–273.

White, K., & Davey, G. C. L. (1989). Sensory preconditioning and UCS inflation in human "fear" conditioning. *Behaviour Research and Therapy, 27,* 161–66.

Wiens, S., & Öhman, A. (2002). Unawareness is more than a chance event. *Journal of Experimental Psychology: Animal Behavior Processes, 28,* 27–31.

Wik, G., Fredrikson, M., & Fischer, H. (1997). Evidence of altered cerebral blood-flow relationships in acute phobia. *International Journal of Neuroscience, 91,* 253–263.

Wilensky, A. E., Schafe, G. E., & LeDoux, J. E. (1999). Functional inactivation of the amygdala before but not after auditory fear conditioning prevents memory formation. *Journal of Neuroscience, 19,* RC48.

Williams, D. A., Sagness, K. E., & McPhee, J. E. (1994). Configural and elemental strategies in predictive learning. *Journal of Experimental Psychology: Learning, Memory, and Cognition, 20,* 694–709.

Williams, J. M. G., Watts, F. N., MacLeod, C., & Mathews, A. (1997). *Cognitive psychology and emotional disorders* (2nd ed.). Chichester, England: Wiley.

Williams, R. J., & Roberts, L. E. (1988). Relation of learned heart rate control to self-report in different task environments. *Psychophysiology, 25,* 354–365.

Williams, S. L., Kinney, P. J., & Falbo, J. (1989). Generalisation of therapeutic changes in agoraphobia: The role of perceived self efficacy. *Journal of Consulting & Clinical Psychology, 57,* 436–442.

Willick, M. L., & Kokkinidis, L. (1995). Cocaine enhances the expression of fear-potentiated startle: Evaluation of state-dependent extinction and the shock-sensitization of acoustic startle. *Behavioral Neuroscience, 109,* 929–938.

Wills, T. A. (1981). Downward comparison principles in social psychology. *Psychological Bulletin, 90,* 245–271.

Wilson, A., Brooks, D. C., & Bouton, M. E. (1995). The role of the rat hippocampal system in several effects of context in extinction [see comments]. *Behavioral Neuroscience, 109,* 828–836.

Wilson, E., & MacLeod, C. (2003). Contrasting two accounts of anxiety-linked attentional bias: Selective attention to varying levels of stimulus threat intensity. *Journal of Abnormal Psychology, 112,* 212–218.

Wilson, R. I., & Nicoll, R. A. (2002, April 26). Endocannabinoid signaling in the brain. *Science, 296,* 678–682.

Wiltgen, B. J., & Fanselow, M. S. (2003). A model of hippocampal-cortical-amygdala interactions based on context fear conditioning. In K. J. Jeffery (Ed.), *The neurobiology of spatial behaviour* (pp. 83–103). Oxford, England: Oxford University Press.

Wiltgen, B. J., Sanders, M. J., Behne, N. S., & Fanselow, M. S. (2001). Sex differences, context preexposure, and the immediate shock deficit in Pavlovian context conditioning with mice. *Behavioral Neuroscience, 115*, 26–32.

Withers, R. D., & Deane, F. P. (1995). Origins of common fears: Effects on severity, anxiety responses and memories of onset. *Behaviour Research and Therapy, 33*, 903–915.

Wolpe, J. (1948). *An approach to the problem of neurosis based on the conditioned response.* Unpublished master's thesis, University of Witwaterstrand, South Africa.

Wolpe, J. (1958). *Psychotherapy by reciprocal inhibition.* Stanford, CA: Stanford University Press.

Wolpe, J. (1973). *The practice of behavior therapy* (2nd ed.). New York: Pergamon Press.

Wolpe, J. (1976). Conditioning is the basis of all therapeutic change. In A. Burton (Ed.), *What makes behavior change possible?* (pp. 58–72). New York: Brunner/Mazel.

Wolpe, J., & Rowan, V. C. (1988). Panic disorder: A product of classical conditioning. *Behaviour Research and Therapy, 26*, 441–450.

Wood, B. S., & McGlynn, F. D. (2000). Research on posttreatment return of claustrofobic fear arousal, and avoidance using mock diagnostic imaging. *Behavior Modification, 24*, 379–394.

Woods, A. M., & Bouton, M. E. (2006). The effects of occasional reinforced trials in extinction on reacquisition of an instrumental lever-press response in rats. Manuscript submitted for publication.

Woodside, B. L., Borroni, A. M., Hammonds, M. D., & Teyler, T. J. (2004). NMDA receptors and voltage-dependent calcium channels mediate different aspects of acquisition and retention of a spatial memory task. *Neurobiology of Learning and Memory, 81*, 105–114.

Yaniv, D., Schafe, G. E., LeDoux, J. E., & Richter-Levin, G. (2000). Perirhinal cortex and thalamic stimulation induces LTP in different areas of the amygdala. *Annual New York Academy of Sciences, 911*, 474–476.

Young, J. E. (1999). *Cognitive therapy for personality disorders: A schema-focused approach* (3rd ed.). Sarasota, FL: Professional Resource Press/Professional Resource Exchange.

Young, S. L., Bohenek, D. L., & Fanselow, M. S. (1994). NMDA processes mediate anterograde amnesia of contextual fear conditioning induced by hippocampal damage: Immunization against amnesia by context preexposure. *Behavioral Neuroscience, 108*, 19–29.

Young, S. L., & Fanselow, M. S. (1992). Associative regulation of Pavlovian fear conditioning: Unconditional stimulus intensity, incentive shifts, and latent inhibition. *Journal of Experimental Psychology: Animal Behavior Processes, 18*, 400–413.

Zajonc, R. B. (2001). Mere exposure: A gateway to the subliminal. *Current Directions in Psychological Science, 10*, 224–228.

Zettle, R. D., & Hayes, S. C. (1982). Rule governed behavior: A potential theoretical framework for cognitive–behavior therapy. In P. C. Kendall (Ed.), *Advances in cognitive–behavioral research and therapy* (Vol. 1, pp. 73–118). New York: Academic Press.

Zhang, W. N., Bast, T., & Feldon, J. (2001). The ventral hippocampus and fear conditioning in rats: Different anterograde amnesias of fear after infusion of N-methyl-D-aspartate or its noncompetitive antagonist MK-801 into the ventral hippocampus. *Behavioral Brain Research, 126*, 159–174.

Zinbarg, R. E. (1990). Animal research and behavior therapy Part I: Behavior therapy is not what you think it is. *Behavior Therapist, 13*, 171–175.

Zinbarg, R., & Mohlman, J. (1998). Individual differences in the acquisition of affectively-valenced associations. *Journal of Personality and Social Psychology, 74*, 1024–1040.

Zoellner, L. A., & Craske, M. G. (1998, November). *Contextual effects of alprazolam or exposure therapy.* Poster presented at the 32nd annual conference of the Association for Advancement of Behavior Therapy, Washington, DC.

AUTHOR INDEX

Herrero, M. T., 66
Herrnstein, R. J., 119
Herry, C., 163
Hertel, P. T., 113
Heth, C. D., 159, 211, 213, 218
Hildebrand, M., 106
Hiss, H., 192
Hitchcock, J. M., 64
Hladek, D., 204, 220, 221
Hodes, R. L., 48, 84
Holmes, E. A., 129
Holt, W., 72
Honey, R. C., 188, 241
Honeybourne, C., 105
Horselenberg, R., 108
Huddy, J. J., 39
Huerta, P. T., 67, 70
Huff, N. C., 65
Hugdahl, K., 41, 77, 78, 94, 96
Hull, C. L., 26
Hume, D., 19
Humphreys, L., 160
Hurwitz, B. E., 48
Hyman, I. E., Jr., 92, 93

Insausti, R., 66
Iwata, J., 60, 64
Izquierdo, I., 164

Jacob, R., 4
Jacobs, W. J., 198
Jacobson, E., 28
Jameson, J. S., 225
Jami, S., 163, 167
Jasmin, L., 63
Jenkins, H. M., 160
Jennings, J. R., 48
John, O. P., 142, 143, 145
Johnson, J. L., 191
Johnson, R., Jr., 47
Johnston, J., 123, 126, 127, 131
Joly, M., 68
Jones, M. C., 8, 24, 25
Jones, T., 111
Joseph, S., 129
Josselyn, S. A., 72, 160
Juliano, L. M., 192

Kagan, J., 6, 80, 144
Kahneman, D., 105
Kairiss, E. W., 68
Kalin, N. H., 64

Kalish, H. I., 60
Kamin, L. J., 60, 119, 120
Kamphuis, J. H., 224
Kandel, E. R., 160
Karekla, M., 146
Kashdan, T. B., 142
Kauer, J. A., 68
Kawahara, S., 68
Kazdin, A. E., 28
Keenan, C. L., 68
Kehl, S. J., 68
Kehoe, E. J., 175, 178, 192, 193
Keir, R., 7, 77
Keller, M. B., 4
Kelly, A., 43, 240
Kelly, M. M., 146
Kelso, S. R., 68, 70
Kendler, K. S., 6, 92
Kenney, F. A., 167, 177
Kent, G., 80
Kessler, R., 4
Ketelaar, T. V., 145
Kheriaty, E., 93, 94
Kida, S., 72
Kihlstrom, J., 22
Kilic, C., 229
Killcross, S., 60
Killen, J. D., 4
Kilpatrick, D. G., 116
Kim, J. A., 8
Kim, J. J., 63, 65, 66, 67–68, 70, 165
Kim, Y., 40
Kimmel, H. D., 39
King, D. A., 159, 164, 204, 207, 212, 220
King, J., 39
King, N., 78
Kinney, P. J., 107
Kintner, K., 113
Kirino, Y., 68
Kirk, J., 129
Kirsch, I., 107
Kirshenbaum, S., 107
Kjellberg, A., 48
Klauer, K. C., 45
Kleinknecht, R. A., 93, 95
Knight, D. C., 58
Knowles, K. A., 95, 110
Koch, M., 50
Kochanoff, A., 145
Kogan, J. H., 160
Kokkinidis, L., 169
Konorski, J., 120, 131

Marshall, P. J., 145
Marshall, W. L., 224
Marsicano, G., 170
Martin, I., 80, 130
Martin, N. G., 6
Marx, B. P., 142
Mason, S. T., 168
Masserman, J. H., 25, 26, 27
Massicotte, G., 160
Mast, M., 59
Matchett, G., 83, 105, 109, 111
Mathews, A., 45, 100, 101, 102, 104, 111, 113
Matzel, L. D., 217
Mayer, B., 108
McCarthy, P. R., 45
McDonald, A. S., 115
McEchron, M. D., 67
McGaugh, J. L., 7, 164, 166
McGee, R., 4
McGlynn, D., 219, 224
McGlynn, F. D., 198
McGregor, I. S., 59
McKenna, F. P., 101
McKenna, I., 109
McLaren, S., 147
McLennan, H., 68
McNally, R. J., 11, 32, 45, 105, 114, 218, 225, 241–242
McPhee, J. E., 42
Medina, J. H., 164
Melia, K. R., 65, 165
Menzies, R. G., 88, 89, 90, 91, 92, 96, 105, 106, 134
Mercier, P., 40
Merckelbach, H., 77, 78, 93, 106, 109
Merikangas, K., 42
Milad, M. R., 163, 164
Mill, J., 19
Miller, N. E., 8, 25, 26
Miller, P. P., 142
Miller, R. R., 177, 208, 217
Miller, S., 82
Mills, I., 218, 219
Mineka, S., 4, 7, 9, 22, 32, 39, 76, 77, 78, 80, 81, 82, 83, 84, 85, 86, 87, 88, 91, 95, 96, 99, 119, 121, 122, 128, 130, 134, 149, 152, 204, 220, 221, 223, 224, 238
Miserendino, M. J., 64, 65, 70, 163, 165
Mitchell, C. J., 124, 126
Moffitt, T. E., 92

Mogg, K., 45, 101, 102, 104, 113, 240
Mohlman, J., 80
Monroe, S. M., 94
Moody, E. W., 12, 175, 181, 182, 183, 184, 185, 186, 187, 189, 240
Morgan, C. A., 7
Morgan, M. A., 163
Morris, J., 58
Morris, R. G. M., 68, 121, 159, 185
Morrison, G. E., 67
Mowrer, O. H., 5, 18, 25, 30, 31, 82, 118, 120, 122, 126
Mowrer, W. M., 25
Muller, J., 61, 68
Muller, R. U., 165
Muñoz, R. F., 140
Muris, P., 77, 78, 93, 109
Musch, J., 45
Myers, J., 92
Myers, K. M., 167–168, 175, 200
Myerson, W. A., 136
Mystkowski, J. L., 13, 191, 204, 217, 221, 223, 230

Nadel, L., 66, 198
Nadel, N. V., 72
Nader, K., 61, 63, 161, 169
Nagy, L. M., 168
Nakajima, S., 177
Napier, R. M., 192
Nardone, G., 133
Neisser, U., 92, 94
Nelson, J. B., 179, 220, 231, 241
Neumann, D. L., 42
Nicholas, T., 122
Nichols, K. E., 145
Nicoll, R. A., 68, 170
Niedenthal, P. M., 102, 114
Nijman, H., 106
Nissim, H., 169
Noriega-Dimitri, R., 147
Norris, E. B., 179
Norton, G. R., 4
Nugent, M., 39

O'Connell, D. N., 39
O'Dowd, B. F., 169
O'Flaherty, A. S., 128, 201, 224
O'Keefe, J., 66
O'Reilly, R. C., 66
Oakman, J., 143
Ochsner, K. N., 142

Waldie, K. E., 90
Walk, R. D., 89
Walker, D. L., 61, 64, 65, 163, 166, 171, 190
Walker, J. R., 4
Wall, S., 82
Waters, E., 82
Watson, C., 25, 62
Watson, J. B., 20, 23, 43, 75, 81, 100, 135, 158
Watson, P. D., 39
Watts, F. N., 101, 102
Watzlawick, P., 133
Weertman, A., 108
Wegner, D. M., 142, 147
Weinberger, N. M., 63, 68
Weinman, J., 104
Weisman, R. G., 121
Weiss, C., 67
Weizman, R., 178
Wells, A., 125
Westbrook, R. F., 132, 167, 185, 211
Westphal, M., 143
Whipple, B., 145
White, J., 101
White, K., 83, 109
Whittal, M., 219
Wickess, C., 107
Wiens, S., 87, 130
Wiig, K. A., 66
Wik, G., 61
Wilcoxon, I. A., 28
Wilensky, A. E., 61
Williams, D. A., 42
Williams, J. M. G., 102, 104, 113
Williams, R., 101, 125
Williams, S. L., 107
Willick, M. L., 169
Wills, T. A., 111
Wilson, A., 164
Wilson, E., 101, 102, 113

Wilson, K. G., 137, 142
Wilson, M. A., 67
Wilson, R. I., 170
Wilson, T., 29
Wilson, W. J., 122
Wiltgen, B. J., 66, 67
Winter, J. C., 167
Withers, R. D., 95
Witter, M. P., 63, 66
Wolfe, G. E., 122
Wolkenstein, B., 77
Wolmer, L., 178
Wolpe, J., 8, 10, 26, 28, 29, 35, 135, 158, 179, 241
Wong, S., 40
Wood, B. S., 198
Woods, A. M., 12, 175, 178, 191, 194, 240
Woods, D. W., 147
Woods, S. W., 42, 168
Woodside, B. L., 72
Woody, S. R., 114
Wynne, L. C., 119
Wyss, J. M., 63

Yaniv, D., 63
Yeh, S.-H., 159, 163, 171
Young, J. E., 114
Young, S. L., 63, 64, 66, 67, 70, 160
Yule, W., 4

Zador, A., 72
Zajonc, R. B., 43
Zettle, R. D., 143
Zhang, W. N., 66, 67, 72
Zilski, J., 187
Zinbarg, R., 76, 80, 82, 83, 96, 129, 134, 149, 152, 223
Zoellner, L. A., 223
Zucker, R. S., 68
Zvolensky, M. J., 145, 146

SUBJECT INDEX

temperament and, 80
Behavioral measures, 8, 45–47. *See also* Measurement of fear learning
Behavioral system of fear, 5
Behavior therapy
cognitive–behavioral approach and, 33–34
criticisms of conditioning approach in, 30–33
development of, 26–30
emotion regulation model and, 148–149, 151–152
origins of, 8, 23–26
Behaviour Research and Therapy (journal), 30, 91
Beliefs. *See* Danger-laden beliefs; Outcome expectancy beliefs
Bell–Magendie law, 19
Berkeley, George, 19
Biased attentional direction, 101–102
BLA (basolateral amygdala). *See* Amygdala
Blink-startle reflex, 47
neurophysiology and, 64–65
Blocking, 180
BNST. *See* Bed nucleus of the stria terminalis (BNST)
Bouton, M. E., 175–196
Breathing strategies, 147
Bridging mechanisms, 12, 190–195, 243
Brown, Thomas, 19

Cannbinoidergic neurotransmitter system, 170
Cardiovascular indices, 48–49
CeA. *See* Central nucleus of the amygdala (CeA)
Central nucleus of the amygdala (CeA), 64
Cerebral blood flow, 49
Childhood amnesia, 92, 94
Childhood events
accuracy of recall for, 92–93
reliability checks on recall for, 93–94
Children, studies of
instructional conditioning in, 78–79
observational conditioning in, 77, 78
reliability checks on recall and, 93
Cholinergic neurotransmitter system, 170
Circle–ellipse experiment, 22
Classical conditioning. *See also* Associative learning; Instructional learning; Nonassociative learning; Observational learning; Two-factor theory

critiques of and, 30–33, 75–76
extinction in, 158
individual differences and, 9, 76, 134–135
modeling of anxiety disorders and, 23–26
modeling of avoidance learning and, 118–120, 122, 123
neurophysiological traditions and, 20–23
philosophical traditions and, 18–19
Clinical practice. *See also* Exposure therapy
early behavioral approaches and, 25
emotion regulation and, 148–149, 151–152
expectancy-based model and, 10, 129–130
extinction as learning and, 199–200
extinction training and, 229–233
mechanisms of renewal and, 206–208
neural bases of extinction and, 171–172
reinstatement and, 213–214
CNS modulation, 5–6, 8–9. *See also* Neurophysiology
CO_2-enriched air procedure, 40, 145–147
Cognitive–behavioral therapy
exposure techniques and, 11
growth of, 33–34
as term, 34
Cognitive mechanisms. *See also* Attentional bias
fear acquisition and, 9, 99–116
fear-relevant stimuli and, 86–87
information-processing biases and, 100–104
outcome expectancy beliefs and, 104–112
Cognitive rehearsal. *See* Mental rehearsal
Conditional stimulus (CS), 7, 21, 158. *See also* Phobic object, nature of
altered presentations in exposure and, 230–231
in fear learning studies, 38–39
inhibitory vs. excitatory, and exposure, 231, 233
Conditioned emotional reaction concept, 23
Conditioned inhibition, 9, 120–122, 227–229
Conditioned reflex therapy, as term, 25n
Conditioned suppression, 60, 187–189
Conditioning procedures in fear learning studies, 41–42

Consolidation, 159

Context specificity of extinction, 240–241. *See also* Relapse; Renewal; Return of fear after extinction
  background cues and, 177
  clinical practice and, 229–232
  human studies and, 12–13
  mechanisms of, 241
  nonprimate behavior and, 12
  return of fear and, 13, 176–178, 204, 211–212, 220–223, 243
  training and, 243

Contextual influences. *See also* Context specificity of extinction
  fear response systems and, 5–6
  hippocampus and, 66–67

Controlled escape, 11

Coping strategies
  control of anxiety and, 147
  outcome expectancy beliefs and, 111–112

Counterconditioning, 179, 195. *See also* Relapse effects; Renewal

Craske, M. G., 3–13, 217–233, 237–244

CS. *See* Conditional stimulus (CS)

CS–CER–CAR schema. *See* Two-factor theory

Cued conditioning
  hippocampus and, 67–68
  single-cue conditioning procedure, 42

Danger, perception of. *See* Imminence of threat

Danger-laden beliefs, 219

Davey, G. C. L., 99–116

D-cycloserine (DCS), 166, 171, 172, 190

Defensive behaviors
  neurobiology and, 72–74
  rodent studies and, 56–58

Delay conditioning, 67, 70, 72

Depression
  experiential avoidance and, 147
  neuroticism and, 6–7
  return of fear and, 219

Developmental factors, 3–4, 89–90

Diagnostic and Statistical Manual of Mental Disorders, Fourth Edition, 4

Differential delay conditioning procedure, 41–42

Direct inhibitory association, 210

Dirikx, T., 197–216

Dishabituation, 219

Distraction, and exposure therapy, 224

Dopaminergic neurotransmitter system, 169

Dot probe task, 45

Drugs. *See* Medications

Dunedin Multidisciplinary Health and Developmental Study, 91–92

Eastern Pennsylvania Psychiatric Institute, 29

Eelen, P., 17–35, 197–216

Eifert, G. H., 133–153

Electrophysiological data, 162–163

Electrotactile stimuli, 39–40

Emotion regulation
  anxiety disorders and, 10, 139–147
  clinical practice and, 148–149, 151–152
  experiential avoidance and, 144–147
  fear learning in context of, 140, 147–152
  flexibility and, 142–144
  future research and, 149–152
  nature of, 139–140

Empiricism, 19

Encapsulation, 86–87

Enuresis, treatment of, 25n

Evaluative conditioning, 131

Expectancies, 104–106, 223–225. *See also* Integrated expectancy model; Outcome expectancy beliefs

Expectancy-based model, 10, 126–130
  clinical practice and, 129–130
  future research and, 130–131
  research on, 127–129

Expectation, concept of, 161

Experiential acceptance, 146–147

Experiential avoidance, 143–144
  inflexibility and, 150–151
  as toxic diathesis, 144–147

Experiential variables, 80–83
  etiology of anxiety disorders and, 6–8, 133–153
  following conditioning, 83
  during learning event, 82–83
  outcome expectancy beliefs and, 109–110
  preexisting, 80–82

Exposure therapy. *See also* Clinical practice
  clinical studies on, 217–233
  context and, 206
  extinction and, 199–200, 217–233
  Eysenck and, 30

generalization and, 12, 205
methodological changes in, 10–11
Mowrer and, 30
Pavlov's description of, 22–23
physiological arousal and, 225–229
process variables and, 219–220, 223–225, 226–227
safety signals during, 227–229
systematic desensitization and, 10–11
trial spacing and, 223–225, 232
Expression, 159–160
Extinction
amygdala and, 162–164, 241, 242
associative strength of CS and, 241
behavioral analysis for, 157–162
clinical findings on, 13
context specificity of, 12, 13, 176, 240–241, 242, 243
critiques of conditioning model and, 31–33
exposure therapy and, 199–200
extinction training performance and, 241–242
future research and, 240–244
multiple contexts during, 186–189, 208, 209–210, 230
neurobiology of, 157–173
as new learning, 12, 37–38, 176, 199, 241 (See also Extinction training)
nonprimate behavioral evidence on, 27, 157–173
in the problem context, 192–195
renewal and reinstatement and, 12, 32–33, 241
response prevention and, 119–120
retrieval cues and, 13, 190–192, 208–209, 210–211
return of fear and, 218–220
synaptic erasure and, 38, 241
as term, 10
underlying mechanisms of, 200–203
Extinction training
excitation during, 242
extinction learning and, 241–242
negative valence at end of, 243
opposing responses in, 160–162
outcome expectancy violation and, 242–243
psychopharmacology and, 243
spacing of trials, 160–161, 242–243
stages of, 159–160
structure of, 242–243

Eysenck, Hans, 26, 29–30

Fanselow, M. S., 55–74
Fear
behavioral analysis of, 157–162
developmental stages and, 3–4, 76
normal vs. disordered, 133–135
as term, 4
Fear learning. See Avoidance learning
Fear learning studies. See also Measurement of fear learning; Individual differences
cognitive processes during conditioning and, 46–47
conditioned stimuli in, 38–39
conditioning procedures in, 41–42
emotional vs. cognitive indices and, 47
measurement in, 42–51
unconditioned stimuli in, 39–41
Fear module, concept of, 87–88
Fear of strangers, 89
Fear-relevant (FR) stimuli. See also Phobic object, nature of; Preparedness theory
associative learning and, 83–88
judgmental bias and, 102–103
Fear response systems, 5–6
Footshock, 59–60
Forgetting, 94–96
Forsyth, J. P., 133–153
Freezing, 57, 58, 59–60
Frontotemporal amygdala (FTA)
afferents and, 61–64
efferents and, 64–65
FTA. See Frontotemporal amygdala (FTA)
Future research
avoidance learning and, 130–131
emotion regulation model and, 149–152
expectancy-based model and, 130–131
extinction and, 240–244
fear acquisition and, 237–240

Gall, Franz, 19
García-Gutiérrez, A., 175–196
Generalization decrement, 206–207
Generalized anxiety disorder
fear stimuli and, 4
neuroticism and, 6
Genetic factors, 6–7
Glutamate, 160. See also NMDA (N-methyl-D-aspartate) receptors

Posterior intralaminar nucleus (PIN), 63
Postexperimental test sessions, 43–44
Posttraumatic stress disorder (PTSD), 7, 73
Posttreatment changes in life, 198
Predatory imminence continuum, 56, 57
Preencounter defenses, 57–58
Preexisting experiential variables, 80–82
Preparedness theory, 32, 76, 83–88
    automaticity and, 86–87
    encapsulation and, 86–87
    evolved fear module and, 87–88
    selective associations and, 84–86
Preventative interventions, 231
PRF. *See* Partial reinforcement (PRF) proce-
    dure
Prolonged extinction therapy, 189–190
Propranolol, 168–169
Protein synthesis, 171
Psychic reflex, 21
Psychoanalysis, 24, 25–26, 28, 29
Psychophysiological indices, 201–202
PTSD. *See* Posttraumatic stress disorder
    (PTSD)

Questionnaires, 43–44
Quinn, J. J., 55–74

Rachman, Stanley, 30
Rapid reacquisition effect, 178, 192–195
Rayner, Rosalie, 23–24, 31
Reasoning biases
    outcome expectancy beliefs and, 108–
    109
Reciprocal inhibition principle, 27–28
Reflexive responses, 60. *See also* Blink-startle
    reflex
Reflexology, as term, 20
Reinstatement, 177–178, 199, 211–213
    bridging mechanisms and, 12, 190–195,
    243
    clinical practice and, 213–214
    context specificity and, 13, 243
    ITI and, 182–186
    mechanisms of, 213–214
Relapse effects, 176–178. *See also* Reinstate-
    ment; Renewal; Return of fear after
    extinction
    optimizing extinction learning and,
    179–190
    prevention of, 178–195
Relaxation
    exposure therapy and, 10–11

as technique, 28–29
Renewal, 159, 176–177, 199, 203
    bridging mechanisms and, 12, 190–195,
    243
    clinical implications and, 206–208
    context specificity and, 13, 176–178,
    204, 243
    human conditioning research and, 203–
    206
    mechanisms of, 206–208
    mechanisms that prevent, 210–211
    prevention of, 208–210
    types of, 176–177, 204
    verbal measures and, 44
Rescorla–Wagner model, 9–10, 120–121
Resistence-to-extinction phenomenon, 31–
    33
Response-focused emotion regulation, 139–
    140, 142
Response prevention, and extinction, 119–
    120
Retrieval cues, 13, 190–192, 208–209, 210–
    211
Return of fear after extinction. *See also* Re-
    instatement; Relapse effects; Re-
    newal
    clinical studies on, 218–220
    context specificity and, 220–223
    phenomenon of, 197–198
RT-based measures, 45–47

Safety signals, 120, 121–122, 227–229
    medications as, 229, 232
Sechenov, Ivan, 8, 20, 21, 22
Second messenger systems, 171
Selective associations, 84–86. *See also* Asso-
    ciative learning
Self-reports
    etiology of phobias and, 7, 88–91
    reliability of recall and, 91–96
Seligman and Johnston model, 123
Separation anxiety, 89
Shifted attentional function, 101–102
Single-cue conditioning procedure, 42
Social contingencies
    and disordered fear, 135–136, 138–139,
    144
SOP ("sometimes opponent process") model,
    179–180, 181, 185
South Africa, behavior therapy in, 26–29
Spence, Kenneth, 27
Spider fear, 191–192, 209–210, 220–223

ABOUT THE EDITORS

Michelle G. Craske, PhD, is professor of psychology and director of the Anxiety Disorders Behavioral Research Program at the University of California in Los Angeles. She has published widely on the topics of fear and anxiety disorders, their etiology, assessment, and treatment. She has been the recipient of continuous National Institute of Mental Health funding since 1991 for research projects pertaining to risk factors for phobias, anxiety disorders, and depression; attentional biases and psychophysiological fear responding; the translation of basic science of fear extinction to human phobias; and the development and dissemination of treatments for anxiety and related disorders. Dr. Craske is associate editor for the *Journal of Abnormal Psychology* and *Behaviour Research and Therapy* and is a scientific board member for the Anxiety Disorders Association of America.

Dirk Hermans, PhD, is professor of psychology and director of the Center for the Psychology of Learning and Experimental Psychopathology in the Department of Psychology at the University of Leuven in Leuven, Belgium. He is director of postgraduate training in cognitive–behavioral therapy at his university. He has published widely in peer-reviewed journals on topics of affective processing as well as learning and memory processes in anxiety and emotional disorders. His most recent research covers the study of evaluative learning in human aversive conditioning, mechanisms of extinction and reinstatement in human fear conditioning, and the use of reaction time procedures in the assessment of fear learning. Dr. Hermans is associate editor of *Cognition & Emotion* and the *British Journal of Clinical Psychology* and is a member of the editorial board for *Experimental Psychology*.

Debora Vansteenwegen, PhD, is the research director of the Psychophysiology Laboratory at the Center for the Psychology of Learning and Experimental Psychopathology in the Department of Psychology at the University of Leuven in Leuven, Belgium. She has published in peer-reviewed journals on the topic of human fear conditioning and emotional learning. Her main focus of research is emotional learning and human fear conditioning. Most recently she has investigated the processes of extinction, return of fear after extinction, and contextual conditioning in human conditioning studies as well as in clinical samples. Dr. Vansteenwegen is a senior member of the educational board of the Dutch Institute for Research and Postgraduate Education on Experimental Psychopathology.